Psychotherapy
of
Schizophrenia

PSYCHOTHERAPY
of
SCHIZOPHRENIA

Edited by

JOHN G. GUNDERSON, M.D.

and

LOREN R. MOSHER, M.D.

JASON ARONSON • NEW YORK

Library of Congress Catalog Card Number: 75-6844
ISBN: 0-87668-208-5

Manufactured in the United States of America

CONTENTS

PREFACE

Drs. Gunderson and Mosher (N.I.M.H.) organized a series of seminars on the psychotherapy of schizophrenia which were the impetus for the present book. There were five such seminars composed of senior therapists, each member selected for avowed expertise in treating schizophrenic persons by some form of intensive psychotherapy. There was a geographical distribution of the groups, with one group in New England, one in Chicago, one in Washington, D.C., and two in California. The author-editors have contributed chapters which give background and orientation to the book, but the seminar proceedings are reported in individual papers by members of the groups and reports of seminar discussions. As is common in compilations of this sort, there is a wide variation in the quality of the presentations, but it is perhaps true that individual papers will be judged good or poor depending upon the orientation of the reader and his concept of schizophrenia and the proper method of treatment. The usefulness of this project as an activity of N.I.M.H. is justified by the time and circumstances of the study.

In the earlier years of this century, Freud, Meyer, Bleuler, Greisinger, Southard, and others initiated studies to support their belief that mental disturbances were the result of failure in adaptation of humans to the circumstances of their world, in a manner appropriate to their age and stage of growth and development. The degree to which these studies focused on genetic ("constitutional") psychological (and metapsychological) or social factors varied with orientation of the worker.

Following World War II, there was a great upsurge of interest in human behavior, with many people believing that proper study of man in his environment would produce a peaceful world with equal opportunity and justice for all. In the United States the basic approach to such issues was a melding of the genetic-dynamic approach of Meyer with the depth psychology of Freud and the sociodynamic work of Southard. In those heady times of the flowering of psychotherapy, most research dealt with the neuroses, psychophysiological disturbances, and character disturbances. But there were a sturdy few who maintained their interest in the study of the major psychoses, particularly schizophrenia. The new era of treatment of schizophrenia by psychodynamic and milieu manipulation was in opposite stance to the application of insulin shock and electroconvulsive and lobotomy treatments for the same set of symptoms. In the mid-fifties the tranquilizers were developed, and these greatly altered the attitude of many psychiatrists to manipulation of the chemical and physiologic processes of the body as one facet in the treatment program for patients suffering from some constellation of symptoms dubbed "schizophrenia."

A number of studies convincingly demonstrated that

proper administration of the tranquilizers could drastically alter schizophrenic behavior, and in many instances, bring about remissions. A few reasonably designed studies tended to show that treatment with appropriate drugs was more effective than psychotherapy or milieu. At least one of these studies however, showed that while drug therapy was very effective for certain types of schizophrenics, a combination of appropriate psychotherapy and drug therapy was somewhat more effective.

In spite of this major change in the principal form of treatment for schizophrenia, there remain those who are dissatisfied with the overall results of pharmacotherapy in schizophrenia and believe that one must investigate further the effectiveness of psychotherapy as either the principal, or as an additional, form of management.

In this setting, Gunderson and Mosher felt it appropriate to foster the further investigation of the processes of psychotherapy in schizophrenia. They hoped as well to establish more objective criteria for the determination of the particular form of schizophrenia under observation in a particular research study, and also to establish objective measurements of change.

The reader will find many of the presentations inconclusive and the interpretations of what went on in therapy highly personal, but this is symptomatic of the field. In some sections, the treatments described are mostly anecdotal, and some of the illustrative cases were reported still "in process." However, within this collection of papers, there are also some evidences of progress toward the editors' original goal. The material on self-object differentiation and the beginnings of organized ways of testing for this are encouraging and, in fact, lay the groundwork for further research in a more restricted and probably better-designed research project. The further development of the study of the effect of therapist choice and therapist-patient match also suggests further research.

This collection of papers will add to the knowledge of persons working with schizophrenic persons and particularly those interested in research on the treatment of this condition. It is an excellent case study in the necessity for well-designed research, using objective criteria for measurement of change. Only by careful subclassification of the group of schizophrenics, will we develop methods for sorting out which forms of treatment are best for which kind of schizophrenia and perhaps also what type person the therapist must be to effectively work with psychotherapeutic aspects of the management of these patients.

J. R. Ewalt, M.D.
Bullard Professor of Psychiatry and
Senior Associate Dean for Clinical Affairs
Harvard Medical School

INTRODUCTION
John G. Gunderson, M.D.

Historical Context

This book was begun in 1970 when a NIMH psychotherapy of schizophrenia program was organized by the professional staff (Loren Mosher and David Feinsilver) of the Center for Studies of Schizophrenia. The idea for such a program quickly elicited the enthusiasm and support of staff from the Psychotherapy and Behavioral Intervention Section (Hussein Tuma and Raymond Friedman) of the Clinical Research Branch at the National Institute of Mental Health. By that winter (1970–1971) the program's form had been decided and initiated. It was possible to implement this program quickly because the impetus for it had already been developing in the field over the past several years.

High among the reasons for this program's formation

was the felt need to redress the balance of interest toward psychosocial interventions at a time when the value of drugs and rapid return to the community were being widely acclaimed. Though I do not wish to minimize the major contributions of either antipsychotic drugs or community involvement, it is nevertheless obvious that these relatively new developments in treatment have their limitations. Statistics from that period confirmed what was already apparent clinically. Only about 15 to 40 percent of the schizophrenics living in the community achieved what might be termed an average level of adjustment (i.e., being self-supporting or successfully functioning as a housewife).[1] About one-third of newly discharged schizophrenics would be readmitted by the end of a year's time and half by two years. Thus the major treatment trends of the 1960s were at best providing only partial answers. By 1970 even their strongest advocates recognized that drugs neither appreciably altered fundamental aspects of personality nor influenced long-term social or interpersonal adaptation. Our impression was that the enthusiasm generated by the discovery of the phenothiazines, coupled with recent studies of the biological and genetic aspects of schizophrenia, had stimulated hope for the future unraveling of schizophrenia's etiology, but that these developments had also spawned a measure of disillusion with the usefulness of presently available psychosocial modalities. Precisely because psychosocial interventions address themselves to the more enduring aspects of personality and function, they seemed to need more adequate recognition. Without this recognition it seemed that, just as surely as the state hospitals had provided an easy way for communities to exclude, ignore, and forget their deviant members, the psychiatric profession was in danger of the same mistake in its enthusiasm for the phenothiazines and rapid discharge into the community.

There were several reasons why, of the many forms of

psychosocial treatment used for schizophrenia, attention was focused on psychotherapy. Individual psychotherapy is the oldest and most widely practiced form of psychosocial intervention. Moreover, the use of individual psychotherapy for schizophrenia was under immediate attack because of the prevailing impression that the outcome studies were being too readily and widely generalized. In contrast, we concluded from those studies that good research design with poor clinical care or poor research design with good clinical care provided inconclusive results. Rather than an indictment of psychotherapy for schizophrenics, these studies demonstrated to us the need for more thoughtful research on newly admitted patients involving experienced psychotherapists (see Chapter 26 and Chapter 16). We were aware that despite the gloomy nature of the conclusions drawn from the existing outcome studies, the therapists who were working with schizophrenic patients remained convinced that their ministrations were effective and that they could produce profound changes in the patient's internal state as well as in his rapport with the environment. It would be a mistake to dismiss too readily those admittedly sporadic but dramatic results reported with the use of intensive psychotherapy by clinicians like Otto Will, Marguerite Sachehaye, Frieda Fromm-Reichmann, Milton Wexler, Gertrude Schwing, and others.

In addition to these problems—or perhaps because of them—other factors would seem to jeopardize the future practice of intensive psychotherapy of schizophrenia. Here must be included the prospect of a national health insurance excluding payment for long-term psychotherapy, the declining influence of psychoanalytic preceptors in training programs, the influx of new treatment strategies promising more for less, and the disillusionment and withdrawal by well-known therapists from intensive psychotherapy with schizophrenics.[2]

It was in recognition of these reasons and trends that the

National Conference on Schizophrenia held by the NIMH in 1970 on research, training, and services placed *highest* on its policy recommendations that the NIMH direct its future attention to the need for controlled evaluation of psychosocial treatments.[3] It is noteworthy that this recommendation arose from the participation of national leaders of training and service programs as well as from the research participants.

These, then, are the reasons for developing a program on psychotherapy of schizophrenia. The purpose of this program was to renew interest in the experienced psychotherapist's efforts to modify basic aspects of schizophrenic disorder and to involve these same therapists in the design of new and better research in this area.

Organization of the Program

Strupp and Bergin,[4] as well as Robbins,[5] emphasize the need to study the work of experienced psychotherapists—a deficiency of much current and past psychotherapy research. There are several possible methods of employing the expertise of senior psychotherapists in research. Perhaps the most obvious and direct approach, although one fraught with great difficulties, is to employ gifted senior clinicians as therapists in outcome research. A second approach that we believed represented a more modest goal— and, to our minds, an essential first step in the direction of the eventual outcome research—is to engage senior clinicians in a task specifying the various dimensions of the often nebulous term "psychotherapy." Only when we begin to specify which type of therapist working with which type of patient employing what specific techniques and in which specific setting will we have identified enough critical variables to begin to initiate relevant outcome research.

By inviting senior clinicians, who as a group have been

distant and at times even hostile to research endeavors, to discuss the therapy they do with potential research in mind, we hoped to address another major problem confronting the field of psychotherapy research which was highlighted by Strupp and Bergin, who have noted that "thus far research in psychotherapy has failed to make a deep impact on practice and technique." We believe that one reason for this limited feedback between psychotherapy research and clinical practice stems from the fact that somewhere in the process of translating the techniques of successful therapy into variables that were included in previous research, clinical relevance was compromised or lost. We believe that one method of strengthening the links between research and clinical practice is to involve the experts—the treaters—in the process of research design and implementation.

Discussion groups were established in Washington, D.C., Chicago, the New England area, San Francisco, and Los Angeles. These areas were selected because of personal familiarity of the center staff with one or several leading therapists in those regions. These initial contacts then helped organize the local groups. Each group was composed of five or six senior clinicians, each having approximately twenty years of experience in the treatment of schizophrenic patients. For the most part, the program participants are psychoanalysts who are well known for their interest in long-term intensive individual psychotherapy with schizophrenics. Although most are psychoanalysts, a broad spectrum of clinical and theoretical positions is represented. Extensive clinical experience, a reputation for success in treating schizophrenic patients, and compatibility as a group member were the criteria generally used for inclusion in the program, and no attempt was made to balance the groups further.

The NIMH mandate to each group was deliberately presented in a hazy manner in order to facilitate group autonomy and to allow each group to define and pursue its own interests. Our stated hope was that their clinically derived intuitive notions could be translated into reliably observable variables and, eventually, testable hypotheses. At the inception of the program no obligation was negotiated with group members and none was intended beyond the first meeting. Their interest and enthusiasm in the groups is even more noteworthy because of the sparse financial remuneration from the NIMH for their time—much less than these men could have gained in clinical practices. Thus their involvement represents their continuing interest and not the fulfillment of a prearranged contract with the NIMH. There was, moreover, a prevailing optimism among the participants for this opportunity to meet and for the implied recognition of their work. Nate Apter noted that "clinical work with schizophrenics is extremely lonely," and attributes to this some of the enthusiasm for this opportunity to work with others. In any event, the groups have met every three to four months since the program's inception.

Initiation of the Program

In order to facilitate and to provide a launching pad for discussion during the first phase of the project, the following questions were distributed to each group prior to its initial meeting:

1. How do you operationally conceptualize the nature of the schizophrenic's difficulties?

2. How do you characterize the kinds of schizophrenic patients who profit or fail to profit from individual psychotherapy?

3. What are the essential characteristics of therapists who work well with schizophrenic patients?

The participants lost little time in beginning to address these questions. The detail and depth of discussion in all groups soon made it apparent that these exchanges were useful and that subsequent meetings would be required to deal adequately with the list of questions. Thus the first two to four meetings for each group were taken up by attending to the above questions. This format provided a structure that allowed the group members to become familiar with each other. In some instances old colleagues who had lost touch with each other became reacquainted. In other instances clinicians who worked near each other but had never met talked at length about their common interest for the first time. There was a general feeling that such meetings were long overdue.

The following paragraphs summarize the areas of agreement in the composite responses to the original questions from all five of the study groups. This material can be seen in outline form in Table 1. It is an attempt to form a synthetic overview of what reasonably might be acceptable to most of the participants in the program. But not all of the questions were taken up in equal depth by every group, and clearly not everyone in the groups would agree with all of the statements presented here.

A Working Definition of Schizophrenia

Loren Mosher has argued that the inclusion of a working definition of schizophrenia in the research protocols of projects concerning psychosocial treatments will enhance the prospects of future replication of findings.[6] Surprisingly, the task of defining the disorder itself produced the least amount of disagreement among the groups. The following is the composite definition of schizophrenia based on the responses of the group participants to this first question:

Schizophrenia is a disorder of ego functioning caused by developmental, parent-child experiences (which may include biological-constitutional elements) which results in an inability to separate out and maintain accurate internal mental representations of the outside real world. This inability, in turn, causes the production of restitutional symptoms (delusions, hallucinations) which are most prominent when the individual is confronted with the stresses of developing independent, mature, trusting adult relationships.

Amendments to this definition would include the emphasis that individuals falling under this rubric are in reality not *that* qualitatively different than "normals"; that it is primarily the mother-child relationship that is disturbed; and that this definition, while implying homogeneity, should recognize the heterogeneous nature of those falling within this category.

On examination of this definition, the following observations seem noteworthy.

1. Except for the nature of the possible inability and the resulting restitutional symptoms, this definition could apply to other categories of psychopathology.

2. There was no rush to advocate a strictly environmentalist approach to the cause of schizophrenia. In fact, there was frequent acknowledgment that some poorly defined constitutional or biological factors may be at work in the schizophrenic. The possibility of a genetic predisposition was not seen as incompatible with the pragmatic approach of doing anything possible.

3. The concept of a schizophrenic inability to maintain internal mental representations was articulated in a variety of ways by group members. Although the participants described many different aspects of the same phenomena, the differences in their descriptions ultimately seemed to be more semantic than real.

4. The basic schizophrenic psychopathology is at least in part a derivative of early primary relationships to parents and the conflicts in those relationships which have led to primitive ego functioning.

Patient Factors Affecting Outcome

The following discussion focuses on patient variables that were hypothesized to relate positively to successful prognosis in therapy:

> Schizophrenic patients who tend to profit the most from individual psychotherapy are young and intelligent (IQ above low normal), "reactive," and present during their first break in an acute manner. They have a past history of achievement at work and in other creative activities, as well as some success in interpersonal, especially heterosexual, relationships. They are motivated and tend to experience "pain" or the sense of a "struggle" and definitely see themselves in need of help. They often appear to be striving actively for higher levels of functioning, and exhibit some degree of the following capacities: self-observation, problem solving, integrating experience, self-control, and delay.

A past history of hospitalization as an independent variable (that is, independent of chronicity) was not felt to be highly related to outcome. Also, the depth of regression (during the acute phase especially) was not considered a significant prognostic variable.

We can only speculate about the rather pedestrian quality of this discussion of patient variables, and offer the suggestion that perhaps the strong emphasis placed on the characteristics of the therapist as being critical for positive outcome overshadows a more in-depth consideration of patient characteristics. However, it may well be that there is simply nothing radically new or different to be added, even by these distinguished clinicians, to the already existing research literature (Vaillant,[7] Philips,[8] Stephens,[9] and others) in this area. An effort to investigate important variables in selecting patients for individual psychotherapy is reported later in this volume (see Chapter 19).

Therapist Characteristics Affecting Outcome

During both preliminary and subsequent meetings the subject of therapist characteristics received considerable attention from all of the groups. Two general characteristics of schizophrenia therapists repeatedly emerged from their discussions. The first concerned the therapeutic zeal necessary for long-term intensive psychotherapy with schizophrenic patients. This characteristic represents a deep personal need on the part of the therapist to help this particular type of patient. There is recognition that such a sense of mission may indeed represent a rescue fantasy or a desire to "play God." Thus, while the virtual necessity of this near-drivenness is recognized, the stipulation is made that such a drive be well integrated into the personality of the therapist so that it is reasonable and manageable, resulting in the maintenance of appropriate interpersonal distance.

The ability to tolerate extreme frustration, despair, helplessness, and often lack of progress in therapy (and imposing this need upon the patient) was the second primary constellation of characteristics associated with success in therapy with schizophrenic patients. Lest this foster the image of the therapist as a paragon of perfection, it should be noted that group consensus exists that schizophrenia therapists have in general suffered painful life experiences that tend to render them "honest," "real" people who have experienced a struggle to attain a strong sense of identity. Perhaps the suggestion of omnipotence which ran like a thread throughout the discussions related not so much to the perfection of the therapist's personality as to the awareness and attempts at mastery of his imperfections, which are so severely challenged by schizophrenic patients.

A third set of characteristics was seen as related to failures in treating schizophrenic patients. While perseverance and even a sense of being driven is necessary for success, therapists who are motivated by a guilt-ridden feeling of omnipotence seem doomed to failure, as are therapists who tend to view schizophrenic patients as superhumanly precious or fragile, or who are overly perfectionistic and excessively critical.

The personality characteristics of the therapist emerged as the set of factors which was hypothesized to be the primary determinant of success or failure in intensive therapy, and issues of technique, while important, were not accorded so high a status.

The Initial Phase of Therapy

The groups were unanimous in identifying the primary task of the initial phase of therapy with the schizophrenic patient as the establishment of contact, a term that defies exact definition, but which includes attachment behavior and a trusting relationship. In the process of establishing contact, offering the patient the possibility of being understood, and beginning to develop a relationship that will allow the patient to view the therapist as a constant, reliable, and predictable person, the therapist is called upon to exhibit a number of behaviors. These include caring for and about the patient, attempting to understand him, fostering dependency, being reliable, and above all, appearing to the patient as a "real person." The therapist will often be called upon to assume the role of an auxiliary ego, helping the patient to deal with numerous daily problems of a here-and-now nature, and to correct his misperceptions of the world.

Evolution of the Program

At the conclusion of the discussions of the initial questions in the summer of 1971, three consultants were asked to apply their considerable investigative experience to the problem of transferring the clinical observations being gathered into testable hypotheses. The background, approach, and eventual impressions of these three consultants vary greatly. Dr. Martin Orne, with a great breadth of experience in the travails of clinical research, was pessimistic about the potential for experienced therapists to attend to or develop researchable hypotheses. Dr. Jack Ewalt, who had been principal investigator of one of the major outcome studies in the 1960s, was guarded in his optimism. Dr. Robert Wallerstein, one of the early workers of the Menninger psychotherapy project and a well-known psychoanalyst, was markedly enthusiastic about the program.

The common theme of the consultants' recommendations was the need to clarify and specify the clinical concepts into quantifiable and scalable indices. As a specific example, Wallerstein suggested the development of a weighted prognostic index for suitability for psychotherapy. (See Chapter 19.) Other areas needing specificity included: (1) theoretical positions and distinctions among the clinicians; (2) labeling therapeutic techniques discriminatively for schizophrenics versus other patients; (3) noting the distinguishing features of clinical stages, for example the initial stage; and (4) discriminating the schizophrenic patient from other patients. Orne also elaborated on the value of having group participants agree on criteria for schizophrenia, so that there was some assurance of being able to compare the group discussions and generalize from them. Considering the needs of outcome measures in psychotherapy studies, he suggested these clinicians might be able to develop an outcome scale reflecting the changes they hope to accomplish by their therapy. Ewalt concentrated on the need for specificity in the clinical language being used. He noted that even such mundane words as "first break" or "reactive" might have quite different meanings to different people. He suggested that a translation of the clinical data into testable hypotheses might require the addition of methodologically sophisticated researchers to those groups where such expertise was lacking.

These suggestions were transmitted to the groups and, as will be seen, some of the ideas were adopted while others were not. To some extent the ideas incorporated by the participants were those that corresponded to the group's preexisting inclinations. This was in part due to the fact that, by the end of the initial discussions, the groups had taken on their own individual identities and were increasingly autonomous with regard to the NIMH. Thus the NIMH's involvement became increasingly facilitative and coordinating rather than directive or organizational. In this context, then, the groups eagerly began to pursue markedly divergent directions reflecting the interests of their members.

The New England Group

The New England group focused primarily on the aspects of patient/therapist interaction which they believed affected therapeutic process. This focus would appear to be the result of the participants' having been influenced by the Washington School of Psychiatry in the 1930s and the work of Adolph Meyer and Harry Stack Sullivan. The influences of this lineage can be seen in the view of schizophrenia as a regressive reaction to life events, the emphasis on the importance of interpersonal relatedness in the origins and treatment of schizophrenia, and the unspoken agreement that the interpersonal relatedness was vital to the therapists' effectiveness.

Interactional factors that contributed to a therapeutic relationship were:

1. Shared affect. This experience in therapy was viewed as drawing two people closer together, whether the affect expressed was positive or negative. The therapist's empathy and "realness" were seen as facilitative of this experi-

ence. This process of sharing tends to increase the patient's tolerance of affect and perspective.

2. Love. "Love remains the ever present active ingredient in the therapeutic relationship." "Love" is used here in the sense of any positive bond. The context established by these bonds permits tolerance of frustrations, motivation to change, and acknowledgment of "missing" or grief. The participants felt it was particularly hard for love to be mutually recognized, acknowledged, and accepted without both feeling guilty and needing to defend against the feeling.

3. Distance. This functions in the interaction to assure separateness, involves respect for the usefulness of defenses, and allows compromises or "equalizing adaptations" to occur between two people. It also encourages the experience of a broader range of mutual responsiveness. This parameter involves the useful aspects of separation (e.g., grief, individuation, and autonomy) and the learning involved in experiencing hate.

4. Identification. This process is therapeutic insofar as it involves use of the therapist's ego strength and, in particular, may be essential in the initial stage of therapy in facilitating a relationship and for the development of an observing ego. Therapists must, however, be aware of and ready to interpret aggressively the patient's assignment of his unwanted parts (i.e., projective identification) onto the therapist.

Among the other process variables discussed by this group were ambivalence, real relationships, insight, interpretation, confrontation, and introjection (see Chapter 2). An effort to assess a therapeutic interview for these and other variables (see Table 2) by using video tape was made without much success. Following the controversies about regression at the Stockbridge conference (see Chapter 5), the group has devoted its attention to this problem and is preparing a monograph on clinical aspects of this topic.

The San Francisco Group

The San Francisco group met regularly for intensive study of a few selected cases. Their principal interest was in what could be learned about the defense mechanisms that psychotic or borderline patients commonly use, rather than therapeutic processes per se. The classical analytic situation was used to study these defenses because it minimized the interference of the therapist's personality with the process of objective observation.

The group discovered early that projection is the predominate defense employed in borderlines and other psychosis-vulnerable persons. The use of projection is not unlike that seen in the everyday life of neurotics except in degree. The predominance of projection presents particular problems to therapists as well as to others who interact with such patients. In brief, the crux of this problem is the consistent misinterpretations of the therapist's comments made by the patient, which allow him to maintain his defenses but which frustrate the therapist, who doesn't understand that he is being misinterpreted.

A by-product of this study has been increasing data on the use of the couch in treating patients who have a capacity for psychotic regression. The group is attempting to specify further the type of patient who is suitable for psychoanalytic treatment using the couch. They have concluded that paitents for whom their method of study (i.e., classical analytic techniques) was appropriate could not be schizophrenic, since the resulting regression seemed unethical. Thus, with mutual regret, they decided that their work did not fit with the NIMH program's format and they discontinued further involvement with it in the winter of 1971–1972.

The Washington, D.C., Group

The Washington-Baltimore area is historically responsible for a number of pioneering efforts in the intensive psychoanalytic psychotherapy of schizophrenia. This clinical heritage, combined with the neighboring research resources of the National Institute of Mental Health, were important in the selection of this group's participants and in the varied projects that have been undertaken.

Starting with discussions of optimal characteristics of patients and therapists, the group has pursued its concern for patient-therapist matching. A list of clinical guidelines for the matching process was enumerated. They ranged from such general principles as "opposites attract but similarities bind" to more specific matching criteria, such as avoiding the combination of an aggressive paranoid patient with an assertive authoritarian male therapist. (See Table 3 for a complete listing.) These impressionistic observations generated a pilot research project at Chestnut Lodge which attempted to specify matching criteria more precisely (see Chapter 23).

A second major concern of the Washington group was the process of change during recovery from a schizophrenic psychosis. This was first discussed in terms of traditional symptomatic changes. Growth was described in terms of change from a paranoid, catatonic, or hebephrenic presentation to one of more overt disorganization, to a clinical picture resembling severe depression and/or borderline states, and from there finally into a more typically neurotic character structure. In more recent meetings this interest led to discussions of differential diagnosis of borderline and schizophrenic patients and the difference between these groups in terms of psychotherapeutic results from intensive therapy.

Change in the course of recovery from schizophrenic psychosis was also envisioned in terms of nonsymptomatic clinical signs (for example, reemergence of a sense of humor, or capacity to recognize imaginings as such). In particular the concept of self-object differentiation emerged as a basic explanatory principle uniting many of the clinical signs that were given as signals of change. Much of the group's attention has focused on the subsequent development of the SOD scale, which may provide a badly needed tool for assessing change during psychotherapy along the axis from undifferentiated toward a stable sense of self (see Chapter 20).

The Los Angeles Group

Despite the common bond of psychoanalysis in this group, there were major conflicts in the members' views on the theories of schizophrenia and their implications for clinical practice. In fact, the workshop found itself immersed in a major ideological debate that had been in progress between Los Angeles psychoanalytic institutions for some time. The major issue in this debate, insofar as this program was concerned, was whether schizophrenia could be best conceptualized as a conflict (see Chapter 11) or as a deficit disorder (see Chapter 10). The implications for therapy growing out of these opposing views were also the subject of controversy. The clarity of these antithetical theoretical formulations made the meetings intense, interesting, and illuminating, but there seemed to be little chance of reconciliation. They could agree that how the basic schizophrenic dilemma was conceptualized largely determines how one approaches therapy. They also would agree that a loss of internal object representations was important in schizophrenia and that in reality there is a continuum between states of deficiency and defense.

Several by-products have emerged from these controversies about theory and technique. First, there was an increased awareness of the need to articulate theoretical allegiances and their influence on clinical practices and ideas. Second, within the Los Angeles group itself a new theoretical position evolved which included aspects of learning theory.[10] Third, the group became aware of the necessity for defining concepts in mutually understandable ways. This brought to light the problems of language and the need for operational definitions. Fourth, the group directed its attention to the problem of designing research so as to test adequately their opposing viewpoints (see Chapter 16). Out of this latter discussion came the conclusion that the technical aspects of treatment were a difficult variable to isolate in research design from (a) the degree and type of patient psychopathology (that is, different technical considerations attained for "sicker" schizophrenics than for "less sick" ones), and (b) the treatment context (for example, office or hospital). Thus, to test the value of competing techniques would require control over many difficult variables. The group has remained interested in the ways by which the number of patients can be kept limited to preserve the research value of the single analyst.

The Chicago Group

From the start the Chicago group contained clinicians with considerable research experience. Although most had previous experience and some notoriety in the practice of treating schizophrenics, only a few of the original members were currently doing intensive psychoanalytically oriented psychotherapy with schizophrenics at the time of the program. The concern with psychotherapy has thus been largely what can be learned from it about the nature of schizophrenia and whether it is an effective method of treatment. In considering this they reviewed previous efforts at research and defined the problems involved in doing research in this area (see Chapter 18). They undertook a retrospective pilot investigation of successfully treated patients with schizophrenia to evaluate what factors distinguished this group from other schizophrenic patients treated similarly who had poor outcomes (see Chapter 24). This latter work has highlighted the need for research on psychotherapy with schizophrenics to take cognizance of phasic changes during recovery and to evaluate whether these phases are related to the schizophrenia or are artifacts of the treatment setting.

The second line of this group's interest has concerned the nature of schizophrenia itself. Using systems theory as a framework, they have been critical of the metapsychological concepts derived from viewing a schizophrenic in a psychoanalytic context to the exclusion of the schizophrenic's performance in other areas (see Chapter 13). Using data obtained from other than psychoanalytic areas, they believe that conflict theories of schizophrenia are inadequate and that treatment techniques must take into consideration the role of a deficit that is unremediable. Paralleling this skepticism about metapsychological formulations, the Chicago group has emphasized the need for more reliably observable descriptive accounts of schizophrenic phenomenology. Accordingly, several of their members have been involved in a collaborative project in which they are seeking discriminating clinical signs for schizophrenia.[11]

Products of the Program

Dissemination of Information

As these groups traveled their divergent ways, it seemed to us that the breadth and depth of the discussions were in many instances unparalleled in the existing literature. On scrutinizing the literature about or derived from intensive psychotherapy with schizophrenics, we found it impressive that almost always the papers reflected the authors' personal experience but rarely reflected clinical opinions derived from collective experience with colleagues or addressed issues that were being raised by contemporary authors on similar topics. One method of disseminating the information coming in this program was by organizing conferences at the annual meetings of national mental health organizations. Some of the more creative and well-stated contents of this program could thus be shared with a larger body of interested professionals.

The first of these gatherings was held at the meetings of the American Orthopsychiatric Association. A panel of research experts who were not direct participants in the program (Fiske, Strupp, and Ewalt) met to discuss and review the existing outcome studies on psychotherapy and to examine ways by which future research might proceed. In addition, an outline of the program was presented and discussed for the first time. There was some consensus about the need for preliminary work before outcome studies should be considered. Ewalt emphasized the complexity of outcome studies while Fiske noted the need for outcome criteria and Strupp emphasized the need to discriminate nonspecific (personality) variables from specific (technical) variables in evaluating the type of therapy that is being given.[12] These comments were confirmed in the impressions derived from a review of previous outcome studies (see Chapter 26) and the emergent diversity among the clinical practices of the participants of our psychotherapy experts within the program.

At the second meeting, the 125th annual American Psychiatric Association meetings in Dallas, May 1–5, 1972, we assembled two papers describing the program[13] and these were supplemented by papers from representatives of the Chicago, Washington, and New England groups. The questions raised by these papers (see Chapters 4 and 18) led one member of the audience to inquire whether the presenters were therapeutic nihilists. The emphatic disclaimer given by Otto Will and Jarl Dyrud led to immediate and hearty applause.

The last convention assembled speakers from four of our groups (Gerald Aronson, Philip Holzman, Stanley Eldred, and Helm Stierlin) for the annual fall meeting of the American Psychoanalytic Association in New York City, December 1, 1972. The topic was "The Influence of Theoretical Models of Schizophrenia on Treatment Practice." Eldred admonished analysts to take the impact of drugs and community-based treatment into consideration in their theoretical formulations of schizophrenia. Aronson outlined the conflict and deficit views as expressed in the Los Angeles group and presented an alternative third formulation. Holzman criticized the use of psychodynamic explanations for schizophrenia to the exclusion of other data sources. Stierlin then briefly delineated a transactional theory of schizophrenia and described the three major disturbances in transactional modes found in schizophrenic families, i.e., binding, delegating, and expelling. Most of the issues raised by these authors are found in the papers contained here by them (see Chapters 13 and 14). A more detailed report on the proceedings of this meeting, moderated by Robert Wallerstein, with discussion by Don Burnham and Harold Searles, has also been prepared and is available elsewhere.[14]

The sessions drew large audiences at all of these conventions, demonstrating the appeal that intensive psychotherapy with schizophrenics still holds. These programs generated a great deal of interest among the groups and sometimes competition between them. In this context it was decided to have a conference for the participants themselves. It was hoped that such a conference would diminish the provincialism and personality cultism that have long been bugaboos of this area, while at the same time generating more direct communication among the leaders of the field. This conference was held as a cooperative endeavor by the NIMH and Austen Riggs in Stockbridge, Massachusetts, October 13–14, 1972. Much of this book reflects the substance of the conference proceedings.

Impact on the Field

Through the papers and work generated in this program, there now exists a new literature that sometimes addresses old problems but often introduces new ideas for others waiting to take up the banner. We feel that an impetus has been given to the field in a helpful way which can only reflect well on the often overlooked interface between research and clinical practice, and their institutional embodiments, the NIMH and psychoanalysis.

As may be readily seen from the preceding descriptions of the program, its original goals have undergone concurrent narrowing and broadening: narrowing in the sense that getting senior clinicians involved in research on psychotherapy of schizophrenia has taken some specific, well-defined forms; broadening in the sense that we have come to see that the content of this program may have its strongest influence not as research per se but as guides to teaching and as a stimulus to further creative work. The whole field of individual psychotherapy has served notice that it is viable, enduring, filled with controversies that are exciting and relevant, and needn't apologize to the scientific establishment for its limitations.

This enthusiastic endorsement must be tempered, however, with recognition of the limited success in one of the program's early goals: asking clinicians to refine clinical notions into testable hypotheses. Rosenthal had previously pointed out, "To ask therapists to describe what they do is analogous to asking artists to explicate their sources of inspiration and techniques of execution—a notoriously difficult task." Participants came face to face with this difficulty early in the program. Although descriptions of clinical experience can permit a listener to share a therapeutic experience, "when one takes the person and persons discussed into the realm of scientific inquiry, the obvious gap between clinician and the impersonal scientists takes on great proportions." This problem was to recur throughout the program, and if even a modest advance has been made toward solving this problem it will be the program's most enduring contribution.

Future Directions

Since the time of the Stockbridge conference we have given considerable thought to defining priorities for the future of the program on psychotherapy of schizophrenia. The general conclusion reached is that the program will continue, but in a more restricted and carefully delineated manner.

Since its inception over four years ago, the primary purpose of this program has been the stimulation and development of research on the psychotherapy of schizophrenics. We did not expect that a program to study two phenomena as complex as schizophrenia and psychotherapy would be quick or easy to develop. On the basis in part of the Stockbridge meeting, it was decided that in the future the discussion groups should be more sharply focused on research issues. This will entail a relative deemphasis on clinical and theoretical discussions. While these are of great importance, we believe that sufficient time and attention have been given them over the past four years to warrant this shift in emphasis. Moreover, these subjects have resumed a natural autonomy of their own which we view as partially a legacy of these meetings and the excellent papers that have resulted. We believe it should now be possible to plan some pilot research on the clinical and theoretical notions that have been under discussion. Each group will, of course, decide which (if any) area(s) it will want to work on. This redefinition may require new or additional members, selective consultation with research methodologists, or other changes in format. It is understood that such pilot work may require more time than that allowed by meeting once every three months. It has been placed in the hands of group members to decide whether they wish to make such an investment or not. The group meetings themselves might then serve a more consultative, progress-reporting, instrument-testing, and coordinating function than was previously the case. We are hopeful this approach will allow a continued and fruitful collaboration with the participants in this program which will help us understand more precisely, in a communicable way, the ways in which psychotherapy does or does not facilitate change.

REFERENCES

1. Mosher, L. R., and Feinsilver, D. *Special report: Schizophrenia.* National Institute of Mental Health publication no. 72–9007. Washington, D.C.: U.S. Government Printing Office, 1971.

2. Burton, A. The adoration of the patient and disillusionment. *Am. J. Psychoanalysis,* 29:194–204, 1969.

3. Klerman, G. Implications of the proceedings of the follow-up conference on schizophrenia: research, training, and services. Lindeman Center, Boston, Mass.: unpublished manuscript, March 1972.

4. Strupp, H. H., and Bergin, A. E. Some empirical and conceptual bases for coordinated research in psychotherapy: a critical review of issues, trends, and evidence. *Int. J. Psychiatry,* 7:18–90, 1969.

5. Robbins, L. L. Traditional reductionism is unsatisfactory. *Int. J. Psychiatry,* 7:153–156, 1969.

6. Mosher, L. R. A research design for evaluating psychosocial treatments of schizophrenia. *Hosp. Community Psychiatry,* 23:229–233, 1972.

7. Vaillant, G. E. The prediction of recovery in schizophrenia. *J. Nerv. Ment. Dis.,* 135:534–543, 1962.

8. Philips, L. Case history data and prognosis in schizophrenia. *J. Nerv. Ment. Dis.,* 117:515–525, 1953.

9. Stephens, J. H. Long-term course and prognosis in schizophrenia. *Seminars in Psychiatry,* 2(4):464–485, 1970.

10. Aronson, G. Defense and deficit models: their influence on therapy. Paper presented at the annual fall meeting of the American Psychoanalytic Association, New York, December 1972.

11. Grinker, R., and Holzman, P. Schizophrenic pathology in young adults. *Arch. Gen'l Psychiat.* 28(2):168–175, 1973.

12. Strupp, H. On the technology of psychotherapy. *Arch. Gen'l Psychiat.*, 26(3):270–278, 1972.
13. Friedman, R. J.; Gunderson, J. G.; and Feinsilver, D. B. The psychotherapy of schizophrenia: an NIMH program. *Am. J. Psychiatry,* 130(6):674–677, 1973. And Gunderson, J. G. Controversies about the psychotherapy of schizophrenia. *Am. J. Psychiatry,* 130(6):677–681, 1973.
14. Gunderson, J. G. (reporter). The influence of theoretical models of schizophrenia on treatment practice. Submitted to the *J. Am. Psychoanalytic Assoc.*, Vol. 22, No. 1.

TABLE 1

Operational Variables for
Psychotherapy of Schizophrenics
from All Study Groups

I. Concept of Schizophrenia

Schizophrenia is a disorder of ego functioning caused by developmental parent-child experiences (which may include biological-constitutional elements), which results in a deficit in the ability to separate out and maintain accurate internal mental representations of the outside real world, which then causes the production of restitutional symptoms (delusions, hallucinations, etc.); and this mode of functioning is resorted to as a result of being confronted with the stresses of developing independent, mature, trusting adult relationships.

II. Patient Characteristics

Individual psychotherapy with schizophrenic patients will tend to be

A. *successful* to the degree that the patient shows the following characteristics:
   1. nature of onset—acute, first break, reactive.
   2. demographic characteristics—young in age, intelligent (IQ above low normal).
   3. a premorbid social history which indicates some success in achieving interpersonal relationships, especially heterosexual.
   4. shows certain kinds of ego strengths:
      a. capacity for self-observation.
      b. capacity for problem solving.
      c. capacity for integrating experience.
      d. capacity for self-control and delay.
   5. experiences "pain" or "struggle," and sees self as in need of help; i.e., is "motivated."
   6. seems to be striving for higher levels of functioning.
B. *unsuccessful* to the degree in which the patient shows the following characteristics:
   1. opposite of above, especially long-standing presence of symptoms.
   2. chronic hospitalization.

   3. organicity.

   4. chronic paranoia.

   5. shows refractoriness to repeated trials of psychotherapy.

   6. shows certain ingrained characterlogical defensive patterns which preclude intervention, such as certain sociopathic traits (e.g., alcoholism, drug dependency) and certain "acting out" tendencies (e.g., relentless self-destructiveness, uncontrollable aggression).

III. Therapist Characteristics

Individual psychotherapy with schizophrenic patients will tend to be

A. *successful* to the degree in which the therapist shows the following characteristics:

   1. has a deep "personal" need to help this kind of patient; (e.g., "play God," be confronted with mystery, challenge, "impossibility," the primary process, etc.) but this need is well integrated and provides gratification, such as in a sense of exhilaration akin to artistic experience, or in intellectual pursuits, scientific productions, etc.

   2. has gone through his own painful life experiences, which he has resolved in some way.

   3. has ability to be honest and real, be "his own person" with patient.

   4. can tolerate intensity of schizophrenic attachment behavior, especially intense affects.

   5. has a capacity to be receptive to the symbiotic needs of the patient—become an auxiliary ego—and still maintain separateness.

   6. has ability to be empathic with the primary process and not be overwhelmed, to "dip in" and "dip out."

   7. has ability to be very active and aggressive with the patient but also, at times, to be very passive and follow the patient, just observing.

   8. shows a balance between field independence and field dependence.

   9. has ability to observe himself and the patient while being involved.

  10. has the ability to make a commitment and to "give to the patient," while not imposing expectations.

  11. has the ability to tolerate little or no movement and not to

need success, and ability to trust in the basic health of the patient.
12. has youthful enthusiasm and optimism.
13. has had therapeutic experience with such patients which has not been discouraging.

B. *unsuccessful* to the degree in which the therapist shows the following characteristics:
1. is overly perfectionistic and hypercritical.
2. is driven by guilt-ridden omnipotence.
3. views patients as suprahumanly "precious" or "fragile."
4. cannot work well together with others connected with the treatment of the patient, such as institutional personnel and family members.

TABLE 2

Evaluation of Interview

Please rate on a scale from 1 (absent) to 5 (prevalent) how much you felt each of these dimensions was in evidence and then check whether you felt this was too much or too little.

Dimensions	*Score 1 - 5*	*Too Much/Too Little*
I. Therapist dimensions		
1. "presence"	————	———— | ————
2. interpretation	————	———— | ————
3. confrontation	————	———— | ————
4. support	————	———— | ————
5. permission	————	———— | ————
6. limits	————	———— | ————
7. activity	————	———— | ————
8. empathy	————	———— | ————
9. "realness"	————	———— | ————
II. Patient dimensions		
1. regression	————	———— | ————
2. identification with therapist	————	———— | ————
3. learning	————	———— | ————
4. insight	————	———— | ————

III. Dimensions of focus
      1. reality   ———   ——————|——————
      2. fantasy   ———   ——————|——————
      3. past   ———   ——————|——————
      4. present—here
         and now   ———   ——————|——————
      5. future adaptation ———   ——————|——————
      6. hostility-anger   ———   ——————|——————
      7. affection-love   ———   ——————|——————
      8. loss-separation   ———   ——————|——————

IV.   Relationship dimensions
      1. distance   ———   ——————|——————
      2. closeness   ———   ——————|——————
      3. ambivalence   ———   ——————|——————
      4. efficacious to patient ———   ——————|——————

3. Predictions of outcome by the time of the next meeting———

_____

_____

TABLE 3

Guides to Patient-Therapist Matching*

1. Specific suggestions
    A. Passive, withdrawn patient needs active, "intense" therapist, not "analytic caricature."
    B. Fragile, shaky patient does better with more passive therapist, and does not do well with active, "intense" therapist.
    C. Acting-out patient needs a therapist who himself is somewhat of an "actor outer," not someone who tends to be moralistic and hyperconventional.
    D. Aggressive paranoid does well with:
       a. woman or man comfortable with passivity (e.g., European),

not with male having need to assert his masculinity (e.g., Texan).

b. a somewhat "paranoid" therapist empathic with the world view of "everybody is against me," but not to the extent of overinvolvement and *folie a deux*.

E. Hysterical, seductive female tends to do well with grandfatherly type who enjoys seductive stimulation, not with young single male having savior fantasies and need for love.

F. Depressive patient needs somebody who is comfortable with all the various aspects of depression within himself (demandingness, emptiness, rage).

G. Hopeless "given up" patients need a charismatic therapist, one who is able to follow through for the long term.

2. General Principles
   A. Liking each other on initial encounter is not a necessary or reliable indicator.
   B. Feeling intensely involved with each other on initial meeting is a negative indicator.
   C. Differences attract but similarities hold together; having similar "ego styles" is good.
   D. Anxiety will be present in any good match, but should not be overwhelming; in other words, should lead to a symbiotic match but one which still allows for self-differentiation.
   E. Some therapists seem to do very well with any kind of patient.
   F. Some therapists may be very good for one phase of therapy but not others.

   a. Charismatic therapist not necessarily good for follow-through.

   b. Empathic paranoid not necessarily good for follow-through.

   c. Therapist good with one depressive phase may not be good in the others.

   G. Not necessarily good idea to go along with the institutional pressures to assign patients to therapists simply because they "have time."
   H. Patient should stimulate (for example, by virtue of charm, appearance, fame, humor, or being "impossible") in therapist a feeling of wanting to work with him and to be of help to him.

*Most of the table reflects the thinking of Washington group members: M. Adland, J. Fort, C. Schulz, and H. Sterlin.

SECTION ONE
CLINICAL PRACTICE

1

MAJOR CLINICAL CONTROVERSIES
John G. Gunderson, M.D.

Background

This chapter will attempt to cite and explicate controversies in the psychotherapy of schizophrenia, trying, where possible, to trace historical sources, and, when relevant, citing contributions from the literature and clinical research. It is hoped that this will provide an overview and guide for the chapters that follow in the clinical section of this volume. It is also hoped that others will be stimulated to consider these thoughtfully derived but often contradictory opinions in arriving at their own conclusions, and that the questions raised by these controversies will stimulate future research on the psychotherapy of schizophrenia to test the important questions raised by these debates.

In the early part of this century Freud and Jung first introduced the idea that schizophrenic pathology might be connected to conflict and be reducible to understandable communications. Freud subsequently reached a rather pessimistic conclusion about the therapeutic value of exploration.[1] This led to a hesitant investment in psychotherapeutic work with schizophrenics. It remained for interest to be reactivated in this country through the concepts of psychotic reactions first fostered by Adolph Meyer and then the pioneering efforts of Harry Stack Sullivan. There followed an era of excited innovations in which Rosen, Wexler, Sachehaye, and Fromm-Reichmann, among others, all wrote dazzling case accounts of the successful treatment by intensive psychotherapy of severely schizophrenic patients. Despite a more recent wave of skepticism about the efficacy of such treatment, many still believe in psychotherapy as the only humanistic and nondegrading method of dealing with very human people in a particularly severe type of dilemma called schizophrenia. Most of the participants in the NIMH program are experienced therapists who advocate individual psychotherapy for most schizophrenic patients. The controversies described here are mainly those that concern these experts; namely, what kind of intensive psychotherapy should be given.

The areas in which the participants of this program most often found significant areas of controversy are divided into the following two types: (1) *focus* (What? What is the area of principal investigation and discussion in the interviews?), (2) *technique* (How? What methods does one employ to pursue the psychotherapeutic goals?). It is understood that the positions to be described here are polar extremes that neither express the mainstream of thinking on these topics nor represent positions that are rigidly adhered to even by those who recommend them. The dichotomies in approach are often not mutually exclusive. The debate is more frequently one of emphasis, priorities, or sequence.

Current Controversies

Where to Focus the Therapy

The controversies about focus have largely emerged in discussions about the initial stage of psychotherapy. Differences can be seen in terms of time parameters in the patients' lives and in terms of differing ego structures being addressed.

Past vs. Present vs. Future

Some therapists focus on the patient's past, others focus on the immediate present, and others orient their approach toward the future.

Those who focus on the past would ask the patient, "What happened?" This approach emphasizes the importance of integrating the precipitating circumstances.[2] The therapist sees the projection as an avoidance technique and asks the patient to remember his painful but real life crisis. In its more limited sense of recent history this approach was first advocated by Whitehorn,[3] while in a broader sense this approach seeks to explore all past developmental history relevant to the patient's presenting problem. It is necessary for a patient to recognize himself in terms of his past and to see his present as a continuation of that experience. The experience of other therapists leads them to question whether many schizophrenic patients aren't either unaware of their precipitating crisis or unwilling to deal with it early in treatment. If so, then they suggest the crisis must be reexperienced and worked through in the relationship to the therapist. Still others see in this approach the danger that the therapist may impose too much of his own theory and expectations on the patient, and not follow the patient closely enough.

The second approach, focus on the present, would address a different question in the initial phase: "What are you experiencing?" This draws the patient's attention to his immediate reality and emphasizes the importance of the interaction with the therapist in ultimately coming to understand himself. Advocates see this process as critical in helping the patient define his psychological[4] and biological[5] self. This approach would directly take up the patient's *feelings* and their connection with the therapist. There would be an effort to understand the function served by the patient's operating defenses. This process might be likened to that used in ego or character analysis. Opponents of this approach say it does not address the patient's presenting psychopathology as a reaction but as a part of his usual personality. Because it may overlook a loss precipitant, this approach may encourage the therapist to function as a substitute for a lost object. This then postpones grief work —which might bring about early recompensation—until terminal phases of treatment.

The third orientation would focus on the patient's future. The question asked is "What do you want for yourself?" This question appeals to the patient's need to make decisions, plan, and organize. This would draw the patient's attention to the aimless course his life had taken and the maladaptive aspects of being psychotic. (See Chapter 18.) It avoids the psychotic productions and sets aside past experiences, at least for the time being, while supporting the patient's developing autonomy by pursuing what he wants independently of family expectations. Hence the phrase "for yourself" is a way of saying that the patient is master of his own destiny and needs to define himself in terms of his wants. Proponents[6] point to the antiregressive function of this approach and emphasize the importance of providing support to the patient's development of competence and sense of efficacy from use of problem-solving capacities.[7] This approach seems vulnerable, however, to the criticism that internal satisfaction depends on more than leaving home, being competent, and pursuing what one wants; it requires interpersonal relatedness. In fact, being competent and being efficient may be of use only insofar as they are rewarded by being loved.

It may be that each approach is most appropriate for different schizophrenic patients. For example, the approach that stresses integration of the precipitant may be useful only for patients with histories of a clear precipitant (acute reactive patients), while the ego-organizing adaptational approach of the last type (future oriented) may be best for those whose schizophrenic condition might be considered chronic.

Reality vs. Fantasy

Another issue of focus is how much attention should be paid to dreams and fantasies and how much to realities. The real life approach views the schizophrenic's dreams and fantasies as avoidance techniques by people already too prone to avoid and distort what is real. The schizophrenic, in this view, is aided by more structure, being reminded of the discrepancy between reality and his fantasy and dreams, and by the therapist's role as a reality anchor.[8] This contrasts with the Jungian view[9] and with the following statement by one participant in the study groups: "To really understand my schizophrenic patients, I need to understand their dreams and fantasies and spend a good deal of the analysis exploring the meaning of these" (see Chapter 11). Such concern follows from where the patient is "at," and movement toward reality must stem from the patient's initiative. This emphasis on fantasy is criticized for containing a danger of providing intellectual depth but no practical reality-based connectedness that improves social adaptation.

Affects

Many therapists would feel that the schizophrenic disorganization is frequently a regressive response from intolerable affects.[10] Often these intolerable affects occur in response to the loss of some important relationship. A recent follow-up study supports the view that the capacity to sustain and deal with loss differentiates schizophrenic patients who do well from those who do not.[11] Opinions would vary, however, as to exactly what affects the schizophrenic encounters in the process of loss which he primarily needs help in learning to deal with. Some clinicians would see the patient's primary difficulty as recognizing and managing his aggression and its affective derivative, anger.[12] By encouraging the patient to express anger directly, they would hope to avert the need for projection and eventually to modify basic concerns about his omnipotent destructiveness which are accentuated when loss is encountered. There is some research evidence that supports this idea, that therapists who focus on patients' aggression tend to have better results.[13]

Other therapists would focus on the patient's need to remember the pain involved in the loss itself. This requires the patient to recognize what was positive or "loved" in the relationship which is now no longer available and is being missed. The primary affect called upon in this process is sadness, and this process is not dissimilar to mourning. Here the patient's aggressive presentation and concerns about destructiveness are seen as defenses to avoid the real pain of dealing with what was once valued but is gone. Searles[14] has concluded along this line that the hateful expressions he chronicled in his early writing are basically "subsidiary to love" and "that such an ugly emotion as vindictiveness is basically a reaction against such positively oriented emotions as separation, anxiety, and grief." Similarly, Wynne[15] has singled out a group of families he calls "pseudohostile" in which constant bickering is used to avoid the threatening affectionate interactions.

There are common themes to the discussions of focus as well as controversies. The older debate about emphasis on psychotic production seems all but settled. No one feels that active exploration and interest in the content of a patient's hallucinations and delusions is of much therapeutic worth. While no one says they are of *no* worth or interest, they are seen as a low-yield and low-priority area of focus. In this respect Frieda Fromm-Reichmann's mandates seem to have survived better than, say, those of Rosen. Consistent with this development, there seems to be little interest in the early suggestion that therapists enter into and go along temporarily with the patient's hallucinatory or delusional world. Almost all of the approaches seem to have in common, as an initial goal, helping the patient define himself, whether this is in terms of past experiences, psychobiological boundaries, biological feelings, or wishes and goals. With respect to affects, several participants emphasized the importance of using the presence of affect as evidence for choosing where to focus and the importance of helping schizophrenic patients label their feelings[16] and connect them to their life experience regardless of whether they are past, present, or anticipatory.

What Techniques to Employ

Whereas the problem of focus concerns mainly the content over which therapeutic interaction takes place, the controversies about technique concern how one interacts with schizophrenic patients. Each of the four axes of controversy described here encompasses a range of opinions.

Exploration vs. Relationship

The process of exploration can be described as a mutual patient-therapist effort to investigate and understand the causes for the patient's dilemma. The goal of this process might be defined simply as understanding oneself, and, in general, it is felt that this achievement will allow change, growth, and improvement. The therapist's ability to maintain objectivity in his observations of the patient is considered important. While a relationship inevitably develops between patient and therapist, this is viewed as necessary for the investigative task but not as primarily therapeutic in itself.

There are therapists, however, who feel that this process is less valuable with schizophrenic patients than with other types of patients. The emphasis on investigation implies that the schizophrenics' problems are predominantly intra-psychic and does not give due weight to their interpersonal origins. They emphasize that what is most helpful to schizophrenic patients is the development of a real relationship.[17] In this view the therapist's value is less one of objective inquirer and more one of subjective participant. The therapist's consistency and concern facilitate his internalization.[18] It is the experience of trusting and being cared about that causes the patient's previous distrust to diminish and his low self-esteem to be improved. The growing closeness of this relationship then provides a vehicle by which the patient's expectations of being hurt or rejected are modified, i.e., an ego corrective experience. Granted that such changes may, in turn, ultimately permit the exploration of past life and defense operations similar to the way this is done with neurotics, this remains a secondary phase of secondary importance. Such observations led Rosen and Fromm-Reichmann to debate in the 1950s whether a schizophrenic patient actually needed two therapists—one for beginning therapy and one for analysis.

Some of those who feel exploration is the primary vehicle of change feel that a real trusting relationship is developed only after the patient is able to see what interferes with his getting close. Such a relationship is fostered by the therapist's active interest in having the patient share with the therapist what he has avoided by himself or by the analysis of the patient's defenses against such closeness. In any event, the importance of the relationship is predominantly or only its usefulness in either allowing investigation or being the subject of investigation.

A third position, perhaps somewhere in between these two, would emphasize that it is the investigation of the ongoing relationship that is important (Will, 1967). The therapist's objective use of his subjective responses to the patient are important tools to aid both the patient's understanding and the developing relationship (Searles, 1965).

Interpretation vs. Support

Closely related to a debate about exploration and relating is the relative importance given to interpretative and supportive techniques. Interpretations have traditionally been considered a therapist's tool for allowing the patient's experience to be enlightened with a new perspective such as facilitating the movement of avoided material into awareness. By this model the interpretation is followed by insight and a learning experience. However, this "interpretation" of what results from interpretation with schizophrenic patients has been questioned. Less interpretive psychotherapists see the danger that interpretation may bring premature closure or cause undue regression (Kernberg, 1972). Even allowing that an interpretation may be beneficial, a new explanation of why this occurs is needed for psychotics, since there is no unconcious in psychosis and frequently no alliance with a reasonable self-observing ego.[19] Therefore, the benefit may arise either out of nonverbal accompaniments to the interpretation (e.g., sincerity, empathy, affection) or from the relief in discovering that the uncovered material can be understood and accepted. Paul Federn[20] was perhaps the strongest critic of being overly interpretive with schizophrenics. He pointed out that these patients require greater repression, not less, and that interpretation could prevent the maintenance of a positive transference.

Support is delivered in an ingenious variety of ways and in greatly varying amounts to schizophrenic patients. Behavioral methods include the actual provision of token supports such as candy, cigarettes, and even lodging. These nonverbal responses are thought to be responsive to preverbal needs. Common forms of verbal support include support of executive ego functions such as advice, problem solving, and reality testing, and support of self-esteem by reassurance and encouragement. A third type of support (neither verbal nor behavioral) arises from the therapist's consistency, dependability, interest, and enthusiasm.

Even if conflicts could be fully verbalized, many therapists believe that supportive techniques help establish contact and build a positive relationship necessary for later interpretive work. Less supportive therapists feel that such supports may sometimes be harmful "acting out," and that supports too often underestimate the patient's strengths (especially his capacity to form an alliance and to verbalize conflict), unnecessarily infantilize the patient, and unfairly limit the potential for growth or, at best, greatly prolong treatment. Searles suggests that such activities stem from a therapist's unconcious need to curtail the schizophrenic's aggression. As with other variables, the two sides to the interpretation-support dichotomy are not incompatible, and invariably the advocates for either polar technique do more of the other than they may at first acknowledge.

Activity vs. Passivity

Activity here refers to the therapist's role in initiating anxiety, defining himself, confronting defenses, pursuing hypotheses, giving support, getting a history, or otherwise selecting the focus. Activity imposes the therapist's preconceptions on the content. Thus, too much activity may keep the content too confined to the present and not permit free expression of other, possibly deeper areas of conflict. This risk is weighed against the belief that such activity may greatly abbreviate unnecessary and prolonged symptomatic distress for the patient. Active therapists may feel that past experience allows them rather quickly to formulate the origins of the patient's problems and thus justify his role in selecting content.

Passivity, of course, refers to the therapist's nonimposition on the patient's associations. The belief here is that by following the patient's own associations one has a greater chance of finding out what is most important as the patient experienced it and, in any event, avoiding the danger that activity may prematurely lead to such experiences before the patient is ready or able to deal with them. It also implies less verbal activity and more opacity for the patient. Such passivity is criticized for encouraging projection, increasing separation, and not providing enough ego support.

Regression

Perhaps more than any other topic in the area of psychotherapy of schizophrenia, "regression" has come to be charged with affect and disagreement. Signals of the extent of these feelings can be seen in the rhetoric used by opposing camps to describe each other's treatment. Treatment that takes active measures to oppose regression is described as "manipulative" and "inhuman." Therapists who attempt to prevent regression are called "impatient," "intrusive," doers who are "intolerant of psychoses and affects" and who have been "poorly analyzed." Treatment that is permissive of regression is described by its enemies as "infantilizing" and "outdated." The therapist who accepts regression is caricatured as an "indecisive," "inassertive" sitter who is "only interested in the patient's pathology" and/or attaining "infantile gratifications" of his own unresolved dependency and power needs.

In a more positive sense, each point of view can present a consistent approach with a persuasive rationale. Those who are permissive and accepting of the patient's psychotic regression see the patient as re-creating the unresolved infantile disorder that must be "lived through" and grown out of in order to attain a stable higher level of ego integration. The unfolding of a primitive transference to the therapist and the formation of a symbiotic relationship require the therapist's permissive acceptance. The resolution of this symbiosis is a process of self-object differentiation by which the patient leaves the previous level of object relations and develops true autonomy. There is disagreement as to whether this reemergence ("rebirth," as Jungians would term it, "inner voyage" for the existentialists) is a healing process that follows naturally, given an accepting atmosphere, or whether it occurs as the result of a conscious process of learning and conflict resolution, as others suggest (Wexler, 1971). This first approach would emphasize that the therapist's attitudes, e.g., accepting, hopeful, are more important than the particular type of verbal engagement. The latter approach stresses the importance of the therapist's verbalizations and has seen the application of traditional psychoanalytic techniques to psychotic patients, including the use of the couch. Viewed from the perspective of such favorable outcomes, psychosis properly "lived through" is believed by some to offer an opportunity not just for return to premorbid function, but for growth.[21]

Therapists who favor active interventions against regression, which might include structured milieu, maintaining contact with family, lending support to defenses, and sometimes ataraxic drugs, stress the importance of the patient's using his ego strengths in the service of integration. The therapist would not do anything for the patient that he could do for himself. The therapist has expectations of maximal performance from the patient and attentively addresses the patient's higher ego functions in the service of observing himself. Too much disorganization and primary process thinking makes working together with the patient impossible. While the therapists in our groups were uniformly hesitant to attribute much lasting benefit to drugs, for some therapists the drugs do play a helpful adjunctive role by compensating patients to a point where their talk is coherent and they are able to tie their affects to their life experiences.

Therapists who oppose long regressions view the exist-ence of a psychotic transference by schizophrenic patients as unnecessary, often unanalyzable, and potentially lead-ing to either the transfer of patients to another therapist or chronicity. The psychotic transference referred to is that where therapist comes to be seen delusionally not as being *like* mother, but rather as actually *being* mother. The pro-cess of such a delusional attachment is fostered by the therapist's passivity, by his reluctance actively to confront the patient's projections and distortions, and by his reluct-ance to be real. In this view the therapist must make it clear that he is not a mother and that he will not take care of the patient in any real sense. The logical extension of this view is that a therapist should not in any way take any physical care of a patient, even if he is willing, since this is not possible over the long run and sets up unrealistic life expectations.

Therapists who are permissive about regression often say that the power to prevent regression is an exaggerated claim and that a psychotic transference is, if not desirable, at least inevitable. The activity, structuring, and partici-pant functions required by a therapist to prevent regres-sions make proper analysis of the infantile vicissitudes of the maternal transference impossible to investigate and grow out of. In response, those who use such active mea-sures to control regression acknowledge that it isn't the prevention of all regression that is their goal, but rather modulation of regression within limits that allow the pa-tient to integrate the regressive content, that don't separate patients from the important people and the business of their lives unduly, and that discourage unnecessary periods of psychotic distress. Within this context they feel there is still room for regression that is in the service of ego growth. The difference is in the emphasis on keeping this within proscribed limits, i.e., what can be reversible within the context of the psychotherapy.

The Narrowing of Theory
and Practice

The description of differences here makes it clear that there has been some narrowing of the theory and practice of individual psychotherapy for schizophrenia.

There is less polarization of opinion about the necessity and value of regression and prolonged hospitalization, with some recognition of the shortcomings to any generalization. There is also some narrowing of the therapist's technique in the direction away from direct id interpretations and away from actual feeding of patients. In keeping with this there seems to be a trend toward acknowledgment that real relationships are needed, but that they are insufficient by themselves, without analysis of the transference aspects. In contrast to a recent report describing therapists of schizophrenics,[22] there was a general impression here of a more sober, businesslike approach to psychotherapy with schizophrenics and less romanticization than in the infancy of this field. This is evident in less interest in the pathology and symptomatology, and more interest in practical issues regarding adaptation. There is less emphasis on the schizophrenic as victim of deprivation and more interest in his role as perpetuator of his difficulties.

Nevertheless, there are at this time major differences among these most experienced therapists about where it is most useful to focus in content, when to interpret, when to be passive, when to permit or prevent regression, and how to conceptualize the factors producing change. This reflects a healthy respect among psychotherapists for the complexity of the basic schizophrenic problem and the inadequacy of present research on psychotherapy with schizophrenics to provide more definitive answers. What one finds is that each therapist has a unique admixture of the parameters of therapy described here. For example, though the divisions of technique made here are interrelated and sometimes artificial, it is surprising to note how often unexpected combinations of these positions take place. It would seem probable, for instance, that therapists stressing exploration would also emphasize the importance of interpretation and tend to be more active—and vice versa. Yet this is frequently not the case. A more pervasive trend would be that most therapists would find "relationship therapy," "support," and "activity" more useful early in treatment, and that they move in their own distinctive styles toward less activity, more interpretations, and more productive exploration with time. The conclusion would seem inescapable that the varying forms of psychotherapy practiced are not simply logical derivatives of clinical observations, but to some degree the style of treatment is an extension of the personality of the therapist. This is consistent with the importance given the therapist's personality and his style of being real, making contact, and relatedness in treating people diagnosed as schizophrenic.

There is a need to synthesize the effects of relationships on technical approach and the influence of techniques on the relationships. For example, the choice of treatment technique probably influences the nature of the identification that patients make with their therapists. Therapists with more active interpretive methods seem to encourage aggressive identifications, and therapists who are very supportive and real may foster ego ideal identifications. While these are both ways in which patients adopt the therapist's ego strengths, they are apt to be applied respectively to different problems—internal conflict and external situations. If left unexplored they provide the so-called transference cures by which patients are cured as long as the therapist is present. Therapists who are passive may be confronted with more projective identifications. The projective identification must be treated as a transference phenomenon to be analyzed. Thus technique strongly influences the patient's use of the therapist for identification. The value given identification itself depends greatly on the theory and goals. There are, of course, many other such unspecified variables.

An implication of the observed heterogeneity is that research efforts on psychotherapy of schizophrenia are better directed toward finding out how different variables within the interaction affect outcome rather than toward trying to compare "psychotherapy" with other treatment modalities. Necessarily this means correlational studies rather than comparative studies are needed. Methods must be worked out for quantitatively assessing the presence or absence of the various variables in the interaction. This same conclusion is reached by reviews of past comparative research efforts (see Chapter 26). It would also be of value to assess A and B type therapists along such variables as passivity, focus, theory, interpretive activity, regression, etc.

Clearly a second area in which these divergent opinions have relevance is in the training of psychotherapists to do intensive and long-term work with schizophrenics. There is room at this stage in the developing science for the therapist to experiment with various techniques and to allow his own personality to exert its influence. At the same time the novice therapist should studiously attempt to observe what factors in his personality and its interactional application seem to induce change in patients. There is room for much more natural experimentation of this kind.

REFERENCES

1. Freud, S. *On Narcissism.* Collected Papers, IV. London: Hogarth Press, 1914.
2. Soskis, D. A., and Bowers, M. B. The schizophrenic experience: a follow-up study of attitude and posthospital adjustment. *J. Nerv. Ment. Disorders,* 149:443–449, December 1969.
3. Whitehorn, J. C. Guide to interviewing and clinical personality study. *Arch. Neurology and Psychiatry,* 52:197–216, 1944.
4. Laing, R. D. *The Divided Self.* London: Tavistock, 1960. Winnicott, D. W. Ego distortion in terms of true and false self (1960). In *The Maturational Process and the Facilitating Environment.* New York: International Press, 1965.
5. Mann, J., and Semrad, E. V. Conversion as process and conversion as symptoms in psychosis. In *On the Mysterious Leap from the Mind to the Body,* ed. Felix Deutsch. International Universities Press, 1969, pp. 131–154.
6. Mosher, L. R. Implications of family studies for the treatment of schizophrenia. Paper presented at symposium on the treatment of schizophrenia, University of California at Los Angeles, March 18, 1972. Schulz, C. G., and Kilgalen, R. K. *Case Studies in Schizophrenia.* New York: Basic Books, 1969.
7. White, R. W. The experience of efficacy in schizophrenia. *Psychiatry,* 28:199–211, August, 1965.
8. Kernberg, O. F. Clinical observations regarding the diagnosis, prognosis, and intensive treatment of chronic schizophrenic patients. Paper presented at the Follow-up Conference on Schizophrenia: The Implications of Research Findings for Treatment and Teaching, Los Angeles, Calif., March 26–27, 1972.

9. Perry, J. W. Reconstitutive process in the psychopathology of the self. *Annals of the New York Academy of Science,* 96:853–876, 1962.
10. Semrad, E. V. A clinical formulation of the psychoses. In *Teaching Psychotherapy of Psychotic Patients,* ed. David Van Buskirk. New York: Grune & Stratton, 1969. Schwartz, D. P. The integrative effect of participation. *Psychiatry,* 22:81–86, 1959.
11. Merrifield, J.; Carmichael, W. G.; and Semrad, E. V. Recovery patterns 15 years after acute psychosis. Paper presented at the 124th annual meeting of the American Psychiatric Association, Washington, D.C., May 1–5, 1971.
12. Grinker, R. Changing styles in psychiatric syndromes: psychoses and borderline states. Paper presented at the 125th annual meeting of the American Psychiatric Association, Dallas, May 1–5, 1972. Spotnitz, H. *Modern Psychoanalysis of the Schizophrenic Patient.* New York: Grune & Stratton, 1969.
13. Shader, R. I.; Grinspoon, L.; Harmatz, J. S.; and Ewalt, J. R. The therapist variable. *Amer. J. Psychiatry,* 127:8, February 1971, pp. 1009–1012.
14. Searles, H. F. *Collected Papers on Schizophrenia and Related Subjects.* New York: International Universities Press, 1965.
15. Wynne, L. C.; Ryckoff, I.; Day, J. *et. al.* Pseudomutuality in the family relations of schizophrenics. *Psychiatry* 21:205–220, 1958.
16. Will, O. Psychological treatment of schizophrenia. In *Comprehensive Textbook of Psychiatry,* ed. A. M. and H. I. Kaplan. Baltimore: Williams & Wilkins, 1967, pp. 649–661.
17. Greenson, R. R., and Wexler, M. "The non-transference relationships in the psychoanalytic situation." *International Journal of Psychiatry,* 1, 1969.

18. Wexler, M. Schizophrenia: conflict and deficiency. *Psychoanalytic Quarterly*, 40 (1):82–99, 1971.
19. Greenson, R. R. The working alliance and the transference neurosis. *Psychoanalytic Quarterly*, 34:155–181, 1965. Zetzel, E. R. *The Capacity for Emotional Growth*. London: Hogarth Press, 1970.
20. Federn, Paul. Psychoanalysis of psychosis. *Psychiatric Quarterly*, Part 1, Errors and How to Avoid Them, 17:3, 1943. Part 2, Transference, 17:246–420, 1943.
21. Mosher, L. R.; Menn, A.; and Goveia, L. Schizophrenia and crisis theory. Paper presented at the annual meeting of the American Orthopsychiatric Association, Detroit, April 7–10, 1972.
22. Burton, A. The adoration of the patient and its disillusionment. *American Journal of Psychoanalysis*, 29:194–204, 1969.

2

PROCESSES OF PSYCHOTHERAPY
OF SCHIZOPHRENIA

S. Eldred, B. Foster, J. Gunderson, L. Mosher, E. Semrad, O. Will, and I are sitting around discussing. Will is telling us of his experience.

Therapeutic Interaction:
A Sample

He sits silently with a young patient in his office at Austen Riggs every day. She crouches, shivering and frightened, in his presence. Her disheveled appearance and mute pain appear largely as they did when friends found her wandering aimlessly through the streets at night a few months previously in Europe.

Occasionally Will talks to her—indicates that she seems to be experiencing considerable suffering, suggests that there must be good reason for her to be as discomforted as she is by either herself or other human beings, that he would be interested in trying to understand what some of these experiences she had had were about. He sees her at the end of the day so that he can extend the time of their appointment, if need be. While she comes of her own accord to their meetings, she is frequently quite late. He doesn't comment on the time of her arrival, since such comment seems to make her later the following day.

She tells him after many silent times a recurrent dream. "It's Christmastime, the snow is pure and white, I'm an old lady, a hundred years old, wearing a shawl with a knot in my hair. Down the hill comes a man riding a sled. He takes me into the woods and I sleep and freeze to death.''

Will talks a little about himself during the silences. He muses about his training and experience, those things he feels someone might reasonably ask if he were free to speak. He includes some details about things that interest him.

After a while the patient tells him another dream in which a large lizard is sitting on the rocks talking and talking while she is swimming in a bay. The talk disturbs her swimming. She tells the lizard to stop talking but he doesn't seem to pay any attention. She then takes a knife, kills the lizard, disembowels him, and then carries his gutless remains up to the house of the psychoanalyst and shows them to the psychoanalyst's wife.

Her psychoanalyst takes this as a cautionary tale, and talks even less—and yet he conveys his continued presence and interest in her experience. The days and the hours pass. The patient gets up and moves around the office. She begins to explore its contents—picks up books, looks at, touches, and smells the rugs and other items. She rearranges various chairs. She asks him who the people are in the pictures he has around his office—Fromm-Reichmann, Sullivan, and a good friend of Will's who had died. Will tells her of these people and of some of his feeling for them and their importance in his life. She seems interested and attentive, but she never directly says anything about Will himself.

At one point she puts the chair in front of the fireplace and sits in it. "Who are we," she says, "sitting in front of the fireplace?"

He says, "Dr. Will and Miss Adams" — not her name.

"Yes, but it's like being home or being married to somebody," she says.

In the 184th hour she punctuates the silence by asking Will if he would bring her a couple of things from his impending short trip to New York City. What would that be? he asks. "Some black cloth," she says, "to make me a dress. I'm a witch and I only wear mourning."

Will responded that he could ask his wife, who was accompanying him on the trip, to help with that. And the other? She says, "A menu." She'd like to know what they eat, when they'd eat out in a restaurant. There is a discussion between them of food preferences. Then Will talks some about his wife—her early experiences, her psychiatric nursing, his interest in her wishes to be a dancer, and his sorrow that she has never been able to follow up fully in the development of that interest. He gathers too, he says, that there are many directions that the patient is sad that she has not somehow been able as yet to follow.

As time passes she talks about her thoughts—she says that "speech hailed her." She didn't find her thoughts sequential, related to subject or object. Once put into words, she felt her thoughts were lost—they seemed more dreamlike, more fantasy, less connected to the experience that they were supposed to represent. They also seemed to reveal her craziness, to her shame. Sometimes she reviewed her thoughts or what Will said, hoping to find a sequence, something that seemed familiar. She said she paid little attention to words, hers or Will's; mostly she listened to the tone.

She tells Will later that he can stop apologizing to her. She means his way of saying, "I don't know if this gets us anywhere," or "Well, I don't think this explains very much," or "It might better be seen this way—but on the other hand . . ." Later she tells him of her fear that she would be trapped in a prison of theory or relationship or words. Gradually they go on walks, drives, shoot pool.

In a year and a half or two years she sees Will from many points of view, and begins to be able to tell him something of her past and her views of the world and her feelings. Very early in life she would imagine she was a witch.

School, she fantasized, was a prison in which she was captured. She felt she had no parents. She herself was not human. She hated herself, and must remain forever isolated. Perhaps, if the future was unaccountably bright, she could live with animals, work on a large animal preserve in Africa as a kind of game warden.

She and Will began to develop what he felt was a promising relationship—she began to talk about her loneliness, her despair, her fright. People must be avoided because they would be destroyed by her. Will was in danger because of the possibility of their closeness—he would be driven mad, commit suicide, die. She herself must always be free to kill herself. And yet, she said, she stayed at Riggs because of Will as a person—not because he was a therapist. She did find some usefulness about him. She was by this time able to live out of the hospital, and concomitant with the greater openness to communication she felt open to intense pain and aloneness. At times she came over to Will's house at night to tell him of her distraught state.

At this point the field of visible action rather abruptly widens. She communicates some of the pain and usefulness of the endeavor with Will to her family. Her father encourages her to leave therapy, the father's and mother's marriage dissolves chaotically, the patient leaves Will and Austen Riggs to live with a young guru and his other woman.

Formulations to Explain

We (the group) discuss this wondrous evolution and tragic shift in the girl—an evolution of her inner world and outer relatedness and tragic shift which occur as a part of the process between herself and her therapist, between herself and her inner world, between herself and her family and the world surrounding it. But it is the betweenness of herself and her therapist and their relatedness to their inner worlds which holds our search for regularities.

Semrad is thinking about the time of her awakening, her finding some aliveness in the presence of another, in Will's presence. Her body finds itself, he thinks, a living thing that has been dead before. Sensations unattached to words crowd and confuse her. One thinks one's going crazy at such a time. The dreadful pain reflects the trouble of integrating her biological self with the rest of her personality. To include this part of her violates old protective and punitive dictates of her conscience and sense of self. It exposes her to the rage of frustration and the risk of demeaning failure in bodily, sexual negotiation with another person.

Will is reminded of another patient of his, mute and secret, who held her inner life, she said, in compartments. And as the compartments began to break down in the process of her growth, she felt confused and overwhelmed. Colors crowded her, noise and music filled her mind, in ways exciting and terrible. She made a suicide attempt at this time of vulnerability.

Semrad says he would be likely to tell a person in such a state that she was feeling some kind of love for him and that this was frightening her. He thought being older than the patient has the advantage that such behaviors aren't so stimulating and frightening as they had been when he was a younger man. But being older had its conflicts, too—one found oneself to be more inhibited or conflictful about one's feelings of sexuality, one felt more open to self-ridicule for regarding oneself as a vital sexual being in the face of one's awareness of bodily decline. One felt unwilling, hesitant in competing sexually in fantasy or thought with younger people. He liked to remind his older colleagues that they were, however old, pretty young at heart.

The fashion in which Foster believes this girl spares herself the agony of integration of herself as a woman is by splitting herself, her impulses, and this task into disconnected parts. She then can relate to others and herself as part objects. If she stays with Will, she must become (integrate) a woman in his male presence, or at least try to

deal with these impulses. With her guru, she can disso-
ciate. She is a child, and yet sexual. She is irresponsible,
and yet passively attached to her inner image of her father.
She cooperates with her father's bidding by leaving her
therapy.

Schwartz is reminded, particularly by the early course of
the therapy, of his children when they were little—how
they liked to explore their mother's face and body. They
smelled it and squeezed it and rubbed against it and got to
know it with their eyes, mouths, and hands. Their mother
provided them with continuity of space and stimulus—no
sudden moves, no sharp drops, no jarring tones, no abrupt
changes in temperature. That "providing" process is active for his wife, though hidden in everydayness and natu-
ralness. Will has that complicated repertoire that
masquerades as a single quality, he thinks—of lending himself to the patient's warming growth.

Eldred is ever aware of the wider context, the nature of
the institutions—family and hospital milieu—and how they
interact, not always supportively, with such patient awak-
enings. Sometimes it helps in such a situation to have another therapist or consultation at this time, to provide the
safety or distance in which the patient, the family, the
therapist can move. Sometimes he thinks one can stay with
such a patient and allow the nature of one's rage to guide
one. While one cannot artificially calculate it, he finds that
at such times his capacity as a therapist to express outrage,
to "blow his cool" at the patient's disruption of their productive work, helps define the task—i.e., the integration of
these parts of herself—and yet the anger provides the distance from what is otherwise too hotly stimulating in
encounter.

Gunderson and Mosher listen to this discussion with an
ear for what one could formulate in terms of testable hypotheses, what one could put in the form of a statement,
either for the training of therapists or for the useful conceptual grid of the researcher.

Seven meetings lead to some agreement as to the way we view the nature of the problem of schizophrenia and the nature of the task of the psychotherapy of schizophrenia. The central portion of the problem is the occurrence and warding off of a variety of intolerable affects within the patient.[1] The nature of the affects appears to vary considerably from rage to grief, from lust to tenderness. The specifically schizophrenic process of warding off these affects appears to be by various degrees of disorganization.[2] The occurrence of this disorganization tends to be regarded as rapidly developing, and having little process to its development—that is, no steps, no partiality, an all-or-none phenomenon.[3] There is some question, however, whether this is an artifact of the moment of observation. There do appear to be different degrees of disorganization.[4] In the milder degrees of disorganization, the affect is simply warded off and the object is given up. In the more severe degrees of disorganization there is loss of focus on the instinctual representation, and a breakdown of a variety of defensive structures, most crucially in alteration of the structure of the self and object representation.[5] If the disorganization proceeds, the breakdown of the integration of the self, object, instinctual representation, involves a sense of rather total loss of the structure of the internal objects and of the overwhelming of the ego apparatuses. That is, not only does the sense of self and object as differentiated images, with clear and stable boundaries, disappear, but the capacity to focus, order, test, delay, modulate thought, impulse, affect, and action are inundated by the disorganization.

Panic is the frequent nature of the person's experience in this state.[6] Attempts to repair, to organize and/or to ward off such a state of disorganization and the accompanying panic can involve suicide, murder, or other desperate withdrawal attempts. A sense of both the disorganization and the structuralized damping down of all affective experience by patients seems implied in their description of having "died" psychologically at the time of this disorganizing state. It is worth noting that processes of affect modulation, of damping down, or of pleasurable emergence, of bodily absorption, or of bodily dissipation are not descriptively or conceptually clear to anyone either intrapsychically, in relationship to defenses, or interactively, in relation to behaviors.[7] Attempts at repair and warding off frequently involve denial, as in acute catatonia, projection as in paranoid restitutions, and fantasy reconstruction as in delusion formation. All of these are accompanied by a concomitant emotional withdrawal from people.

The sense of inner deadness, the denial, projection, or delusion formation, clearly do not promote or integrate the warded-off impulse, action, thought, or associated affects. Once one begins interacting with such a person again (interfering with his withdrawal efforts) the affect and its disorganization reappear.[8]

Among these affective storms as organizational attempts evolve are those that hold the self beneath contempt, those that contain a grief beyond repair, that envision a rage, venomous and unforgiving.

With this in mind, we put aside the nature of the stresses that precipitate the schizophrenic episode, and the developmental problems that lead one to be vulnerable to such an occurrence. We leave these aside except as they are crucial to the psychotherapeutic action.[9]

Our group focus then becomes the nature of the evolution of a psychotherapeutic interaction with a person subject to schizophrenic disorganization.

Attachment

The development of a mutual, structured attachment between patient and therapist with the aim of fostering the growth, the integration, the ultimate separation of the patient from the therapist appeared as a condensed statement of our common activity. Of what processes does this development of attachment consist?[10] How do these people come to matter to each other?[11]

The therapist does things in the early times of therapy. He spends time in the presence of the patient, he tries to appreciate the nature of the patient's dilemma and the patient's activity in relationship to that dilemma. He attempts to lend himself to the activity (however dimly perceived) of the patient in dealing with this dilemma.[12] He does this within the limits of his continued survival in the presence of the patient. To these ends he acts and talks in such a way as to favor continuity of himself and continuity of his relatedness to the patient in the face of the patient's attempt to deal with chaotic disorganization of thought, of impulse, and of affect. To these ends he provides himself as a rather regular, not easily disorganized human object in the face of the patient's panicky certainty that all human objects (inner and outer) are subject to his destructive rageful activity.[13] He notices and moves toward honest naming of what the patient communicates in words or actions about the patient's state, feeling, observations, and effort—and he does that within his sense of respect for the distance required for safety, and the essentially inviolable privacy of a separate human being. He appreciates the vulnerability of the sense of self to degradation and panic which make withdrawal and disorganization genuine and dangerous. He openly acknowledges the patient's accurate observations about himself or his surroundings, veiled or direct, painful or flattering. And he does this as real in the face of the patient's conviction of the unintegratable nature of accurate perceptions. He notices differences between them. The patient's body and its functions—presenting its refusal to be ignored through anorexia, fecal smearing, sexual gesture, or chill fear—is allowed space and words in the therapy.[14]

Where ego function is less inundated and disrupted,

much of this can be done verbally. The contexts, then, of that person's life experience, of traumatic events leading to despairing schizophrenic disorganization, and of the developmental history describing the growth of that vulnerability to schizophrenic disorganization are definitions of the work-related task between therapist and patient as well as important in their own right.

What the patient gets from all of this seems clear: his inundated ego functions find a human being willing to modulate, establish constancy, provide stimulus barriers, apply controls to action in life-threatening situations, focus and name accurately, sequence and remember, distinguish a self from a nonself, a living from a dead, an inside from an outside.[15] That person nevertheless respects the capacity and value of the patient for whom he is providing these partial functions. The repetitive experience of this allows the patient to become attached to that other person.

It is, of course, a mutual attachment, however different the quality of the bonds. Not a few therapists describe the loss they experience when such functions are no longer required by their (*sic!*) patients. But for the therapist the process of attachment too is a complicated process. There are qualities of charm, various kinds of beauty, qualities of enigma, of challenge, and so on that various therapists find invite for them an investment.[16] These qualities and their investment in them precede their work with any particular patient. Intensity of feeling, poetic expression, searching honesty, and bodily insistence, so much an inevitable part of the schizophrenic dilemma, seem attractively alive, and attractively frightening to many of us as therapists. Each of us noted that our occupation with the inner world of ourselves and other human beings had deep roots.[17] Each in our early years as children had found some fascination and fascinating pain in the sight of and contention with a deeply troubled parent. The search of each of us for the principles by which our own and others' inner worlds and relatednesses are governed has become a rewarding and independent activity. It continues to have importance. This search for a regularity contributes to the attachment, and one notices that in each new therapy, new rules of inner experience are being painfully taught to the therapist by the patient.

The Patient Leads

Early on in any therapy a remarkable shift seems to occur. The patient begins running the therapy and the therapist. The way the hours go, their content, the direction of the movement, their pace, the language, the mood, and the limits of playfulness are determined largely by the patient.[18] The patient described by Will makes him sit silently while she finds her time to reach out and explore him and his environs. Another patient gets intolerably anxious whenever Will uses words referring in any way to electricity—so he learns to eliminate such words as "shocking," "turning off," and "switch" from his language. (Much later she asks him why he quit talking about sex to her, and when he inquires as to what this is about she appears to be referring to his elimination of electrical imagery from his language.) Semrad's patient, for example, at such a time arranges a full and pleasing participation in her analysis and in her relationship with her analyst till he notices that she is systematically excluding any participation of her body or its feeling from the analytic experience, just as she does from the rest of her life and her interactions. Foster has a patient who tells her a story of a boy who cuts down the only tree on an island he inhabits to provide himself with a canoe for his harrowing travels over the ocean, and how he returns then at the end of his travels to sit on the stump of that very tree. The patient, after telling the story, proceeds to "travel" through a rather harrowing and painfully long period of regression, to which Foster must be support, witness, and rooted stump, to whom the patient can return.

The therapist's experience of this change is not dissimilar from that of the mother who, having given suck to her tiny, fascinating, and cuddly infant, suddenly finds herself after eighteen months (and it not infrequently takes that long with patients, too) confronted with an extraordinarily strong-willed, muscular, negativistic (that means he decides what he wants to do where and when without his mother) young person who runs her house, life, and person for the next few years. It is often after such experiences that patients begin to describe their having evolved an inner image of their therapist and occasional glimpses of their own sense of self. This ruthless, unwitting imposition of the patient's problems and activity upon the therapy and therapist is a regularity of the attachment process.

Identification

Therapists lend themselves to this with varying degrees of grace. The probability is that it is not just a state but a process; that is, that the work involved is that artful and yet-to-be-described endeavor by which one allows oneself to be moved without being changed, to be passive without being inactive, to merge and yet retain one's integrity. The task and its dictates provide the support and limits for the therapist at such trying times.[19] This essential part of the process is described as the therapist's having evolved a partial identification with the patient, which can then be appreciated and resolved through the process of interpretation.[20] Out of this must, for the therapist, come an inner image of the patient, and of himself as a part, however temporarily, of that patient which contributes to his own evolution as therapist (and person?) and which "attachment" is part of the process of therapy.[21]

The part processes of interactive, intrapsychic nature in

projective identification—as it shares in the development of attachment and evolution of the sense of self and of the image of other—need to be specified. The further evolution of the image of the other—the manner in which one's tender and passionate, aggressive and sexual capacities create the image of the other, then mimic it, and then identify with the image they have created in the process of organization of the sense of self and its object—need to be more thoroughly understood as they occur between and within two people.[22]

We leave this attachment of self and object partially evolved, however, and move to other aspects of what therapists do to and deal with in patients. These other aspects have to do with the maintenance of intrapsychic structure, of organization in patients, and of their developing individuation.

Regression

No one having witnessed a schizophrenic in acute panic would willingly contribute to such a state. And without ever specifying that there must be degrees of regressive disorganization, or of what these degrees consist, we in fact, as therapists, expect—though we usually do not say that we create—and indeed search for some degree of regression compatible with integration and growth.[23]

It is, of course, not only classical analysis that is a regressive therapy; the psychotherapy of schizophrenia, in spite of the avoidance of the couch, the avoidance of free association, and the avoidance of withdrawal into fantasy, in spite of the avoidance of anonymity of the therapist which is so useful in the classical analytic situation, invites regression. One can highlight this by comparison with the behaviors involved in those treatment plans of frequent use in emergency rooms, for example, which are designed to be antiregressive. They (1) are oriented to the task of immediate adaptation and (2) allow a very short time. They focus on the here and now exclusively, and rather simplistically are concerned with immediate decision making and choosing courses of action. They minimize closeness and avoid one-to-one relationships, avoid communication about one's inner world, encourage the expression of affect only in response to outside stimuli, avoid investment in or dependency upon the therapeutic personnel, freely use rigid control and punitive and judgmental responses. By contrast the psychotherapy of schizophrenia has as its task the evolution of an intimate relationship that will allow integration and growth, and this requires a considerable length of time spent with another human being. In this pursuit we allow confusion to exist from time to time, we are interested in the inner world of the patient, we explore all of the person's experience including his past, we follow affect regularly and respectfully, we allow dependency, encourage intimacy, are loath to be judgmental or to control behavior. All of these together with the goals of mutual honesty and completeness of communication—especially about the nature of the forces at work and interaction between therapist and patient—inevitably involve the hallmarks of regressive potential,[24] that is, (1) intensity of affect, (2) attempts to include that affect and its relevant impulse and thought within the field of mutually conscious interaction, and (3) change or alteration of previously established intrapsychic structures and interpersonal interactions as well as their corresponding experiences.

Therapists know of this continuum between regressive disorganization and "regression in the service of the ego."[25] They delicately handle the way in which they relate to the patient's momentary and overall state. The degree to which intimacy is shown, the level of intensity, the nature of the task of confronting a patient about a particular aspect of his life or behavior, all are modulated by the therapist with this continuum in mind.[26] We tend to note those behaviors of ours which modulate such things by referring to the affect that the interaction has evoked; this intervention "made the patient too anxious," this "attitude on our part was too seductive," or "scared the patient," or "allowed him to feel too guilty." We tend not to classify the behaviors themselves. Yet it seems that therapeutic behaviors that provide distance and privacy, which are open-ended, don't close off options to action or thought, are respectfully listening, are nonintrusive, that acknowledge and appreciate separateness and complexity are all useful and provide room in which a patient can learn to modulate intensities and evolve structures.

The Therapist's Aggression

Similarly, we cause pain regularly to the patient and we modulate that sensitively. Yet we rarely codify the nature of these behaviors or their intrapsychic states or fully their results.[27] For example, we stay in the presence of someone in whom our very presence evokes terror. We talk about unpleasant things, and at times in a rather tactless (direct) manner. We notice behaviors, feelings warded off, and bring them by naming into the center of our interaction with our patients; we invite their tears at times when they are with effort attempting to avoid crying. We locate losses that seem at times to have been so devastating as to have required denial and disorganization in past dealings with them. We call spite or vengeance by name when we see them, and speak of love in the face of the patient's associated sense of vulnerability to shame. That we act in this pain-producing and aggressive way—at times which are not fully of our own making, but in fact are signaled as readiness by the patient—need not distract one from the fact that it feels aggressive, it violates previous behaviors or thought-feeling pattern rules of the patient and his upbringing, and the patient regards this, quite correctly, as aggressive and painful behavior. And after considerable experience of this kind and crucial interaction with his therapist, the patient finds himself able to alter the boundaries of his own interaction within himself and with other people in the face of their own and his discomfort.

Identification with the aggression of the therapist and his therapeutic function, and with his interactive capacity to tolerate separateness, are among the hallmarks of a patient and therapist who have traversed the territory between integration and disorganization.

Description and study of such processes, of intrapsychic and interactive modulation of the therapist's sensitive aggression, are an integral part of the attempt to understand the patient's maintenance of and change in organizational level. These processes are also crucially involved in the development of individuation for the patient, in the support of integrity for the therapist, and ultimately for their mutual capacity for and sense of separateness.

Finally, what we call hope in a therapeutic interaction (only there?) are those elusive perceptions of mutual direction, in regressive states and behavior, which convey a space for action about to be, for a viable inner world, for a human future.[28]

REFERENCES

1. Freud, S. Letter to Wilhelm Fleiss (Draft H[1895], p. 109). *The Origins of Psycho-Analysis.* New York: Basic Books, 1954.
2. Bak, R. Regression of ego-orientation and libido in schizophrenia. *Int. J. of Psychoanalysis,* 20, 1939.
3. Freud, S. Psychoanalytic notes upon an autobiographical account of a case of paranoia (p. 458), 1911. *Collected Papers,* vol. 3. New York: Hogarth Press, 1925.
4. Fenichel, Otto. *The Psychoanalytic Theory of Neuroses* (p. 418). New York: Norton, 1945.
5. Burnham, D. L., et al. *Schizophrenia and the Need-Fear Dilemma* (p. 15). New York: International Universities Press, 1969.
6. Sullivan, H. S. *Schizophrenia as a Human Process* (p. 198). New York: Norton, 1962.
7. Rapaport, D. On the psychoanalytic theory of affects. *Int. J. of Psychoanalysis* 34:177–198, 1953.
8. Semrad, E. V. *Teaching Psychotherapy of Psychotic Patients* (p. 32). New York: Grune & Stratton, 1969.
9. Lidz, J.; Fleck, S.; and Cornelison, A. R. *Schizophrenia and the Family.* New York: International Universities Press, 1965.
10. Will, Otto A., Jr. Schizophrenia and psychotherapy. In *Modern Psychoanalysis,* ed. Judd Marmor. New York: Basic Books, 1968.
11. Semrad, *Teaching Psychotherapy.*
12. Pious, W. L. An hypothesis about the nature of schizophrenic behavior. In *Psychotherapy of the Psychoses,* ed. A Burton. New York: Basic Books, 1961, pg. 43–68.
13. Fromm-Reichmann, Frieda. *Principles of Intensive Psychotherapy.* Chicago: University of Chicago Press, 1950.

14. Hill, Lewis B. *Psychotherapeutic Intervention in Schizophrenia.* Chicago: University of Chicago Press, 1955.
15. Hartmann, H. On the metapsychology of schizophrenia (1953). In *Essays on Ego Psychology*, p. 202. New York: International Universities Press.
16. Eissler, K. R. Remarks on psychoanalysis of schizophrenia. In *Psychotherapy with Schizophrenics*, ed. Brody, E.D. and Redlich, F.C. New York: International Universities Press, 1952.
17. Freud, S. Letters of S. Freud. Letter to the members of B'nai B'rith Lodge (no. 220, p. 367). New York: Basic Books, 1960.
18. Ibid., no 12.
19. Wexler, M. The structural problem in schizophrenia. *Int. J. of Psychoanalysis*, 32: 157–166, 1951.
20. Strachey, James. The nature of the therapeutic action of psychoanalysis. *Int. J. of Psychoanalysis*, 50:275–292, 1969.
21. Tower, L. E. Countertransference. *J. Amer. Psychoanalytic Assoc.*, 4:224–255, 1956.
22. Segal, H. *Introduction to the Works of Melanie Klein.* New York: Basic Books, 1964.
23. Kris, E. Psychology of creative processes. In *Psychoanalytic Explorations in Art.* New York, International Universities Press, 1952.
24. Gill, M., and Brenman, M. The metapsychology of regression and hypnosis. In *Hypnosis and Related States.* New York: International Universities Press, 1959.
25. Kris, Psychology of creative processes.
26. Tower, Sarah S. Management of paranoid trends in treatment of a post-psychotic obsessive condition. In Mullahy, P., *A Study of Interpersonal Relations.* New York: Grove Press, 1949.
27. Wexler, M. The structural problem in schizophrenia:

the role of the internal object. In *Psychotherapy with Schizophrenics*, ed. Brody and Redlich.

28. Erickson, E. H. Growth and crisis of the healthy personality. In *Identity and the Life Cycle*. New York: International Universities Press, 1959.

3

CRUCIAL ASPECTS OF THERAPEUTIC INTERACTION
Gerald Aronson, M.D.

The problem of schizophrenia is its stability. Of course, to the schizophrenic, the problem is the sheer terror of it all. But to us who treat these bewildered and bewildering sufferers, and who write about it and occasionally experience a touch of it, the problem—which gathers us together in lectures, seminars, and books—is the glacial stability of the experience amid its shifting expressions.

Does the very refractoriness of the response to treatment—which is none other than stability facing intervention—tell us that we are on the wrong track entirely? Or does it urge special concern upon us that we not neglect crucial elements? The wrong-track possibility cannot be discounted so long as etiology eludes us. But in the absence of curative molecules we attempt to use curative people. We then begin to talk of therapeutic interaction.

Everybody has a list of elements crucial to the therapeutic interaction; so much so that the laurel of cruciality passes quickly from one element to another in a manner reminiscent of the indecisive/overdecisive dither of the schizophrenic himself. My list is brief: (1) the nature of intolerable affects, (2) pair-formation, (3) the love-internalization dilemma, (4) the problem of entering the wider world, and (5) the nature of the therapist.

Intolerable Affects

The New England group (see Chapter 2) views schizophrenia as having something to do with the warding off of intolerable affects by disorganization. One can tackle this from two sides: Why does the schizophrenic experience his affects as intolerable? Why does he react to these affects by disorganization?

I would suppose that some schizophrenics do experience affects as intolerable. All affects? Specific affects? Those that create or result from guilt, shame, humiliation, longing, anxiety, fear? Maybe some, maybe all. But it seems likely to me that those affects that are intolerable are characterized not so much by their intensity as by their special quality of intentionality and action in the human sphere. When a person is awed at the sight of the Grand Canyon or a marvelous mountain, his intention is to look more upon it. It would be interesting to know whether such affects, regardless of their intensity, are felt by schizophrenics to be intolerable. I would think not, unless the mountain or the Grand Canyon has some symbolic correspondence with something human. Hypothesis: If the affect does not have, as its provenance, origin, or goal, something human, and if there is no link with intentionality or congruence with action, then, no matter how intense, it would not be experienced as intolerable.

A more general speculation: Affect is a signal that is itself the result of a taming process. Something occurs in the reticular activating system or limbic system—wherever the home of feelings—which is filtered, tamed, and otherwise modulated. If there is no taming, what does it feel like? Perhaps we have an inkling at times of confusion, dreaming, disoriented states, catastrophic illness, and so on. What gets through the barrier of taming we call affect. But that must be only a very small portion and very different in quality from what starts toward the barrier. Perhaps it is not the affects (the postbarrier residual) which are intolerable; perhaps the taming process is deficient and what is experienced, unmodulated, is the preaffect precursor. Something closer to the visceral and the somatic, giving an eerie feeling-tone to what is usually experienced in quite a different manner. Perhaps riddance, autotomy, or disorganization are the only methods to deal with such protopathic experiences. The schizophrenic specificity—if such there is—resides in the character of the affect-barrier, or taming process, rather than in the nature of the affects themselves. Perhaps the disorganization is in response to, or companion to, those untempered visceral storms rather than to the more readily verbalized, already tamed affects. This thin band-aid of theory cannot cover up the fact that I have invoked two specificities: a deficiency in the taming process and the special place of those affect-precursors that have to do with intentions and actions involving other humans or parts of humans. Perhaps we might unite these seemingly unrelated elements when we remember that the mother-child relationship serves as a stimulus-barrier and hence an affect-tamer.

The therapeutic implications of these speculations would seem to favor the use of a barrier, soother, pacifier, buffer, or tamer. Perhaps, in some measure, drugs—with the usual caveats—play such a role. In large measure, human influence can serve such a taming and modifying function. The question "What kind of human influence?" touches upon the old debate of schizophrenia as a deficiency disease or a defense syndrome. If the former, then the human influence should tend toward the pacifying, barrier-making side rather than the interpretive stance called for by the defense theory.

A word about disorganization in response to affect: If a neurotic were in his right mind, he too might try to disorganize himself, to unhinge the structures securing secondary process, but he cannot. He simply does not have that mechanism or that deficiency or that psychic situation available—except in sleep, in toxic conditions, and the like. The nonschizophrenic has to work very hard to achieve this disorganization. Baudelaire used to set for himself a program, "the systematic derangement of the senses," but he was forced to use opium, hashish, or sensory isolation.

Pair-Formation

In the case reports of Dr. Schwartz (Chapter 2) and Dr. Foster (Chapter 5), examples of pair-formation abound. Schwartz: (1) A dream—the old lady with hair tied in a knot, a man on a sled comes down a hill, they go into the woods and she dies—a pair is formed, followed by death. (2) The patient kills the talking lizard and bears the gutless creature to the therapist's wife. Three pairs are formed or recognized: patient-therapist, therapist-wife, and patient-wife. And two are dissolved by the therapist-lizard's death, leaving only the patient-wife pair. (3) The therapist is going to New York with his wife; the patient talks about being a witch and wanting to know about the menu. She is curious and intrusive about the pair. (4) In another illustration, Dr. Schwartz notes the patient's feeling that there is danger to the therapist from her association with him. If there is a pair, particularly if it is newly formed, then there is danger. (5) After a very effective, therapeutically oriented pair has been formed with the therapist, the patient tells her father, "Look what a wonderful pair I'm in." Following this communication the father and mother break up *their* pair, and the patient goes with the guru and *his* wife, abandoning potential and actual pairs with therapist, father, and mother to hide herself in a threesome—providing another piece of evidence of the dangers of constructing and maintaining pairs. Foster: In this case there are intimations that as the relationship lurched on between therapist and patient, another pair was solidifying between patient and an art teacher.

Hypothesis: Therapy will not succeed in the absence of pair-formation between therapist and patient. No surprise so far! But success will not occur with the formation of only this one pair. The patient must make a pair with the therapist and at the same time—not before, not after, but at the same time—make a pair with someone else, who may be unknown to the therapist, arranged by the therapist, or provided by the therapist.

Corollary hypothesis: The therapist must be in a pair with the patient and, at the same time, with someone else as well—spouse, friend, supervisor, co-therapist, whoever.

Our theories provide amply why this should be true, if true, but could not necessarily have predicted its truth. Speculations abound: the prevention of engulfment-symbiosis, correctives to mutual idealization, the reconstitution of Oedipal and pre-Oedipal triads, the splitting and projection of mental contents into good and bad parents, the construction of relatively conflict-free chumships, the necessity to have cognitively fixed structures amidst the storms of the therapeutic relationship, etc.

The Love-Internalization Dilemma

Another dilemma? As if not burdened enough with the need-fear dilemma and the dependency-autonomy dilemma, the schizophrenic suffers a further intersection of dilemmas.

By the nature of his disorder, by virtue of being human, and because he is in therapy, the schizophrenic is subjected to an intensification of an everyday phenomenon consequent upon pair-formation. If you love someone, you are joined to him and he is vividly in your mind. Gradually, if you have an ability at all in this sort of thing, you internalize some aspects of your partner; you begin to become like him and you think a bit more like him.

But as this process of internalization goes on, with its consequent identifications, is there not a degree of loss of interest in him? As we internalize significant aspects of valued/loved/feared objects and we succeed in constructing those identifications that form the cornerstones of the ego, we need our parents and teachers less and less. Perhaps we come to love them less.

As internalization and structure-building proceed in therapy, the therapist is delighted. But as the patient starts to internalize certain aspects and functions of the therapist, he needs the therapist less. And object-loss, a trauma to all, is markedly so to the schizophrenic. As this loss occurs, the patient begins to feel alone in a world emptied by his successful internalizations. (Up to that point he may have felt alone by virtue of his refusal or inability to internalize what he considered to be a noxious element.)

The patient, experiencing the losses consequent to his micro-internalizations, attempts to reinvest himself in the therapist by divesting himself of the internalizations that have caused these grievous losses. Further, he attempts to reinstate by a variety of maneuvers (increased illness, aggressiveness, propitiation, placation, withdrawal) the external vigor and vividness of the therapist's presence or to remove himself from it entirely in order to prevent the painful losses.

The therapist's aim is to provide an auxiliary ego which he hopes will be taken in by the patient. The therapist wishes to make it possible for an internalization to replace an external relationship. When this process succeeds to any degree, countermeasures are set in motion by the patient to prevent the object-loss. Hence, the patient experiences great ambivalence. However, the ambivalence is not only those of love-hate, libido-aggression, etc., but largely one of ego-integration vs. object-loss.

I have simplified this point greatly in the interest of clarifying a poignancy that must be endured by both therapist and patient. A practical point: Love leads to internalization, which leads to lessened love after a certain time. If lessening of love (or object-relationship) has not occurred, the patient has not yet finished his major internalizations.

Entering into the
Wider World

Forming a pair and suffering through the love-internalization dilemma are, of course, not events but processes in sequence and cycle. The love-internalization dilemma threatens the pair with dissolution and leads repetitively to renewed attempts at pair formation by both therapist and patient, though not necessarily at the same time. If all goes well, bit by bit the therapist begins to function as a model for identification, object of internalization, namer of emotions, container of anxiety, and so on. These functions bring into the newly formed arena between the two persons the wider world of language and ideas. Private experience begins to be transformed by, and into, public speech.

But what the therapist considers a gain the patient may view as a loss.

I cite Albert Einstein as an example. It is said that he did not begin to speak until much later than the usual age. Although evidence is sparse, I conjecture that something like this might account for the delay: "If I spoke the language of men, then what would I do with my own ideas? I would be using a foreign tongue, using the currency of others trying to coin my thoughts, and thereby altering something very precious to me."

This conviction, I suggest, is common to many geniuses: they experience their own thought, ideas, and feelings as treasure. The schizophrenic has a hard time drumming up very much in the way of clear ideas and clear feelings; whatever he has, paltry though it may be, is his treasure and he wants to hold on to it, preserving it against foreign debasement and contamination. Side by side with the urge to dissipate perplexity and confusion (an urge shared by the therapeutic pair) is the necessity to maintain untarnished the private icons. This latter trend makes the patient turn a fearful, hence deafened ear to the therapist's "Oh, what you mean is . . ."

We try to help the neurotic person so that what is private (i.e., secret and unknown) becomes public, to us and to himself. The schizophrenic may experience this effort as one that insinuates a public language, public views, and public thought processes (secondary process) into private places. Relieved though he may be of his loneliness by virtue of being understood, he feels like a nationalized industry without self-determined goals, idiosyncrasies, or independent judgment.

To the extent that the patient experiences the language of secondary process as a relatively neutralized, de-instinctualized form with a low frequency of metaphor, his own images are perceived, though terrifying and bewildering, as textured, vivid, and exciting. If his words-images-thoughts have achieved thing-cathexis (as Freud posited), they throb to a degree that makes public language seem lifeless. He suffers so much lifelessness already that he struggles to retain what he can of life.

If the therapy goes well, the therapist also enters a wider world of language and thought. He comes to use the patient's metaphors and suffers (enjoys?) a twist of rhetoric that may deform to an extent, great or small, his own language uage and thought, threatening (at worst) or (at best) playing fast and loose with his own secondary process.

The Nature of the Therapist

The reader has noted few suggestions for technique in this discussion. The nature of the therapist as the therapeutic agent puts technique in the shade. Words treat neurotics; people treat schizophrenics.

Whatever else these statements convey, the inferences are *not* to be drawn that technique or knowledge of some characteristic courses of the schizophrenic reactions (Chapter 24) are not of great importance, or that the nature of the therapist is preternaturally fixed and unalterable.

Forming the pair, weathering the love-internalization dilemma, entering the wider world are activities in which both therapist and patient are involved. These broad categories, like a symphonic movement or a tapestry, can be aided, served, and catalyzed by a variety of techniques informed by wide and minute knowledge. The master hand, guiding and shaping, mainly midwiving—these massive movements are the therapist's nature.

What can be said of this most important of therapeutic agents? Not as much as needs to be said—but some elements can be caught sight of from Dr. Foster's case description (Chapter 5).

The therapist is an anchored, solid person who takes her own emotions seriously and who takes the patient's emotions seriously. The therapist has within her what I would call, for lack of a better word, a certain validity, a *force majeure*, and feels similarly that what is in the patient is a major force. The patient comes to know these facts about the therapist. This anchorage and solidity within the therapist give her a special and specific courage: the courage to stop medication, to play, to ban, to interpret, to threaten, to become important to the patient. It is not that this courage in itself emboldens the patient but that since it stems from the therapist's validity and substantiality, the courage communicates to the patient that he is in touch with a quality of immense psychic weight, for which even a term like "charisma" would be too pale.

How vague the words and how tangible the quality! Such gravity of purpose and character contains both gusto and anguish. Can these be of no use to a patient in whom the capacity for pleasure has been extinguished by the chronic expectation of terror?

4
THE CONDITIONS
OF BEING THERAPEUTIC
Otto Allen Will, Jr., M.D.

Introduction

During the past year and a half I have met on several occasions with a group of senior and experienced colleagues for day-long discussions about psychotherapy and schizophrenia. For all of us this has been a personally enriching and professionally valuable experience, whatever its consequences may be in terms of demonstrably productive "hard" research. In the meetings there has been a remarkable lack of defensiveness, competitiveness, envy, and jealousy, despite our disagreements and arguments. All of us have spent much of our working lives as therapists of seriously troubled people. Some of our patients have improved; others have not. We know enough to recognize that in this complicated field one cannot, in a simple sense, be expert. We tend to be sanguine but cautious. For each of us psychotherapy is hard work, but gratifying. We do not hold a romantic view of schizophrenia, but look upon it as one of the complicated and crippling endeavors to continue life. Our attitude toward disorder is serious, but is salted (as all existence must be) with a trace of humor.

We discovered—if we did not know before—that we had no great triumphs to reveal, no shameful secrets to conceal, no grandiose need to bewail failure, and no tricks or easy shortcuts as substitutes for thought and labor. We can't say precisely what schizophrenia "is" or just what can or should be done about its behaviors in all instances. But we are not as uncertain as these comments may suggest. We think of schizophrenic phenomena as attempts to cope with what are experienced as overwhelming requirements of existence. To a large extent the form of these efforts is learned in the process of growing up and can be modified, for better or worse, through further learning.

For me, the most important lesson derived from these meetings is that in our work one must share respectfully what he does with associates who know something about this business—its challenge, pleasure, risks, and loneliness. What follows does not reflect exactly what each member of the group would advocate, but they would not cast the remarks aside; they would use and mold them in discussion.

The following comment by James Baldwin is timely:

> I have always felt that a human being could only be saved by another human being. I am aware that we do not save each other very often. But I am also aware that we save each other some of the time. . . . [T]he miracle on which one's unsteady attention is focused is always the same, however it may be stated, or however it may remain unstated. It is the miracle of love, love strong enough to guide or drive one into the great estate of maturity, or, to put it another way, into the apprehension and acceptance of one's own identity.[1]

Delineation of the Problem

I do not think that it is useful for me to attempt an account of the generality of states labeled schizophrenic, or of a therapeutic approach somehow designed to resolve all problems listed under that rubric. Some investigators insist that the term "schizophrenia" is misleading, if not destructive to useful thinking on the subject, and deny that there is such an entity. The word does include, at least, a wide range of behaviors—transient or prolonged, overt or obscure, occurring in a variety of circumstances, and observed from different points of view.

Therapy, as I speak of it, cannot be defined as an entity, or as a technique that can be applied impersonally by an operator without reference to the personalities of the participants. Each therapist has his own style. A part of what he does he may not notice (important though it may be); other parts he may not wish to recognize, rationalizing or explaining these with often irrelevant "theory." It is to be hoped that he knows a good deal about what goes on—but not to the extent that he is immune to surprise and further learning.

In view of the above it is advisable to refer specifically to a patient. M, twenty, was the older of two children; her brother was three years younger. Both parents were successful professional people, their marriage said to be satisfactory despite its vicissitudes. M had been known as a quiet, seemingly compliant, and happy girl—a good student and well liked by friends. In her senior year of high school she withdrew from social activities, lost interest in her work, was "moody," complained of fatigue, and left her classes and home to live in a commune. She had a bad trip with LSD, was injured in a car accident, was hospitalized for treatment of a fracture, and had consultation with a psychiatrist. She refused to talk with him and later (on the insistence of her parents) met with another and found him "unsatisfactory." A third therapist she liked, but showed her regard for him by attempting suicide with barbiturates. After a brief hospitalization she returned to treatment, but soon spoke of feeling strange, and after cutting herself and attacking the physician spent several months in a sanitarium, where she was treated with insulin coma and electroshock. With the aid of ataractic drugs she managed to live for a few weeks as an outpatient, but again took an overdose.

Many of the patients with whom I am concerned in these

remarks resemble M in several respects. They usually present a combination of the following characteristics: (1) the disturbance is recognized in adolescence or the early adult years; (2) they withdraw from people, drop out from school or work, become increasingly isolated, and may seek solace in drugs; (3) when they get into so much trouble that the community is disturbed, they are labeled sick and exposed to various forms of treatment, which they tend to reject; (4) they distrust doctors, hospitals, adults, prescriptions for living, and themselves; (5) they have no well-defined goals, they fear their own destructiveness and that of others, and they tinker with thoughts of suicide or magical freedom from restrictions; and (6) they often keep tottering along with the aid of drugs, prescribed or otherwise, attempting to conceal despair, sleep disturbances, nightmares, hallucinations, and a sense of personal emptiness.

This person does not seek out treatment; he has no enthusiasm for me or my work; he doesn't fit in anywhere, and his future is not promising of anything but disaster. There are several forms of living called schizophrenic, but for the present I am concerned with the foregoing profile. It may be worth noting that all psychiatrists might not agree that what has been briefly described is evidence of a schizophrenic process.

A Concept of Schizophrenia

A therapist works, more or less consciously, with a concept of the processes with which he concerns himself professionally. The concept may not be "true," it may be inadequate for the conditions to which it is related, and it may be flawed by inconsistencies, lack of proof, prejudices of the possessor, and so on. It may be treasured by the therapist as if his honor and existence depended on its maintenance, in which case it is not likely to be subject to growth and may be used to mangle, if not destroy, what substance it has. Nonetheless, a grouping of ideas about how something comes to be, and how it works, should be recognized, exposed, formulated, and used—not left to operate covertly.

The difficulties of M and her kind I consider to be schizophrenic, a condition characterized by qualities summarily sketched in what follows.

(1) The origins of the trouble may be found in the infant's relationship with the mothering one in the context of the family organization, prior to the refinement of speech skills, the formation of clearly defined object relations, and the development of dependable constructions of the body image and the self. For survival the mothering relationship must be maintained; persistent severe discomfort in it (the early forms of anxiety) is dealt with by withdrawal and the beginnings of denial and dissociation. Perceptual distortion is used in order to live with some degree of emotional comfort and security.

(2) Whatever genetic, congenital, or constitutional problems may exist, environmental factors are required to bring about the behavior eventually called schizophrenic. That is, we learn to be much of what we are.

(3) Shakow describes the schizophrenic difficulty as being a lack in the ability

to achieve a generalized set. . . . He has difficulty in focusing on the relevant aspects of the defined situation, while being more susceptible to the influence of the peripheral and extraneous. . . . [He] appears to be doing this at least in part as indirect and symbolic efforts to attain the satisfaction of fundamental needs which, in contrast with the normal person, have never been adequately satisfied in the ordinary course of events, particularly those deriving from the familial setting.[2]

I think that the person here described may not focus on factors that seem to be relevant to an observer because attention must be given to all manner of details in any one of which it is feared may lurk a threat to remaining fragments of self-esteem and security.

(4) In adolescence there is an acceleration of being. Along with physical maturation come cultural and social demands for change. The young person is neither child nor adult, and may be treated indiscriminately as one or both— confusion, contradiction, and transition. He is asked (often indirectly and obscurely) to enter into intimate and self-revealing relationships, form acceptable and satisfying patterns of sexual behavior, separate from accustomed family ties, think in terms of a career, consolidate systems of value, and give up certain illusions—and probably acquire others. Again I refer to Shakow:

> The situation is made even more complicated by the fact that with chronological development the schizophrenic finds himself in an *environment* which also changes concomitantly. It changes in the sense of being organized to provide fewer and fewer outlets for infantile or childish need satisfaction. Further, the environment constantly makes demands of its own which the organism must at least make stabs at meeting.[3]

(5) This situation is complicated and something must be done about it. The demands must be met in some way; there must be a response. Change, growth, and separation are required—and while desired, are feared. If one is to enter into more "personal" relationships, he will reveal more of himself. If important aspects of that self have been concealed, dissociated, their revelation is likely to be disconcerting, frightening, and nightmarish. The person may now be exposed to himself and others as something less than human, and as a consequence be rejected and abandoned, becoming nothing. Human relatedness is essential to survival and growth, and yet, in its invitation to revela-

tion, it threatens disaster in disorganization of the personality—a state of panic. This last condition is intolerable. It
is a nightmare in which a problem exists and must be
solved, but has no definition and is unknown. The self is
being lost, meaningful relationships are disappearing, and
there is a great sense of urgency to do something—to bring
to chaos a semblance of order.

(6) Attempts at resolution of this extremity include the
following: (*a*) withdrawal into fantasy, with a denial of
external demands and the exertion of control over "inner
events"; (*b*) suicide, with the implication of redoing and
magical rebirth; (*c*) preoccupation with fragments of experience and unrelated details of the bodily economy, as in
hebephrenic abandonment; (*d*) the paranoid "solution"
with its oversimplified and grandiose response to living; (*e*)
further dissociation of the distressing sentiments of the
nightmare with the accompanying need to live thereafter
cautiously lest the old ghosts return; (*f*) the elaboration of
behavioral patterns—such as the obsessional—whereby a
pseudoexistence is maintained by moving from one scene
and person to another, none being satisfactory or sufficient, despair and isolation increasing as they are denied,
and loneliness hidden by success; and (*g*) there can be a
recovery with profit, the dissociated aspects of experience
becoming an acceptable portion of the self, permitting
growth to occur.

Certain of these "solutions" to disorganization are not
promising therapeutically. Suicide is an end. The hebephrenic and paranoid answers are without joy, but they
work too well; the road back is likely to lead through terror, and few dare to take it. Well-established obsessional-
ism, denial of disorder, and fascination with the personal
constructs of fantasy can be intruded upon, but not without
pain for all concerned. The person of my interest here has
found a problem, not a solution.

Note that the schizophrenic phenomena as described in

this account may seem to appear inexplicably as well as suddenly, but are the culmination of a lengthy series of interpersonal experiences and affronts to self-esteem and a sense of personal integrity. Crazy and incomprehensible as it may look, the behavior is goal-oriented, problem-solving, and purposive. The therapeutic relationship is designed to help the patient gain sufficient trust in human relationships to the extent that he can give up or reduce ineffective and unnecessary avoidance maneuvers, and get on with more productive learning and action.

Conditions for Being Therapeutic

Patient Selection

It is often said that one wishes to work with a patient in the early, acute stages of his trouble. To do so isn't as easy as it might seem to be. In those early stages the disorder may go unrecognized or be denied, or there is hope that it will be outgrown. Proffered therapy may be rejected, its need denied, or prematurely terminated. Various approaches are used as quick results are sought. Guilt and shame push us to find an organic disease or even to welcome death rather than to face up to the possibilities and realities of our interpersonal-social imperfections. The patients with whom I meet have, in a metaphorical sense, had the roof cave in on them; they are trapped. They don't see a way out in what I do, and they usually try to get rid of me. Sometimes they succeed, but as best I can, I interfere with their flight and try to insist that the "buck stops here."

This person—the M mentioned earlier—is not "well motivated" for treatment, and I don't look for, or ask for, confidence, trust, hope, respect, and liking. I look for evidences of struggle with the problem. How do you get what you need (security and satisfaction in a human relationship) without losing what you have (some organization of personality, shaky though it may be)? I want to find out if the tie to human beings is strong (it must be there for life to have continued thus far), and if the patient is aware of it, and values it even as he fears it. If he knows what he needs and fears, our task is not easy but simplified.

On the basis of what has been said so far, anyone who desires to do so can—with thoughtfulness, carefulness, respect, and a trace of daring at times—find ways of approaching a fearful and distrustful human being without driving him away, or being driven away himself. In what follows I shall venture a few suggestions about procedures that for me have value, but are not presented in the sense that "this is what to do." I refer here to the patient in a hospital, in this instance an open institution.

The First Step

As a beginning I want the patient to know something about me, and I tell him a little about myself and what I do. I assume that something ails him, and I'd like to know more about it, but I don't talk about change, or achieving "good health," or getting "better," because to do so would lead me to voicing platitudes, and the patient has probably endured enough of those by now.

I avoid at the start material that might lead me to form prematurely an opinion about the patient that is not based primarily on my own contact with him. I don't want to get caught up in what others have said about him, accounts of what he has done, his misadventures, his perhaps multiple and differing diagnoses. I could be influenced too easily by such reports and lose the person in the verbiage. I try to find out how this person views the world, how he came to be who he is, how much he values his life, what he can envisage for his later days, and how he perceives me. I don't push with questions—I can wait. But if I am unclear about something, I say so. I don't want to get into pseudo-agreements in which neither one of us knows what he is talking about. My wish is to learn what I can about this person as he is now; I don't know what he can—or should —become because he is to me a stranger. I shall attempt to learn with him what roads are open to him and which he will follow; together we may discover what will constitute good health for him. As I see it, my task is to help this person look at, and evaluate, his life and his prospects. I don't know how he should live, but I may be able to help him in discovering this for himself. I am not an expert in living. My professional skill is in the area of working with an anxious human being in such a fashion that he can attend with discrimination to what goes on in his life.

It is necessary that the patient and I meet with each other, despite the fact that we are at times reluctant to do so. I plan to meet with the patient for an hour (sometimes longer) five or more days each week. We usually meet in my office, but I may visit his room, or go for a walk or a ride in my car if space seems too restrictive and movement is desirable. The essential rules are that we do get together, that violence is to be held in check, that no one is going to get hurt physically (and not seriously otherwise), and that we will not run away from each other during our work.

I expect that bonds of relationship will form as the meetings continue and there is an arousal of emotion. Drugs are used only during times of prolonged and dangerous disturbance. I usually remain with a patient when he is near or in panic, using a wet sheet pack when indicated. My purpose is this: I want him to learn that whereas the human relationship can lead to panic, it can also be a major factor in allaying panic. A person in a nightmare needs someone to be with him; he requires human contact—and frequently its presence makes the use of medication unnecessary.

Dependency

The procedure described will lead to a situation of dependency, often long denied by both participants. The therapist may recoil from what he experiences as excessive demands on his energy, time, and emotions; he speaks of being devoured, manipulated, enveloped, and so on. The patient may express fears of being controlled, brainwashed, and killed. They seem to be caught up in formless, hateful symbiosis from which there is no escape. At this juncture the therapist may "discover" that his patient can't change, is hopeless, and should be abandoned. The patient suspects that his therapist will sicken, die, commit suicide, or go crazy. The theme of all of this is the fear of the growing attachment and its inevitable accompaniment, separation.

Dependency with security is a necessary preliminary to relationship and independence. The therapist may become strongly attached to his patient, but the pleasure derived from the latter's growth and increasing effectiveness is greater than the pain of separation. There will be many farewells for the patient as he turns from illusions, fantasy, and once reassuring symptoms. He will often protest that the state of "sickness" is better than the state of "health," the former being by now more fixed and predictable. I know of no calming answer, for what he says is to an extent true. Life is to be lived, not avoided; therapy is not designed to lead to a form of blandness or happiness, but to an increased ability to deal openly with uncertainty and the limitations of human existence.

Regression

Regressive behavior may occur as an attempt to escape from an intolerable situation. We seek for possible causes in the patient's relationships with other people—relatives, patients, staff members, and the therapist himself. Psychological murders can be carried out quietly in seemingly benign hospital situations. Regression may occur when social demands are felt to be excessive, in which case we usually reduce the input of stimuli and group pressures, for the time being.

We don't attempt to produce a state of profound regression, there being no guarantee that recovery from it will occur. On the other hand, we don't recoil from evidences of regression or attempt to prevent its development through a rapid resort to such modalities as drugs and electroshock. We have asked the patient to show us who he is, and he may reveal significant aspects of himself in what we call regression and "acting out." If the behavior endangers the patient or others, we limit it; otherwise, we attempt to learn from it.

The "Team"

The therapy that is outlined briefly here is not done alone, but requires the close coordination of the efforts of a group of people. A team is more than several individuals with assigned tasks. The members of an effective team must get to know each other, share responsibility, and talk to each other openly about their hopes, doubts, fears, discouragements, pleasures, loves, and murderous impulses. The reason is not a wish for narcissistic displays, but for the development of mutual support and the reduction (and hopefully avoidance) of covert disagreements that promote the phenomena of mutual withdrawal in patients and staff members. Meetings with members of the patient's family are part of the "teamwork."

It should be noted that we encourage attachment in those who both need and fear it. While the bonds of relationship are forming but are yet fragile, separation should be avoided; so one does not abandoñ a young child, the hurt being too great to be repaired easily, if at all. Whatever we do, we attempt to maintain contact until there is the strength to endure separation.

Conclusion

Very little has been said directly about psychotherapy; rather the conditions of its being have been suggested.

If schizophrenia is some sort of disease to be done away with, what I have spoken about is no answer to such a problem. Should schizophrenic behavior be one of the paradigms of human living, it should be studied in many ways. The slow and costly concern with the individual in these times of great demand and need and haste may appear to be frivolous and impudent, if not simply callous and even wicked. I think, however, that we should persist in this task, hopefully uncovering as we do certain truths about man, pleasant and otherwise. Schizophrenia is largely an example of our ignorance about ourselves, our disregard for life, and our (sometimes blind) cruelty to each other. From this point of view we might, through our science and improved methods of control, do away with schizophrenia —and be left with the problem of schizophrenia; that is, the willful nature of man himself. Bitter though the cost may be, and great the need for cure, let us reveal and not conceal; let us learn and have the courage to use our knowledge. There is likely to be no second chance.

REFERENCES

1. Baldwin, James. *Nothing Personal.* New York: Atheneum, 1964, p. 3.
2. Shakow, David: Some observations on the psychology (and some fewer, on the biology) of schizophrenia. *J. Nerv. and Mental Dis.*, 153: 300–316, 1971, p. 311.
3. Ibid., p. 312.

5
THE RECAPITULATION OF DEVELOPMENT DURING REGRESSION: A CASE REPORT

Beatriz Foster, M.D.

The following is a condensed operational account of some aspects of the first three years of treatment with a schizophrenic patient.

I have focused primarily on the developmental history and some phases of its replication during the period called "regression." I have omitted for reasons of space other important aspects, such as the importance of the nonhuman environment and its impact on the patient, and a detailed account of the work of a team (nurses, activities, maintenance, dietary, etc.), without which a patient such as this cannot be treated.

Identification of the Case

Marianne N. is a twenty-eight-year-old, unmarried, white Protestant from the Midwest who was referred by a psychiatrist. She came accompanied by her parents for admission to the Austen Riggs Center in November 1967.

Summary of Background Information

Sources of History

Most of the history has been obtained from the patient. Additional information was made available from several visits of the parents, whom I interviewed with and without the patient, and from several family visits that included the older sister. Also available were letters from four of Marianne's eleven previous therapists.

Family History

The patient's paternal grandfather is described by his son as an extremely competitive man who measured his children's work by their tangible accomplishments. The grandfather invented and designed machinery, was successful financially, and died at the age of sixty-seven.

The family was steeped in a tradition of science and the children were trained to be "rebels" and "nonconformists." The patient's father saw his family as being different from other families, and he valued this quality of uniqueness. Although Marianne's grandfather died when she was three, she felt for a long time a strong tie to him, and to honor his memory she wore white blouses daily to emulate his ritual of wearing white shirts. This fact distressed her father, who regularly wore blue shirts in an effort to be different from his father, whom he hated.

The paternal grandmother is eighty-seven and lives with a female companion near the home town. She dislikes and distrusts men as much as her own father disliked women.

Paul N., the patient's father, age fifty-six, is president of the family business, N. Laboratories, Inc., and is in charge of engineering, designing, and manufacturing commercial food-processing equipment. The second of three brothers, Mr. N. is a driven, aggressive, soft-spoken man who enjoys nothing more than grappling with problems that demand immediate and complete solutions. He proudly told me that his company produces a large percentage of the food-processing machinery used in the United States, that he likes to "steer his own ship," and that he detests socializing or anything resembling conformity. Even in his youth Mr. N. was "independent." At ten he was running the machine tools in his father's shop and had already played an instrument in the town band for two years. Earning his way through the use of his mechanical skills, he visited all of the forty-eight states, Canada, and Mexico before finishing high school. He did not graduate from college, saying that the courses seemed to be elementary and irrelevant to his interests. He educated himself by reading books on mechanical science. Mr. N. describes himself as "generally friendly," but his wife speaks of him as charming only in social situations with people whom he likes. According to her, he is preoccupied with solving problems even in his sleep, and has little sympathy or understanding for her. The patient sees him as "a God who judges everything"; he is critical of her and her mother, saving his praise for the older sister. In Marianne's judgment he wages a persistent psychological warfare with his wife, pointing out at every opportunity her "psychological weakness." Lately he has periods in which he allows himself relative inactivity— reading, sleeping, or taking trips with his wife.

The patient's maternal grandfather, age eighty-two, is described by his daughter as a quiet, gentle, kindly man who is understanding with his daughter and concerned about his grandchildren. He worked for a railroad, and participated in town choirs and bands.

The patient's maternal grandmother, who died in 1964 at the age of seventy, wished for her daughter the "culture" and advantages that she had not possessed. She is described as a loving but unsentimental woman who, after Mrs. N. and her two younger brothers left home, was hospitalized for a short period because of alcoholism.

Sarah N., the patient's mother, age fifty-seven, is a timid, withdrawn, humorless woman who impressed me as being very depressed. She sees herself as quiet, unassuming, uncertain of herself, and prone to turn her anger against herself, becoming physically ill. She is described by the patient as a martyr, someone who must be neat and tidy in everything she does and who has had the life drained out of her by her husband. According to the husband, she occasionally has temper tantrums and reacts in a highly dramatic fashion.

Mrs. N. met her husband in high school, and they married when they were both twenty. The marriage has never been satisfactory to either partner. She is frightened by such things as his daredevilish flying, his interest in mechanical endeavors, his traveling, and so on. He, on the other hand, is bored by her concert-going, museum-visiting, etc. Mr. N. has tried to deal with his disagreements by tackling them head on. Mrs. N. deals with them in a passive-aggressive way, complaining and eventually giving in. In 1958, after twenty years of marriage, the parents mutually decided on a divorce. This decision was made because of a growing dissatisfaction with their continual conflicts and mutually exclusive tastes. After the divorce they lived together for a few months while the girls finished school and then Mrs. N. and Marianne lived in California for two years. During this period Mr. N. decided that his old habits were too important to relinquish and that starting all over again with someone else was too difficult for him. He then proposed marriage to his ex-wife and they were remarried in 1960. Remarriage brought no major changes; when Mr. N. wanted to do one thing, Mrs. N. wanted to do another. Mrs. N., however, compromised more often now, would not complain, and would try in every way to avoid an open fight. Each parent describes the other as removed and unrelated. It is difficult to imagine the manner in which the family lived together. From their descriptions, they seemed to live almost like four strangers, each in his own separate world.

Marianne's sister, Ann, age thirty-three, is a mathematician and has recently divorced her husband, retaining the custody of their ten-year-old daughter. Ann tries to appear as someone who shares her father's self-sufficient, aggressive, and competitive orientation, as well as his scientific interest. Currently she appears to be increasingly depressed.

Developmental History

As Mrs. N.'s first pregnancy was difficult, her physician recommended that she have no more children. The N.s wanted another child, however, and Mrs. N. went through another pregnancy. She recalls the period as "one of the happiest times in my life." The delivery itself was uneventful, labor lasting fifteen hours. The baby weighed approximately seven and one-half pounds and cried immediately after birth. Regarding sex preference, the parents insist that they were happy with another girl. (My impression is that they wanted a boy.) When asked about the choice of a name the mother said they had "already used up our favorite girls' names for our eldest daughter so the closest we could find was Marianne."

During the delivery the mother suffered vaginal tearing, which needed surgical repair, and the postpartum period was difficult. She hemorrhaged heavily on two occasions and bled continuously for approximately three months. After two weeks in the hospital she returned home. Because of Mrs. N.'s weakness, fatigue, and increasing depression, the baby was cared for by a housekeeper, who stayed with the family for eight years.

Marianne was breast-fed for six weeks, shifting to a bottle when Mrs. N. developed a breast abscess. At this time Mrs. N. had a fever and the housekeeper took over the duty of feeding the baby. Marianne is described as an alert baby who had difficulty taking to bottle feeding, with the result that everyone involved became impatient. At six months she was started on spoon feeding, but would spit the food up and cry while being fed. The housekeeper is described as being harsh, stern, and unfriendly to children. Marianne disliked and mistrusted her intensely.

The baby did not share the parents' bedroom. At first she

slept with Ann, the older sister; shortly afterward she was put in another room because of her difficulty in falling asleep, her wakefulness, and her incessant crying. From an early age Marianne seemed to resist sleep and often awakened as if from a nightmare.

Teething started at eight months. Marianne bit on pieces of cloth and spoons to such an extent that the mother was concerned that she might seriously injure her gums.

Locomotor development was within normal limits.

As toilet training was started by the housekeeper, there is no information available on this. Marianne does recall using a potty until she was old enough to carry it to her crib. Often she would fill the pot with her mother's favorite kitchen utensils, cover them with a bowel movement, and derive pleasure from her mother's resulting rage. She wet her bed until age eleven.

When Marianne was a year and one-half old her mother developed pneumonia and was hospitalized for approximately two months. The patient was not allowed to see her mother at this time, and her father reports that she cried almost continuously. During this period she was cared for by the housekeeper, and by an elderly married couple. This couple entered the family scene and remained close to them for several years. Marianne liked them, and they looked forward to the times when she would be left in their care.

After Mrs. N. recovered from pneumonia, both parents decided to enter psychotherapy. Mrs. N. was seriously depressed, and Mr. N. had taken some tests that diagnosed him as an "ambulatory schizophrenic." Mrs. N. sought help locally and Mr. N. moved to another town to work with a therapist who was on the staff of a psychiatric institution, as it was thought that he might need hospitalization at some time during his treatment. For the next three years (from the patient's age one and one-half to four and one-half) the father was home only on weekends. He would arrive on Friday night and shortly after arrival would become involved in arguments with his wife. Marianne recalls hiding under the furniture and filling her ears with tissue paper so she couldn't hear what they were saying. On occasions Mrs. N. and Ann would visit the father in the town where he lived, Marianne being left with the older couple. She felt abandoned, rejected, and frightened, but also relieved that she would not have to go through the hassles and battles of their meetings.

During these years Marianne had numerous somatic complaints. When she was two and one-half she was diagnosed as having a heart murmur, and for three months her activity was restricted. At age three she had a tonsillectomy. The mother did not stay with her during hospitalization. When she awoke from the anaesthesia, the hospital personnel had great difficulty calming her. Postoperative hemorrhaging was severe.

There was very little physical contact between the mother and Marianne. The patient recalls that she would go to her mother to be held. After a brief contact the mother would ask, "Is that enough?" When the father was present, even this gesture was omitted. (At one of the parents' visits, Marianne asked them if this account was a misperception or an accurate statement. Mrs. N. admitted that she herself had had a lot of difficulty touching or being touched. In addition, Mr. N. said that he was very jealous if his wife had any physical contact with the girls. In view of this fact, Mrs. N. made it a point to avoid touching her daughters in the presence of her husband.) The father's jealousy and the competitiveness with the daughters extended to other areas. She recalls his bringing her toys, and as soon as she set these in motion he would himself play with them while Marianne cried and waited her turn. If he gave her crayons and a coloring book, he would take them away and color himself. His explanation at the time was that Marianne would break the toys or crayons; his explanation to me was that he felt an urge to play when he saw her do so. Marianne experienced these interactions with her parents as very confusing and frightening. The father insisted that the daughters call him Steve, not Dad. This was the pseudonym he used for signing his paintings and short stories. The patient's one happy memory of the father is at age four when he offered her a bottle of 7-Up and let her drink all of it. Marianne remembers this age period as one of loneliness and rejection. At the age of three Marianne wanted to be held by her mother while they were being photographed. Mrs. N. insisted, however, on holding a dog. The picture was taken with the mother holding the dog and Marianne crying.

Another set of memories around age five were introduced by Marianne as "the three animals I have killed." First, she let the family dog out of the house and it was killed. Second, she tied a stray cat to a swing set, feeling it would otherwise run away by morning, and the cat strangled itself. The third memory was of her taking a pet turtle outside during the winter, forgetting about it, and letting it freeze to death.

Until she was six years old the N.s lived in a middle-class neighborhood. Marianne's memories of herself during this period are of an unhappy, tense child who was always crying, dirty, and friendless. This is recalled as a period of constant unrest, fear of parental fights, terror of her father, and dismay at her mother's reactions. Marianne often did not go to bed before one or two A.M., had frequent violent temper tantrums, bit her nails, chewed her hair (until the mother had it cut so short she could not get it into her mouth), and had difficulty eating. When Marianne was six Mr. N. designed a very unusual modern house for the family and they moved to an upper-class neighborhood. At this time Marianne started school.

In the new home Marianne was racked with a variety of preoccupations that kept her in a state close to panic and effectively excluded her from the family. At night, with her head against the pillow, she imagined the sounds of her own heartbeats to be the footsteps of the woman on the Old Dutch Cleanser can (imagined without a face and with a head shaped like an ax) coming up the stairs to get her. She would often shake without apparent cause, was afraid of dying, and would beg her parents to take her to a physician. She had frequent skin rashes, and was told if she continued biting her nails the rash from her hands would extend to her brain.

At the age of eight she developed an auditory hypersensitivity, particularly to noises made by inhaling cigarettes, chewing food, and running water. She wrapped faucets in towels and placed blankets under the windows on rainy nights, all to muffle the sounds of water. The N.s were startled by Marianne's running away from the table or out of the living room, pressing her hands against her ears in an effort to avoid hearing the noise they were making as they smoked or ate.

Little by little Marianne withdrew from the family life. She would eat alone and spend time in her room. She did not puncture her eardrums only because she thought that at a later time she would wish to hear. At this time she began to wear ear plugs. Even now she wears these occasionally. She was afraid of being kidnapped, of dying, and had fantasies of seeing bodies cut in half. She became aware of people's genitals—wishing that she could make them disappear. In school she was extremely anxious and unhappy. She felt inadequate, and her time was taken up with a fear of either urinating or defecating in public areas. Her attention was poor, and she had difficulty learning. She ate little for breakfast and skipped lunch, hoping thus to avoid the necessity of going to the bathroom while in school.

Notwithstanding these difficulties, during this period Marianne recalls some happy memories of times she spent outside of the house in the company of friends. She did not relate well in groups, but did develop a one-to-one relationship with a girl, and also spent time with three other girls, two of them her age and one older. It was around this time that she was sexually informed by an older girl, who played sexual games, one of which included Marianne's introducing crayons into this girl's vagina. Information about menarche was provided by the mother when the patient was approximately nine.

When I asked the parents what they thought of Marianne's behavior at the time, they said she was timid in school, had violent temper tantrums, and seemed worried; they looked upon these as passing concerns. They did, however, take her to see a psychologist for a checkup. He is reported to have said, "Everything is okay." Only as an afterthought to my question did they recall being concerned about finding a dead mouse Marianne had kept in a jar, and an unexplained cut she had made near her eye. At age ten she reached her menarche, and was frightened when her mother said she was now "a grown-up woman."

According to the parents, at age twelve Marianne began to compete with her older sister. She began going out with a gang called the Black Leather Jacket Group. She described them as "hoodlums" and was thrilled by their dark, mysterious, exciting world. This was the first group in which she did not feel like an outcast and was not regarded as an unwanted, tag-along "strange one." It was the first group of peers to which she belonged. She would dress in denim clothes and a black leather belt; would climb out of her window at night and spend until dawn riding around on motorcycles in the park. On occasion she spent the night at one of her boy or girlfriends' houses. It was some time before the parents became aware of this behavior. When they did they tried to set limits to it, with the result that she became irate, threw temper tantrums, and flouted their limit-setting. At thirteen she was in an automobile accident, sustaining lacerations of the scalp and wrist. Her parents were unaware of this because they were traveling, and returned home to find her in the hospital. After Marianne's recovery Mrs. N. threatened to put her in a boarding school, but Marianne refused to give up her friends. She says that from age twelve and a half to fifteen and a half she never lacked a boy friend.

When Marianne was fifteen the N.s were divorced and she moved with her mother to California, where they lived in an isolated corner of a trailer park. She spent two years there, again had no friends, felt betrayed and terrified, and did very poorly in school. Mrs. N. worked during the day, went to school at night, and often returned home to find Marianne waiting on the doorstep because she was afraid to be in the trailer alone. At this time Marianne had a recurrent nightmare of falling from a precipice and disintegrating. When she was seventeen her parents remarried and she returned with them to her home town but dropped out of high school. She withdrew to her room, ate poorly, and slept little, and her thinking became increasingly disorganized. She was interviewed by a psychologist—the first of a long list of consultants and therapists—and eventually, at the recommendation of one of them (February 1961), entered a school in New Hampshire which was a protective, parent-oriented community (a residential home for "disturbed" adolescents).

In the summer of 1962, at age eighteen, she returned home. Her sister, who was now married, had become pregnant. Marianne recalled this period of her life as "pure hell." She had somatic delusions, could not be left alone, could barely eat or sleep, and eventually was hospitalized for a month in a general hospital for "exhaustion."

In the fall she returned to the same school in New Hampshire and with the help of her therapist was able to organize herself enough to complete high school in 1963. At this time a longstanding interest of hers became one of her time-consuming occupations: ballet. Some people said that she had great talent as a dancer, and for the first time in her life she found gratification in something that made her special within the family and gave her the hope of being able to dedicate her life to this discipline.

She decided to stay in the school for one more year to consolidate her improvement, but during the latter part of that year (1964) an administrative quarrel over the manner in which the school should be organized created a split among the staff members. The therapy staff withdrew en masse. The situation became chaotic, students were taking sides, and she lost the second group in which she felt she had belonged and been accepted.

That summer, at age nineteen, she lived with a possessive and intrusive woman who was a trustee of the school and who sheltered an odd assortment of eccentrics and artists in her Boston home. Much of this time Marianne hid in her room. She took a course in remedial reading and occasionally met with her therapist. In the fall she enrolled in a small, philosophically oriented, experimental college with the understanding that her therapist would be on the staff there. He was not. Consequently, throughout that year she drove ninety miles several times a week to see him. This experience proved to be disastrous, as the previous one had been. She began regular classes but found them to be too advanced for her abilities. On the other hand, some of her artistic talent was now more evident, and it was arranged that in the third term she should have a single tutorial class for her regular courses and a private class in modern forms of expression. She worked on a film that was shown in an exhibition, and the school kept it in its archives because of its excellence.

Early Signs of Onset

Her social life was reduced to fleeting contacts. Her experience of loss, both of the "hoodlums" and of her previous school, made her afraid of becoming attached to this school and the group. She did have a boy friend, who served as a source of comfort, particularly after dark, when she became extremely anxious and afraid of being alone. The janitor would allow the patient and her boy friend to sleep in the school library together. During that year she started drinking heavily, and near the end of the year, while drunk, had sexual intercourse for the first time. After this she was sexually promiscuous. In the summer of 1964 she went on a trip with three young men. She drank heavily, was very anxious, her thinking frequently was disorganized, and on several occasions she was in a state of terror. On one of these occasions she awoke to find herself naked in the middle of the night on a beach, disoriented and screaming. Somebody heard her and brought her a blanket, and she spent the night on that beach. The next day she walked down the coast for several miles and found her friends, having no recall of the incident. She then began using marijuana and amphetamines. On one of the occasions, under the influence of marijuana, she had a hallucination in which the devil pursued her.

On a trip with her parents—a period of six weeks—she was extremely anxious and delusional, and took tranquilizers and alcohol to reduce the level of anxiety. Following this trip (in 1965) she rented a studio apartment in Greenwich Village (New York City) where she lived with a girl friend and two young men. She spent her days taking ballet lessons and wandering through the city. At one time, while drunk, she was "awakened" while being "raped" by two men. When she failed in an audition for ballet, she left the studio in tears, walking for hours in a daze.

Hospitalization

Marianne sought out her previous therapist and on his recommendation she was admitted to a psychiatric institution on September 8, 1965. She says that she entered the hospital expecting to receive a lobotomy and left it two years later with a feeling that this was exactly what had happened. Although the hospital therapist told her that he would stay with her until she felt better, he left for military service eight months later. She experienced the next therapist (a man) as unresponsive and controlling, stifling her creativity, causing her to lose her integrity as a person, and denying her access to any feeling. Therapeutic sessions were punctuated by her tantrums and complaints that she was being destroyed by him and the ugly confines of the city. Her major complaint was that the therapist was a "cynic," who secretly hated life. At first the therapist felt that the patient was transferring to him the negative part of her feeling for her departed therapist. There were ups and downs in the relationship. The therapist found many signs that she "approached me and the therapy in a very positive manner, but just when you'd think you were getting close to her she would become afraid and withdraw." During the last half of her hospitalization there was a determined effort to enforce limits and structure to Marianne's day, and the result seemed to have been a settling into a protracted struggle. Classes and group meetings were compulsory, and the attending staff was perceived by Marianne as being sadistic. Mornings were an agonizing ritual of dressing quickly and hiding in an effort to avoid the noise on the floor made by the people who came to clean the ward. She did like some of the staff and especially enjoyed trips to the park, where she and one special staff woman watched children and made up stories. In spite of this comforting relationship the patient watched in alarm as she regressed through stages of prolonged sleep, depression, and social isolation. In December of 1966, Marianne requested another therapist. When this request was refused, she felt she had no choice but to insist on being transferred to another hospital. In the first hospital she was treated with a number of ataractic drugs, including Librium, Elavil, Vivactil, Miltown, Stelazine, Thorazine, and Cogentin, given at different times. She was admitted to the Austen Riggs Center on October 2, 1967. From the time of admission to August 31, 1969, she was seen in therapy four times a week by a young man. During these first two years her behavior was generally quiet, obsessional, and phobic, and she presented some somatic delusions. This early part of her treatment is not summarized here.

Initial Phase of Therapy

First Contact

I saw Marianne for the first time shortly after my arrival at the Austen Riggs Center during the July 4th (1969) picnic. I found myself observing her while she was involved in some competitive games. She is a five-foot, six-inch slender young woman, with long, black, straight hair and unusually large blue eyes. She was dressed in a shabby blue dress (the type a six- or seven-year-old would wear) and looked very serious. I noted that although she participated in the games by going through the motions, I had the impression that she "wasn't there." I found myself interested in the patient and asked the director of psychotherapy if I could work with her.

At this time Marianne met with the director of psychotherapy to discuss her future plans for therapy. He suggested that I had time but she said she would not work with a woman or with a junior therapist. She did, however, reluctantly agree to go through the motions of meeting with me.

First Interviews

Marianne arrived late for the first appointment, wearing the same blue dress (she had six of that kind) and a man's woolen coat, notwithstanding the fact that it was a hot day in August. She sat on the edge of the chair, her fists clenched. There was a wooden expression on her face, but her eyes seemed to show great anger. This was the first of three interviews. In brief, she said the following: She had been in treatment for many years; she hated women (and added "no offense intended"); she didn't trust them and would never be able to reveal herself to a woman. She told me that at the time she was taking 400 mgs. of Thorazine and 15 grs. of chloral hydrate for sleep. She suspected that should I become her therapist I might want to take her off drugs, in which case she might go into a panic as she had in the past. She then asked me a question: "Would you take me off the drugs?" I answered that should she become my patient I should eventually do so. She then added that I seemed to be forceful, a trait she didn't like. When I asked her what she thought of herself as a woman, she angrily replied, "What do you mean? I am not a woman; I am a girl."

She said that as a child she had had some nightmares and was afraid that if she started working with me they would come true. She then volunteered to tell me something about the nightmares. The first one took place in the woods. She was lined up with several other people, approaching a huge frying pan in which she was to be fried. She said that she always woke up from the nightmare in a state of terror. In the second nightmare she was about to dive into an empty swimming pool. She added that in the dreams these horrors never happened because she woke up. She felt that should she start seeing me, all of these would become true.

During the interviews I found myself puzzled about myself and very interested in the patient. I was puzzled because I felt she disliked me, she openly rejected me and didn't want any part of me. Although I felt intrusive, I was still willing to work with her. After several meetings with other available therapists, she was assigned to me in the middle of September 1969. She didn't show up for the first several appointments, and when she finally came, she angrily started off by saying, "This is the history of my life. I have always gotten what I don't want, and of that I get the worst."

The blue dress and the man's coat that she wore at the initial interview were her uniform for the next several months. During the sessions, for which she always arrived late, she would complain about life at Riggs, her unhappiness, my lack of warmth, and her increasing dislike of me. She said that the only thing that was currently helpful in her life was the Thorazine. From the very beginning of the treatment I was in daily contact with members of the nursing staff. I found out through them that Marianne would establish contact with them by requesting 25 or 50 mgs. of Thorazine several times in the day. Since I wanted her off the Thorazine and the chloral hydrate, we agreed that she would try to eliminate the drugs herself. Given the tenuous quality of our relationship, I did not want to get into a power struggle. I had told her that, instead of asking for drugs, she might try getting in touch with me and perhaps we could then try to understand what her anxiety and fear were about. I had from the beginning made myself available to the patient at any time that she might need me.

Beginnings of Attachment

The last Sunday of November 1969 she called me at nine P.M., saying she was very frightened and would like to talk with me. We met in the library of the patients' residence. During that meeting she told me that she had had eleven therapists. She often became attached to them, but they left her, and now she was afraid of becoming attached to me. She then asked me what kind of contract I had with the Center. I told her that as far as I knew, I should be staying here for quite some time. She then spoke of her childhood, giving me more information during this meeting than during the previous two months. She talked at length about her parents' divorce and their remarriage. While we were together, she excused herself twice, saying she would return immediately, which she did. We were together for one and a half hours. After this meeting the nurses informed me that she had taken 100 mgs. of Thorazine after telephoning me and 50 mgs. each time she left the room.

Removal of Tranquilizers

As I felt that this testing situation could be prolonged indefinitely, I decided to discontinue the use of the drugs. It was the first of a series of occasions on which I interdicted Marianne's behavior. She became angry at this decision, but was also relieved. From September through December, Marianne spent her days somewhat as follows: She would get up at six A.M. and go to the house of a neighbor, a Mrs. W., with whom she practiced yoga for approximately an hour. She felt very close to this woman, who was in her sixties. She also hired a ballet teacher and would practice in her room several hours a day, planning to study at Jacob's Pillow (a famous dance center) the following summer. By the end of December, at which time (presumably the effect of the drugs was wearing off) it became increasingly difficult for her to continue her activities, she began to withdraw. Her contacts with Mrs. W. became sporadic, and her last social event or activity before withdrawing altogether was constructing a raft which she named after her friend and in whose company she floated it on a nearby river.

The Fear of Loss—The Need-Fear Dilemma

From the middle of December Marianne would come to the hours and sit on the edge of her chair, become increasingly silent, and rock back and forth with her eyes closed. Many times when she opened her eyes I had the impression she had come out of a dream. I asked occasionally what she was thinking about or feeling and she would invariably answer, "Nothing." Whenever she spoke during these hours the main topic was the fear of separation and fear of loss. She said she felt she had once had a belonging. If she gave this up (this memory or introject, however unclear) she would not recognize it should it come her way again. An example of this concept was that she would never use a public phone. Should she put a dime into the telephone it would seem to disappear. Should the dime be returned, she would never know that it was the dime she had owned before.

At this time I discovered that in the attic of the Inn (the building where the patients live) Marianne stored dozens of garbage bags in which she kept cheesecloths through which she had filtered the bathtub water, fingernail clippings, hairs that had fallen out of her head while combing, used menstrual pads, etc. Then I recognized more clearly her need for attachment and her fear of separation.

As her anxiety grew more apparent she also spoke of the things that she had been afraid of all her life: her fear of suffocating and choking, the loss of sphincter control, the fear of being kidnapped, her fear of decaying, of disintegrating, etc.

By the end of January 1970 she told me that she wanted an IUD (which she had had for three years) removed. As she has a phobia about traveling, she did not want to go to the office of the gynecologist, and the IUD was removed at the Center. After this event took place she withdrew into her room and began restricting her intake of food.

Second Phase

Withdrawal

During the period described so briefly above, Marianne was also engaged in a lot of compulsive ritualistic behavior. She spent long hours in her room bathing, hand-washing, cleaning her room, and in an assortment of other rituals that were to protect her from evils coming from the "within" and from the "outside." In March 1970, more was revealed openly. Marianne was in the Center's greenhouse (on the grounds) when another patient of mine mentioned that some flagstones were going to be placed in the solarium. Marianne asked how this was to be done. Explaining the procedure, the other patient mentioned that an acid was going to be used to modify the structure of the stone. At this juncture Marianne ran out of the greenhouse, thinking that some of the acid might have gotten inside of her. She began scrubbing her body with a Tuffy pad (a synthetic fiber used to clean Teflon) until she bled. Both her chest and her hands were raw, and while she bathed she would scream for help because she felt contaminated and feared disintegration. (She would not go near the greenhouse for one and a half years after this event.) She stopped coming to my office for fear of bringing acid into it and contaminating it. I met with her in the Inn, where we would sit at a distance of several feet from each other in respect for her fear that she would also contaminate me.

Then came the "event of the patients' kitchen" at the Inn. The drain of the sink was clogged. Marianne asked what substance was used to unclog the drain, and one of the workers told her that it was acid. Marianne ran out of the Inn in panic; she refused to return, saying that the kitchen had become contaminated with acid, that the acids had extended to the halls of the Inn, and she feared that coming closer to the Inn would cause her disintegration.

Attempts to Control the Phobias

After every bath she needed a complete new uncontaminated outfit. Some of the nurses helped her to get clothes. Many times she would buy a complete new outfit and yet something would happen to it and she would dispose of it, feeling that if she so much as came close to it she would die. When she moved out of the Inn she bought a number of tents. Soon each became contaminated by a thought, a ritual carried out in an inappropriate manner, or a "contaminated" person walking by. Then Marianne would purchase another tent, move into an "uncontaminated area" for a day or two, and the process would repeat itself.

Her room was mapped out into "good places" and "bad places," and she jumped from one spot to another. In a similar fashion the outside was divided into contaminated and uncontaminated areas. I would always attempt (at any inconvenience to myself) to see her in one of the uncontaminated areas. We would meet on the front lawn of the Inn. She would stay about ten feet away and then lead me to some place where we could talk. Once this happened to be the white line on the center of the main street.

I would see her twice a day for varying lengths of time. The rest of the day she spent in the woods, washing in the swamp, performing her rituals, and talking to the trees, who she said liked her. During one of these meetings she told me a story about a little dog who lived in a circus. He was allowed to live in the circus because he was so small that everyone wanted to look at him. His tininess made him a place in the circus. The dog was very well liked by the people of the town but although he felt at home in the circus, all was not peaceful. One day a tragedy occurred, and the dog grew bigger. He was now grown, and since there was now no place for him, he went away. The people of the town cried but did not know what to do. Time went on, and the little dog (now not so little) lived in the woods and felt lonely. He was what many people (and dogs, perhaps) call normal. Then something happened that changed the dog's life. He began growing and became abnormally large, and he realized that he was again unusual. No longer was he an ordinary size—he was huge. He returned to the circus and everyone was glad to see him again. Marianne then said that one can be accepted only if he is "different."

Regression

While Marianne was living in the woods she stopped eating, lost weight, and looked filthy. Neighbors complained, saying that she was seen running naked in the woods and was often heard screaming. I was concerned about these matters. I brought food with me to our meetings, and she accepted this from me. I would offer her milk, juices, cheese, and so on. At first she would take only the liquid and for a period of about three weeks I spoon-fed her milk. Eventually she let me hold a paper cup from which she drank. She would not allow me or anyone else to touch her. Thus it was that each morning and evening I would go out and feed her. In the middle of April, on a very cold morning, we met as usual, and she looked cyanotic from the cold. Her eyelids were swollen (I found out that she had been wrapping her contact lenses in leaves) and she looked ill. I told her she could not live in the woods any longer, and that we should have to find another arrangement. I went to my house (it is very close by) and got one of my sweaters and put it on her (touching her for the first time), and brought her to the medical office building. Here, with some help, we cleansed her and I gave her some warm milk and found for her a room in a guesthouse nearby.

For two weeks she lived in the guesthouse, but this also soon became "contaminated." For the landlord there was an increase in the heating bill because Marianne spent so much of her time in the bathtub. Then I found her another place in the house of a woman who works in the dietary department. Marianne lived with her for approximately three weeks, happy at feeling that for once she belonged to a family.

At the end of May I felt (I'm not certain why) that the need to live outside had been fulfilled and that the behavioral pattern was becoming routinized. Once again I said no. I told Marianne that I wanted her to come to my office and to return to the Inn. She refused, but I said I would not see her on the lawn any longer. (I think that at this time I would not have been fulfilling a need, but just meeting a demand.) Her need to be outside (and in the process understand some of her motives and strengthen the bond with me) had been transformed into a demand to be special, unique, and unchanging. She returned to the Inn, but in an effort to avoid contamination she would not touch anything with her hands, resorting to the use of her feet instead. She opened doors with her feet, operated faucets, and even turned records on her record player. She missed her hours for about two weeks and then angrily stomped in one day. For the next several months we didn't have one quiet session. She would enter my office, leave the door ajar, would stand on one foot with her hands away from her body, or squat on the floor at the other end of the room and scream without interruption. She was in an unrelenting rage, crying and complaining about my cruelty, lack of understanding, incompetence, etc. I was then seeing her seven days a week.

Her compulsive behavior was increasing; she was unable to eat, and she lived in constant fear of dying or disintegrating. During these sessions I rarely said anything. In the month of June 1970 she again missed sessions and withdrew into her room. I met with her there. On my first visit to her room I was startled and shocked. She had removed all the furniture with the exception of her bed, and it looked like a seclusion room. She would squat naked on one side of the room and I would sit on the floor at the other end. She would scream and bang her head with her fists or against the wall. At one time she banged her head so badly that she bled from one of her ears, but there was no evidence of concussion. On a weekend I saw her at her request morning and afternoon—each time to hear her screaming unpleasant things about me. At one point she asked me if I was angry (this question was asked repeated-

ly) and I told her: "No, I am simply fatigued." She asked
me what about, and I told her that for a year she had said
many unpleasant things about me and that on that day I had
finally felt the impact of these. She then said: "In the time I
have known you, you have done two things right." I asked
her what these were and she said: "You touched me—two
times."

At that time it was not only impossible to touch Marianne but it was also impossible to talk much with her. The
only thing I felt that I could do was to sit with her, try to
understand whatever I could about her rage, her fear, and
the feelings she stirred up in me (obviously responsive to
what was going on in her). I made myself available twenty-
four hours a day and worked in close contact with the
nursing staff.

In September 1970 Marianne began defecating and urinating on the floor in her room and in other parts of the
building. She stopped eating and lost thirty pounds, her
weight falling to ninety-nine pounds. She would be fed only
by me and by some of the nurses whom she trusted. For a
long time she had had difficulty flushing the toilet, fearing
that a part of herself (feces) would be lost, and that even if
she saw it again she wouldn't recognize it. At this time
there was great fear of object loss. I was then concerned
with the way in which she expressed her rage. She would
soil in her blue jeans, but wouldn't change them for days.
She would defecate in public areas (the television room and
sstairwells), and also in hidden places that were very difficult to find, except for the stench. (Later when we talked
about the significance of this behavior she agreed that some
of the reasons were those mentioned above. She said that
she found comfort while sitting in a warm puddle of urine,
but I have no explanation for this act.)

In October 1970 her parents visited. It was a painful visit
in every sense. I knew then that much of what Marianne
had told me about them was probably so. They impressed
me as distant, cold, and very disturbed people.

When they left, Marianne regressed even more. She spent her days on a small blanket on the floor, crying like a baby, rocking and sucking her thumb, and masturbating. As she didn't eat or drink any fluids for three days, there was serious concern about her physical health. Later she told me that at this time she had let go feelings that had been dammed up in her for many years. She had been relieved by her parents' acceptance of the fact that she was a very disturbed person. During this time she had a dream in which a nurse, to whom she was strongly attached, offered her a cupful of Thorazine and she refused it, saying she did not deal with problems that way.

In November 1970 I left for a conference for four days. It was one of the few separations I had from the patient in the first two years of treatment. The night before I left she asked to see me. She was crying, her nose was running, and for the first time she admitted she was very frightened at my being away. As I was leaving she asked me to hold her in my arms, and I did so. The first night I was away she flew into a rage and with a hammer tried to break into the medicine closet. When the nurses asked her what she was doing, she said that she had learned that she could rely on people, not on pills. If people were not around, however, she wanted the pills. (She had known for a long time that people could cause pain, and now she could accept the idea that people could also bring relief and comfort.)

In December Marianne's parents visited again, this time with her sister. Although the separation was again very disturbing, something had changed. After each family visit I met with her to review what had taken place at the meeting, attempting to verify or correct her perceptions. This was a useful experience for both of us. Marianne feared that her perception of her family as disturbed (particularly her views of her mother and her sister) was a gross distortion. She was often relieved to find out that I shared many of her impressions.

At this time members of the staff expressed concern

about the state of the patient's physical health. Her hands continued to bleed, but they were not seriously infected, and I did not wish to impose physical contact on Marianne. I knew that the time would come when she, on her own, would ask for care. In early January 1971 she stepped on a broken glass, cutting her foot. She voluntarily asked a nurse, with whom she had developed a good relationship, to remove the glass from her foot. When the nurse saw her injuries she was concerned about the possibility of an infection, and thought that the patient should be seen by a physician. My opinion was requested, and I suggested that the nurse alone take care of the lacerations. There was some difficulty in removing the slivers of glass, but the patient would not let her feet be touched by anyone but this nurse. She also let the nurse put some ointment on her sore hands.

It is perhaps worth noting that I felt increasing pressure from the members of the hospital community to do something. The fecal soiling was becoming a major social issue, and the community meetings at which I acted as consultant were taken up with the difficulty of living near Marianne. Many people wanted to move far away from her on account of the odor. By that time she was well established as the craziest patient in the community.

As much as the nurses and I shared in her treatment, I found myself feeling as if I were somehow solely responsible for the things that were happening with her.

During this time the nurses were attempting to find a substitute for Marianne's soiling. We were trying to toilet-train her. We then put a bucket in her room, in which she defecated. Eventually she allowed us to put disinfectant in the room to reduce the odor.

At this time she decided that the bathroom had a "cold" appearance. It was painted white, and to her it looked like a surgical operating room. She said that she wanted to make it more cozy, perhaps as a step to begin using it. It was my impression that she experienced the bathroom as a surgical room in the sense that there she lost parts of herself (feces, bits of hair, nail clippings, dirt) which she never retrieved.

She obtained paint from the maintenance department and completed a neat job of painting. When the work was done she flew into a rage, smeared the walls with paint, and broke the windows with the bucket. I was called over to see her. When I knocked on the door she wouldn't let me into the room, "because it was a mess." I asked her, "What else is new?" and went in. She was indeed in the midst of a huge mess. There was a bucket full of feces on one side, and pieces of glass were all over the floor. She was picking up the debris and cleaning the room by herself. She showed me where she had smeared the new paint, and smiling she said: "It will be hard work but eventually it will come off." I hesitated for a moment when I saw her in the midst of that mess. Should I help her clean it up? I thought that if I did so I should be telling her that I did not think she could do it by herself. Therefore I stayed with her for a few minutes without helping. She continued to clean and soon I left her to her work.

In the month of January the patient requested to see me on a weekend. As a general rule I visited her twice each day. On a particular weekend I came over at her request five times, each time to hear horrors about myself. Eventually, and seemingly for no particular reason, since this day was not greatly different from any other day, I became angry. I jumped out of my chair and shouted at the patient. In the process I told her some of my feelings about her, both good and bad. I became aware of myself. Marianne looked very startled. Afterward she told me that she was reassured at what I did, as one of the questions she had asked me over the months was the possibility of my being angry with her. From then on she would never have to ask me whether or not I was angry, because when I was, my feeling was obvious.

At this same time, January 1971, she developed an intense hatred for a certain nurse. This nurse became the repository of everything bad that happened to and around Marianne. The nurse, by the way, resembled the mother physically and in an uncanny way. Marianne would not then allow nurses to come to her room. She nailed the door shut, and went in and out of the Inn through the windows. On five occasions she became assaultive to nurses. There was a serious question regarding our ability to treat Marianne in this hospital, and it was suggested by many members of the staff-patient community that she should be transferred to another institution.

In the month of April 1971 I told Marianne that she would have to make a choice between her feces and our relationship. Should she feel that she could not control her necessity to soil on the floor, she would be transferred to another hospital. She wept and then told me that her relationship with me, notwithstanding the rage and hostility, was the most meaningful relationship in her life, and that she would never soil on the floor again; and she never has.

In the month of May I became aware that her compulsive behavior included spending large sums of money. She made an arrangement with a cab driver to shop for her, and over a period of two months he purchased $7,000 worth of clothes—mostly blue jeans and T shirts. Everything was used once and then sent to the laundry or thrown away. At the time I thought again that this behavior was not meaningful and I set limits to it by putting her on a "spending ban," and I also told her that from now on she would have an allowance of $100 a month. She looked at me in dismay; this was approximately what she sometimes spent in a day. Marianne would not touch money (the reason being the same as the one for not using a public telephone; should she touch the money she would not recognize it should it come her way again). Under the new system she could charge up to $100 a month in the local stores. At the end of the month we would figure out her expenditures and then she would pay her bills by check.

Community meetings are held three times each week. They are chaired by a patient with three staff consultants. In these meetings community issues, social matters, personal problems, etc. are dealt with. At this time Marianne was often referred to this group because of the vast spectrum of her behavior that was considered antisocial by her peers. She would enter the living room, where these meetings were held, by opening the door with her feet. Often she would throw objects around the room, kick, spit at other patients, scream, and sob. During all of these referrals I was present, and during them I remained silent.

At the end of June three men arrived in the area to visit another patient, and she became attached to one of them. From June until the end of August she did not appear in my office. She did not come to her hours, and she did not live in the Inn. She lived with this man, often staying with him in the woods. On occasion I met Marianne on the street; once she turned her face, and on another occasion she stopped to speak with me very briefly. She told me that she was enjoying life and that she did not want my interference. I understood and did not insist on meeting with her.

At the end of August 1971 I again met her on the street and told her that I had learned that her parents would soon be visiting. I thought it could be useful for us to discuss some matters before this meeting. She did not come to see me, however. We did meet with the family, spending most of the sessions in collecting data about her early history and about the family transactions.

Marianne did not look at me during these meetings, but I insisted that we meet after them. Though the relationship with me now appeared to be at its worst, she was able to spend some days at a local hotel with her parents, had a picnic with them on the lawn, and went out with her father to the top of a hill to sketch the landscape. She went shop-

ping with her mother, bought some beautiful Indian dress-
es, and expressed concern about her sister's apparent
emotional disturbance. When her parents left she did
something that had never been done before in this family.
She told them that she wanted to hug each one. She then
went up to each of them in turn to give a hug. Needless to
say, I did not hear this from the patient, but heard it a
month later from other sources.

The separation from the parents was much less anxiety-
ridden than in the past. I said to Marianne that in order to
continue her relationship with me she would have to give
up the relationship with her boy friend. I found myself no
longer tolerant with waiting for her in my office. She said
that if she had to make a choice again she would choose
me, notwithstanding my lack of warmth and understanding.

I realized both during the parents' visit and after they left
that there had been a remarkable change in the patient. I
did not know to what I could attribute this, but I felt that a
certain integration of the patient's personality was taking
place.

After separating from her boy friend Marianne secluded
herself in the Inn and requested that I see her in her room.
She said that she had given up her boy friend and that in
return I should to something for her. She could not come to
see me in my office because she was afraid to leave the Inn.
Her fear of leaving the Inn was related to the idea that she
would float away, and thus the only way she could see me
safely would be to meet with me in her room. I refused to
do so because I felt that she was experiencing a certain
amount of change, and that her dealing with her family and
the boy friend had been ostensibly different from her transactions the year before; this change entailed with it some
progress, and was frightening, as anything that could be
equated with moving toward an integration of herself was
viewed as a loss rather than an asset. I felt that if I went to

see her in the Inn I should be giving in to her need to feel sick and excessively dependent. I feared that she might resort to a regression of the nature that had taken place the winter before.

Marianne thought that I was lacking in understanding. She asked the head nurse to tie a rope around her waist; should she walk out of the Inn, the rope was to prevent her from becoming lost. Interestingly enough, at the time there were several new people on the nursing staff and it was generally said that I was an ungiving, unsympathetic person to this sweet girl. Even the head nurse, a very capable and experienced woman, told me that I should give in and meet Marianne "halfway." I told the head nurse that I would not put one foot outside of my office, and that if it required six months for Marianne to come to the office, I was willing to wait this out. My feeling at the time was one of loneliness, of isolation, and also of insecurity. In time Marianne called me on the phone, and for about a month and a half I had "hours" with her by telephone. There was a reason for my doing this. In the past Marianne was unable to pick up a phone, feeling that she could not relate to the isolated voice of a person. If the person were not present she felt that the contact was unreal. Only if the person were visibly present could she maintain a conversation. During these telephone conversations I felt that she was learning to deal with me at a distance, forming a dependable and constant introject of myself. What might have looked like a setback was, in my view, a step forward.

After about a month and a half I felt again, as with other patterns of behavior, that the telephone calls were getting routinized and should be interrupted. I told Marianne that I would not speak with her on the phone any longer and that she should come back to my office. She screamed, yelled, and said that she needed to continue speaking with me on the phone. I replied that each of us had her own needs, and that I had mine. I did not wish to continue talking with her

on the phone. Thereupon Marianne had a sequence of temper tantrums. She said that she felt like killing herself, and
spoke of carving my name on her forehead so that everybody could see what evil I had done to her. I sent her a
message saying that it was her life she was taking, not
mine. She then came to an hour and talked to me about her
boy friend, saying that she missed him. She said that she
had given him up for me, and I hadn't given her anything in
return. I said to her then that in order to continue working
with me she had to be on a "boy ban" (that was the name
that I gave to the limit-setting). By this I meant that for an
undetermined period of time she was not to get involved
with any men, as it seemed to me that she used men in the
same way that she had used her compulsions or Thorazine,
i.e., to allay anxiety. She accepted this demand with a
certain sense of relief.

Third Phase

Reentry to the Community

Marianne became involved in several community projects. One of them involved the painting of the patients'
kitchen. It was her first community collaborative effort
with other patients, and as I was involved with this too we
spent a weekend painting the kitchen together. On a Sunday, after we had spent the day painting, we were at last
alone in the room. We sat on the floor and talked about
what it meant to be painting the kitchen together. She said
that she thought something very important had happened,
as her period of regression had first manifested itself after
she ran out of this kitchen a year and a half before. At that
time she had felt that the kitchen was contaminated with
acid. Now she had come back and was repairing something
of the past through the painting. I think that the repair of
the patients' kitchen was an externalization of what she
was experiencing as an inner repair.

At the time the patients' kitchen was painted, she felt ashamed about her own room, and said that it was of the utmost importance that her room be redone. She thought that if she had a room to which she could take people she would feel more at ease. This would be better than going to public areas or to other people's rooms. The floor of her room was stained in such a way that it was beyond repair. She sent a note, saying that she was willing to pay for a new floor should the hospital allow her to do this. I thought at the time that it was very important that her floor and her entire room be refinished. Little by little the patients began having some contacts with her, although they continued to be very much afraid of her; they feared her temper tantrums, her assaultiveness (both physical and verbal), and her bizarre behavior.

After the month and a half that she was able to hold telephone conversations with me she was able to touch money. For several months I gave her a weekly allowance of $25 in cash. She continues to be on the "spending ban," and discusses any major expenditures with me. We now budget her needs for the coming several months.

Little by little she found her way into the community. Her first social event took place on Halloween. On that occasion she dressed up as Miss Muffett and persuaded one of the aides to dress up as a spider. She spent the first part of the party sitting next to the spider, and then began jumping up and running away from it. She told me later that at Halloween parties she had always dressed to show how she felt: the first year she was here she dressed up as a dog; the second year she dressed up as a statue; the third year she didn't go to the party because she was in her room screaming; and this year she came as Miss Muffett.

As time went on she became more involved with the community, and began joining small groups of people in carrying out their various projects. In December 1971, despite much apprehension, she ran for the post of Activities Planning Group Chairman (which is one of the patient subcommittees in the hospital). To her amazement (and to mine), she was elected. She did the job with much anxiety and uncertainty, but carried it through for two months. Her impulse control was then remarkably increased, and she could go to the meetings and control her behavior and perform effectively despite anxiety.

In the middle of November she asked me to come to her room one Saturday night. She had selected some clothes and was trying to be personally neat. She told me that she had accumulated things in the attic, but that it was very frightening for her to go up there. I suggested that we go together, and we spent approximately three and one-half hours working in the storage bin in the attic. It was an experience for both of us. For me it was a direct contact with an aspect of her psychotic experience which I had not seen previously. For her it was taking a plunge into a part of the past that she was trying to forget.

We searched through many bags of garbage. There were the cheesecloths that she had used to filter the bath water, the saved hair, the fingernail clippings, the menstrual pads, and all manner of things. We sorted them out and threw some away. Some of the clothes she saved for further use.

On her birthday I brought her a gift which she was able to accept—a lavender-blue Irish shawl. It was a Sunday morning when I gave it to her. She was very pleased, and we went for a short walk. There was snow on the ground and the day was beautiful. We walked about the Center property and picked up some pine cones, from which she makes necklaces. Having filled our pockets with these cones, we returned to the building. I was on medical call that day, and in the afternoon I wanted to do something with her. We returned to the Inn and together we finished the patients' kitchen, cleaning out all the shelves. I brought some things from my house which I did not need—pots, pans, and a blender. While we were in the kitchen several patients dropped by and brought her gifts. She told me this had been the happiest birthday of her life.

Attempts to Control Complusions

The floor of her room was replaced; the room was painted, and everything was "new." One day I asked her what her room looked like. She told me that she had not been able to enter it, as she was very frightened and couldn't go into it without me. I walked with her to the Inn, and we went into her room together. It looked very beautiful. She was startled and said several things that I think are worth mentioning: (1) that she remembered the room as being much larger than it really is; (2) she walked on the floor and said she really knew where the stains (from the soiling and urinating) had been, but that they were not there any more; and (3) she said she was very frightened. When she said these things I realized that as she was saying them she was mapping out the floor into the "good" and "bad" parts. At this I decided to put her on a "compulsion ban." She asked me what I meant, and I told her that from that moment on she must relinquish all her compulsions. She looked astonished, but said she would do it. She gave up the compulsions apparently without much difficulty and began arranging her room. She received a record player from her parents for Christmas, and enjoyed playing records. She was given many gifts by her mother and by patients, and obviously enjoyed receiving them (in the past she had not been able to accept gifts from anyone).

Soon after New Year's she flew into a rage and returned to the compulsions. She cleaned the floor with Q-tips, scrubbed it, and ran water in the bathroom for hours. She missed sessions with me and for the next two weeks I didn't see her. Her compulsions had apparently multiplied, and the general feeling of the staff was that the compulsions were not fulfilling her needs. I felt very unsympathetic with the patient and was also angry. I took note of this because I had not felt anger with Marianne as I did at that time.

Eventually she showed up in my office and told me that

she felt more compulsive than ever before. The compulsions, however, did not serve their purpose. Once they had been as good as Thorazine, if not better, but now she had to find new ones in order to be able to reduce anxiety. She also told me that she knew now what the compulsions meant, that when she started feeling anything that would make her uncertain, anxious, afraid, or have any other unpleasant feeling, she would resort to the compulsions and the undesirable feeling would disappear. She told me I had done something bad to her by taking them away from her. I said that she would have to make a decision. If she wished to continue with her compulsions I did not want to work with her. I said that I respected the ways she had developed to behave crazily because she showed a great deal of expertise in their use. I also thought she could make a first-rate career of being a mental patient, but I was not willing to share her life in this fashion. Again, as I did when she was soiling, I told her that she had to make a choice between the compulsions and the relationship with me. The difference this time was the absence of social pressure, or pressure from the institution that she stop the compulsions. The pressure was only from me. As far as I was concerned, if she chose to live in a mad way I should recommend her transfer to another institution. She wept and said that she used the compulsions out of spite. She did not want to be told what to do, but she knew that she would do anything to enable the relationship to continue. I told her at this point that I found myself not giving a damn about what the relationship meant to her; I was no longer tolerant of her behavior, and unless she was able to take a look at her problems and the feelings covered up by these compulsions, I was willing to stop treatment. She replied that she would make an effort to take a look at what really was happening in her life, and I cut the hour short and told her to get out.

After this hour I went to the medical director and spoke with him about my feelings. I found myself enraged at the patient, realized that this rage could be partly mine, but also could reflect the rage that this girl was experiencing behind the compulsions. I was really feeling for her, so to speak.

She returned to the hour the next day and told me that she had made a choice. She was frightened, but was willing not only to give up the compulsions, but to try to speak to some of the "contaminated" people. We talked about my rage the day before, and I told her that I was willing to admit some of the rage was mine, but that I experienced her as an extremely cruel woman, and that the cruelty, rage, and murderous feelings must be explored. She then went to different people, one by one, with whom she had been in a feud over a long period of time, and with each made her peace. Since then she has continued to come to the hours.

For a long period after she gave up the compulsions (approximately two months) I would get three or four calls a day from her, particularly in the evening. She would begin experiencing some unpleasant feeling and she would then resort to the compulsions. Sometimes the feelings started out by being pleasant feelings. She hadn't experienced such feelings before, and perhaps their strangeness stirred up the anxiety. She would wish to resort to the compulsions in order to stop the anxiety, but then realized that she had to make a choice between accepting the feelings (and with the feelings, accepting me) or resort to the compulsions and in the process annihilate me. We would talk either in person or on the phone, trying to identify what she was feeling and find a name for it. At this time she began to write regularly every night. She wrote letters addressed to me describing some of the feelings evoked at the times when she would feel like resorting to a compulsion. Little by little she would then be able to tell me that what she was experiencing was anger, or jealousy, or rejection, or love, or being able to admit to envy. (I have currently approximately 150 pages typed by the patient.)

She formed a relationship with Mr. G., an art teacher who has been of utmost importance in her treatment. Even during the time of her regression he would go to the Inn and leave some sketching pads and finger paints in her room. Sometimes she would use them, and on the next visit would show him what she had done. He always criticized her work honestly without regard for what she might be going through personally. I think that his respect for her as a person had an invaluable effect on her. Marianne had never shown me any of her paintings until May 1971. Mr. G., at an art exhibit, showed me some of the paintings she had allowed him to exhibit without her name being attached to them. At that particular time I was feeling very burdened by the patient, and Mr. G. showed me an aspect of her which gave me some hope.

In May 1971 she came to my office with approximately fifty paintings, some of which were old and some not yet dry. The couch in my office had just been reupholstered, and in putting some of these paintings on the couch she stained the couch slightly. She said, "Oh, I've stained your couch." I replied, "Oh?" and continued looking at the paintings. She said later that my response had been very important to her, because she was more important than the mess she had made. She did not give me any of these paintings. The first gift I received from her was at Christmas, 1971. This was a collage, a very beautiful piece of art, I thought, made with small pieces of colored paper torn out of magazines and glued together. The picture is the face of a woman who is freeing a white bird. She gave it to me on Christmas Day, wrapped in a necklace made of the pine cones we had picked up together on her birthday. This picture is a close representation of how I feel she experiences our work together—putting herself together, piece by piece, like the little pieces of paper in the picture.

Sharing

As Marianne gave up her compulsions, she felt she had

to keep busy, as she didn't know what to do with her free time. I then went with her to various places. We would go to the nursery school and spend time there with the children, or we would go to the shop, where she would paint while I sat on one side. We would also go for short walks.

On a Sunday in February 1972, I was on medical call and had spent considerable time over at the Inn taking care of a very disturbed patient. Marianne and I saw each other several times during that day in the corridors, but she didn't talk with me—just nodded as she passed by. At eight P.M. there was a knock on the door of my house. It was snowing heavily. There stood Marianne, holding a bowl of soup in her hands. She said, "You've had a very tough day and must be tired. I made some soup. Maybe this way you won't have to cook." I invited her into the house. We made some tea and sat by the fire while I had the soup.

It was the first time Marianne had been in my house and she was interested in some art objects and books. We talked about art and various things for about two hours. It was the first time we had not talked about her problems and the first time the patient acknowledged my own needs overtly. Since then she has been in my house several times and has felt free to give me many gifts, which, as a rule, she has made herself.

In May 1972 I went on a vacation for two weeks. This was our first long separation. She handled the separation adequately. She organized the Free University (sponsored by the patient community, and involving many group meetings), and she chaired the Free University, calling people on the phone, inviting them to lecture, sending out invitations, enrolling people for courses, and so on.

When I returned she came to her hours regularly, and I am now seeing her five times a week. Since then much of the time has been spent in trying to analyze what is happening with her currently, and also in trying to understand what has happened between us during the past three years. Her freedom to express both thoughts and feelings has increased remarkably, as has her ability to interpret what is happening to her. She continues to write at night what has happened during the day and brings it to me the next morning, sometimes to request that I look at it and sometimes just leaving it with me.

Discharge

In June, after her parents announced that they were visiting, Marianne and I started to talk about the possibility of her being discharged to outpatient status. I was hesitant because of her "traveling phobia," but I thought that it would be worthwhile to take the risk of discharging her to the halfway house as an outpatient. A discharge date was set for July 15, 1972.

Marianne spent a week with her parents at a hotel near the Center. She then applied for a job in a nursery school conducted in a church nearby. All of this seemed to be done without particular strain or anxiety. She came to her hours on time and we would discuss not only what was going on with the family but also her projects for the future. When her parents left, I visited with her in her room on the last day that she was to spend at the Inn. She told me that as much as she looked forward to the change, it was difficult to give up the room. She felt that in this room she had "been born" and that this birth had taken place between her and me. She knew that other people were involved, and she feared that once she walked out everything would change. I said that I understood, and we sat for approximately two hours—a great part of it in silence—and I helped her pack.

The night before she left the Inn, the patients and some ex-patients and former staff members gave a party for her. On the day of her departure she asked two of the nurses, who had been very close and involved in her treatment, to accompany her to the door of the Inn to see her walk out. The nurses did this, and she kissed them goodbye as she left the Inn alone. The nurses said it was like seeing a child who has grown up leave the family home and go, perhaps to college. She moved to the Elms (that is, the Center's halfway house) without major difficulty. I saw her on her regular appointments after that, and since then things have gone relatively smoothly.

I wish to mention here a gift I am to receive. While Marianne was extremely disturbed she painted on the door of her room a picture of a woman holding a child in her arms. She has purchased the door because she wants me to have it as a gift.

Marianne is currently involved in several classes outside of the Riggs program—that is, drawing, painting, and pottery. She also is holding a regular job in the nursery school. In the hours we talk about several issues, two of the very important ones being her difficulty in traveling and the relationship of this to what seems to be a family phobia (everyone in the family is afraid of traveling). She is also dealing with her grief at having spent the last ten years of her life in institutions and in the process having to give up many of what may have been her major interests, primarily dancing.

One of the subjects that has been talked about freely in the hours currently concerns her sexual fantasies, previously avoided in her conversations with me. She is relieved that her "boy ban" continues, as she is afraid that should she become angry at me, or at the institution, or at the last ten years of her life, she might run away and live for a period of time with some man, escaping the need to deal with her current reality. Her thoughts about the future concern the possibility of eventually being able to marry and have children. She has some doubts as to her ability to form a close relationship with a man, but feels that so many changes have taken place in her life that eventually she may be able to accomplish this. I do not think the patient will wish to return to school, as her major talents lie in the field of art. She herself expresses a desire to continue perfecting her talents as a painter, sculptor, and potter.

We have also talked about her experiences during her regression, and what happened between her and me. I asked her at one point what had been useful to her in my relationship to her as her therapist. She replied that in the first place I was a very quiet therapist and that I spoke very little during the hours. This was helpful, she said, because she felt that words confused her. She did not know what they meant, they acquired multiple meanings, and when people spoke to her she didn't know exactly how to relate the words they used to what these words represented for her. She said that I had used few words in the hours. She had also found it helpful to note that I used my body very freely. When I asked her what she meant by that she said that I had never been concerned about touching her, or feeding her, or putting her to bed. If I had been uneasy at making such contacts she would have been unable to accept them from me.

Summary

In a very condensed and somewhat informal fashion, an account has been given of the first three years and one month of psychotherapy with a schizophrenic woman which is still in progress. A number of topics have been dealt with briefly and lend themselves to discussion. Among these are: (*a*) the nature of a family relationship and the possible effect of this on the patient; (*b*) the developmental history and the concept of the "onset" of schizophrenia, i.e., when did it "begin"?; (*c*) the difficulties of adolescence and the patient's inability to solve those problems, except in the ways described; (*d*) the early clear signs of onset; (*e*) the decision re hospitalization, i.e., being officially named a patient; (*f*) the first two years at the Austen Riggs Center lived without major change—regression, exposure, etc., i.e., the stability of the defenses; (*g*) the initial contact with me (the current therapist)—i.e., the problem of the first interview; (*h*) the decision not to use ataractic drugs; (*i*) the need-fear dilemma; (*j*) the patient's isolation and dealing with this in the community of an open hospital; (*k*) regression and threat to life; (*l*) the beginnings of attachment; (*m*) limit setting, called "bans"; (*n*) the cooperation of a group—the "team"; (*o*) acting out—assaultiveness, not coming to hours, the boy friend, etc.; (*p*) the therapist's feelings; (*q*) the depression in the patient; (*r*) in conclusion, the problems of detachment from the institution and separation.

Psychological Retest Report

The current test diagnosis is of longstanding schizophrenia as a decompensation in a once basically obsessive-compulsive personality; depressive features are also present. This represents a change from the 1967 and the 1971 test diagnoses (which were virtually identical) in that agitated and paranoid features now seem markedly reduced and obsessive-compulsive defenses more prominent and adaptive. Indeed, she used up an entire eraser in adhering to the standards of the Bender-Gestalt designs; her perfectionism and scrupulousness were not, however, accompanied by unduly harsh self-criticism, and there was even the suggestion that some not very sneaky acts of "naughtiness" were to be considered playful rather than evil. Her general emotional tone seems considerably lighter this year, not quite so grim, and the self-monitoring, the greater interest in the usual, and wish to accommodate herself relatively more to the outer world, all noted a year and a half ago, have continued to develop. For instance, this time the patient was able to engage in a much broader range of test situations with no detriment to her performance. Dogged signs of life, hope, and indeed of feeling inextinguishable are many (not in a grandiose way, however); these are perhaps most graphically captured in her Rorschach percept of "a mole climbing through layers of rock." Though her thinking can still become quite fluid, overinclusive, loose, and circumstantial, she is considerably clearer and less autistic now, more able to express herself, and more in control of a once irresistible tendency toward psychotic synthesis. The generally greater modulation of internal drives, that is, of the unmediated outpouring of raw, primitive, aggressive affect and polymorphous sexual processes observed in 1967, has led to a considerably greater productivity and to the greater availability of her emotional and cognitive resources, albeit in the context of a still definitely schizophrenic picture.

Though these gains seem obvious, this shy but flirtatious, enjoyable but enigmatic young woman also conveys the unsettling impression that she currently has a stubborn investment in facelessness, that important matters are being evaded and unrevealed, that perhaps her current emotional productions are not quite authentic, and that she is reluctant to commit herself to and to "own" anything or to define herself as real. She gives at once the feeling of being beyond her psychosis but also of needing to touch base with it. She consistently elaborates alternative perceptions of both herself and those around her, shifts her perspective quickly and continuously, and seems far more inclined to endow, "contaminate," and spoil what is distinctly good with detracting bad aspects, often very willfully, it would appear. On rare occasions she fleetingly integrates the vulnerability and the power within herself as well as the insubstantial and the overwhelming in her world.

Concomitant with what appears to be greater differentiation in her view of people is lessened fragmentation in her view of herself and a greater awareness of and tolerance for internal conflict. In addition, the patient seems far less inclined to feel victimized now and less likely to get "locked into a paranoid position." Depression, themes of what has been lost, broken, and closed, are now seen where provocation and vengeance occurred last year. Though she is still vigilant to the destructive potential of others, particularly as feelings of closeness develop, her wariness and belligerence are triggered less this year and seem more clearly associated with specific fears of being attacked. Gone are the "stillborn," "dewinged," and autistic anatomical percepts of last year, suggesting that issues of bodily damage may be less pervasive now. As in 1971, "her sexuality and femininity are extremely unsettling" to her because they seem fused with both her sense of utter dirtiness and of secret neediness. Sexual wishes in the most general sense call into play a gamut of defensive operations—withdrawal, reaction formation, and denial being most prominent—that render seemingly nonexistent all other intense feelings related to issues of identity and incorporation as well as the currently glaring ambivalence about reproduction. In the process, she herself as a person can seem impoverished and even lost to those around her, neither touching nor touchable, and obviously helpless to articulate her inner experience.

Her current Wechsler-Bellevue II scores of Full 117, Verbal 117, and Performance 116, are no different than either her 1971 WAIS scores or her 1967 Wechsler-Bellevue II scores. The consistency of these scores reflect, as before, "the longstanding status of her difficulties and their inroads into her functioning."

6

BREAKING THE RULES

Dr. Foster's presentation emphasizes the activities of the therapist in response to countertransference-transference relationships. She has provided neither psychodynamic explanations for the content of the patient's psychosis nor justification for the technical aspects of her work with the patient. Dr. Foster supplies much evidence for significant clinical improvement and for the emergence and development in her patient of more effective mental structuring, a prerequisite for enduring improvement in schizophrenic persons. In consideration of the clinical state of the patient when Dr. Foster undertook psychotherapeutic responsibilities—at least eight years of psychotic behavior, the last six continuous; eleven previous therapists; and clear signs of deeply regressive behaviors—the probabilities for attributing the amelioration of the schizophrenic symptoms to a spontaneous remission are remote.

There are, of course, extratherapeutic elements that contributed to Dr. Foster's success with this patient. They were provided by the patient's parents. They are: the parents did not intrude into the therapy; the patient may live wherever she wishes, the parents did not press her to return to their home; and their permissiveness and affluence enabled the patient to indulge her psychotic urges in a most profligate fashion. Otherwise the patient might now be languishing in a state hospital.

The psychotherapeutic relationship is but one subsystem in the entire system affecting a therapeutic result. We have heard the comments "Psychotherapy does not exist in a vacuum" and "The milieu is an essential ingredient of the process" previously. A systems approach requires that the position of the observer be identified in relation to the process being observed and described. In this connection, let me characterize our dilemma with a short nonclinical vignette.

Prior to the launching of Sputnik, a child was examining a miniature replica of our world, a multicolored globe. The preliminary questions were: "Why is there so much blue?" and "What do the brown and green mean?" The simple answers "Water, mountains, and forests" were politely but unenthusiastically accepted with slow assenting nods. There was a moment of silence. But then the youngster turned and asked, "Daddy, where do you have to stand to see our planet this way?"

This fragment of my fatherhood characterizes the current status of research in the psychotherapy of schizophrenia: it is highly personal; complex relationships are simplistically reduced and thereby distorted; the problem extends over the entire earth; there is pride of possession and participation in the experience; and the communication of the experience is accepted sympathetically only by persons who can report similar stories of their own.

How, then, can we extricate ourselves from a highly personalized, individual perspective? How do we convert idiosyncratic experiences into more general forms and questions, and eventually into testable hypotheses? I propose to dissect out two elements of the psychotherapeutic relationship which may be used for comparison with the work of other therapists who venture into the perplexing world of psychotherapeutic relationships with chronic schizophrenic persons.

In order that we may start from common ground, I present a summary of technical sequences I have used for involving schizophrenic patients in psychotherapeutic endeavors. It consists of four steps:

1. Accept the psychosis by respecting the patient's inability to tolerate physical and emotional closeness. Regard regressive behaviors as the patient's mode of communicating current problems in a highly indirect way.

2. In recognition of the patient's individuality, utilize inquiring and observing attitudes, and thereby initiate a nonintrusive relationship as one of two persons interested in understanding the patient's behaviors. The therapist's repeated and frequent self-presentations provide a patient with opportunities for identification. The identification process is established when the patient uses the therapist's observing power to modify behavior, however slightly. Most effectual are comments on how the patient's behaviors affect others. To be avoided are interpretations of what the patient says and does.

3. The continued utilization of the therapist as a perceptual agency leads the patient to reassess the external world and reestablish reality testing functions.

4. Extended contact with a nonobstrusive but enthusiastic therapist forms the base for a corrective emotional experience that will activate the feelings of hope so necessary for the reentry into the world of interpersonal relationships. When these four steps have been successfully taken, the previously reluctant schizophrenic patient may enter voluntarily into a psychotherapeutic program with some possibilities for reconstructive work.

With minor emendations, this suggested approach is endorsed by many American psychoanalysts who have chosen to work with psychotic patients. Implicit in the technique is that the therapist will continue to maintain the analytic posture although accorded certain liberties. During the critical periods, psychotic patients may be reassured, encouraged, safeguarded, and given medication.

With these considerations out front, I wish to demonstrate that Dr. Foster obtained her most spectacular effects with her patient when she *broke* these rules.

In reviewing the case summary, I found thirteen in-

stances in which the therapist interdicted the patient's behaviors. The first occurred during the fifth month of
treatment in November 1969 when the phenothiazine medication was stopped. In April 1970 the order was "to come
out of the woods" where the patient had been living. A
month later, the doctor demanded: "Return to the Inn!
Come to my office!" The fifth was a year later, in April
1971: "No more soiling; otherwise, go to another hospital!" In May 1971 the "spending ban" was invoked. The
seventh occurred in September 1971 when Dr. Foster insisted that the patient meet with her parents. Shortly thereafter, the patient was told to give up her boy friend. The
two subsequent prohibitions had to do with office visits and
hours over the telephone. The eleventh interdiction was
that the patient must relinquish her compulsions. The
twelfth reinforced the former when the patient was in-
structed: "If you wish to use compulsions, I do not wish to
work with you!" And the thirteenth asserted that the doctor was not willing to continue treatment with a chronic
mental patient.

However, as you have just heard from Dr. Foster's report, interdictions were a small part of the therapeutic exchanges. The interdictions only punctuated long intervals
in which the patient observed her doctor to be understanding, tolerant, concerned, caring, available beyond ordinary
duties, loving, and with a sense of responsibility not only to
her but to the community for her antisocial behavior. Before ordering the patient to give up her life in the woods,
the doctor fed her and nourished her. In June 1970, eleven
months after the treatment began, the therapist expressed
her own sense of frustration about the course of treatment,
but the patient knew that she was available to her seven
days a week. In November 1970, just before her physician
left Stockbridge to attend a meeting, she was held in her
arms. In January 1971, when the members of the community were expressing their feelings of revulsion at the

patient's soiling behavior, the doctor felt as "if I were somehow responsible for the things that were happening to her." That feeling prompted the therapist to intrude into the patient's stinking room, which in turn provided the incentive for the patient to clean up the mess herself. Almost a year later, when the patient had completely refurbished her living quarters, and upon the insistence of the therapist had discarded the "garbage"—the accumulated excrescences from her body—she began to keep house for herself with the aid of some utensils given to her by the doctor.

How different these experiences were for the patient, considering that her mother turned her over to others for care and could not bear to touch her! How new a series of relationships compared with the parents who had not known that she sneaked away from home every night for months during early adolescence to be with her motorcycle friends! When we examine the flow of the psychotherapeutic exchanges, we discover an alternation between indulgence and restriction on the therapist's part. The doctor's variable responses, caring and concerned on the one hand, on the other frustrated and restrictive, contrasted sharply with the parents' unremitting bitter struggle with each other, neither budging from fixed attitudes. It was this contrapuntal rhythm in the therapeutic encounter that formed the basis for a corrective emotional experience. When I have myself felt desperate and communicated that feeling to my patients, major changes in patients' behaviors and in our relationships have occurred. Under given conditions, it is constructive for the patient to hear: "This is enough!" The problem is, of course, when to intercede and when to be permissive. In any event, these considerations led me to suggest earlier that the so-called rules governing technique may have to be modified with certain schizophrenic patients. A longer follow-up on Dr. Foster's patient will be required to justify this suggestion. (Many can remember another rule-breaker, Dr. John Rosen, who achieved multiple successes with back-ward patients but whose improvements did not endure.) Nevertheless, I submit that a therapist who can tolerate frustration, communicate that feeling at an appropriate time, recover from the sense of despair, and continue exploratory work without rancor presents a self that can be massively internalized, and provides the patient with a larger ability to master previously uncontrollable impulses, a major problem for schizophrenic persons. When the therapeutic endeavor possesses this rhythmic quality, the impoverished or even deficient ego may be partially repaired.

There is another related quality of the therapeutic relationship, hardly ever mentioned, which is suggested in Dr. Foster's presentation. This event occurred in January 1971, in the nineteenth month of treatment:

> We were trying to toilet-train her. We then put a bucket in her room, in which she defecated. Eventually she allowed us to put disinfectant in the room to reduce the odor. . . . She decided that the bathroom had a "cold" appearance. It was painted white and to her it looked like a surgical operating room. She said that she wanted to make it more cozy. . . . She obtained paint from the maintenance department and completed a neat job of painting. When the work was done she flew into a rage, smeared the walls with paint, and broke the windows with the bucket. I was called over to see her. When I knocked on the door she wouldn't let me into the room, "because it was a mess." I asked her, "What else is new?" and went in.

Dr. Foster's "What else is new?" appears to be a wryly humorous comment, not too sardonic, considering the magnitude of the mixed mess. "What else is new?" also maintains the analytic posture of inquiry and curiosity. It has a quality of playfulness from which exploratory attitudes as well as creativity are partially derived.

The data I have about patients in general with respect to the play relationships between them and their parents suggest three major types:

1. The parent enters into the play spontaneously and has empathy for the child's abilities as well as its likes and dislikes, and encourages all efforts. The emergence of new activities is recognized and acclaimed. Both participants experience the play activity as pleasurable.

2. The parent enters into the activity out of a sense of duty and compulsively responds to the exchanges, sometimes empathically and sometimes without synchronous cooperative behavior. While there is also a possibility for integrative and creative experiences in this type of play, spontaneity and pleasure are unilateral; only the child experiences the joyful time.

3. The parent enters into the play activity with a deadly seriousness because the self-representation is that of a sibling who has been deprived of the opportunity and who now wishes to compensate for the past privations. The patient-to-be is bewildered and confused and is the passive participant waiting for leads from the adult. Spontaneity on the part of the child is absent. The child's activities are dictated by the parent's behavior. Winning and losing are equivalent. The experience is disruptive and prevents the distinction between work and play, youth and age, reality and unreality.

Dr. Foster's patient's father fits the last category. In all likelihood, her mother did also. Here is the passage from Dr. Foster's report:

> The father's jealously and the competitiveness with the daughters extended to other areas. She recalls his bringing her toys, and as soon as she set these in motion he would himself play with them while Marianne cried and waited her turn. If he gave her crayons and a coloring book, he would take them away and color himself. His explanation at the time was that Marianne would break the toys or crayons;

his explanation to me was that he felt an urge to play when he saw her do so. Marianne experienced these interactions with her parents as very confusing and frightening. The father insisted that the daughters call him Steve, not Dad. This was the pseudonym he used for signing his paintings and short stories. The patient's one happy memory of the father is at age four when he offered her a bottle of 7-Up and let her drink all of it. Marianne remembers this age period as one of loneliness and rejection. At the age of three Marianne wanted to be held by her mother while they were being photographed. Mrs. N. insisted, however, on holding a dog. The picture was taken with the mother holding the dog and Marianne crying.

Even though it may be judged unprofessional, I believe that the therapist should be ready not only to regard some of the schizophrenic person's activities as playful but to respond playfully. This approach does not deny the reality of the illness but recognizes the reality of the regression. This approach sets, side by side, the deadly seriousness of the illness and the prospects for recapturing a lost opportunity for partial resolution of the illness. It is, moreover, a powerful way of communicating that the therapist is not as fearful of the patient's impulses as the patient is.

In summary:

1. It may be more constructive to examine the ebb and flow, the dialectic process of the treatment relationship, than the specific short-term problem-solving issues because they may be at variance with the previous rhythms in the life processes of the patient, and provide the base for a corrective emotional experience.

2. The therapist must be prepared to view the patient's problems with deadly seriousness and simultaneously be ready to pick up clues from the regressive process which indicate the patient's desire and need for playfulness. This flexibility on the part of the therapist may also provide the patient with an opportunity for a corrective emotional ex-

perience—especially when the differentiating and integrating experiences of play have been denied the patient previously.

I return to the vignette of the child looking at a colored globe. Blue stands for oceans, brown for mountains, and green for forests. Simple answers! But the distant perspective is not yet available to any of us.

7

REGRESSION IS UNNECESSARY
Herbert Y. Meltzer, M.D.

My views differ considerably from those expressed in Dr. Foster's work with her patient, yet there is no question of my respect for the integrity, perseverance, and devotion of Dr. Foster to her patient, often at the expense of considerable personal sacrifice and suffering. Because my views are different, the conference organizers believed it would be useful to include my opinions in the published proceedings in the hope that they might stimulate empirical studies of outcome which could help to decide the issues. Put simply, I bleieve that the risks to life and the suffering experienced by this patient in the course of her treatment should and could have been avoided without compromising the extent of her improvement.

Dr. Foster's basic approach to the treatment of a schizophrenic is in significant contrast to my own. The contrasts can be seen more clearly in diagrammatic form, and I have therefore set out some of the main characteristics of our two approaches side by side in Table 1. My two years of experience with intensive one-to-one psychotherapy of schizophrenics and seven years of experience with the type of treatment of schizophrenic patients described in the table form the base of the clinical practice from which I will discuss Dr. Foster's work with this patient.

TABLE 1

Foster	*Meltzer*
1. Intensive individual psychotherapy	Milieu therapy
2. No pharmacotherapy	Adequate pharmacotherapy
3. Toleration of regression	Strive to end regression as rapidly as possible.
4. Hospitalization of patient for period of years, away from family and friends	1–3 month hospitalization near home with frequent home visits during hospitalization
5. Exclusion of family and friends from direct participation in treatment	Insistence upon family participation in treatment
6. Therapist makes critical decisions for patient	Patient shares with entire staff, patient group, and his own family as well as family of other patients in making decisions regarding passes, privileges, posthospital plans, and discharge date for himself and other patients

Based on a minimum two-year evaluation after discharge —an evaluation that considers outcome criteria such as symptom remission, social functioning, and rehospitalization rate—the treatment approach that I now use has been highly successful in achieving a good outcome for the majority of two hundred schizophrenic patients. These results are achieved with relatively short hospitalizations, and I emphasize with minimal regressive behavior on the part of the patients.

A first question about this patient is whether, after having been hospitalized for five years and having had two or three individual therapists at Riggs plus eight others before that, she should have been reassigned to a twelfth therapist. Did the staff ever consider that another institution with a different clinical approach might be able to offer her more effective and efficient treatment *if* further institutionalization was needed? Indeed, it is not clear why Marianne was still hospitalized at the time her work with Dr. Foster began. Was it ever considered that she might be discharged and worked with as an outpatient, that she didn't need institutionalization twenty-four hours a day? For example, there is a three-month upper limit on an inpatient stay on my ward at the Illinois State Psychiatric Institute. The few schizophrenics who have not significantly improved by that time are almost always discharged to their families and provided intensive outpatient care, and in most instances they show considerable improvement outside the hospital. We have on one occasion transferred a destructive patient to another institution, where that patient improved much more than he had at our hospital. We have accepted treatment failures from long-term intensive psychotherapy institutions and achieved rapid and significant success in their treatment. Thus with changes in therapeutic milieu and regimen many apparently intractable patients improve dramatically. Perhaps one of the reasons such a change was not considered for Marianne was an overcommitment to one-to-one psychotherapy as the *only* form of treatment for schizophrenics.

Once having undertaken the treatment, Dr. Foster made two interrelated decisions that set the tone for the entire therapy. Dr. Foster decided (1) to take Marianne off phenothiazines and to tolerate the ensuing massive, acknowledged life-threatening regression of more than two years' duration which affected many other patients and staff at Austen Riggs, without resuming neuroleptic treatment; and (2) to accept exclusive responsibility for decision making for Marianne in many areas of her life after a long period of total permissiveness.

Dr. Foster decided to take Marianne off phenothiazines

within the first hour of their meeting and communicated
this directly to the patient. Later on we are told that the
medication had to be stopped because the patient was using
it to allay anxiety, a process that Dr. Foster believed inter-
fered with psychotherapy. I will discuss the latter idea subsequently, but it is my purpose now to consider the fact
that Dr. Foster committed herself regarding medication in
the very first hour. It is highly unlikely that she could have
known that *this* patient would use medication to interfere
with psychotherapy since it had barely started at that point.
I believe that there were two important reasons for the
decision to stop medication in that first hour. One is the
belief of some psychotherapists that the neuroleptics are
nonspecific tranquilizers without significant antipsychotic
effects, and that they interfere with the capacity of schizophrenics to engage in psychotherapy. The second reason is
that the statement had little to do with pharmacotherapy
per se. Rather it was a device that Dr. Foster used to
disengage Marianne from her previous therapists, who had
prescribed drugs, and to define the style with which decisions will be made between them; i.e., Dr. Foster will uni-
laterally decide what is or is not to be permitted for
Marianne. Support for this view is, I think, offered by the
fact that the next issue that they discussed was that Marianne felt like a girl and not like a woman. It was, I believe,
most unfortunate that Dr. Foster used the medication issue
to communicate her intent to exert unilateral control in the
therapeutic situation. Almost any other issue used to
achieve the same end would have had less unfortunate
consequences. It is my belief that Dr. Foster should not
have sought a relationship of dominance with Marianne.
Had Marianne, her family, other patients, and staff had
formal roles in the decision-making process regarding Marianne's treatment, as is the case in the therapeutic community in which I work, Dr. Foster could have received
valuable help in planning a therapeutic program for Mar-

ianne. I believe both Marianne *and* Dr. Foster suffered greatly and needlessly, Marianne much more so, because Dr. Foster tried to establish dominance and control and because there was no effective system for input by other people in the Austen Riggs system. The power struggle that developed between them was, I believe, the result mainly of Dr. Foster's thrust for control and led directly to much of the bizarre behavior over the next three years. This struggle accomplished little, if anything, in the working through of it that could not have been accomplished by an adequate contract based on mutual respect which was then effectively implemented.

Throughout her report, there are indications that Dr. Foster herself, as well as Marianne, other patients, and staff, held Dr. Foster responsible for Marianne's deterioration, and that Dr. Foster found the assumption of responsibility and many other aspects of her relationship with Marianne a cruel burden. While there are occasional references to other people who participated in Marianne's treatment, there is little doubt that the main aspect of treatment was the relationship between Dr. Foster and Marianne. As Marianne deteriorated, Dr. Foster had to endure criticism and pressure from Marianne and other staff members. Surely Dr. Foster feared for the patient's life and must have agonized about her clinical decisions as Marianne was picking her flesh, sobbing for help, squandering thousands of dollars. Advocacy of the idea that the therapist, through his one-to-one relationship with the patient, is or should be the major determinant of clinical outcome is a common aspect of intensive individual psychotherapy. Elvin Semrad, clinical director of the Massachusetts Mental Health Center, has written (1964): "Any regression is evidence of too much pain in the relationship, and means the patient feels you do not accept him as he is, as a real person in his own right, with and without his transferance overloads. This immediately requires reevaluation of the therapist's role in the relationship. Has the patient picked up your impatience, your frustration, your anger with his demands?'' This statement puts the blame for a regression such as Marianne's on the therapist. I believe Semrad's statement is correct, particularly in a case like Marianne's, where the therapist has taken responsibility for so many crucial decisions, eliminated drug treatment, and given short shrift to enabling the patient to engage in adjunctive treatments such as activity therapy and schooling. The fault, however, lies as much in the system as with the therapist. I believe all therapists who engage in one-to-one psychotherapy over a prolonged time with difficult patients feel the agony of this type of responsibility, or of temporary or prolonged failure. These are some of the crucial reasons why so few psychiatrists remain in inpatient work with schizophrenics. Such agony *is not present* in a milieu unit where all staff share the professional clinical responsibility, and share decision making with each other and with patients and their families.

The lack of input by Marianne and her family into the decision to stop medication raises the ticklish issue of informed consent and ethical responsibility. If Dr. Foster anticipated a regression of the type that ensued once medication was stopped, it seems to me that she would have been obliged to inform Marianne, who could have decided whether she wished to risk that regression in return for whatever benefits Dr. Foster might have been able to hold out as possible. Marianne might have spelled out some limits on the maximum duration a drug-free trial might be conducted, or what type of behavior on her part, if it developed, might be intolerable to her; e.g., defecation in public places, suicide attempts, public nudity, or extravagant spending. That Marianne could have been engaged in the decision is indicated by her telling Dr. Foster of her fears of panic if her medication was stopped and of her fears that the nightmares of self-destruction might become reality if she started working with Dr. Foster. I believe that Dr. Foster should have actively worked to give the patient the opportunity to participate in decisions that directly influenced whether or not these nightmares would become a reality and what to do about them if they did occur. I believe such an involvement of patients in decision making affecting their treatment also has a very useful therapeutic purpose. Infantilizing patients by making crucial decisions for them is antithetical to the development of autonomy and good judgment, which should be among the major goals of any type of treatment of a schizophrenic patient which aspires to be more than just somatic treatment or custodial care. Dr. Foster's unilateral decision not to use medication with this patient was the first step in depriving Marianne of responsibility for herself. In allowing her to become as regressed as she did, Dr. Foster passively condoned a situation in which the patient could not be responsible for herself. Similarly, in the final stages of inpatient treatment, there was little evidence of any effort on Dr. Foster's part to get the patient to learn to make effective decisions for herself; rather, demands and threats were made with unusual frequency. There is little question in my mind that adequate neuroleptic therapy would have helped Marianne to control her own behavior and would have prevented the massive and life-threatening regression.

I shall now discuss Dr. Foster's decision not to use neuroleptic drugs in terms of the proper place of pharmacotherapy in the treatment of a schizophrenic patient. First, it might be argued that drugs had been tried with this patient to no avail, so why continue? One must, however, evaluate the quality of drug treatment provided. Was the right drug prescribed in adequate dosage and for sufficient time? In the hospital Marianne was in prior to Austen Riggs, she was given three different classes of psychotropic medication, two of which, the minor tranquilizers and antidepressants, have little or no role in the treatment of schizophrenic patients. One has doubts, then, whether the phenothiazines were prescribed adequately. Prior to Dr. Foster's assuming responsibility, the patient had received 400 mg. of chlorpromazine (Cpz) per day plus prn meds. Despite this, she was apparently not thought to be sufficiently improved to be discharged, although, as I have indicated, we are not given any clear reason why continued hospitalization was indicated. Four hundred mgs. per day is a moderate dose of Cpz, one which we have found adequate for many patients, but some patients do indeed not have optimal improvement at this dosage. When this occurs, a number of options are open. The first one should be to raise the dose in 200 mg. increments. After two or three weeks at each new dosage level there could be a review of progress and a decision to maintain or raise the dose. A maximum might be at 2,000 mg. per day, as this patient fits the criteria for benefit by high dose phenothiazine treatment: patients under forty years of age with less than ten years of hospitalization (Prien and Cole, 1968). A second strategy might be a phenothiazine of another class, such as fluphenazine. A third alternative would be a butyrophenone or a thioxanthene neuroleptic. Given that the neuroleptics are proven antipsychotics in *groups* of schizophrenic patients, it seems important to determine if *this* patient could derive benefit from adequate amounts of the type of neuroleptic best suited for her. Stopping the drug should have been the last resort if there had been no improvement shown with all the options indicated above.

The issue of correct drug management in this case also requires consideration of the use of prn medication. At the same time that Dr. Foster deplored the fact that medication may be used to allay anxiety, she allowed the patient free access to medication via prn orders of which we are told the patient availed herself whenever she felt anxious. Regular daily doses of medication or biweekly injections of fluphenazine enanthate with elimination of the prn orders should have markedly attenuated this problem which Dr. Foster claimed accompanies the use of phenothiazines. Dr. Foster's failure to eliminate prn medication or even to discuss her reasons for not considering stopping it in the report again raises my suspicion that the decision to stop medication had little to do with the stated reasons of facilitating psychotherapy.

The question remains, however, do daily doses of neuroleptics, by diminishing anxiety or by causing other changes, interfere with the psychotherapy of schizophrenic patients? This is a question that connot be easily dismissed. The recent work of Goldstein et al. (1969) and Rappaport et al. (1972) suggests that some nonparanoid schizophrenic patients may do less well clinically when given phenothiazines. Although this work needs independent corroboration, there are certainly some patients with schizophrenic-like symptomatology who do not require any medication to go into remission. These can be identified by a one-to-two-week trial without medications. It has been my overwhelming experience that with the appropriate dose of the right medication (at least in the clinical setting of my treatment unit at the Illinois State Psychiatric Institute) the large majority of schizophrenics are able to achieve a state of lowered anxiety with minimization of thought disorder that permits them to engage in psychotherapy. They can then go on to learn interpersonal skills and self-awareness, which enhance their capacity to identify and achieve their goals and to avoid or withstand stress without further regression into psychosis.

The concept of the adjunctive role of drugs in the treatment of those schizophrenics for whom drug treatment alone is not sufficient is shared by a number of clinicians experienced in one-to-one psychotherapy. For example, Semrad has stated that neuroleptic drugs could be used in the intensive psychotherapy of schizophrenics "when recovery could not be initiated or maintained on a relationship basis" (1964). Dyrud and Holzman have put it eloquently: "Drugs will reduce thought disorganization, quiet an unruly and excited patient, or mobilize a withdrawn patient. It remains for psychosocial interventions to teach and to train, to reassure and to raise self-confidence, and to help with skills for living that some patients may never have learned or may have learned badly" (1973). There is also relevant physiological data. In states of underarousal or massive overarousal, learning is markedly inhibited, whereas it is facilitated by an appropriate level of arousal, of which anxiety may be a component (Hebb, 1966). If drugs are used wisely, they can be one means to achieve a level of anxiety which facilitates learning. There should be no stigma attached to the doctor or patient who uses drugs as one means of attaining this level of anxiety.

Thus, from both a clinical and a humane perspective, I do not believe it was wise to withdraw and withhold neuroleptic medication from Marianne and thus precipitate and prolong her long and terrible descent into madness. I do not believe much if anything that was useful happened to Marianne during that period. On the way back, yes. But on the way down, and in the purgatory she endured for two years, no. There was such massive anxiety, such chaotic, demented thinking, such empty ritual, such pointless game playing with Dr. Foster that no learning could occur. To the extent that Marianne recalls her primitive behavior in subsequent years, it can have little salutary effect on her self-esteem and probably is of some harm. On our unit, we have, with only the rarest of exceptions, been able to terminate a psychotic regression within at most weeks of admission to the hospital, and then been able to engage in psychotherapeutic work for the rest of the moderate hospital stay. During the brief period of regression, it is possible to acquire data about the patient's basic conflicts which can be utilized during the treatment process, but I have seen no advantage to allowing the period of regression to run its course without medication when that course is of many months' duration, and includes any serious danger to physical health and severe inconvenience to other patients and staff, whose daily existence is made extremely unpleasant by the behavior of the severely regressed patient.

To me one of the most distressing aspects of this case was the total permissiveness toward bizarre behavior early in treatment and the frequent and arbitrary restrictions both of bizarre behavior and of adaptive behavior, such as dating men, in the latter half of treatment. In this latter phase, Dr. Foster's first verbalization of a limit was apparently able to get the patient to make rapid, profound behavioral shifts. This indicates to me that the patient was able to modify her behavior long before Dr. Foster decided that the behavior had to change, that the early cues that change was possible were missed, and that had these cues been observed, the patient could have been encouraged to work on her own toward behavior change rather than through orders to change.

The decision to hospitalize Marianne thousands of miles from her family, the frequent statements in the report of the psychopathology of the family and the pernicious effect of their visits on Marianne's behavior are very much related to the emphasis on one-to-one therapy in this case and to the antimedication bias. The underlying assumptions here are that schizophrenia for all intents and purposes is a "psychogenic" disorder based upon pathological interactions between child and parents which begin at birth and persist throughout life. The pathogenic family must be kept apart from the patient, especially in the first phases of treatment. Somatic approaches in such a psychogenic disorder would be of limited value. I believe these assumptions are false and lead to innappropriate treatment decisions. While there is every reason to believe "psychogenic" factors are important in the phenotypic expression of schizophrenia in most patients, there is now unassailable evidence for a genetic role in the etiology of schizophrenia (Wender, 1969), and hence biochemical causes and consequences, some of which have been defined (Meltzer, 1969; Meltzer and Engle, 1971; Fischman, Meltzer, and Poppei, 1970; Murphy and Wyatt, 1972). When psychiatrists accept the notion that there are organic aspects of schizophrenia, I believe that they become less zealous in their commitment to a particular form of psychotherapy. It is now well known that separation from the schizophrenic parent at birth does not alter the incidence of development of symptomatology (Heston, 1966; Rosenthal et al., 1968). There is no evidence that separation from the family during treatment will alter the disease process. The efficacy of schizophrenic treatment programs that include family therapy is just beginning to be tested, but it looks promising (Massie and Beels, 1972). In our own center, families of schizophrenics have been included in the treatment process for a variety of reasons: as information givers throughout the treatment process; for the opportunity to observe family interaction over an extended period; for the opportunity to work with crucial members of the patient's household to effect changes in interaction patterns; for the opportunity to educate the family about the patient and vice versa; and to assist in maintenance of ties with prehospital social functioning to prevent permanent disruption of this functioning and to facilitate return to it. In addition, despite the frequent assumption that the families of schizophrenics exert a pathological influence on the patients, it is my experience that many families provide strong support to the patients to remain in the hospital, actively engage in therapy, including taking medication, and thus become invaluable colleagues in the therapeutic process. This is especially true in the early stages of hospitalization when patients have not yet developed a positive alliance with the treatment staff. We have successfully integrated multifamily group therapy with milieu therapy and pharmacotherapy. I see no reason why it could not be used with one-to-one therapy as well. As I previously stated, had Marianne's family been actively engaged in the treatment process, it is unlikely that the life-threatening regression that developed and persisted for two years would have been permitted.

In closing, I would like to reemphasize that I am not opposed to one-to-one psychotherapy of schizophrenics. I believe it has a significant place in the treatment of some schizophrenic patients. But it should not be valued to the extent that it was in this case, so that in order to engage in it, other forms of treatments are prohibited or downgraded, hospitalization for years is accepted as the appropriate time span to engage in work, life-threatening regression during its course is tolerated, and separation from family and friends is encouraged. We have referred selected patients for one-to-one psychotherapy several months *after* hospitalization, when social functioning has been reestablished. At that point, they frequently can benefit from the psychological work and interpersonal relationships that skilled psychotherapists can offer. What is required from the psychiatrist during the inpatient phase of treatment is not the establishment of dominance or an overemphasis on the importance of the doctor-patient relationship, but to be a reliable friend, a sensitive listener, an able counselor, a sage psychopharmacologist, and an effective coordinator of the many other potentially therapeutic elements present in a good clinical setting.

REFERENCES

Dyrud, J. E., and Holzman, P. S. The psychotherapy of schizophrenia: does it work? *American Journal of Psychiatry*, 130 (1973): 670–673.

Fischman, D. A.; Meltzer, H. Y.; and Poppei, R. W. The disruption of myofibrils in the skeletal muscle of acutely psychotic patients. *Archives of General Psychiatry*, 23 (1971): 503–515.

Goldstein, M. J.; Judd, L. L.; Rodnick, E. H.; and LaPolla, A. Psychophysiological and behavioral effects of phenothiazine administration in acute schizophrenics as a function of premorbid status. *Journal of Psychiatric Research*, 6 (1969): 271–287.

Hebb, D. O. *A Textbook of Psychology*. Philadelphia:W. B. Saunders Co., 1966, pp. 234–239.

Heston, L. L. Psychiatric disorders in foster home reared children of schizophrenic mothers. *British Journal of Psychiatry*, 112 (1966): 819–825.

Massie, H. N., and Beels, C. C. The outcome of the family treatment of schizophrenia. *Schizophrenia Bulletin*, no. 6 (1972): 24–36.

Meltzer, H. Y. Muscle enzyme release in the acute psychoses. *Archives of General Psychiatry*, 21 (1969): 102–112.

Meltzer, H. Y., and Engel, W. K. Histochemical abnormalities of skeletal muscle in patients with acute psychoses, pt. 2. *Archives of General Psychiatry*, 23 (1970): 492–502.

Murphy, D. L., and Wyatt, R. J. Reduced monoamine oxidase activity in blood platelets from schizophrenic patients. *Nature*, 238 (1972): 225–226.

Prien, R. F., and Cole, J. O. High dose chlorpromazine therapy in chronic schizophrenia. *Archives of General Psychiatry*, 18 (1968): 482–495.

Rappaport, M.; Hopkins, K.; and Hall, K. Auditory signal

detection in paranoid and nonparanoid schizophrenics. *Archives of General Psychiatry*, 27 (1972): 747–752.

Rosenthal, D.; Wender, P.; Kety, S.; Schulsinger, F.; Ostergard, L.; and Welner, J. In *The Transmission of Schizophrenia*, ed. D. Rosenthal and S. Kety. Oxford: Pergamon Press, 1968.

Semrad, E. V. Long-term therapy of schizophrenia (formulation of the clinical approach). Presented at *Psychiatry in the Mid-Sixties*, New Orleans, 1964.

Wender, P. H. The role of genetics in the etiology of schizophrenia. *American Journal of Orthopsychiatry*, 39 (1969): 447–458.

8

IDENTITY AS A WAY
OF CONCEPTUALIZING THE CASE
Clarence Schulz, M.D.

Dr. Foster has revealed, in a remarkable way, perhaps not so much what she did in the way of interpretive work, but some of the feelings she experienced, and the changes that I think the patient evoked in her. A second point has to do with conceptualizing the whole treatment along the lines of self-object differentiation, the struggles against fusion, and the attempts on the patient's part to create a delineation and a differentiation.

The second line of thinking has to do with the identity aspects as a way of conceptualizing the case. She has described identity features that go all the way back to the grandfather and the father. The patient's grandfather wore white shirts and the patient's father wore blue shirts to be different or to differentiate himself from the father. The patient, in her identification with the grandfather, wore white blouses so that she would at the same time be different from her father. You see attempts on the father's part to blur role identities. He didn't want to be called Dad and he played with her toys. One notices the patient attempting to find some kind of identity by being "the craziest patient in the community." I trust she succeeded because I hope you don't have any that are crazier than this description. This is an open setting, I am told, but I don't think we have anybody sicker than this at Sheppard Pratt. I'll come back to comment on her regression.

I would postulate that self-object differentiation is where the first glimmerings of identity begin. These first fleeting senses of differentiation are the start. I think much of what we can see in the way of the clinical phenomena described here can be subsumed under the whole struggle around the issue of identity as it relates to self-object differentiation, the struggles against fusion, and the patient's attempts to create a delineation and a differentiation. I would diagnose the deficiency, as discussed by Wexler (see Chapter 10), as a failure in this crucial developmental task of a firm delineation of self from object. I view many of these things, like the patient's scratching herself and causing herself injury and so on, as attempts at stimulus input to define some kind of body ego, as Freud called it. The rocking that she would do, the head-banging that she participated in, the scrubbing her body until she bled were ways of establishing a very primitive, rudimentary sense of self. That is why the patient was so impressed by and appreciative of the therapist's physically touching her. Another confirmation of the importance of differentiation can be found in the patient's dog story which concluded with ". . . one can be accepted only if he is different."

Her refusal to let go of menstrual pads, nail clippings, and hair and so on, these are all body parts whose loss means loss of self.* These losses are experienced in a very concrete way for a person at this level. Similarly, her clothing—the wearing of the soiled blue jeans—was regarded as part of herself. Sometimes patients will hang on to clothing for a very long time. I think her use of the leather jackets, when she belonged to that group, gave her an identity by belonging.

While I regard the treatment result as really astounding in what has happened here, I am going to be the devil's advocate and raise the question of whether it had to go this way. This issue is part of what we have been struggling with in some of our research discussions. Since we can't

*We could conceptualize these as "transitional self" in parallel to Winnicott's "transitional object."

run the same patient through twice, I don't know if anybody can ever answer this kind of question. I shall ask what if the therapist had drawn the line earlier? I am really raising an issue of timing. After all, the therapist did come to the point of no longer allowing the patient to live in the woods and also would not continue to see her on the lawn. Supposing the attempt to draw limits to assist this differentiation and so on had come about sooner? Could the whole process have had a different course, where the patient would not be physically endangered living in the woods, and so forth? That would scare the hell out of me. I guess there was more tolerance for it here, or at least we haven't heard much about the staff reaction during this phase.

Supposing you interposed greater structure in the life of this patient? What if you had the art therapist move in much earlier? Suppose you had put greater organization around her—not necessarily a locked hospital, but perhaps you could do it with more staff or staff that was integrated with the therapist. I realize we are hearing this from the standpoint of the therapist's report, and maybe much was left out by way of conferences with the staff, involvement of other patients to help set limits and provide structure. I am thinking of the use of other people—patients and staff alike—to structure a more organized, a more programmed, if you will, approach with the patient. My conjecture is that it would not have allowed the extensive regression, or the depth of it, or the length of it perhaps. These are real questions that are, unfortunately, unanswerable.

Dr. Foster stated that she was reluctant to impose something physical on the patient but would rather wait for the patient to ask for it. I am not so reluctant. I know that some people are reluctant to do certain things, such as set limits, because it's similar to the way the patient's parents behaved toward the patient. That doesn't bother me as much because I think that if the patient reacts to this by way of transference anger toward me, the transference aspect can always then be dealt with. I do not recommend avoiding all authoritarian approaches or engaging in something really totally different from what the patient has experienced in the past. So, for my own taste, the limits would have been established earlier. They would have come in a combined form of trying to integrate the other staff and patients in setting those limits, together with an attempt to be interpretive about it.

SECTION TWO
CURRENT THEORIES

THE CURRENT
METAPSYCHOLOGY OF SCHIZOPHRENIA

Background

Disputes about the metapsychology of schizophrenia have traditionally focused on the question of schizophrenia as a deficit or schizophrenia as a defense, i.e., conflict. A derivative argument has concerned the schizophrenic as qualitatively different from other people, or, as in the conflict model, the schizophrenic as being on a continuum with other people. Both the conflict and the deficit theoretical models can trace their beginnings to Freud. Those who adhere to a conflict view are in sympathy with Freud's early formulations on schizophrenia,[1,2] while those who further the deficit view cite Freud's later formulations, beginning with his analysis of the Schreber bibliography.[3] The subsequent development of these two disparate theoretical views have come to incorporate more modern psychoanalytic thinking. Changes in the theoretical concepts of schizophrenia since Freud largely parallel the growth of psychoanalytic theory in general. Thus, while Freud's formulations stress the topographic model (i.e., conscious-unconscious systems) and the vicissitudes of intrapsychic energies (i.e., cathexis-decathexis), later theorists have emphasized structural components of intrapsychic life and more recently the dependence of intrapsychic structure on object relations. There are, in addition, some innovative theoretical developments—some of which have arisen during the course of this NIMH program—which hint at the direction in which future theoretical formulations of schizophrenia are likely to go. These theoretical developments have been reviewed elsewhere[4-7] but are briefly described here as an introduction and overview to this section of this volume.

Deficit Theories

Prominent among the efforts to take up the deficit banner where Freud left off are the contributions by Milton Wexler. In Chapter 10 Wexler traces the development and sources of his theorizing to its present state. His hypotheses about the vulnerability of those who become schizophrenic to the loss of their internal object representations is founded in the conceptual framework prepared by Freud in the Schreber case and in "Mourning and Melancholia." It remains a broadly accepted and widely cited psychoanalytic formulation of schizophrenia. In brief, this theory states that the preschizophrenic child, because of a deficient perceptual apparatus, central organization, or learning capacity, does not normally internalize from his early parental experiences a stable sense of self. Thus, in times of later stress, these brittle internalizations evaporate, leaving the schizophrenic "selfless." This overwhelming experience leads the schizophrenic to attempt object restitution (and thus self-restitution) in ways that constitute the familiar clinical symptoms of schizophrenia—hallucinations, delusions, and so on.

Among the reasons why this theoretical position is generally accepted is that it allows for but doesn't require an organic or genetic base to schizophrenia. Moreover, it focuses attention on an internal developmental deficit that recurs catastrophically in the adult schizophrenic and thus is consistent with or explains much of the dramatic clinical phenomenology of schizophrenia. Finally, it uses familiar language and is closely wedded to early psychoanalytic traditions. Yet, despite these strengths, this formulation is also vulnerable to the following criticisms:

(*a*) It does not specify the nature of the deficit or why the schizophrenic has his particular deficit of memory traces, learning, or internalization. In other words, it describes the what, but not the how and why of a deficit, and not whether it is specific to schizophrenia (vs. other disorders).

(*b*) It fails adequately to consider the role of nonmaternal family members or the nonfamily environment.

(*c*) The concept of internal object representations is not well defined (i.e., some feel that what is really unstable are those object representations that have become self-representations), is not well understood developmentally, and is not a readily recognized inference from clinical observations (i.e., like all metapsychology, it is at least a second order inference).

For further critical comments, see Chapter 14, in which Harold Searles presents his eloquent and impassioned viewpoint of the deficit view.

Multiple variations of deficit theories have been advocated. Arieti[8] earlier used a conflict model to explain schizophrenia, but more recently he prefers to talk of "deficient internalization," which may involve nonpsychological factors.[9] Rado[10] provided a theoretical view of schizophrenia specifically based on the presence of a genetically determined "schizotype" personality. Kessler[11] postulates that the genetically determined deficit is an exaggerated "inhibitory defense," i.e., a neurologically determined inability to repress selectively. In a recent report Aronson has attempted to modify Wexler's deficit view by introducing the controlled observations from animal experiments done by Harlow and Lorenz.[12] The principal impact of these studies in Aronson's revision of the deficit theory is the increased emphasis given to the strength and adaptive quality of the vulnerable infant's learned responses to his early frustration experiences. These response patterns become maladaptive when confronted with other demands in life.

This modification would help explain the deeply ingrained characterologic pathology of the adult schizophrenic in addition to the more acute fulminating symptomatology explained by Wexler.

Defense Theories

For purposes of simplicity, the development in the conflict theories of schizophrenia can be divided into three models. The first of these, and the one most frequently and vociferously argued about by those who don't accept deficit models, is derived from the observations of children by Melanie Klein[13] and has subsequently been elaborated on with respect to schizophrenia by her followers Hanna Segal[14] and Herbert Rosenfeld.[15] This theoretical position stresses the importance of internal-external, good-bad, part-object splitting during early infancy. This position is described in Chapter 11 and further observations related to it are found in Chapter 24. Like the deficit theory, it posits a defective process of early internalization (called introjection by Kleinians), but does so without hypothesizing that this is due to a constitutional deficit. Rather, the core conflict in internal object images occurs when the three-to-six-month-old infant experiences predominantly destructive impulses toward the mother. This provides a prototypical confusion between good and bad or love and hate (called the paranoid-schizoid position), which is reactivated in adult life when there is danger of internalizing whole objects. The infant who is unable to surmount (i.e., bear) the fear of being hurt which results from his destructive impulses is vulnerable to later development of schizophrenia. The paranoid-schizoid position is reactivated in adult life when there is a danger of internalizing whole objects. This occurs when the vulnerable person loses an object who has been the target of his split-off (projected) badness or when he becomes attached to an object to whom he cannot project his badness (i.e., some form of intimacy is called for). The flight from internalizing his own badness (becoming a whole object) and the ensuing loss of internal object representation is thus an active rather than passive defensive process by the ego.

This viewpoint has been criticized both for the inferences Klein drew from childhood observation and for the predominant role given very early experience while comparatively neglecting the impact of later environmental conditions. The concepts and language defy ready correlation with clinical observations, leading even sophisticated metapsychologists to admit they aren't sure they understand the position being taken. Freeman complains that this theory would fail to account for similar psychopathological content appearing in organic and toxic psychoses.[16] Moreover, like all conflict theories, it tends to overlook the potential role of genetic predisposition. Finally, as James Grotstein points out in Chapter 11, the Kleinian metapsychology can be adapted to include possible genetic predispositional factors. In his comments on Grotstein's paper, Ralph Greenson addresses some of these criticisms and the technical implicat᠁ ᠁s derived from them.

The second development in the conflict theory of schizophrenia is attributable largely to the work of Arlow and Brenner, who renounced the topographic model as used by Freud and placed the responsibility for schizophrenia squarely on the shoulders of a defective ego.[17] This defective ego, however, is not to be confused in their formulation with the presence of some deficiency which would be inexplicable by environmental determinants. They view the psychosis as a defensive effort to avoid the emergence of anxiety from inner conflicts. These defenses differ only in the degree of disruption of reality contact they cause, not in any qualitative difference.

Elvin Semrad extends this ego psychology view of schizophrenia. He sees schizophrenic psychoses as defensive operations designed to avoid intolerable affects including but not limited to anxiety.[18] These defenses (denial, projection, distortion, and identification with the aggressor) become habitual means of warding off the pain that had accompanied depriving or overindulgent early childhood relationships. By not attending to unpleasant percepts, the child prevents internal turmoil from occurring. This produces severe handicaps in later life when internal affect is handled as if it were an external danger. Therefore, in children who rely on these defenses, capacity to delay responses, to bear painful experiences, and dissipate tension within the body are developed only to a limited extent. The preschizophrenic thus avoids relationships as a means of controlling the danger of developing intense affects. Ego decompensation, regression, and clinical psychosis occur in later periods of intensification of affect. At such times the impossible pain of the early relationship to a parent is evoked. Some of the clinical sequelae of this formulation are commented on by Daniel Schwartz (Chapter 2). Like Arlow and Brenner's, this theory emphasizes the defective ego structure and quantitative—not qualitative—differences in the defenses used by the schizophrenic. But it also goes further by stressing the central role of affects in the pathological childhood development which predispose to later schizophrenic psychoses.

The theory of affect intolerance can be commended for its coherence and its close affiliation with clinical observation. Many others have noted the importance of affect intolerance in schizophrenia. Grinker,[19] among others,[20] [21] has stated his clinical impression that the inability to experience anger lies at the base of schizophrenic decompensation. In some respects this resembles the central role given flight from destructive impulses in the formulations about schizophrenia by Harold Searles and by the Kleinians. Yet this theory, like most others, can be viewed as descriptive rather than etiological. Thus, the reasons why one child and not another develops pathological defenses against affects is not explained, nor does the theory explain why one affect may be particularly unbearable as opposed to another for a given schizophrenic patient. Like the Kleinian theory, this theory also infers a grossly disturbed early parent-child relationship as the basis of the disturbed relationship that the adult schizophrenic shows toward a therapist. But retrospective reconstructions of early mother-child relationships remain unconfirmed hypotheses, awaiting prospective evaluations.[22] Further discussion of the affect theory is found in Gerald Aronson's paper (Chapter 3).

It may be readily appreciated that all of these theories, both deficit and conflict, have in common a reliance upon the metapsychological language of psychoanalysis as has been derived from observations in the analytic situation. None of the traditional theories of schizophrenia has taken into consideration the newer observations about schizophrenia which have arisen out of the community movement and the widespread employment of antipsychotic drugs. Philip Holzman (Chapter 13) is critical of the limitations of data derived solely from the analytic situation and questions the applicability and appropriateness of psychoanalytic metapsychology to schizophrenia. Other, newer theories about schizophrenia employ new data bases and all try to avoid the traditional controversy of deficit vs. conflict viewpoints.

Reconciliatory Theories

One means by which recent theorists have sought to overcome the old split between conflict and deficiency is to delineate central or organizing issues which may be viewed with equal comfort either as a cause of defective structure or as being superimposed on and perhaps caused by weak structure. In this respect, Burnham[23] emphasizes the need-fear dilemma and links this to specific aspects of weak internal structure, namely the systems for self-control and self-regulation which are either too tenuous or too rigid and which the person has difficulty maintaining autonomously. Similarly, and more broadly, Mahler has stressed the central role of separation-individuation in normal and pathological development.[24] Helm Stierlin in Chapter 15 and Clarence Schulz in Chapter 20 join Searles,[25] Jacobson,[26] and Freeman[27] in employing this developmental axis as a central organizing theoretical construct to explain adult schizophrenia. In brief, this theoretical position states that there are normally occurring autistic and symbiotic phases in the relationship of the infant to its mother. During these phases the infant has a poor sense of itself as independent from the mother, and it is only through a gradual process of separation that individuation occurs with its accompanying formation of a stable and assured sense of self. Failure to emerge successfully from these developmental phases predisposes such children to later development of schizophrenia. In Stierlin's family work, described below, he implies that he is dissatisfied with the prominent role given the dyadic symbiotic experience in this theory. Likewise, Searles criticizes Mahler's formulation for underestimating the degree of interpersonal, intrafamilial trauma that schizophrenic patients suffer despite a relatively normal genetic endowment. The result of this, according to Searles, is an underestimation of the role of aggression in a schizophrenic. From a different vantage point, Wexler has criticized the self-object differentiation formulation of schizophrenia for not being specific to schizophrenia and for being descriptive rather than being an explanatory theoretical formulation.

Transactional Theory

A second major trend in new theories of schizophrenia has been the recognition that the schizophrenic develops his pathological vulnerability over an extended period of time and in circumstances that are extended beyond the early infantile parent-child relationship. This has necessarily meant that theoretical formulations must allow for, if not actively include, the impact of the interpersonal network and social climate in which the individual developed. For example, several studies have demonstrated that the father's psychopathology may be just as influential on development of schizophrenia as the mother's.[28] Growing out of the active and relatively new research and therapeutic interest in the families of schizophrenics has come the first, albeit preliminary, theoretical formulations of milieu transaction. One of the difficulties required in moving out of the dyadic relationship—as postulated to occur in early development and as recapitulated in the analytic situation —has been the need to develop a new language along with new metapsychological concepts.

Wynne[29] has formulated schizophrenia as a disorder of psychological and emotional transaction between people, not as a process located exclusively within a person. The infant learns to interact in his family and particularly with the mother. If this primordial experience is disrupted, either because of the mother's distractions (a failure to teach) or because the child for organic and probably genetic reasons is unresponsive (or responds idiosyncratically), a failure to learn to use language meaningfully takes place. Thus response dispositions interact with interpersonal (particularly intrafamilial) transactional processes to create the schizophrenia-vulnerable person. Such families tend to interact in rigid, oversimplified, and distant ways in which any readjustments to accommodate growth or change are not tolerated. Thus schizophrenic symptomatology is reflective of a crisis in development in which change or intimacy is required. In extending this interactional conception of schizophrenia, Stierlin[30] has focused on the centripetal and centrifugal forces within family constellations and applied these concepts to the schizophrenic family. In this context he's borrowed the concepts of self-object differentiation and formulated the development of schizophrenia in terms of the degree, amount, and type of distance or differentiation which the index child is permitted from his parents. Although this conceptualization owes something to the concept of self-object differentiation, the language is transformed into the language of transactional systems.

Systems Theory

In a more ambitious effort to expand theoretical formulations of schizophrenia beyond the infantile experience, Grinker has employed "systems" theory.[31] This systems theory, like Hughling Jackson's theory of neurological development, views the organism as the product of an unfolding logical progression whose course is influenced in succession by constitutional, nurturing, familial, economic, social, and interpersonal factors. According to Grinker, we know that all of these factors are involved in the ontogeny of schizophrenic disturbance as well as so-called healthy development. The schizophrenic state can then be viewed as a system composed of difficulties in heredity, early family systems of communication, in early peer experiences, with trauma, etc. This view means that we aren't able to focus on any one factor in our concern for the various etiologies of schizophrenia, but to note that all factors are necessary in varying combinations. There is no such thing as spontaneous change, we are just not presently able to pinpoint the factors in the schizophrenic's system which can explain his changes. Holzman points out that this view of development and more specifically of schizophrenia envelops the considerable contributions of nonpsychological factors (e.g., genetic, biochemical, and neurological) which he views as necessary in light of current scientific understanding of schizophrenia. Yet, as comprehensive as the systems theory would appear to be, it provides little specificity for the problem of schizophrenia. Thus it fails to provide testable hypotheses, guides to clinical practice, and predictions for course and behavior. Holzman employs it mainly as a prescription and rationale for further systematic observations before expanding psychological theory. In this sense it is closer to describing the criteria for a theory of schizophrenia than actually providing one.

Summary

The more recent developments in the clinical theories about schizophrenia have in common the impulse to encompass observations from sources other than the analytic situation. In the effort to do this, no theory has emerged which is both sufficiently specific to schizophrenia to readily provide predictions and thus testable hypotheses or which is general enough to encompass known information about schizophrenia. It is certain that among the criteria for a modern theory of schizophrenia are the following:

1. It must encompass what is known from the clinical phenomena in the schizophrenic as a patient (i.e., style of relating or transference).

2. It must draw viable implications from such phenomena to conform with what is known about the schizophrenic's early child development.

3. It must incorporate nontransference phenomena, including information about the schizophrenic's response to drugs, community, and family.

4. It must allow for and hopefully embody a role for constitutional or biological factors in at least some members of the schizophrenic group.

5. It must encompass factors derived from nondyadic interactions, including social circumstance, drug precipitants, and spontaneous remissions.

Fortunately a group of prospective studies of children at risk for subsequent development of schizophrenia are currently under way. These studies are looking at and systematically assessing early development, including parameters such as interpersonal relatedness, mother-child interaction, use of language, and ability to express affects. Since a fraction of these children (about 10 to 15 percent) will later develop schizophrenia, there will be a chance to test the validity of some of these theoretical models and delineate a better informed conception. Risk children have now been differentiated from others by prolonged separation of mother and child,[32] the difficulty of dealing with positive affect in three-year-olds,[33] the compliance of female vs. hostility of male preschizophrenics in school,[34] etc. [35,36] Such findings are still tentative and sketchy, but it is noteworthy that none of the clinical theorists have thus far cited this highly relevant literature.

Even more difficult is the task of connecting metapsychological concepts of schizophrenia to the burgeoning literature on the nature of a constitutional deficit in schizophrenia. This is largely due to the current absence of a unified, generally accepted biochemical, neurological, or genetic theory of schizophrenia. Yet biochemical theorists like Kety[37] are taking some steps toward delimiting symptoms that might be attributable to one biochemical hypothesis vs. clinical phenomena not explainable in that way. Likewise, an essentially neurological hypothesis like Shakow's[38] that schizophrenia is due to an inability to sort out relevant stimuli lends itself to metapsychological extrapolation. Indeed, Wynne[39] and Will[40] have tried to employ this model. Even conflict theorists need to attend to the interface between biology and psychology. Here, for example, Mednick has suggested and provided some empirical substantiation for the idea that the autonomic nervous system is unstable in those children who later develop schizophrenia and that this instability is the product of environmental events like separations from mother.[41] Despite the speculative nature of metapsychological correlations with such results, bridging this gap from biological to psychological is the most important step lacking in most current metapsychological theories. This step must be taken to make any theory comprehensive and usefully predictive and to change descriptive metapsychological theories into true etiological theories.

It would seem somewhat misleading, in any event, to accept without further investigation the common belief that one's theoretical view of schizophrenia guides one's techniques of treatment. Among the participants in this NIMH program the concatenation of technique and theory was varied, often confusing, and certainly not predictable. This observation flies in the face of the intense emphasis given to specific theoretical positions by many experienced psychotherapists. This raises the question whether the intense belief in a theoretical construct which allows the therapist to organize and systematize his observations is an important concomitant for successful treatment even if it is not accurate in its content. Moreover, it suggests that an organizing principle can be useful to a therapist, perhaps in reducing anxiety, even if it is not true about the particular patient. Certainly the observation that theory doesn't dictate technique is consistent with the impression that personality factors in the therapist are considered more important than technique in treating schizophrenics.

It would seem likely that in future years new theoretical positions about schizophrenia will emerge which incorporate the best features of the advancements made by some of the authors in this volume. This would appear to be the direction in which the metapsychological theories explaining schizophrenia are headed. There is a growing dissatisfaction with traditional theories and old debates and a healthy exploration of new theoretical constructs. For the present, the plethora of theories reflects the uncertainty of our understanding of schizophrenia.

REFERENCES

1. Freud, S. Neuro-psychoses of defense. *Standard Edition*, 3:41–68. London: Hogarth Press, 1953.
2. Freud, S. Further remarks on the neuropsychoses of defense. *Standard Edition*, 3:157–185. London: Hogarth Press, 1953.
3. Freud, S. Psychoanalytic notes on an autobiographical account of a case of paranoia. *Standard Edition*, 12:3–82. London: Hogarth Press, 1958.
4. Bellak, L., and Blaustein, A. Psychoanalytic aspects of schizophrenia. In *Schizophrenia: A Review of the Syndrome*, ed. L. Bellak. New York: Grune & Stratton, 1966.
5. Freeman, T. *Psychopathology of the Psychoses*. New York: International Universities Press, 1969.
6. Rubins, J. G. Schizophrenia as conflict and defense: implications for therapy and research. In *Research and Relevance*, Vol. XXI of *Science and Psychoanalysis*, ed. J. Masserman. New York: Grune & Stratton, 1972.
7. Pao, P. Notes on Freud's theory of schizophrenia. Presented at the fall meeting of the American Psychoanalytic Association, December 1, 1972.
8. Arieti, S. *Interpretation of Schizophrenia*. New York: Robert Brunner, 1955.
9. Arieti, S. Schizophrenia. *Am. J. Psychiat.*, 128:3, 1971.
10. Rado, S. Schizotypal organization: preliminary report on a clinical study of schizophrenia. In *Psychoanalysis of Behavior*, vol. 1. New York: Grune & Stratton, 1956.
11. Kessler, M. Use of familiar dynamic considerations to explain the schizophrenic process. *Dynamische Psychiatrie*, 2:40–49, 1969.
12. Aronson, G. Defense and deficit models of schizophrenia. Presented at the fall meeting of the American Psychoanalytic Association, December 1, 1972.

13. Klein, M. *Contributions to Psychoanalysis.* London: Hogarth Press, 1948.
14. Segal, H. Some aspects of the analysis of a schizophrenic. *Int. J. Psychoanal.*, 31:285, 1951.
15. Rosenfeld, H. *Psychotic States: A Psychoanalytic Approach.* New York: International Universities Press, 1966.
16. Freeman, T.; Cameron, J.; and McGhie, A. *Chronic Schizophrenia.* New York: International Universities Press, 1958.
17. Arlow, J., and Brenner, C. *Psychoanalytic Concepts and the Structural Theory.* New York: International Universities Press, 1964.
18. Semrad, E. V. A clinical formulation of the psychoses. In *Teaching Psychotherapy of Psychotic Patients*, ed. D. Van Buskirk. New York: Grune & Stratton, 1969.
19. Grinker, R. Changing styles in psychiatric syndromes. *Am. J. Psychiat.*, 130:146–155, 1973.
20. Spotnitz, H. *Modern Psychoanalysis of the Schizophrenic Patient.* New York: Grune & Stratton, 1969.
21. Searles, H. F. *Collected Papers on Schizophrenia and Related Subjects.* New York: International Universities Press, 1965.
22. Yarrow, M.; Campbell, J.; and Burton, R. Recollections of childhood: a study of the retrospective method. *Monographs of the Society for Research in Child Development*, 35(5):138, 1970.
23. Burnham, D.; Gladstone, A.; and Gibson, R. *Schizophrenia and the Need-Fear Dilemma.* New York: International Universities Press, 1969.
24. Mahler, M. S. On human symbiosis and the vicissitudes of individuation. In *Infantile Psychosis.* New York: International Universities Press, 1968.
25. Searles, *Collected Papers.*
26. Jacobson, E. *Psychotic Conflict and Reality.* New York: International Universities Press, 1967.
27. Freeman, *Psychopathology of the Psychoses.*

28. Cheek, F. E. The father of the schizophrenic. *Arch. Gen. Psychiat*, 13:336–345, 1965.
29. Wynne, L. Communication disorders and the quest for relatedness in families of schizophrenics. *Am. J. Psychoanal.*, 30:100–114, 1970.
30. Stierlin, H. Some therapeutic implications of a transactional theory of schizophrenia. Presented at the annual fall meeting of the American Psychoanalytic Association, New York, December 1, 1972.
31. Grinker, R. Changing styles in psychoses and borderline states. *Am. J. Psychiat*, 130: 151–152, 1973.
32. Mednick, S. A., and Schulsinger, F. Nature-nurture aspects of schizophrenia: early detection and prevention. Unpublished manuscript.
33. Grunebaum, H. Cited in Mosher, L., and Gunderson, J. Special Report on Schizophrenia, 1972. *Schizophrenia Bulletin*, 7 (Winter): 27, 1973.
34. Watt, N. Longitudinal changes in the social behavior of children hospitalized for schizophrenia as adults. *J. Nerv. & Ment. Dis.* 155(1): 42–54, 1972.
35. Mosher, L., and Gunderson, J. Special Report on Schizophrenia, 1972. *Schizophrenia Bulletin*, 7 (Winter):10–52, 1973.
36. Garmezy, N. Children at risk: the search for antecedents to schizophrenia. *Schizophrenia Bulletin*, in press.
37. Kety, S. Prospects for biochemical research in schizophrenia. The Paul Hoch Memorial Lecture. Am. Psychopathological Assoc., New York, March 1–2, 1973.
38. Shakow, D. Psychological deficit in schizophrenia. *Behav. Sci.*, 8:275–305, 1963.
39. Wynne, Communication disorders.
40. Will, O. Psychological treatment of schizophrenia. In *Comprehensive Textbook of Psychiatry*, ed. A. M. Freedman and H. I. Kaplan, pp. 649–661. Baltimore: Williams & Wilkins, 1967.
41. Mednick and Schulsinger, Nature-nurture aspects of schizophrenia.

10

THE EVOLUTION OF A
DEFICIENCY VIEW OF SCHIZOPHRENIA

Early Clinical Experiences

In 1948 a sad event for the Menninger Foundation turned out to be somewhat fortunate for me. The misfortune in Topeka was that Margaret Brenman, Merton Gill, and a number of other remarkable people left the Foundation to take up residence at the Austen Riggs Center and, in the process, left behind some loose grant money. I was happily the beneficiary of this grant remainder. The Menninger Research Department thereupon freed half my time to do some clinical investigations in the treatment of schizophrenic patients.

At an earlier date, John Rosen had paid a visit to Topeka and a number of our staff wanted me to emulate his techniques to see if they were effective in the treatment of schizophrenics. You may remember that Rosen had reported success in a series of twenty-one cases over a relatively short period of time.

As I set up my own research, the staff asked Dr. Jan Frank, one of our senior analysts, to select a nice "process" schizophrenic for me to treat with Rosen's techniques on the assumption that such patients were organic and quite uncurable. I began my research with that patient and, to a considerable extent, I was ultimately successful. This "incurable" patient was able to leave the hospital and is, even at this date, living on her own outside of a hospital some twenty-five years later.

At the time I began treatment, she had been hospitalized

for five years; she had had shock treatment plus nearly every other form of therapy then available. Despite these efforts, she continued to talk in a word salad and was wildly delusional and hallucinated. To the best of my ability, I tried (probably ineptly) to emulate John Rosen's techniques, using deep interpretations, feeding the patient hamburgers, doughnuts, and other goodies, and spending an inordinate amount of time with her seven days a week. The rewards she gave me for such dedicated and kindly investments were mainly sexual and aggressive assaults and what seemed an exacerbation of the schizophrenic symptom picture. With some hesitance even at this late date, I must confess that one very sudden and monstrously aggressive assault by the patient triggered a response in me which was embarrassingly aggressive on my side. I actually slapped her in a kind of reflexive anger. To my amazement the patient responded with the first coherent, understandable words I had ever heard from her. She asked plaintively, "Why did you do that?"

At that time I wanted to report this exchange in a paper I was writing about the patient, but I was quite correctly warned by Karl Menninger against being too explicit about the details of this incident in public print. He had said to me, "You know that despite all of your protestations this was a reflexive act, you will be forever after known as the 'superego psychotherapist' and you will never be forgiven for that action by your colleagues, who will inevitably misunderstand you." To a large extent his sage advice has been only too true. If I may digress for a moment, there is a relevant incident to report on this matter. I once had a rather delightful visit with Bert Lewin, who came to my office and almost immediately greeted me with the question, "Milton, are you still slapping schizophrenia patients?" I said to him, "Bert, you know I don't do that!" and he said, "I know you don't, but think what a marvelous practice you would have if you did!"

The Superego Theory

Anyhow, I developed a theory about schizophrenia at that point—a very simple-minded theory, which in essence stated that between the pressures from urgent instinctual drives and the rigidity of a very cruel, very primitive, and very savage superego, the ego got squeezed out of existence. What I had to do technically in order to help the patient was to side with one or the other of the warring psychic instances. Either you were going to be on the side of the id and support its claims or you were going to be on the side of the superego and support its strictures.

Essentially in responding with such uncontrolled anger to the patient I had committed what must certainly be considered psychoanalytic idiocy; namely, hitting a patient. This memory has proved a source of mortification ever since. Yet I could not help thinking that this was the external representative of a punitive and restraining superego and seemed of some therapeutic value at the moment. Subsequently, I experimented with more restrained but perhaps equally irrational superego restrictions by telling this good Catholic patient that she shouldn't smoke, she shouldn't swear, and that she must forgo all masturbation, an open and repetitive activity of hers on the ward. I added many similar restrictive injunctions.

I was quite impressed not only with the considerable improvement that seemed to occur in the patient as a seeming by-product of these injunctions, but also with the kinds of regressions that occurred when I became more permissive, more liberal, and more giving in the situation. Rather naively, at the time, I assumed that it really works to be on the side of the superego and that this approach could be generally used for schizophrenia, which quite justifiably bears the title "the masochistic neurosis." You must also remember that, at the time, I held the fairly simple-minded theory that in schizophrenia the ego was squeezed out of shape by virtue of the intense struggle between id and superego.

Subsequently, I realized that this was much too naive an approach, and I began to speculate on what I considered to be a more sophisticated level. In connection with the patient above, a Catholic woman with an IQ of approximately 90, it seemed unlikely to me that the major therapeutic benefit came from merely supporting the superego against unacceptable drives. What suddenly seemed more reasonable to me was that these superego injunctions really spoke an understandable language to her. I could really contact and establish communication with this patient since I was using a language that was truly synchronous with her personality both premorbidly and in her illness. And in relation to this kind of patient, the establishment of communication contained within in it the real potential for building psychic structure, and therefore for enhancing reality testing. I presented that view to the Yale Symposium on Schizophrenia in 1951 and it was subsequently published in *Psychotherapy with Schizophrenics* (International Universities Press). I notice with some unhappiness that this later and more plausible publication is frequently omitted from consideration by those making reference to my work.

Later Clinical Experiences and Theoretical Revisions

Around that time, I intensified my therapeutic involvement with schizophrenic patients. I had some very special and very interesting experiences in this area when, in 1951, I moved from Topeka to Los Angeles. For a number of years I had a fairly large number of emergency referrals of patients who decompensated in classical psychoanalysis and began to exhibit acute psychotic symptoms. This represented a quite marvelous research ground for me. It constantly raised a question in my mind as to what elements in classical psychoanalytic treatment might precipitate a decompensation to such an extent in such a large number of patients (approximately twenty over the course of five to seven years).

I became more convinced than ever that my earlier hypothesis concerning schizophrenia had merit. With the analyst sitting behind the patient and removed even from visual contact, and with a refined analysis of the patient's relationships to past objects, there could only be an increasing detachment of the patient from his past object representation and even from his current representation of the analyst. This situation created a kind of deficiency before which the patients rapidly decompensated into an acute psychosis.

I also became increasingly convinced that certain clinical phenomena characteristic of schizophrenics could be understood in the light of this growing loss of object constancy, this detachment from object representation. Among these clinical phenomena were: (1) the considerable confusion and uncertainty concerning personal identity; (2) the malignant loss of distance in early transference reactions; (3) the psychic disasters that often occurred following separations; (4) the inability to distinguish between wish and reality; (5) the large variety of restitutional efforts made in the light of the desperate need to regain objects; (6) as one variety of restitutional effort, pointed out by Freud, the stilted and precious speech; (7) the excesses in oral behavior.

I felt these phenomena had an underlying unity and coherence that served to reinforce my conviction concerning some kind of core object deficiency in schizophrenia with both loss of representations and restitutions being involved.

Historical Precursors
in Freud

This deficiency theory of schizophrenia seemed, at first, to be in direct contradiction to the mainstream of psychoanalytic thinking, which fell more nearly into what was termed a "conflict theory." In the beginning, I had some grandiose notions concerning what I considered to be a profound discovery, until I rediscovered what I probably had somewhere known all along: Sigmund Freud had preceded me in this line of thinking by many years, having very carefully enunciated precisely this theory concerning schizophrenia in several classical papers.

It may be of some use to trace very briefly the development of Freud's thinking about schizophrenia in order to make his final formulations more definitive. As early as 1894, in "The Neuro-Psychoses of Defense," Freud undertook to differentiate the mechanisms of hysteria, obsessions, and psychosis. At this point in his thinking, it seems clear that all three maladies were seen in the same fundamental frame of reference, i.e., conflict. By the time of Freud's writing of the Schreber case in 1911, a significant alteration had taken place in Freud's thinking about psychosis. The mechanisms of paranoia were still described in terms of conflict, but it seems clear that in no way was this considered by Freud as the core of the psychosis. What is fundamental to the schizophrenic illness occurs "silently" by way of the detachment of the libido from people or things. In fact, a careful reading of the Schreber case would indicate that Freud thought Schreber's world destruction fantasies were more central to the development of the psychosis than the paranoid ideation.

These ideas were developed further by Freud in his metapsychological paper on narcissism, and came to full development in Freud's 1915 paper "The Unconscious." Here we find the most fully evolved statement of a deficiency theory of schizophrenia. In "The Unconscious," Freud stated most clearly that he meant more than a withdrawal from external reality objects. This statement, in fact, was a bow in the direction of Jung, who had indicated that any withdrawal from external objects would merely result in the development of a hermit. Now, Freud specified repeatedly that "in schizophrenia, this flight consisted in withdrawal of instinctual cathexis from the points which represent the unconscious presentation of the object." This, in fact, differentiated schizophrenia from neurosis, in which unconscious presentations of the object were maintained with great tenacity.

It is in this paper on the unconscious that Freud also came upon that remarkable insight into the meaning of the precious speech of many schizophrenics. The schizophrenic utilizes words as if they were objects, and so the words become pale shadows of the lost object representations. Like delusions and hallucinations, they represent "the first attempts at recovery or cure which so conspicuously dominate the clinical picture of schizophrenia." But they are poor and inadequate substitutes for the original object representations and lose the quality of meaningful and drive-invested reality.

The Deficit View—Loss of Object Representation

The fundamental theme that unifies all the clinical data offered in somewhat random form earlier may now be stated more clearly. As the silent inner disaster proceeds, due to a progressive disintegration of higher level, more complex and elaborated object representations, involving both ego and superego, there is a progressive loss of identity, both at the psychic and the physical levels, accompanied by enormous anxiety and energetic but unrealistic efforts at reconstruction or restitution. The clinical picture is dominated by intense interactions involving the primitive residues of mature, whole objects—namely, part objects and the symbolic substitutes for objects. These interactions are both intrapsychic and involved with objects in the external world.

It became apparent to me that this progressive disintegration of object representation resulted in a very large structural loss or damage. It also became clear that this would result in significant economic alterations, since both aggressive and libidinal drives would become detached from object representations and become available for other investments. From the genetic point of view, earlier and more primitive conflicts would emerge.

It seemed obvious that the maintenance of object representations was essential for all functions of the ego. The loss of object representation would undoubtedly damage or destroy reality testing. These memory traces or representations were indeed what David Rappaport used to call "the internal road map" for assessment of the external world. As Freud had earlier pointed out, the function of reality testing was not a discovery of reality but a rediscovery process. This function depends on a kind of reverberating circuit in which we recognize reality as an echo from memory traces or internal object representations. Only these provide us with the capacity for knowing the external world.

Even more important is the inevitable consequence that self-representations must also disappear progressively, since these are so intimately linked with object representation. It is most certainly true that we know ourselves, develop our sense of identity as we are mirrored in the eyes of others. The loss happens silently. Immediately following this regressive destruction of one's physical or psychic identity are the noisy, life-saving, restitutive struggles; and what dominates the clinical picture in schizophrenia is certainly the ineffectual, unreal object searching and clinging, whether in fact or in fancy. This simplified metapsychological statement roughly summates my theoretical understanding of the nature of schizophrenia.

Technical Implications

On this basis I began to explore the technical implications. In general, theory derives from clinical observation, but technique derives mainly from theory. With the foregoing basic theory of the nature of schizophrenia, it seemed I would have to infer certain technical consequences that would be consistent with this theory. I was certainly aware of the fact that schizophrenics are also terribly neurotic, and, in some areas, even quite normal. I was therefore quite sure that there were situations and circumstances in which one would interpret to a schizophrenic along classical psychoanalytic lines. But the primary aim, the technique most consistent with the theory as above stated, would orient around restoring structure or even building a structure anew.

At one point in my thinking, I returned more intensely to the question of the applicability of the usual psychoanalytic technique in dealing with schizophrenics. Two of the most significant accoutrements of psychoanalytic practice, the couch and free association, seemed both inappropriate and dangerous with psychotic patients. Given the idea that withdrawal from objects and from object representations are central to the schizophrenic problem, then the separation involved in the use of the couch could only serve to reinforce the sense of object loss, increase the anxiety, and destroy the potential for increased internalization processes, which are at the core of the recovery process. Moreover, free association would serve to increase psychotic fantasy. Inhibiting free association and directing the pa-

tient's attention to reality objects would serve a reconstruction process far better, provided, of course, one is
convinced that the nature of the illness lies more in the
direction of ego deficiency than in the realm of conflicting
impulses and ideas, however rich these factors may also be
in the clinical picture.

These are more or less negative considerations. I felt it
more or less imperative to eliminate both the couch and
free association as part of the therapeutic technique in the
treatment of schizophrenia. In a more positive vein, the
primary problem to which I addressed myself was the development of what I considered to be a set of techniques
specifically designed to establish and to maintain contact
with the schizophrenic patient and to utilize a language that
communicates with the basic inner experience of that type
of patient.

As with the statement of theory, I must also abbreviate
my thoughts concerning the curative process. In general, I
would emphasize the facilitation of internalization by the
patient of a consistent, reliable, trustworthy object to replace the lost representations that have so impoverished
the ego and undoubtedly the superego. Sudden separations
of any type and radical alterations in the patient's environment or daily routines represent a danger in the therapeutic
process. I would therefore be quite chary of those easy,
comfortable recommendations to hospitalize patients or to
remove them from their families. While this may certainly
be necessary in a number of cases, we must carefully assess the risk that every loss of contact entails—namely, a
further threat to object representation with its potential for
pushing acute conditions into chronic illness.

If our desire is to make contact with our patients, to give
them a sense of the possibility they will be understood, to
offer them an object for imitation if not for identification,
then we shall take a somewhat different distance from the
patient than is true in classical psychoanalysis. It may
prove quite relevant to give support to the patient's supere-

go in the struggle to control rampant and dangerous drives. Or it may prove wise to side with one impulse over another. In psychosis, we may have to select the point of least resistance, the point of greatest contact, and even on occasion assume parental roles. Otherwise, we may find ourselves extruded, rejected, and devoid of any leverage in the treatment situation. The same is true in dealing with delusions and hallucinations. However clear to the therapist the meaning may be in some deep unconscious sense, a challenge by way of interpretation will always carry some danger. It is more useful to center attention not so much on the symbolic meaning of the delusion or its falsity, but rather on the significance of the urgent object-seeking generally being expressed.

So that you may know the degree to which I have carried out this type of thinking, I have, for example, structured my office so that it is always possible for the patient to sit with the desk between us, if such protection is needed. It is also possible for the patient to sit beside me if less protection is needed. Or he could sit some distance away on the far side of the room. I did this because I felt that the patient's ability to vary the distance and even control the distance was a very important factor that would enable me to maintain some kind of contact and to establish that kind of communication which is a condition precedent to the building of structure and without which there can be no remission from the illness.

I will not elaborate further on the technical recommendations that emanate from the theoretical position. This is a chapter or book in its own right, and I only wish to suggest the logic of a technique that flows from theory.

Deficit vs. Conflict

Despite occasional lapses in language, I believe that Freud maintained this basic position which differentiated neurosis and psychosis until the very end. Yet despite the clear-cut separation of these entities, it must be understood that the differentiation is between mechanisms and not people. If this is clearly understood, then it will also be understood that every psychotic may be considerably afflicted with mechanisms that are neurotic in character and that every neurotic and even normal may have a core of psychosis. It will also be clear that ego deficiencies may no longer be considered as mere incidents, occasionally and even indifferently associated with neurosis and psychosis. It will be necessary to clarify and define our thinking in order to come to some deeper understanding of the difference between conflict disorders and deficiency disorders.

In practice this understanding will prove the basic orientation point around which we decide how much of a "real relationship" is called for in therapy and how much we can rely on classical or orthodox modes of psychoanalytic treatment. There is a considerable difference between interpreting conflict and building structure. It often proves illusory to assume that inevitably, regardless of ego defect, clarification and interpretation of conflicting elements will automatically provide the atmosphere in which ego growth and development take place. In my experience, it is rarely if ever true in schizophrenia or in related deficiency disorders.

Remaining Questions

With regard to the Los Angeles discussion group, I do not feel able to do justice to the positions taken by the several participants during the course of our meetings.*

On the basis of a general sense of the discussions within the entire group, I would suggest the following items as central questions:

(1) Is the deficiency of internal object representation the key problem in schizophrenia, or is it merely one item

*Arthur Goldberg, Gerald Aronson, Arthur Malin, Ralph Greenson, James Grotstein, and Milton Wexler.

among a series of problems, all of equal importance? Would, for example, the significant schizophrenic phenomena be equally well understood as a by-product of conflict, splitting between good and bad objects, etc.? One position would hold that all these mechanisms are of equal and separate importance. Another viewpoint would indicate that schizophrenic symptoms are basically due to a loss of object constancy, a deficiency of representation. It would suggest that such a deficiency may come about either by developmental failures or by reaction to extreme conflict. Conflict may be seen in every aspect of the schizophrenic picture. But the loss of reality, the splitting of objects, the narcissistic developments, and so on, all come about by way of failure of internal object representations. Psychotic elements appear when portions of the inner world, especially those that are later and hierarchially more developed, drop out of existence as a road map to reality. This loss of representation may come about as an aftermath of conflict; but conflict, by itself, mainly produces such things as anxiety, doubt, and guilt, but not loss of reality.

(2) A somewhat related question deals with the problem of loss of object representation put in terms of a defense in the face of extreme conflict or in the face of difficulty with a painful reality. If this is so, isn't schizophrenia precisely the same in form as neurosis, with a special defense attached (decathexis of object representation, disavowal, etc.)? On that basis, isn't conflict and resolution of conflict still the central issue? In a sense, this may be unobjectionable, but it omits the fact that the psychotic picture may also appear on the basis of a developmental failure (as in infantile autism). It also neglects an obvious conceptual problem. If conflict is universal in neurosis and psychosis, the conflict, in a sense, is not the important differentiating element. It is the defense applied that is crucial. If schizophrenia appears as a by-product of a special form of defense by way of decathexis of internal object representations, then this is the crucial differentiating element making it separate

from all neurosis, and requires our most urgent attention.

(3) All members of our group, in one form or another and to one degree or another, accepted the idea that a loss of object constancy and representation is a vital element in the development of schizophrenia. Similarly, they accepted the relatively universal presence of conflict. Proceeding from this base, they differed widely as to the technique that would be applicable to the treatment of schizophrenic patients. Certainly many analysts here and abroad are using what Dr. Grotstein calls the "psychoanalytic approach to the treatment of schizophrenia." By this a classical, interpretive approach, including the couch and free association, seems to be meant. On the other hand, Freud, Federn, Nunberg, Knight, and a host of others would probably join those of us who think that the techniques applicable to the transference neuroses are not suitable for the treatment of schizophrenics.

In the main, our study group, in varying degrees, accepted the idea of making contact with the patient as a crucial element in the treatment. The ability to re-arouse old memories, the capacity to offer oneself as a figure for internalization and identification, plus the warding off of overwhelming conflict were more or less agreed upon as central technical maneuvers. The interpretation of conflict and of transference, especially negative transference, was also considered to be an important element. To a considerable extent, the majority of the group felt the classical approach involving free association and the couch, with main emphasis on interpretation, contained some dangers and some threats with cases of true schizophrenia.

While other issues and questions existed in our discussions, and some other points of agreement (i.e., the genetic element in schizophrenia), it was felt that clarity on the above issues would represent a long step in advancing our understanding of both the theoretical nature of schizophrenia and the technical problems of treatment.

11
A THEORETICAL RATIONALE FOR PSYCHOANALYTIC TREATMENT OF SCHIZOPHRENIA

James S. Grotstein, M.D.

Introduction

The treatment of schizophrenia by psychoanalysis has not been accorded the universal reception by psychoanalysts that has been true of neuroses. The reasons for this are due not only to obvious clinical difficulties in approaching most schizophrenic patients, but also to theoretical conceptualizations of schizophrenia which have tended to differentiate it from the neuroses so qualitatively as to render it a different category of psychopathology, and one that is not reachable by psychoanalytic treatment as a consequence. In this presentation I shall attempt to offer a rationale for the psychoanalytic treatment of schizophrenia and shall attempt also to reconcile some of the principal controversies in the psychoanalytic theory of psychoses which have overshadowed the consideration of its treatment.

The apparent unreachability of schizophrenics seems to speak for itself as a clinical objection to psychoanalytic treatment, and I shall deal with that aspect later in this paper. The theoretical objections have centered around a concept of schizophrenia as a narcissistic disorder which can also be expressed as a basic ego defect, a consideration that precludes the primacy of importance of psychic conflict. I should like therefore to reexamine the psychoanalytic theory of psychoses with a particular view toward illuminating archaic object relations and ego structures re-

I wish to give special thanks to Dr. Ira Carson for his help in formulating many of the ideas in this paper, particularly in regard to the metapsychology of Dr. Wilfred Bion.

levant to schizophrenia. In so doing, I hope to shed light on the importance of the role of the Oedipus complex in schizophrenia, and via the Oedipus complex to show the importance of fantasy in general as a vehicle for understanding the disturbed thought processes of the schizophrenic and also as a reconciling medium for bridging the divergent theoretical and clinical postures, the "ego defect" and the "conflict" schools.

Deficit Theorists

The history of this discordant theoretical leitmotif began with Freud's first major statement about psychoses in "The Neuro-Psychoses of Defense," in which psychosis was considered the symptom of a conflict with reality.[1] His second major statement was in "The Schreber Case," in which he defined psychosis as resulting not from defense per se, but from the decathexis of objects.[2] Ultimately he was to consider psychosis as due to the withdrawal of narcissistic cathexis from internal objects.[3] Narcissistic decathexis corresponded to a decathexis not just of the verbal presentation, but also of the thing presentation in which all traces of the object are removed from the psyche. It is this second point of view (the abolition of the object in the psyche through decathexis) which is held widely by so many analysts today, particularly by Wexler[4] and Freeman,[5] who therefore conclude that psychoanalytic treatment is not praticable in psychosis. The ego is felt by them to be too defective and its capacity to utilize interpretations too precarious. Therapeutic regression is thought by them to be exceedingly dangerous and, unlike the situation in neuroses, threatens a collapse of ego structures. An active regression becomes a passive route. As a consequence, a "real" relationship is suggested by these proponents in which the therapist offers himself as a meaningful and reliable object to fill the gap, as it were, and help to replenish the defective internal world and to control the depth of regression at the same time. The proponents of this school feel either constitutional defects or early environmental traumata are instrumental singly or in combination.

Conflict Theorists

Arlow and Brenner,[6] Boyer,[7] and Giovacchini,[8] on the other hand, feel that psychosis represents a psychic conflict and is therefore defensive in nature. They feel that psychosis is a quantitative more than a qualitative modification of neurosis and that the unique psychopathology of psychosis emanates from increased destructiveness, the depth and extent of regression of ego functions, mainly reality testing, and the regression of superego functions. They feel that a significant number of psychotic cases can be successfully analyzed by classical analytic technique by making allowances for the uniqueness of psychosis as a regressive extension of the infantile neurosis.

Other significant contributions to the literature on this subject have been made by Sechehaye, Bychowski, Burnham, Searles, Frosch, Kernberg, Bion, Segal, and Rosenfeld. Sechehaye in particular has described a technique which is an alternative to an interpretive one in an ambience of "symbolic realization" where a symbol is offered in lieu of interpretations in a permissive, symbiotic setting.[9] Searle's technique seems to be a more interpretive modification of Sechehaye's but the context seems to be one of a relaxed, accepting, transactional encounter in which the "symbiotic relatedness" is the therapeutic instrument.[10]

Kleinian Views

Segal,[11] Rosenfeld,[12] and Bion,[13] all members of the Kleinian school, have developed and elaborated a psychoanalytic metapsychology and treatment that reflects a separate but equally authentic development of classical Freudian ideas. According to these workers, schizophrenia is felt to be the result of a defective development of the ego caused by either heredity or early environmental circumstances and is characterized by a tendency in later years to enter into a state of psychotic identification and/or confusional states. The resultant infantile maldevelopment is seen by them to be due to overdefensive attacks by one part of the psyche upon other aspects which can sense and perceive its needs and upon the perception of the objects that meet these needs; thus the mind, which unites the necessary need awarenesses with the awareness of the objects that can satisfy these needs is felt to be attacked or mutilated by inborn primitive destructive fantasies sponsored by the "death instinct" in its role as an inborn defensive agency which warns about the awareness of danger. If too excessive constitutionally, its uncontrolled destructiveness is experienced as a "primitive catastrophe."[14] The result is nevertheless an impoverished and maldeveloped psyche which has great difficulty in utilizing and internalizing helpful objects.

The rationale for the plethora of techniques under the psychoanalytic rubric emerges not only from the conceptual conflicts between the dichotomy of ego defect and defense but also from serious clinical difficulties that emerge in the treatment of schizophrenia. The lore of the psychoanalytic treatment of schizophrenia is replete with experiences of patients worsening and deteriorating under the impact of analytic technique via uncontrollable regression or being unaffected or unreachable if they are not made worse. The difficulty the psychotic has in being able to contain and represent thoughts as well as understand the interpretation (rather than the "thing itself") and his inability to be separate from the therapist have been cited. This difficulty is the result of defective reality testing due to defective ego boundaries or to a defective cathexis of internal objects resilient enough to withstand excessive stimuli from within and without which are mobilized by analytic regression.

Ego Defect Views

Federn was the first observer to point out that the critical problem in psychosis was the decathexis of the ego boundary and that the withdrawal from reality was secondary to that.[15] Jacobson extended this observation and fitted it into the conception of the representational world.[16] She found that the withdrawal of cathexis from the ego (self) boundary in the self-representation eventuates in the latter's importuning its object representation for a supply of neutral energy which results in two separate but related phenomena: (*a*) an impoverishment of the energy of the internal object representation, thereby leading to deneutralization and thus to reaggressivization and relibidinalization of psychic energies, and (*b*) a spatial approximation of the self and object representations as a consequence of the energy changes tending toward fusion, with resultant psychotic confusion.

Hartmann amplified Jacobson's contribution by positing that psychosis may be due either to the effect of a defective apparatus of primary autonomy, which has difficulty in establishing and maintaining a threshold against internal and external stimuli, or to a defective object representation which cannot facilitate the neutralization of stimuli.[17] The first would be an example of an inherited ego weakness or defect, and the latter would be an example of the internalization of a defective environment, thereby causing an acquired ego defect. Room is left in his conception, however, for the defectively acquired object to be defensive and thus treatable through interpretive means.

Thus the failure to be given the constitutional endowment of an inborn threshold or a neutralizing barrier, in addition to the failure to experience and to internalize objects capable of neutralizing impulses, are thought by Hartmann to be critical for the development of schizophrenia. The lack of this "neutralizing frontier" compromises the schizophrenic's ability to establish a repressive barrier, which is needed not only for the repression of unconscious impulses and their derivatives, but also to create and maintain such a psychic space as the unconscious in the first place. Thus the "neutralizing frontier" or the "repressive barrier" are ways of talking about an aspect of an ego apparatus known as "reality testing" or "ego boundary." In order to test reality, a repressive barrier is necessary to create a boundary and to make distinctions, such as between conscious and unconscious, wakefulness and sleep, inside and outside, front and back, past, present, and future, background and foreground, etc. The lack of this boundary also compromises the schizophrenic's capacity to represent the "thing itself" as thought. This is of great importance in the psychoanalytic treatment of schizophrenia. If the schizophrenic has no capacity to repress, then his main defenses against awarenesses emerging from therapeutic insights would be passive regression and the denial, rrepersonification, projective identification, and splitting of the ego and objects. Thus analytic treatment would be contraindicated if that were the only situation obtaining.

In order to bring to bear other points of view that mitigate the severity of this conclusion as espoused by the ego defect school, it must first be pointed out that "ego defects," "barriers," and "defective objects" are reified constructs based upon the observation and deductions in a dyadic relationship where the observations are made from the vantage point of adult reality. Thus an analyst may observe a patient's regression after an interpretive confrontation, and should the regression descend into psychosis, he may attribute the causation of the psychosis to an ego defect. On the other hand, one may hypothesize that the experience of the "ego defect" is in the mind of the patient. Is he really aware that he is defective per se, or does he experience more proneness to conflict by virtue of his poorer ability to repress his thoughts and/or to represent them symbolically rather than concretely? Is he not all the more defensive by virtue of his tendency to take things more personally? In short, what is the schizophrenic's *fantasy* of his defect? How does he *experience* his "defect"? With what object is it associated?

The Role of Fantasy

Fantasy, which is the biography of internal reality and the reconciling medium of relations among all agencies in the internal world, has been neglected as a key consideration in the debate between the ego defect and the conflict schools, and can perhaps effectively reconcile them. A word must be said, however, about the so-called dangers of interpreting fantasies to schizophrenic patients whose minds are already suffused by them to the exclusion of "reality." This consideration ignores the probability that the schizophrenic patient is haunted by destructive fantasies that are unmitigated by reparative fantasies associated with more benign identifications. This mitigation of a destructive fantasy by a benign fantasy is the usual occurrence in normal infants, according to Isaacs.[18] A solid ego development can take place only upon the scaffolding of these benign fantasies that are related to good identifications. Thus the preponderantly destructive fantasies of schizophrenics prevent the development of a stable ego that can perceive reality. A treatment technique that seeks to mitigate the omnipotent destructiveness of the fantasies in the schizophrenic so as to allow ego development seems therefore to have some rationale to it.

Hartmann's implication of the defective object representation, for instance, can be cited here as a deduction from observation on the one hand, and on the other, as the fantasy held by the patient of the quality and effectiveness of his internal objects. His fantasies about these objects are due, in the first instance, not to logical observations alone, but to complex feelings and attitudes that were "assigned" or "put into" these objects to account for their goodness or badness. It is important to remember that the origin of internal objects in the infant is not by simple introjection of external objects but, as Freud,[19] Ferenczi,[20] Tausk,[21] Nunberg,[22] Kohut,[23] Klein,[24] and so many others have pointed out, by discoveries in terms of their similarities to parts of the self, a phenomenon Melanie Klein has termed projective identification. Thus the infant's internal world is populated by objects that he narcissistically feels he has created himself, first through identification by projection and second by reintrojection with subsequent identification of ego parts with these internalized objects.

Insofar as the infant fantasies he has created his internal objects, he also experiences the capacity to modify them through reparation, i.e., a careful separating out and withdrawal of fantasied projections into the internalized objects so as to defuse the omnipotent and polarized badness of them, thus restoring them to a more reasonable perception. At the same time the examination of the projected attacks can help the patient understand how he might actually have altered the real objects' responses to him. Whether or not the mother or the primal family plays a large role in the genesis of schizophrenia is of great current importance investigatively.[25] However, we can see how fantasies can create through projective identification the image of a bad mother or can "project into reality" and thereby seemingly confirm such an omnipotent fantasy. Yet one can also see that a projective-introjective identification with a truly bad object can also have the adaptive function of internalizing the badness of the object in order to protect the goodness of the object.

From the point of view of fantasy and internal reality, therefore, the scene in the internal world of the psychotic is not necessarily so rigid and fixed as we would be led to believe by such concepts as "ego defect" and "defective barrier." Fantasy helps us to picture an internal world that is dynamically active, rather than static, notwithstanding external observation to the contrary. The schizophrenic could well be suffering from an ego defect on a hereditary or acquired basis and still be seen as having an internal psychic conflict against which he defends himself by active and passive regression of his ego, superego, and instinctual functions. In the psychoanalytic treatment of the schizophrenic, the irruption of overwhelming instinctual components can be seen as revealing the following three transference revelations of the contents of the internal world:

(1) The analyst is experienced as a stimulating agent whose very presence inaugurates and maintains an inexorable unfolding of psychic contents and instinctual components as the psychic labyrinths are opened. As the feelings of hate and desire are mobilized and magnetized into the transference, the schizophrenic patient feels they are being forced upon him by the purposely tormenting and sadistically manipulating analyst. This fantasy, formerly called transitivism, represents a delusion of the patient's being a robot under the control of a sinister influence from the outside. One can see that this fantasy is an intrapsychic way of expressing the condition of a hapless ego feeling it is being controlled by instinctual feelings against which little or no defensive barrier has been erected. The absence of the defensive barrier or repressive barrier is the same thing as being persecuted from within at the behest of outside forces because no distinction between inside and outside really exists.

(2) The defective repressive barrier itself is fantasied by the patient to be an internal object that will not or cannot protect against the instinctual attacks. If the object is one

that cannot protect him, it is fantasied by the schizophrenic patient to have been due to repeated damaging attacks against the object by his multiple invasive projections, which have so punctured and perforated the object (hostile symbiosis) that the object is subsequently internalized as a perforated object without structural integrity or boundaries to withstand the invasion of hostile objects from inside and outside.

(3) If the object is an obstructing object that is felt to be one who will not contain the patient's desperate and dreaded feelings, the fantasy is that it is the retaliatory counterpart to the damaged object in 2 and is therefore an archaic superego object that is felt to hate the patient and refuses to contain his projections. It thus attacks his capacity to think and to link thoughts together.

Thus we can see that Hartmann's postulates of a defective inborn threshold apparatus and a defective internal object for neutralization, Jacobson's consideration of a self-representation importuningly invading an object representation for neutral energy and making matters worse, the ego deficit of Wexler and Freeman, the transference psychosis of Rosenfeld, and the dynamic postulates of Arlow and Brenner, Boyer, and Giovacchini come together in a reconciling synthesis made possible by exploring the internal world of the schizophrenic through the medium of fantasy. The internal world of the schizophrenic is populated by objects that hate and which are desirable. They irrupt into awareness under the "command" of an external object such as an analyst, in which case a delusional transference is created. This delusional transference pictures the analyst as the cause of the patient's troubles because he stimulates awareness from the outside and also contains the projections of the feelings he stimulates, such as hatefulness, malevolence, and sadistic and sexual craving for the patient. At the same time he is felt to be identified with the badly damaged threshold or repressive barrier. Not only, therefore, is he felt to be causing bad feelings to emerge, but he is also bad in being defectively unable to stop the feelings from flowing, feelings that can ultimately eventuate in chaotic psychotic regression. Additionally, the analyst is also felt to attack the residually intact mind the schizophrenic tries to use to think about his problems.

At the center of the therapeutic dilemma of contacting the schizophrenic is the problem of the unrepresentability of his thoughts. This unrepresentability is due to a defective barrier that can also be seen as a defective agency of reality testing, or a defective ego boundary, or a defective neutralizing frontier to slow down the high velocity of the quasar-like particles of the "things themselves." Interpretive treatment in a psychoanalytic setting is in danger of mobilizing the "things themselves" without being able to harness them for thoughtful consideration and interpretation. Psychotic regression can certainly result if the apparent unrepresentability of unconscious contents is not taken up in the delusional transference, as suggested above. Interpretations of the schizophrenic fantasies about the malevolence of the analyst and his defectiveness as a protector against thoughts can be very helpful in mitigating these feelings and, what is more important, beneficially altering his capacity to repress and therefore to represent thoughts so that he can think about them more rationally and effectively. The capacity to repress connotes the capacity to think or to represent thoughts. The schizophrenic cannot think because he cannot repress.

One of the principal difficulties that has stood in the way of the psychoanalytic approach to schizophrenia has been the use of a psychoanalytic conceptual model based on the treatment of the neuroses. This model reflects the genetic hypothesis of an infantile neurosis that is not infantile but rather one of childhood, suggesting the time period of the phallic Oedipus complex. Historically, the time prior to the Oedipus complex has been thought of as zonally autoerotic and was subsumed under the rubric of narcissism. Many advances in our knowledge of early psychic functioning have been flooding the literature lately. Our growing knowledge of early object relations is giving us cause to lift the veil from narcissism so as to see a hitherto undreamed-of richness of archaic object relations which long antedate and anticipate the later phallic Oedipus complex. A technical approach devised for the neuroses which halts at the frontier of narcissism divides psychoanalysis into two theories and two techniques, the one for psychosis not having been clearly elucidated as yet by those who espouse it and not thought to be needed by the ego defect analysts who disavow its rationale in the first place.

Arlow and Brenner, Boyer, Giovacchini, and others feel that the classical technique for neurosis is applicable for many cases of psychosis, as stated above, and suggest furthermore that the critical differences between neurosis and psychosis are, from the standpoint of technique, quantitative ones and are thus regressive, primitivistic extensions of the infantile neurosis. Giovacchini even feels that correct interpretations are effectively "structuring" in schizophrenia, and Hoedemaker[26] and Boyer feel that the maintenance of the classical technique without parameters helps to promote boundary resotration.

The school of Melanie Klein and her followers in their unique development of psychoanalytic metapsychology and technique has become quite familiar with archaic object relations which have until recently been subsumed under the rubric of narcissism. Through the expansion of the concept of projective identification, which Freud stated was the form of relationship prior to anaclytic object choice, they have been able to develop a concept of transference via projection antecedent to transference via displacement of past object relationships. Thus the Kleinians can observe the ever present transference via projective identification in current analytical materials in which elements from the earliest infantile period are repeated *in statu nascendi*. This permits them to reconstruct the fantasies that determined the creation and internalization of narcissistic objects which are the components of the psychotic core, according to Bychowski[27] and Bion.

Problems in Providing an Object Replacement

The technical choice of dealing with a psychotic core that consists of primally bad object identifications is either to "replace" them by good external object relations, as suggested by the adherents of the ego defect school, or to analyze them and to hope that these objects undergo a beneficial modification in their sojourn in the analyst as they are projected into him, modified there, reintrojected, then repaired.[28] The resolution of psychotic identifications can be achieved through an analytic technique that emphasizes the schizophrenic's difficulty in maintaining and internalizing object relationships. The delusional transference, which was discussed previously in more detail, facilitates a recapitulation of the transference psychosis, which includes the earliest narcissistic and archaic identifications long before the "infantile neurosis" of the Oedipal period. A technique that is honed to splitting, which is the forerunner of repression, and to projective identification, which is regressive dedifferentiation, which allows greater access to that dawn of personality development where the groundwork of future psychosis is laid down and can more effectively facilitate its modification.

The idiom of such a technique is well able to grasp the archaic mental catastrophe that the chaotic internal world of the schizophrenic continuously re-creates. What this technique has in common with the classical technique espoused by other workers with schizophrenia is the conviction it conveys to the psychotic patient that his chaotic fragmentation is containable, able to be sorted out, representable, and ultimately able to be thought about and analyzed. A human relationship is set up where the emphasis is on the containment of terror and nameless dread until, through patient interpretation, coherent thoughts and feelings can finally emerge to be analyzed. In the meantime an object exists which is protecting the analytic relationship against all intrusive assaults and is resisting the tendency to act out collusively with the patient as a symbiotic friend because of the belief that that would only intensify the patient's obligatory "dependency" and ultimate terror. The analyst is thus one who allows the "thing itself," the ultimate dread, to be contained, particulated, and analyzed. He thereby allows for an emotional experience with an object which can create a precedent for being able to withstand and withhold, thereby defusing and discrediting the fear of the omnipotent terror of the "thing itself" and allow it to be harnessed by mental representability (reality testing). A boundary is therefore established with the help of a boundary object, and sorting out takes place with a sorting-out object.

Those techniques that use symbiotic relatedness in which the therapist is a coparticipant in an ongoing human relationship claim as a rationale that the psychotic must take in a good object to make up for his ego defect. What is not so simple to comprehend is how the psychotic perceives a good object. A coparticipant who deals with the parametric requirements of the patient must probably run the risk of perpetual obligatory "dependency" without ego growth because of the projective identification implicit in such a process. It is hard to envision how a really good object can be internalized by a schizophrenic anyway, because of the hugeness of the greed and envy that spoil the goodness of the object prior to internalization. A good internal object cannot be supplied by external stuffing. It can be supplied only through the capacity of symbol formation consequent upon the mourning of the loss of an object, a task that is incredibly difficult for the schizophrenic. Perhaps the success of external object relationships with schizophrenics have more to do with reinforcing the nonpsychotic portion of the personality to overcome the effect and power of the psychotic portion and thus cause it to become submerged but never resolved.

Furthermore, there is undoubtedly enormous theoretical confusion about what it is that is internalized, anyway. Fairbairn and Bion have both approached this problem and question whether it is the product of the object rather than the object itself that is beneficially internalized. In short, the awareness of separation from the object heralds a new kind of internalization, that of the product, ultimately the memory of the object. To take in the object is to identify with it and not to grow or differentiate, which is the paradox of the schizophrenic. The schizophrenic actually has access more often than not to good objects but cannot utilize them because of the "need-fear dilemma," as Burnham names it.[29] In short, the question is: How can one get a schizophrenic to take in those needed aspects of object relationships and of psychoanalytic treatment which could help him repair himself and differentiate? The question can be extended to: How can the schizophrenic relocate the sensory modalities which he has lost and yet which he requires to find his feelings and his needs? And how can a schizophrenic relocate the mind he has lost, which is needed to think about and act upon these needs? These questions are at the center of any therapeutic approach to schizophrenia. I personally know of no better way than the psychoanalytic to approach them.

Still another aspect of the treatment controversy of schizophrenia must be mentioned. The classical analytic technique, often thought to be cold and forboding, has been greatly criticized in its use with schizophrenics because of the emphasis on the unimportance of the reality of the analyst so as to allow a maximum of transference fantasies to occur. A treatment technique that emphasizes the importance of the real relationship to the analyst runs the risk of confirming in the schizophrenic patient, who already distrusts his own mind and its thoughts and intuitions, that the therapist's mind is the healthy one, and that the therapist's mind is needed to be depended upon for thinking about his own problems. I suggest this attitude runs the risk of oracularizing the therapist at the expense of the sanity of the patient and subverts the patient's attempts to make use of his own all but discredited thinking abilities to heal himself. In short, classical analysis is even more appropriate for psychosis than neurosis because the margins are less in psychosis.

Psychotic and Nonpsychotic Parts

Another important aspect of the psychoanalytic approach to the schizophrenic has to do with the availability of the psychotic part as differentiated from the nonpsychotic part to analytic treatment, as alluded to above. Katan,[30] Bion,[31] and Arlow and Brenner[32] in particular have brought forth the idea that not all of the psychotic patient is involved in the psychotic process. Bion especially has emphasized the splitting of the psychotic and nonpsychotic parts, the latter of which functions more on the neurotic level and may underlie the psychosis, be covered over by it, and/or be assigned to the object via projective identification for safety but at the expense of psychic impoverishment and confusion. At the same time this concept constitutes a construct that can account for the psychotic patient's ability to understand and to respond to interpretive interventions which can facilitate his unconscious healing. By unconscious healing I am referring to Bion's important clarification of Freud's concept of dream work. Bion recognized that aspect of ego function which makes use of primary process in creating a dream that preserves the sleep which is necessary for a narcissistic repair of all mental functioning. Not only do dreams preserve sleep, but they also transform unconscious sensory awarenesses into elements of thought and feelings that can then be thought about by secondary process. To Bion primary process normally is a very important and purposeful function which prepares unconscious sensations for feelings to be thought about and taken care of. It is the relative inability of the psychotic to dream, according to Bion, which confuses sleep with wakefulness for him, thereby precluding sleep and wakefulness and altering his state of consciousness and awareness as a result. What is even more, his inability to dream (that is, to dream continuously, night and day, including free associations, daydreams, random thoughts, etc.) disables his hypothetical capacity to locate the unconscious awareness of his sensations, needs, and feelings. Thus he cannot think about his needs in any rational way. In short, he is literally and figuratively out of contact with himself. The psychotic portion of the personality misuses what sensory modalities it has access to in order to evacuate the psyche by excessive projective identification in lieu of being able to introject awarenesses or be able to think about them. It is the nonpsychotic portion of the personality which not only can participate in psychoanalytic treatment, but also can come to the reparative rescue of its hapless counterpart by trying to use its own sensory antennae, as it were, to locate the feelings that the psychotic portion refuses to acknowledge and tries to evacuate. It now tries to facilitate their transformation into meaningful awarenesses for secondary process thinking, for appropriate action, and for analysis. Thus the continuing dream work, which Bion calls "alpha function," constitutes the salvation of the psychotic patient in particular and all human beings in general. It is probably the ability of psychoanalysis to locate, preserve, and facilitate alpha function which constitutes the truest meaning of the therapeutic alliance. It is this unconscious, not conscious, function which is the patient's and analyst's most trustworthy ally.

The Role of Sensory Perception-Awareness

One interesting ramification of the concept of a defective primary process or defective alpha function in the schizophrenic is the new light it sheds on the pathology of the id itself, in addition to the ego and superego in schizophrenia. Thus a defective primary process helps us to understand that a schizophrenic is not merely psychotic, which implicates the threshold barrier or ego boundary, but is also defective in terms of his inability to transform sensory impressions of need-awareness into coded elements of instinctual messages. These untransformable and untranslatable sense impressions agglomerate rather than condense, fragment rather than displace, but still urgently clamor for recognition with invasive force. Bion has found that, because of the schizophrenic's intolerance of reality, he attacks his organs of perception of unconscious and conscious awareness as well as the impressions themselves, hurls them in fantasy outside of his psyche into an object, and experiences their return as eerie, mysterious, bizarre objects, one of the pathonomonic features of schizophrenic delusional thinking and the precursor of the transitivistic passivity of the schizophrenic who is ultimately under the robotic control of the Influencing Machine which contains a rearrangement of these discarded fragments. This concept also helps to clarify a differentiation between psychosis and schizophrenia, terms that are often used interchangeably but which now deserve more rigorous redefinition and separation. Schizophrenia would therefore reflect a bizarreness consequent upon a long-standing mutilation of the sensory and thinking processes (id and ego as well as superego), whereas psychosis would merely reflect the consequences of a defective ego boundary with or without long-standing mutilation of psychic processes. Thus one can speak of schizophrenia with or without psychosis.

A case example of a schizophrenic patient in psychoanalytic psychotherapy may be illustrative.* The following is a summary of the material of a Wednesday hour of a twenty-year-old young man who has been in analytic treatment for the last two years:

> I am only going to smoke half a pack of cigarettes. . . . I am thinking about writing a widow in Florida who has some children and marrying her. . . . Last Friday I heard three different voices. . . . Did you see the tongue beside my chair? . . . I had a girl friend once in high school, F.G. She was very attractive and was down on my using drugs. . . . I often think of calling her. . . . I just had a thought about Uncle W., who died at Menninger's. He had a mental problem too. Also he had a wife and child. . . . Most of my friends are already married. . . . I can't stop thinking of F.G. . . . Now I am working more at my father's store and am noticing women. . . . It's silly, but I'm thinking of an older woman who was bending down in my father's store to get some liquor and I was looking at her from the rear and saw a tongue licking her vagina. . . . I used to know a guy who could sleep with his eyes open. . . . There are only a few more days left until the weekend. . . .

I should like to use this case material to illustrate the importance of the sensory modalities of awareness and

*I am indebted to Dr. Duke Fisher for this case material.

their fate in schizophrenia. I should also like to use this case as a vehicle for discussing the archaic part-object relationships which take place in the analysis of the schizophrenic. The patient spoke tangentially of eyes ("I used to know a guy who could sleep with his eyes open") but more directly of his tongue, which existed isolatedly in space after having been disowned by him. It is the tongue that principally contacts the nipple of the breast in the infantile state. The awareness of need (hunger) and the desirability of the breast, which can satisfy this need, are thus recreated in the transference with the analyst, who is to be the desirable person. The tongue is therefore disowned by splitting and projective identification. It is further degraded by contacting a spoiled image of the analyst-mother in the vaginal area from the rear. The envy of the analyst-mother is further confirmed by the struggle the patient has with smoking, which in previous hours was linked up with fantasies of anal masturbation, which was resorted to in order to compete with the breast. The "half a pack" represents Wednesday, the midpoint of the week and the midpoint between the weekend separations when the struggle with ambivalence with the therapist is maximal. He is now aware that the more he reverts to fantasies of anal masturbation, the more he loses an object relationship with a desirable woman (F.G.). The reference to marrying a widow with children has to do with his fantasy of having to marry a "spoiled family" rather than create his own because of his fear of retaliation from one aspect or another of an internalized damaged parental couple ("Uncle W., who died at Menninger's. . . . He had a wife and child"). The "sleeping with his eyes open" association also refers to this fear. Thus the need to possess a ready-made family through intrusion into the parental intercourse was also of great importance. The disavowal of the tongue was in order to break up lingual communication with the object and to deny the goodness of the taste of the object because of envy, which was mobilized by the realization of the forthcoming weekend separation and a subsequent Easter holiday break. The instrument of speech and taste was thus attacked, split off, and discarded, thereby depriving the patient of an instrument of awareness and an instrument of communication. It was reconstituted as a hallucinatory bizarre object which obsessively sought reentry into the patient's reluctant awareness in proportion as he sought to deny his transference feelings and disavowed the sense organ involved with them. In short, the tongue was the sense organ that mediated the awareness of need to the awareness of the desirable object which could satisfy the need. The tongue was thus discarded and the desirable object degraded, and then they returned as hallucinations because of the patient's conflict about his ambivalence towards the therapist and his loneliness.

The Role of the
Oedipus Complex

A common finding in schizophrenic patients is the presence of undisguised oedipal material. It has been a disconcerting point in analytic technique as to how to handle this phenomenon, which is due to the withdrawal of the repressive barrier. More often than not, direct interpretations of the already irrupted material have a perverse effect in worsening the patient or in having no therapeutic result at all because the elements are already conscious. Phenomena such as this have led to the oft-spoken advice to "interpret upward" away from the flagrant oedipal level. Much of the confusion in technique over this point parallels another, more extensive confusion about the Oedipus complex itself. First of all, from the point of view of technique, it is probably not advisable to interpret phallic oedipal material in a schizophrenic patient initially, because it is most likely not just an instinctual irruption, but also an omnipotent defense against psychotic regression characterized by a precocious march away from the mouth-breast zonal conflict to the genital area. When interpreted as a wish to have intercourse with a parent, the interpretation confirms the patient's omnipotence to a dangerous degree. Fairbairn[33] and Klein[34] have pointed out that the incestuous wish constitutes an omnipotent interference with the parental intercourse, and this wish is consequent upon the early traumatic awareness of the primal scene which it seeks to interrupt. The paradoxical result of interpreting the incestuous wish is therefore that the patient worsens as his omnipotence is confirmed.

What is more to the point, however, is the need to revise the concept of the Oedipus complex to account for all the object relations prior to the phallic period, rather than dismiss them perfunctorily as narcissistic and pre-oedipal, and view the Oedipus complex as an extended metaphor for psychic development from the very beginning. Even in using the autoerotic-narcissistic framework, Freud was trying to emphasize the importance of the father complex in the Schreber case, which he did not call Oedipus although he had already used the term by this time. Freud envisioned the importance of autoerotic sensations in mobilizing the countercathectic father complex to curtail them, thereby establishing the ego ideal and later the internalized father as countercathecting structures. The homily of the father helping the son to control his masturbation would emphasize this point. What I am trying to emphasize is that the Oedipus complex is needed to establish psychic structure, particularly those countercathectic structures that internalized objects assist the repressive threshold in maintaining. Interpreting the Oedipus complex blindly, therefore, runs the risk of dismantling the structure-laying function this panoramic myth has been ordained to develop. Thus it would be incomplete in a case of schizophrenia to say, "You wish to have intercourse with your mother!" It would be incomplete also to say, "You wish to have intercourse with your mother but fear your father's castration of you!" It would be more pertinent to say, if I may take the liberty of giving an extended and collective oedipal interpretation which is applicable to nearly all the schizophrenic patients I have seen, "You feel you wish to have intercourse with your mother and fear your father's castrative threats and also fear that he will not and cannot stop you at the same time. Your desire for intercourse with mother is really felt to be an omnipotent invasion of the parental intercourse so as to repossess mother for yourself because you could never stand her leaving you, and you feel her leaving you inside your mind at this moment as you experience confusion!"

I am trying to develop two themes around the Oedipus complex. The first is to extend it retrospectively to the earliest oral period and observe its transcendence from the relationship of the self to its first part object with the dawn of the fear of the third person, the stranger as intruder. The first stranger is any internalized agency, like envy, which intrudes into the infant's relationship to the breast. The mysterious intruder later becomes the mother's other relationships, ultimately the father, and finally the child is the intruder into their relationship. The second point is that the intrusive or possessive wish counterposed to a natural unit such as the mother's breast or the father's penis, for instance, constitutes a necessary biological dialectic in which psychic structure is developed. A biological dialectic can be defined as the necessary competitive struggle which undeveloped portions of the ego require for definition, maturation, and later integration. The dialectic of the father complex opposes autoeroticism so as to compel the infant to be object-seeking, not self-seeking. The exclusiveness of the mother-father bond dialectically opposes the infant's possessive wishes, thus compelling the necessity of the awareness of separation and the loss of omnipotence. It can be said ironically that one cannot have too much of an Oedipus complex. It is through the Oedipus complex and the conflicts relevant to it that one can facilitate the internalization of objects that serve as permanent psychic structurers. From the technical point of view it would then be desirable to interpret the deeper layers of the Oedipus complex preferentially and the impediments to its unfolding which prevent the development and the epigenesis of the later phallic Oedipus complex. This procedure, so important to Kleinian technique, is not advanced in the classical technique. How else, for example, can the little boy's penis be transformed into a healthy reparative, giving penis if his oral problems with the breast are not worked out? If unresolved, the unsolved problems with the breast are carried forward by the principle of genetic continuity altering all the subsequent phases of ego, superego, and instinctual development.

The ramifications of the Oedipus complex are thus everywhere to be found in schizophrenia because, if the schizophrenic lacks psychic structure and the Oedipal complex is to give structure, then this complex must have gone awry from the very beginning. One important example of this is the attack against thought linking in schizophrenia. For instance one may cite the "archipelago-like," disconnected thought fragments that are commonly seen in chronic schizophrenia. Thus early attacks in fantasy against the concept of parental intercourse become linked up with the thinking process itself as thoughts, like sexual parents, come together to make new babies (conceptions). As a result, thoughts themselves in schizophrenia are attacked as well as the organ of thinking itself, so that secondary process as well as the forementioned primary process is attacked by the schizophrenic's hatred of a reality that conceives of the mother's other relationships which can exclude him. It is the early, precocious awareness of the parental genital relationship which therefore mobilizes a precocious augmentation of envy by jealousy which makes the task of the infant who is to become schizophrenic so difficult in attempting to master this situation. This precosity of developmental awareness has been mentioned by Bergman and Escalona.[35] Another way of stating this phenomenon is that the development of the Oedipus complex is pathologically expedited and precociously mobilized in schizophrenia without a graduated, sequential epigenesis, resulting in maldevelopment of psychic structures. It is perhaps the absence of a selective filter that can permit a gradual unfolding of needs to this painful compression of altered oedipal fragments from early and more advanced periods. It is no wonder, then, that anhedonia is such a prominent symptom in schizophrenia. Just as bizarreness emerges from the distortion of primary process and its consequences, as alluded to previously, anhedonia emerges from the attack against the contact with the object just as bizarreness emerges from an attack against the unconscious sense organ of need awareness, as alluded to above (attack against primary process or alpha function). Anhedonia emerges, as the case example demonstrated, from an envious attack against the conscious sense organ which locates the desirable object. If the desirability of the object is felt to be painful because of envy, then the perception of its desirability must be eradicated, leading to anhedonia. Excessive envy, greed, and jealousy from a precocious oedipal development can precipitate such an attack against the desired and needed object. It may also precipitate an attack on the organs of perception of the object. Anhedonia is a defensive result of the internal catastrophe once it is set in motion. The anhedonia is not just the destruction of the awareness of the needed and desired object, but also the avoidance of any awareness of need and desire to obviate envious, greedy, and jealous attacks against the psyche.

The depressive position, as the Kleinians call it, or the separation-individuation phase, as Mahler terms it,[36] is a staging area where the disparate fragments from multiple splitting of egos and objects are invited to reunite and a reconciliation with objective reality to take place. The ultimate paradox of schizophrenia is its hypersensitivity to reality which inaugrates an attack by instinctive destructiveness in the first place against the mental apparatus, its products, and its relating objects. The attempt at ambivalent reconciliation places the schizophrenic in all the more jeopardy as the unifying perception of reality integrates and congeals, revealing a holocaust of an internal world and harsh superego objects which attack and negate reparative attempts. The failure of optimal superego analysis at this point can be crucial in disallowing reparation, thereby precipitating massive ego-object splintering of a secondary type which can end in seeming permanent insanity or suicide.

Summary

The dialectic of ego defect and conflict in schizophrenia can be effectively reconciled by the employment of the concept of fantasy. Thus the defect becomes dynamic from the standpoint of the schizophrenic's experience of his internal world. The psychoanalytic approach to schizophrenia has been handicapped prior to the technical innovations of Mélanie Klein, particularly her concept of projective identification, because of a technical and conceptual difficulty in understanding those archaic object relations which are subsumed under the rubric of primal repression and narcissism. It is also suggested that the concept of the Oedipus complex be broadened and reconsidered in light of its ego and superego structuring capacities. This would require the abandonment of such instinctual drive-defined terms as autoerotism and narcissism and allow a redefinition of the Oedipus complex to begin in the early oral period. Thus a psychoanalytic technique in psychosis could realign itself to this concept of development. If schizophrenia be a defective ego due to defective objects, then the psychoanalysis of archaic object relations in fantasy allows for an alteration of this dynamic situation. If psychoanalysis falls short in its attempt to understand and treat schizophrenia, it is the fault of the relative ignorance we are compelled to tolerate until further conceptual and technical advances improve the analytic instrument so that it need not be diffident before schizophrenia.

REFERENCES

1. Freud, S. The Neuro-Psychoses of Defense. *Standard Edition*, 3:43–68. London: Hogarth Press, 1958.
2. Freud, S. Psychoanalytic notes on an autobiographical account of a case of paranoia (dementia paranoides). Ibid., 12:3–84.
3. Freud, S. The unconscious. Ibid., 14:159–217.
4. Wexler, Milton. Schizophrenia as conflict and deficiency. *Psa. Quart.*, 40:83–100, 1971.
5. Freeman, Thomas. Aspects of defense in neurosis and psychosis. *Int. J. Psychoanal*, 40:199–212, 1959.
6. Arlow, Jacob, and Brenner, Charles. Psychopathology of the psychoses: a proposed revision. *Int. J. Psychoanal.*, 50:5–15, 1961.
7. Boyer, Bryce L. Psychoanalytic technique in the treatment of certain characterological and schizophrenic disorders. *Int. J. Psychoanal.*, 52:67–87, 1971.
8. Giovacchini, Peter L. The influence of interpretation upon schizophrenic patients. *Int. J. Psychoanal.*, 50:179–187, 1969.
9. Sechehaye, M. A. *Symbolic Realization.* New York: International Universities Press, 1951.
10. Searles, Harold. *Collected Papers on Schizophrenia and Related Subjects.* New York: International Universities Press, 1966.
11. Segal, Hanna. Some aspects of the psychoanalytic treatment of schizophrenia. *Int. J. Psychoanal.*, 31:268–278, 1950.
12. Rosenfeld, Herbert. *Psychotic States.* London: International Universities Press, 1965.
13. Bion, W. R. *Second Thoughts.* London: William Heinemann, 1967.
14. Ibid.
15. Federn, Paul. *Ego Psychology and the Psychoses*, ed.

Edoardo Weiss. New York: Basic Books, 1952.
16. Jacobson, Edith. *Psychotic Conflict in Reality*. New York: International Universities Press, 1967.
17. Hartmann, Heinz. Contributions to the metapsychology of schizophrenia. *Psychoanalytic Study of the Child*, 8:177–198, 1953.
18. Isaacs, Susan. The nature and function of phantasy. In *Developments in Psychoanalysis*. London: Hogarth Press, 1952.
19. Freud, S. On narcissism: an introduction. *Standard Edition*, vol. 3. London: Hogarth Press, 1958.
20. Ferenczi, Sandor. *Contributions to Psychoanalysis*. Boston: Richard C. Badger, 1916.
21. Tausk, Victor. On the origin of the "influencing machine" in schizophrenia. In *The Psychoanalytic Reader*, ed. Robert Fliess, 1:52–86. New York: International Universities Press, 1948.
22. Nunberg, Herman. The course of the libidinal conflict in a case of schizophrenia. In *Practice and Theory of Psychoanalysis*, pp. 24–60. New York: Nervous and Mental Disease Monographs, 1948.
23. Kohut, Heinz. *The Analysis of the Self: A Systematic Approach to the Psychoanalytic Treatment of Narcissistic Personality Disorders*. New York: International Universities Press, 1971.
24. Klein, Melanie. On identification. In *New Directions in Psychoanalysis*, ed. Melanie Klein, Paul Heimann, and Roger Money-Kyrle. New York: Basic Books, 1957.
25. Wynne, Lyman. Schizophrenics and their families: recent research findings and etiologic implications. Paper presented to the Mental Health Research Fund, London, February 21, 1968 (in press).
26. Hoedemaker, Edward. The psychotic identifications in schizophrenia: the technical problem. In *Psychoanalytic Treatment of Characterological and Schizo-*

phrenic Disorders, by Bryce Boyer and Peter Giovacchini. New York: International Science Press, 1967.

27. Bychowski, Gustav. The problem of latent psychosis. *J. Amer. Psa. Assn.*, 1:484–503, 1953.

28. Malin, Arthur, and Grotstein, James S. Projective identification in the therapeutic process. *Int. J. Psychoanal.* (47) 1966, pt. 1.

29. Burnham, Donald L. Schizophrenia and object relations. In *Schizophrenia and the Near-Fear Dilemma*, by Donald L. Burnham, Arthur I. Gladstone, and Robert W. Gibson. New York: International Universities Press, 1969.

30. Katan, Maurits. The importance of the non-psychotic part of the personality in schizophrenia. *Int. J. Psychoanal.*, 35:119–128, 1954.

31. Bion, *Second Thoughts*.

32. Arlow and Brenner, Psychopathology of the neuroses.

33. Fairbairn, W. R. D. *An Object Relations Theory of the Personality*. New York: Basic Books, 1952.

34. Klein, On identification.

35. Bergman, P., and Escalona, S. K. Unusual sensitivities in very young children. *Psychoanalytic Study of the Child*, 3/4:333–352. New York: International Universities Press, 1949.

36. Mahler, Margaret. Study of the separation-individuation process: and its possible application to borderline phenomena in the psychoanalytic situation. New York: International Universities Press, 1966, pp. 403–425.

12
THE LIMITS OF
AN INTERPRETIVE APPROACH
Ralph R. Greenson, M.D.

I believe that my ideas are in essential agreement with Dr. Wexler's, which are essentially in agreement with Freud, Federn, Balint, Winnicott, and a host of others. However, I cannot resist the opportunity to make a few points because there is room for additions to such a huge and confusing subject.

I agree that schizophrenia is best understood as a deficiency in the development of ego functions, resulting in a failure to develop self and object representations, mental representations in general, and memories, all of which leads to the revival of the most primitive ego states, inability to integrate what is left of ego functions with the id strivings, resulting in chaotic states or stupor. The causative factors are usually a combination of constitutional deficiencies, a lack of good enough mothering in the first year of life, and later traumatic experiences. The basic clinical characteristics are the inability to distinguish between goings on in the self and others, an unstable self-image and an absorption with one's inner world. If later traumatic experiences play any role at all, which is the usual case, then we see the primitive regressive phenomena described above plus remnants of healthy and neurotic ego functioning.

The therapeutic endeavor, as I see it, is to repair the major damage, i.e., the effects of traumatically bad mothering and the failure to establish object constancy, to develop a stable concept of the self as differentiated from others, and a concept of mother as a whole, an ambivalently loved and hated person. The therapist should work with the patient in such a way as to give him an opportunity to make up for this defect and offer himself as a reliable, concerned, caretaking, accepting person. This is far more important than interpretations, which are mainly useful to indicate to the patient that he is understood, you are in contact with him. It is important not to interpret material that may be correct but which the patient cannot cope with.

My major disagreement with the Kleinians is based on these last points. They believe that the method of treatment should not be changed to suit the patient. All patients —neurotic, borderline, and psychotic—are to be treated in the same way. (See especially Rosenfeld 1965 and Segal 1967). Segal believes that interpretations should be made as often as possible because it gives the patient the feeling you are in contact with his unconscious and this gives him a sense of separateness. I suggest it can also scare him to death, makes you seem like an omniscient person, and will cause the patient to run or to submit passively to the insights. He then can repeat parrot-like what has been said, but he has developed a new psychosis or neurosis which is superimposed on the original unchanged psychosis. I have seen such patients.

I also suspect that the giving of deep interpretations is a counterphobic act on the therapist's part, his way of overcoming his fear of the patient's primitive fantasies. I further believe that the improvement of patients under Kleinian treatment results from their noninterpretive activities which they do not acknowledge as important. For example, Hanna Segal reported eight years of "analytic" treatment of a psychotic-borderline male patient. She mentioned that for years he used her lavatory for several hours after each session to his "postanalytic" work. Dr. Segal mentions this but does not believe her permitting him to do this was an important therapeutic factor. It is regrettable that the Kleinians seem to believe in the omnipotence of interpretation and downgrade or ignore all their other therapeutic interventions.

13
PROBLEMS OF
PSYCHOANALYTIC THEORIES

In this chapter I am presenting the ideas of our discussion group, which includes Roy R. Grinker, Sr., Jarl Dyrud, Nathaniel Apter, Herbert Meltzer, Lawrence Kayton, and myself. Essentially I shall try to describe our view that a conflict theory of the schizophrenias is not tenable, and that therefore treatment techniques derived from such a view are poorly conceived. Our group has emphasized a systems view of the schizophrenias, which takes account of much of the accumulating knowledge of the schizophrenias.

Psychoanalysis as
a Data Source

Psychoanalysis developed as an interpretive discipline rather than as an observational science. Its special strengths derive from its unique access to the patient's inner experiences, his fears and hopes, dreams and fantasies, his prides and his shames, both those he can consciously grasp and those that conceal their influence beyond the reaches of awareness. Psychoanalysis concerns itself with the patient's beliefs and with their significance and meaning within a particular life. We draw our evidence from the associative material and behavior of our patients within the psychoanalytic interview, and particu-

Presented at a panel discussion, the Psychotherapy of Schizophrenia, American Psychoanalytic Association, New York, December 1, 1972.

larly from within that special set of behaviors we call the transference. Our interpretive work has forced us quite correctly to undervalue other sources of information, like extra-analytic reports, laboratory examinations, biochemical and physical studies, information about learning, memory, coordination, sociological data, reports from employers, family members, and so on. It has always seemed that our deemphasis of these para-analytic disciplines aided the development of our own discipline of "hermaneutics," as Ricouer (1970) calls our interpretive system. No other discipline has been able to plumb the depths of inner experiences, to explore with such sensitivity our most intimate feelings and behaviors, and to give to them meaning and significance. This interpretive thrust has been our strength, such that our clinical and general theories have had profound influences on Western thought.

The Language of Psychoanalytic Theory

It has seemed to me strange, however, that we have felt some measure of discomfort, perhaps even of inferiority, about the way in which we have proceeded to develop our discipline. I suppose that we have continued to live out Freud's own self-conscious split between his physicalistic, scientistic allegiances on the one hand, and his proclivities for introspection, romanticism, and humanism on the other. Whatever the reason, we have adopted as *the* theory the physicalistic language of forces and counterforces, the language of mechanism and of cathexis, to restate our own language of interpretation. This metatheoretical language has had a beguiling effect on our own theoretical efforts and has diverted us to unfortuate imitations of the experimental and observational sciences. The physicalistic language of cathexis, it seems to me, explains no more than do the statements of our clinical theories, but they convey far less meaning. Nowhere is this pseudotheoretical effort more hampering than in the language we have adopted to explore schizophrenic pathology.

Our clinical theories—for example, that of unconscious psychological processes, of the power of sexuality and aggression, of the epigenetic development of personality, of the tendency to repeat actively that which was passively experienced—we have fashioned from our studies of neurotic patients. There the data base has been sufficient to enable us to unlock and unfold meanings. But in the study of the psychoses, and in particular the study of the schizophrenias, we come upon a different set of phenomena from those presented by the musings of our neurotic patients.

The Need for a Specific Theory

Psychoanalysis has been able to discern the sense in much of the schizophrenic's apparent nonsense. We have been able to penetrate to the meanings of many delusions, to the messages in the schizophrenic's thought slippage. Particularly in the acute schizophrenias we have contributed an understanding in terms of the patient's attempts to come to grips with an inner world that is falling away from him. Our theory of schizophrenia, however, is a theory of restitution and not of etiology, yet our language of theory pretends to more. Schreber reported a "profound internal change," an "internal catastrophe," as Freud interpreted this phenomenon. Basic and profound disturbances in reality testing and relations to himself and to others followed this profound internal change. To speak of a process of decathexis in respect to these changes is merely to rephrase the description in another language. The theory of schizophrenia promulgated by Freud was a theory of adaptation to a deficiency or dysfunction whose precise nature was beyond the scope of psychoanalytic observation. Freud, in several places, protested that his own experience with schizophrenic patients was limited and he therefore could not detail the nature of the inner catastrophe. Theoretical endeavors to deduce a theory of schizophrenia from the psychoanalytic view of neurosis seemed destined to fall of their own top-heaviness. No data support a conflict theory as the common etiology of both schizophrenia and neurosis, while much can be cited to support a special psychoanalytic theory of schizophrenic restitution.

Any theory of schizophrenia must account not only for the apparent "withdrawal" from personal contacts, but for strange and awkward body movements, unusual sensitivities, thought slippage such as dereistic thinking or autistic logic, confusion and uncertainty in personal identity, body image distortions, extraordinary dependency, pleasurelessness, characteristically poor competence, the flat and spotty modulation of affect, disproportionate rage reactions, hypochondriasis, sensory input compulsions, panics when alone, and many other behavioral symptoms not seen in neurotic conditions. Of course, all of these symptoms do not appear in the same patient and some of these may never be manifested in any one particular patient. Our own view coincides with that of the Los Angeles group and with that of N. London (1973), which regards these symptoms as having a coherence that reflects a deficit in internal organization and which manifests itself in a sense of "some internal catastrophe." This sense of inner disaster is thus regarded as an outcome not of conflict, as in neurosis, but of a deficiency in important psychological functions necessary for growth, development, and adaptation. Neurosis and schizophrenia are thus not to be conceived of as a continuum; schizophrenic and neurotic behaviors are uniquely different. The schizophrenias do not, in our view, reflect compromise resolutions of conflict; rather they are a behavioral manifestation of some psychological deficits. Rather than subsuming the schizophrenias under the theory of neurosis, we shall more profitably understand them as outcomes of a major internal disorganization which may psychologically be represented as personal or world destruction experiences and so on. Decathexis here refers not to defensive withdrawal, but to basic disturbances in thinking and in relating oneself to things and to people.

One would be hard pressed, I believe, to make a case for one psychoanalytic theory of neurosis and psychosis. Both the Chicago and Los Angeles formulations do not imply that the schizophrenias are primarily functional disorders. We leave room for the considerable contribution of genetic, biochemical, neurological, and other nonexperiential variables. The behavior manifestations of schizophrenic pathology may thus be either psychological expressions of nonpsychological factors or, as Waelder suggested, psychological consequences of organic factors. It seems to me that the views expressed by both the Los Angeles and Chicago groups are consistent with the study of organic conditions which, I believe, cannot be ignored either in etiological theory or in the treatment of schizophrenic disorders.

The Need for More Data

Heinz Hartmann in 1951 reminded us that progress in psychoanalysis, as in any discipline, is based on clinical discoveries. Faulty theoretical concepts lead to faulty techniques, and may even block clinical discoveries. In psychoanalysis, unfortunately, there has been a tendency to let theory order what data will be looked at and indeed even the appearance of data. The proper methodological procedure would have theory emerging from the activity of putting things known into a system. To many of us in psychoanalysis it has seemed—to paraphrase J. J. Thomson—

that theory has been a creed rather than a policy. This worshipful attitude toward theory has resulted in the eliding of explanation with observation.

Now, the language of cathexis and of drives belongs to the metapsychology, the metatheory of psychoanalysis. As such, it represents Freud the physicalist and not Freud the clinician and keen observer. My late colleague George Klein has written persuasively on this. He has shown how Freud's drive-cathectic theory of sexuality acquired the status of *the* theory of sexuality, when indeed that theory ignores the essentials of infantile and adult sexual life, of the experiences of sensuality, and of other pleasures. These metapsychological constructs, designed to "explain" clinical observations, actually distract one from the task of enlarging observations and of constructing the clinical theory. The concepts of drive discharge, libido, cathexis in fact aid in intellectualizing and therefore in keeping one away from the facts of sexual craving and arousal, their development and their vicissitudes. I do not want to get into a discussion of psychoanalytic metapsychology at this juncture. But I do want to stress that just as the metapsychology has distracted us from the essentials of the psychoanalytic exploration into neurotic phenomena, so it has misled us in understanding the schizophrenias. We require empirical generalizations which are prior to theory, laws describing behavioral regularities that can later be brought into systematic relationship with one another, but only after they have achieved the status of reliable empirical generalizations. New facts about the schizophrenias are emerging from many of the life sciences, and to ignore them is to play ostrich. Thus we must—all of us—be students of the literature on behavior genetics, of biochemical findings, the psychological deficits discovered in laboratory experiments, the nature of family interactions in schizophrenia, and of the ways in which drugs affect the appearance of the psychosis.

It is becoming increasingly apparent that schizophrenic psychosis may be the decompensation of what Rado has called the schizotype. It is an attractive hypothesis that vastly more schizotypes remain compensated than do not. It would seem that just as a continuity exists between the obsessive character and obsessive neurosis or the hysterical character and hysterical neurosis, so a continuity may exist between the schizotype and the clinical schizophrenias. The psychoanalytic clinical theory is based on an intensive study of the "transference neuroses" and not the so-called narcissistic neuroses. A study of "normal" schizotypes would seem to offer valuable data on the character and behavior of those who may decompensate into psychosis. Such a view would suggest that although the schizophrenias are not conflict disorders, schizophrenic people, like others, can have neurotic conflicts. But we should not delude ourselves into thinking that by treating these neurotic conflicts in schizophrenic people we are treating the schizophrenic psychosis or even the schizotypic characteristics.

Probably all of us have been impressed by the effectiveness of psychosocial interventions in the treatment of some schizophrenic patients. We have also seen that the effect of such intervention has a gentler slope than does that of pharmacologic treatment, perhaps taking several months for its effects to be seen, in contrast to several days or weeks for the effects of drugs to be seen. Psychosocial intervention also affects different aspects of functioning than do the phenothiazines. Some questions thus suggest themselves: (1) Do psychotherapeutic interventions require as intensive a schedule as does psychoanalysis with nonpsychotic patients? (2) Can the same psychotherapeutic effects be achieved by paraprofessional people or even by groups of patients themselves? (3) Does the mere stable presence of other interested persons provide the necessary support for helping to order the internal disorder and thus

to help restoration? The common element in these questions is a plea to search for the essence of what is accomplished in all psychotherapies with schizophrenic patients
and to find out what may be special—if anything—to some
therapies. What can be dispensed with as not useful or
redundant or distracting or irrelevant or as gratifying merely to the psychotherapist? And what are the elements that
are absolutely necessary?

During the last two decades, progress in understanding
and in treating the major functional psychoses, including
the schizophrenias and manic-depressive illness, has accel-
erated. Progress has come from many sources but principally from sources outside of the psychoanalytic
consulting room. Behavior genetics, biochemistry, psychopharmacology, family studies, epidemiology have all made
important contributions to our understanding. Thus it is no
longer possible to ignore the system aspects of the schizophrenias. The schizophrenic syndrome is a process, with
varied and protean pictures. It may develop in early or late
childhood or in early or late adulthood; it may develop
insidiously, with no acute psychotic disruption, or it may
erupt suddenly and unexpectedly; it may never recur or it
may never go on to recovery or it may reoccur once or
many times, each time with a poorer remission. The symptoms may be mild or serious. The premorbid pictures may
range widely, too. A theory that takes account of only one
manifestation of schizophrenic illness can only be an ad
hoc and incomplete theory. Thus the process of decathexis
seems to apply only to that which had once been cathected,
leaving the gradually unfolding schizophrenias and the
nonpsychotic schizophrenias outside the realm of coverage
by the unitary theory, with decathexis as the fulcrum. Psychoanalytic theory is not a hierarchical one, with precise
deductions from first principles. It is rather a concatenated
theory, organizing what is known into an orderly system
and linking one empirical generalization with another, thus

guiding new searches for data and suggesting new and un-expected relationships.

A Systems Theory and Its Treatment Implications

A systems approach has the power to envelop the broad sweep of schizophrenic phenomena. Whether one chooses to study etiological factors—genetic, biochemical, familial, demographic—or the responses to such factors, including the inner resources of the person to resist or to succumb, or the healing processes—whether within the person or exogenously administered—depends upon one's proclivities and interests. But we should not mistake any of these aspects of the pathology for the disease or *the* treatment. It is the imbalance among all these factors—between internal and external threats and pressures on the one hand, and the organism's efforts to maintain itself by thoughts, feelings, somatic shifts, and changed social relationships—that may be called the disease.

When we adopt a systems approach we can view insist-ence upon only one special kind of intervention as either benignly quixotic or unconscionably unethical, depending upon our titer of indignation.

Treatment interventions, from this theoretical vantage point, would direct themselves to several parts of the system.

1. One could focus on the form that genetic counseling could take at this stage of our knowledge, whether indeed such counseling would be helpful or harmful. We are aware of the very high risk of schizophrenic pathology among the children of schizophrenic persons, whether children are reared by biological or adoptive parents. Can such genetic counseling be developed responsibly as an aspect of prevention?

2. Although approximately 9 to 17 percent of children born to one schizophrenic parent will develop schizophrenia during their lives, 83 to 91 percent of such children will not become schizophrenic. What can we learn from those who escape the ravages of psychosis that will help in prevention? Are clues to prevention to be found in sophisticated child-care practices, and particularly from the insights of psychoanalytic studies of child development? Are there specific traumata, for example, certain narcissistic injuries, separations, physical illnesses, that are associated with schizophrenia in vulnerable people? If so, can the dissemination of child-guidance information and work with the family prevent the development of clinical schizophrenia?

3. What role do antischizophrenic drugs, like the phenothiazines, play in treatment? Can they be used effectively for all kinds of schizophrenias? There is some growing evidence, for example, that the phenothiazines are not particularly effective with nonparanoid schizophrenic patients with a good premorbid history, and that there may be some therapeutic advantage in not administering phenothiazine medication to these patients at some phases of the illness. But does it make clinical sense to withdraw such medication uniformly from all patients in our care?

4. The acute outbreak of the schizophrenic psychosis has effects on a family that differ from those of an insidious onset or those with a chronic course. What help can and should be given to the family during the phase of disorganization? Can we treat the family as a group with a focus on support, understanding, and guidance, and perhaps thereby prevent the outbreak of a psychotic response in yet another family member?

5. A close study of a number of schizophrenic patients permits the therapist to divide the clinical course during treatment into four phases, which have been well described by Kayton (See Chapter 24). Kayton describes phase 1 as that of "internal disorganization." During this period the

patient is preoccupied with sinister, persecutory forces, with bad objects, and with powerful grandiose forces. Thought slippage, clogging, and flooding are common at this phase. The patients are also preoccupied with good objects and with hopes of rescue, yet extreme vulnerability to rebuffs and feelings of panic are common. During phase 2, the phase Kayton labels "postpsychotic regression," there are feelings of aloneness, weakness, badness, emptiness, with many hypochondriacal concerns and severely impaired concentration, attention, and reasoning. Withdrawal from other people is typical, as are silences during therapy sessions. Reversal of the sleep-waking pattern is typical and there are dramatic shifts in body image. During phase 3, concentration begins to improve and disorganization begins to subside. The patient begins to become concerned about his appearance, and social relationships begin spontaneously to reappear. During this phase regressions can be terminated rather expeditiously by interpretation, firmness, and structure setting. Phase 4, that of the termination of the regression, is ushered in by feelings of inner strength, by the initiation of activity. A normalized diurnal cycle appears, and there is a return of some self-confidence, although it is accompanied by lowered ambitions.

It has seemed to us that during the phase of psychotic regression, working with internal conflict is less appropriate than it would be during the recovery phase. Although a unitary theory of neurosis and schizophrenia would dictate a standard psychoanalytic technique, our procedure relies upon the empirical experience that a classical approach deepens the regression. During the early phase of the psychotic regression, techniques of making contact with and reassuring the frightened patient, of assuring proper nutrition and other health standards should receive priority. There is a real question in our minds whether the acutely psychotic schizophrenic patient "requires" a prolonged period of regression in order to recover and to heal. We have, of course, argued within our own group about whether premature resolution of acute confusional periods may interfere with later phases of the treatment, and that there may be advantages to the patient in learning to live with his confusions for a while. We have, however, come to the conclusion that this position, on either theoretical or empirical grounds, is not warranted. Our program of treatment tries to limit the regression as best it can. Of central importance is the effort to provide stable object ties between the patient and the staff of the hospital, and later to continue these ties after the patient has been discharged. The threats of object disappearance, of fragmentation, and of the fragile nature of human relationships require dependable contacts with understanding persons. These, and not interpretation, in our opinion, are the nutriment that the ego deficit of these patients requires.

All during the patient's hospitalization we advocate working with the family as both a kind of crisis intervention technique and a way of inquiring into the pathogenic aspects of the family interactions.

Our postpsychotic treatment techniques emphasize an exploration not only of antecedent conflict—neurotic in content—but of the complications in the patient's life wrought by the psychosis itself. During this phase much work can be accomplished on the feelings of inner badness, the relationships to the congeries of good and bad introjects, and the experiences of inner emptiness. Yet we avoid a classical psychoanalytic technique treatment situation, for the reasons already spelled out by Wexler, Freeman, Fromm-Reichmann, London, and others. These reasons include the danger of increasing feelings of separation, of loss of structure, of encouraging regression, and of uncontrolled fantasies.

The postpsychotic program emphasizes training and habilitation, the learning of new skills, the relearning of old skills, help in rebuilding internal structures such as delays over actions, and brakes on fantasies. These, in our opinion, aid in strengthening a sense of stability and confidence.

The use of all adjuncts is critical. Which work best in which circumstances is an empirical matter. It seems to us blind parochialism to continue to interpret rather than to observe, to rely upon only one mode of intervention deduced from theory, and to ignore other aspects of the social-biological-psychological milieu. A systems approach introduces a dimension of complexity that we are only now beginning to appreciate. Yet our maturity, our healthy narcissism, if you will, surely can help us to absorb the blow to our self-regard that is represented by the smaller prospective given to psychoanalysis in this view of the treatment of the schizophrenias. We can appreciate the great irony that Freud's observations and the theory he drew from them, which gave us an understanding of man's apparent irrationality, should find a limit at the most irrational of all human conditions, the schizophrenias.

REFERENCES

1. Klein, G. Psychoanalysis: Two theories or one: *Bulletin of the Menninger Clinic*, Vol. 37:102–132.
2. London, N. An essay on psychoanalytic theory: two theories of schizophrenia. *Int'l J. Psycho-Anal.* 54: Part 1 & 2, 169–178. Part 2, 179–193, 1973.
3. Thompson, J. J. *Recollection and Reflection.* New York: Macmillan Co., 1937.

14
COUNTERTRANSFERENCE
AND THEORETICAL MODEL

My own working theoretical model for the treatment of schizophrenic patients includes the following elements:

1. The analyst's own more primitive modes of experience, and of interpersonal relatedness, have not been permanently resolved through his own personal analysis and other maturing experiences, but are subject to being revived in the course of his ongoing adult life experience, and this is indispensably true in his work with schizophrenic patients. His analysis is effective insofar as it has given him ready access to, rather than somehow effaced, his capacities for primitive feelings of jealousy, fear, rage, symbiotic dependency, and other affective states against which his patient's schizophrenia typically is serving to defend the patient from experiencing in awareness.

Mahler's repeated emphasis upon what the Los Angeles group calls "genetically prepared tendencies" is related to her seeming obliviousness of the therapeutic necessity for the analyst to gain access to, and utilize in the treatment of the psychotic patient, his own (the analyst's) intensely bad-mother identity components. Thus Mahler underestimates the degree of interpersonal, intrafamilial trauma the patient has suffered despite a relatively normal genetic endowment. By the same token, she underestimates the degree of personally intended sadistic and murderous trauma that the patient inflicts upon the analyst and evokes in retaliation from the analyst.

2. There is thus some basis in reality for all the patient's

"delusional transference" reactions, such as his perceiving the analyst as being the personification of the patient's ego-fragmented mother, or emotionally remote father, or what not. The analyst's working in implicit acknowledgment of these nuclei of reality perceptions in the transference—rather than maintaining relentlessly an assumption that the patient embodies all the disturbingly intense ambivalence, for example, in the treatment situation—is necessary to the patient's developing a better integrated and more comprehensive reality relatedness.

3. A healthier reindividuation on the patient's part requires an experience of therapeutic symbiosis in which the analyst participates at a feeling level, although to a manageable deg.ee, subject always to his own analytic scrutiny, and quite different in nature from an acted-out *folie á deux*.

4. The patient's own therapeutic strivings toward the analyst, including the patient's guilt and grief-laden feelings about his having failed to enable the fragmented mother to be a whole and fulfilled mother to him, are of fundamental importance in the therapeutically symbiotic phase of the work.

5. The most basic problem in schizophrenia is the patient's having failed to develop a human identity, either subjectively or, in the more severe and chronic cases, objectively as well. It is in the phase of therapeutic symbiosis that a process of mutual rehumanization, as well as reindividuation, is enabled to occur, through the therapeutic relationship's having become sufficiently strong to enable both participants to let come into play, in the ongoing exploration of the transference, subjectively nonhuman identity ingredients which heretofore had been split off from awareness and acted out in behavior.

Those analysts who view schizophrenia predominantly as a deficiency disease are typically needful of maintaining under repression the bad mother components of their own identities, and of seeking to reaffirm, in their attemptedly warm and giving approach to the schizophrenic patient, their own good-mother aspects. They are in effect asking the patient to rescue them from their own feared bad self, or bad mother introjects.

I, like the members of Dr. Holzman's group, have my own differences with classical analysis. Further, I have known at firsthand the value, for therapy and research, of the family approach. I have seen phenothiazines, when used in a moderate and well-timed fashion, facilitate analytic therapy, although I do not employ them. In addition, I regard general system theory as an exciting and promising new field of scientific thought.

Nonetheless, I find Holzman's chapter both dangerous and disturbing. It is dangerous because, in the midst of repeated and incontestable appeals for open-mindedness, it would set schizophrenic persons apart, qualitatively and indelibly, from their fellow human beings as, in their very essence, something less than human. The chapter's aura of high-sounding, up-to-date scientific versatility evokes feelings of inferiority and self-doubt in the listener who is committed to an essentially psychoanalytic endeavor, and who well knows that he has reason for humility.

Where I think of the phases of treatment in terms of patient-analyst interaction, Kayton (See Chapter 24) interestingly conceptualizes them in terms of the patient's inner experience. It is significant that Holzman, who states, "During the last two decades . . . progress has come principally from sources outside the psychoanalytic consulting room," says nothing about the analyst's own inner experience of the work. My approach focuses, by contrast, upon the countertransference realm, in the broadest sense of that term, as being of the greatest and most reliable research and therapeutic value. This focus is not intended as a means of providing narcissistic gratification to the analyst-researcher; quite the contrary, his personality and especially his sense of identity are found, in one practitioner after another, to be most sensitive and reliably informative scientific instruments providing data as to what is happening, often in areas not verbally articulable by the patient, in the treatment situation.

In my monograph on the nonhuman environment and in a number of subsequent papers, I have described the necessity of the analyst's helping the patient to become established as both subjectively and objectively human, and for the analyst to become able, in this process, to tolerate and even to enjoy various "nonhuman" transference positions, positions that are experienced by him at first as a frightening threat to his own subjective humanness.

Holzman would have us join him and his colleagues in taking flight from the necessary and unremitting exploration of the so-called countertransference dimension of the intensive psychoanalytic treatment of the schizophrenic person and, to the psychiatrist's own relief, take refuge in relegating the patient to a supposedly separate realm of existence, a qualitatively not quite human realm, a realm beyond the psychiatrist's human empathy. I strongly surmise that, when the therapeutic interaction starts to evoke subjectively nonhuman aspects of these authors' identities, they would turn relatively quickly to the latest information from such scientific fields as behavior genetics, biochemistry, psychopharmacology, epidemiology, and so on to find reassuring evidence that the schizophrenic patient is, after all, qualitatively different from truly human beings; so that it is pointless to risk one's own sanity by persisting in this disturbingly conflict-ridden effort to work psychoanalytically with him.

The Holzman chapter contains this passage:

Some questions thus suggest themselves: (1) Do psychotherapeutic interventions require as intensive a schedule as does psychoanalysis with nonpsychotic patients? (2) Can

the same psychotherapeutic effects be achieved by paraprofessional people or even by groups of patients themselves?
(3) Does the mere stable presence of other interested persons provide the necessary support for helping to order the
internal disorder and thus to help restoration?

Now, each of these questions has some worth in itself; but,
taken together, they are the kind of thing said in this paper
which, to me, seem to be a downgrading of schizophrenic
patients.

Psychoanalysts are essentially the only group of therapists who, by reason of their commitment to a courageous
and unceasing exploration of their own inner lives in the
service of their treating of their patients, are equipped to
discern, explore, and rescue the components of common
humanity in the patient who is overwhelmed by a schizophrenic illness which, to less informed eyes, marks him as
essentially nonhuman. The estimated 47 percent of all mental hospital patients who suffer from schizophrenia are
there, many of them for decade after decade, not only
because they have written off their fellow human beings as
not kin to them, but also because their fellow human beings
have come to accept this as functionally true. If the psychoanalytic movement itself takes refuge in what I regard
essentially as a phenothiazine-and-genetics flight from this
problem, then the long dark night of the soul will have been
ushered in, not only for these vast numbers of schizophrenic patients—for the current ones who are already
largely lost, and for the multitude who will follow them in
the future—but also for those relatively few psychoanalysts who are particularly interested in this field. It will
have been ushered in for the profession of psychoanalysis
generally, and for the patients, generally borderline and
neurotic and so on, whom psychoanalysts treat. For once
we give up our heretofore unremitting, open-mindedly observational effort to discern, through an empathic explora-

tion of our own so-called countertransference responses to our patient, the human essence in him which is struggling against the psychopathology which besets his humanness, there is no end to this flight on our part.

The Holzman group says that "neurosis and schizophrenia are . . . to be conceived of not as a continuum, but schizophrenic and neurotic behaviors are uniquely different." I find this so-called unique difference to be explicable and resolvable in terms of very primitive, preindividuation, and even presymbiotic, processes—described by Mahler and others—which all human beings, including those suffering from schizophrenia have in common, as can be discovered, with reliable repetitiveness, if we remain sufficiently open-mindedly observational of the so-called countertransference realm of clinical phenomena.

15

SOME THERAPEUTIC IMPLICATIONS OF A TRANSACTIONAL THEORY OF SCHIZOPHRENIA
Helm Stierlin, M.D., Ph.D.

The Concept of Transactional Modes

So far, no generally accepted family theory of schizophrenia seems in sight. Rather, we find competing viewpoints, some of which include psychoanalytic perspectives while others reject them. With each of these viewpoints the therapeutic implications differ. Unfortunately, I can do no more here than outline one possible viewpoint and trace some of its therapeutic consequences—and even this at the risk of massive oversimplification and distortion.

This viewpoint tries to incorporate a psychoanalytic perspective, even though this is problematical. For psychoanalytic theory and practice grew out of the special analytic situation, delineated by Freud, which obtains between analyst and analysand. Any practical and theoretical deviation from this situation plunges us into a muddle. But it seems to be better to make the plunge and struggle with the muddle than to segregate psychoanalysis from one of the presently most exciting fields of research and therapy—the family, specifically the family with schizophrenic offspring.

My chosen viewpoint, supported by the work of our Washington group and my own therapeutic and research experiences with approximately forty families, involves a

Presented at the fall meeting of the American Psychoanalytic Association, New York, November 30–December 3, 1972.

rather elaborate concept which I have described and illustrated elsewhere (1972a, 1972b, and, with Ravenscroft, 1972c). This is the *concept of transactional modes*. These modes try to grasp and reflect the interplay and/or relative dominance of centrifugal pushes and pulls in families throughout all stages of the individuation and separation process. In this interplay, the transactional modes operate as the covert organizing transactional background to the more overt and specific child-parent (or therapist-patient) interactions. When age-appropriate transactional modes are out of phase, too intense, or inappropriately blended with other modes, the negotiation of a mutual individuation and separation between parent and child (or therapist and patient) will be impeded. We may therefore speak of *transactional mode disturbances.*

The transactional modes bring into view salient contributions of the parents *and* of the children to the ongoing interpersonal process, but also reveal systemic properties of the evolving relationship. We can call them *transitive* and *reciprocal.* They are transitive in that they denote the parents' active molding of an offspring who is still immature, dependent, and hence remains captive to parental influences. They thus reflect the fact that parents, from the beginning, impress on their child their "stronger reality" (Stierlin, 1959). They do this often unconsciously by using covert and subtle signals and sanctions. To this "stronger reality" the child must adapt lest he perish. But also, these modes are reciprocal in the sense that there is always a two-way exchange. In this exchange, the children mold and influence their parents as much as the latter mold and influence them.

Binding, Delegating, and Expelling

Elsewhere I have delineated and illustrated the three major modes of *binding, delegating, and expelling,* which bring

into view the transactional fates of binder-bindee, delega-
tor-delegate, expeller-expellee. In briefest summary, these
modes operate as follows:

When the *binding mode* prevails, the parents interact
with their offspring in ways that seem designed to keep the
latter tied to the parental orbit and locked in the "family
ghetto." Such binding can operate on three major levels.

First, it can operate primarily on a dependency level
where primitive affects are strong. The child then appears
bound by the exploitation of his dependency needs as he is
offered undue regressive gratification. We are inclined to
speak in this context of id-binding.

Second, binding can operate on a more cognitive rather
than an affective level. When this happens, the binding
parent interferes with his child's differentiated self-awareness and self-determination by mystifying the child about
what he feels, needs, and wants. Bateson (1969), Bateson
et al. (1956, 1963), Searles (1959), Wynne and Singer
(1963a, 1963b, 1965a, and 1965b), Haley (1959), and Laing
(1965), among others, have illuminated various aspects of
this interactional process. We can call cognitive binding
"ego-binding" as the binder forces the bindee to rely on
the binder's distorted and distorting ego instead of developing and using his own discriminating ego.

The binding mode can, finally, operate on a third level
where an intense and archaic loyalty and guilt come into
play. Children who are chiefly bound on this level are likely
to experience any thought, not to mention attempt, of separation as the number one crime for which only the harshest
punishment will do. These children, whom we may call
"superego-bound," are prone to suffer maximal primitive
"breakaway guilt" that operates often unconsciously and
gives rise to acts of either massive self-destruction or heroic atonement.

Where the *mode of expelling* prevails, we find an enduring neglect and rejection of children who tend to be considered nuisances and hindrances by their parents. A strong

centrifugal force pushes many of these children into premature separations. These children appear not so much exploited as neglected and abandoned.

Where, finally, the *delegating mode* is predominant, binding and expelling elements blend. The child is allowed and encouraged to move out of the parental orbit—up to a point. He is held on a long leash, as it were. Such qualified "sending out" is implied in the original Latin word *delegare*, which means, first, to send out, and second, to entrust with a mission. The latter meaning implies that the delegate, although sent out, remains beholden to the sender. Also here the loyalty to the parents must be strong, but unlike the more primitive and archaic loyalty mentioned in the binding mode proper, this loyalty must allow for selectivity and differentiation. Otherwise, the delegate could not fulfill his missions. Such missions may include his becoming a famous artist or scientist in an attempt to fulfill the parents' unrealized ego ideal, or it may be the mission of enacting the parents' disowned delinquent impulses. Whatever the mission, the delegate is encouraged to differentiate and to separate to the extent that his specific mission requires this. (An overview of various types of missions is given elsewhere. See Stierlin, 1972a.)

The above transactional modes of binding, delegating, and expelling imply a long-term view of the process of individuation-separation. Such a long-range view makes it evident that parents who bind, delegate, and/or expel their children do not necessarily act in a pathogenic manner. These modes become exploitive and damaging to the child only when they are inappropriately timed or mixed, or are excessively intense.

Extremes of Binding in Schizophrenia

In many of the most severe cases of schizophrenia, a given

child appears intensely bound on all three levels described above—the affective, cognitive, and loyalty levels. This results in mutual thralldom between parents and child. Frequently such a state is termed *symbiosis* or *symbiotic union*. This symbiotic union distorts, exaggerates, and prolongs the normal symbiotic phase of development which M. Mahler (1969) described. It is difficult to convey the oppressive strength of such a pathologic union.

A parent and a child, [write Ricks and Nameche (1966)] form an inseparable unit, prolonged over a long period beyond the usual end of symbiosis (as described by M. Mahler). The child is not considered a separate person and boundaries between the parent and child are not recognized. The parent may therefore bathe the child well into adolescence, be so intrusive as to deny the child any privacy in action or thought, and be impervious to any desires that the child expresses in his own right. The child is expected to comply to parental distortions of this environment, physical restraint, and socialized relations . . . the child must remain functionally helpless, have no other close relationships, and not attempt to escape. The record contains no evidence that the child has ever been permitted outside the walls of the home to visit relatives or friends or has ever attended overnight camp.

Extremes of Delegating in Schizophrenia

In addition to and interweaving with maximal binding, delegating, when extreme, may give rise to schizophrenic disturbances. Such schizophrenic disturbances can be expected to differ, however, in phenomenology, prognosis, and treatment implications from those where excessive binding operates. Delegated patients who become schizophrenic are torn asunder by conflicts of missions and loyalties. Yet they can be expected to have a better long-term prognosis than more pervasively bound patients. For these delegated schizophrenic patients, even though gripped by conflicting loyalties and missions, can get a foothold in the world of peers and alternate adults and can thus promote their final liberation. We can expect them to become acutely, rather than chronically, disturbed, and to be released at least off and on from psychiatric institutions. My own— mainly psychotherapeutic—experiences with schizophrenic patients and their families bear this out, as does the research reported by Nameche *et al.* (1964), Scott and Montanez (1971), and others.

In order to fathom the intensity of conflicts and stresses to which such delegates can be subjected, we must reflect on the missions they are expected to fulfill. Many of these missions imply extreme demands—made on the delegate and his reconciling capacity—and seem incompatible with what his age and ordinary adaptation would require.

Several "missions impossible" particularly stand out here, such as, first of all, the mission to destroy one parent out of loyalty to the other—the mission for which Hamlet, hovering on the brink of a schizophrenic breakdown, provided the classic paradigm.

We must, second, mention the mission to embody and actualize a parent's grandiose ego ideal. The more such a parent senses that he or she cannot realize this ideal alone, the more desperately he or she turns to the child for salvation. This child, of only average endowment, must reach dizzying heights of achievement and fame and must share these willingly with the delegating parent. In other cases, he might have to embody all the beauty and vitality which this parent feels lacking or wanting in himself or herself.

Third, and this is perhaps the most fateful mission, such a delegate might become recruited to embody and externalize the badness and craziness which a parent, in his innermost self, feels and fears to be his fate. This child must then serve his parent's self-reservation, which Freud defined as one of the three functions of the superego (besides ego ideal and conscience; see S. Freud, 1923). Living under the (disowned) threat and spell of madness, such a parent seems often impelled to search for—and, in this process, create—madness in the child. Often such parental fear of and concern with madness seem understandable. Scott and Ashworth (1969), particularly, have shown that parents who unwittingly seek and implant madness in their children are often haunted by the shadows of mad relatives or ancestors. Hence, they grow up with the notion and expectation, frightening beyond comprehension, that madness again will strike their tainted family. It is then in the attempt to control, contain, and neutralize this feared and ever present madness that a child becomes delegated to enact it—i.e., becomes the mad family member.

Some Therapeutic Implications

Given the above model, the therapeutic tasks differ depending on how the various modes dominate and/or blend with each other. Space permits me only a few comments. First, let us consider some therapeutic implications of extreme binding.

Where such extreme binding prevails, the therapist has a short-term and a long-term task to fulfill—the short-term task of preventing what Scott and Ashworth (1967) have called "closure," and the long-term task of helping the parents and schizophrenic offspring to "un-bind."

"Closure," according to Scott and Ashworth, threatens when a patient—ordinarily an adolescent offspring—comes to be perceived as " 'ill,' mad, beyond human influence or concern. . . ." In fact, he seems condemned to a living death—a shadow existence to be led in a mental hospital. But—and this highlights the seeming paradox of extreme boundness—this "dead" patient, condemned to live in a shadowy Hades, retains the power to fill his parents' lives with never ending terror, concern, and guilt. The patient's dead body, although removed from the house, remains available for continuous ritualistic observances. Thus, unlike the dead described by Virgil and Dante, who fear (and perhaps relish) being forgotten, many living dead, who are called chronic schizophrenics, are refused Lethe's drink: although maximally alienated, they stay yet maximally bound to their parents.

Scott and Ashworth have perceptively traced how "closure" comes about. "When the 'child' first breaks down," we learn, "he becomes as a rule the center of a peculiarly intense parental awareness. He becomes the object of parental scrutiny, usually silent and oblique," while "conflict between the parents, often deep and unresolvable, now invariably takes place through the patient to a greater extent than before." At this point many psychiatrists become agents in sealing for good such closure. They spell out and hence officially sanction a "diagnosis" and sentence of "mental illness." And it is here that a psychiatrist's short-term intervention may become crucial. For this psychiatrist is typically brought into the picture when parents, after varying periods of agony and ambivalence, are about to evict their child dramatically. These parents then try to enlist his help to tip their ambivalence definitively. They recruit him as a surgeon who is expected to diagnose and cut off the bad, gangrenous family flesh, to effect its radical sequestration and expulsion. They expect this psychiatrist to label the patient as sick and in need of institutionalization. By giving official medical approval, he has to sanction the rejecting side of the parents' ambivalence and relieve their guilt about expelling their child.

Thus this psychiatrist is placed at a critical juncture in the patient's and family's life. He can use his influence to keep the potential expellee within the family orbit and, in so doing, can try to redistribute to the family the patient's badness and symptoms—that is, he can try to keep alive and "workable" the parents' ambivalence; or he can, by the power of his authority, provide the definitive, expelling push, which, as we saw, does not imply real separation, but a tragic boundness in which all parties forfeit their chances for growth and happiness.

But such prevention of closure is only the beginning of what is therapeutically required. The immensely difficult job of loosening the multiperson bind is still to begin. Above everything, the therapist must now be sensitive to a seeming paradox—the paradox that every prospect of the patient's making progress in his individuation and separation will inevitably trigger a systemic backlash in renewed binding. This affects, among other things, many a bound patient's evolving "positive" transference to his individual therapist, as I. Boszormenyi-Nagy has shown. For, by developing such a positive transference, the patient commits the number one crime of betraying his loyalty to his parents. Hence, he is (increasingly) driven to atone for this crime by presenting himself as sicker and more unworthy of a fulfilled life than ever before. In brief, he suffers or engineers a "setback," i.e., he acts out or becomes more crazy.

Through such a "setback"—and this opens up another therapeutic angle—the patient-victim punishes himself while, at the same time, he gains leverage for making his parents guilty: he delivers himself as the living proof of their failure and badness as parents. When this happens, it is important that the therapist can empathically share the plight of the victimized victimizers (the parents) while he also appreciates the victim's power inherent in his suffering.

Where we find extremes of delegating, similar backlash phenomena and power ploys need to be dealt with. In addition, the delegate's conflicts of missions and conflicts of loyalties, as mentioned above, need to be analyzed and "redistributed." For example, all family members may have to realize that one and the same adolescent delegate cannot very well, at one and the same time, serve the mission of being his mother's vicarious thrill-provider (i.e., become a precocious sex athlete) and also serve the mission of realizing her virtuous ego-ideal (i.e., study properly for the ministry). Such insights may then cause parents to "re-own" traits, needs, and conflicts which they "disowned" by exploiting the services of their delegate. At the same time, they may cause this delegate to "own" the anguish of his grief and loneliness—experiences that await him once he plans and executes those goals and missions in life which are truly "his."

REFERENCES

Bateson, G. Double bind, 1969. Paper presented at the symposium on the double bind, annual meeting of the American Psychological Association, Washington, D.C., September 2, 1969.

Bateson, G.; Jackson, D.; Haley, J.; and Weakland, J. Toward a theory of schizophrenia. *Behav. Sci.*, 1:251–264, 1956.

Bateson, G.; Jackson, D.; Haley, J.; and Weakland, J. A note on the double bind. *Family Process*, 2:154–161, 1963.

Freud, S. (1923) The ego and the id. *Standard Edition*, 19:3 –68. London: Hogarth Press, 1961.

Haley, J. The family of the schizophrenic: a model system. *J. Nerv. Ment. Dis.*, 129:357–374, 1959.

Laing, R. D. Mystification, confusion, and conflict. In *Intensive Family Therapy*, ed. I. Boszormenyi-Nagy and J. L. Framo. New York: Harper & Row, 1965.

Mahler, M. *On Human Symbiosis and the Vicissitudes of Individuation.* Vol. 1, *Infantile Psychosis.* New York: International Universities Press, 1968.

Nameche, G.; Waring, M.; and Ricks, D. Early indicators of outcome in schizophrenia. *J. Nerv. Ment. Dis.*, 139:232–240, 1964.

Ricks, D., and Nameche, G. Symbiosis, sacrifice, and schizophrenia. *Mental Hygiene*, 50:541–551, 1966.

Scott, R. D., and Ashworth, P. L. "Closure" at the first schizophrenic breakdown: A family study. *Brit. J. Med. Psychol.*, 40:109–145, 1967.

Scott, R. D., and Ashworth, P. L. The shadow of the ancestor: A historical factor in the transmission of schizophrenia. *Brit. J. Med. Psychol.*, 42:13–32, 1969.

Scott, R. D., and Montanez, A. The nature of tenable and untenable patient-parent relationships and their connexion with hospital outcomes. Unpublished manuscript, 1971.

Searles, H. (1959) The effort to drive the other person crazy: An element in the aetiology and psychotherapy of schizophrenia. In *Collected Papers on Schizophrenia and Related Subjects*. New York: International Universities Press, 1965, pp. 254–283.

Singer, Margaret, and Wynne, Lyman. Thought disorder and family relations of schizophrenics, IV, Results and implications. *Arch. Gen. Psy.*, 12:201–12, 1965.

Singer, Margaret, and Wynne, Lyman. Thought disorder and family relations of schizophrenics, III, Methodology using projective techniques. *Arch. Gen. Psy.*, 12:187–200, 1965.

Stierlin, H. The adaptation to the "stronger" person's reality. *Psychiatry*, 22:143–152, 1959.

Stierlin, H. Family dynamics and separation patterns of potential schizophrenics. In *Proceedings of the Fourth International Symposium on Psychotherapy of Schizophrenia*. Amsterdam: Excerpta Medica, 1972a, pp. 156–166.

Stierlin, H. Interpersonal aspects of internalizations. *Int. J. Psycho-Anal.*, 1972b.

Stierlin, H., and Ravenscroft, K. Varieties of adolescent "separation conflict." *Brit. J. Med. Psychol.*, 1972c.

Wynne, Lyman, and Singer, Margaret. Thought disorder and family relations of schizophrenics, I, A research strategy. *Arch. Gen. Psy.*, 9:191–8, 1963.

Wynne, Lyman, and Singer, Margaret. Thought disorder and family relations of schizophrenics, II, A classification of forms thinking. *Arch. Gen. Psy.*, 9:199–206.

SECTION THREE
RESEARCH

16

PSYCHOTHERAPY RESEARCH
Loren R. Mosher, M.D.

Research Decline

As noted in the introduction, a major reason for the initiation and development of this program on the Psychotherapy of Schizophrenia by the NIMH was our concern about the lack of ongoing research on the topic. The studies of the late 1950s and 1960s (reviewed in Chapter 26) have been completed, their results reported and conclusions drawn. Unfortunately, the interpretation of the results of these studies has varied widely; indeed, the greatest thing the supporters and detractors of the usefulness of psychotherapy have in common would seem to be their ability to see in the studies only findings that bolster their own point of view. For example, psychoanalysts committed to the psychotherapy of schizophrenia found so many flaws in the studies that it became possible either to disregard their findings completely or interpret them as proving once again that psychotherapy research is irrelevant. On the other hand, those committed to an organic view of schizophrenia, who by this time had available to them tranquilizing drugs with known and established efficacy, could point to the lack of clearly positive results and say, "I told you so." Both groups tended to overgeneralize about the research; the psychotherapists overgeneralizing as to its fruitlessness and the organicists overgeneralizing that psychotherapy was conclusively proven ineffective with schizophrenics. Too few have placed this generation of psychotherapy studies in its proper context. That is, while each study was flawed in its design, much could be learned from it. Had the field been less divided into warring camps, the knowledge these studies contributed might have been more easily employed in the design and conduct of a new generation of more sophisticated studies. Unfortunately, this has not yet happened.

Clinicians as Researchers

For the most part the members of the groups assembled in the Psychotherapy of Schizophrenia program have as their principal professional indentification that of "clinician." Asking clinicians, as we did initially, to spend significant amounts of time deriving research questions is a high-risk undertaking indeed. Their definition of research is a naturalistic one, based on careful observation and description of cases. More experimental research, focused on issues like sampling, diagnosis, controls, bias, and statistical manipulation, tends to be viewed suspiciously and resisted by many clinicians.

There appeared to be several reasons for this resistance. First, as therapists, and within the context in which they operated, they esteemed the individual hour (*not research*) most highly. Opening these hours to the scrutiny of peers, especially from outside their own institutions, was viewed as an uncomfortable process. In addition, the research, rather than clinical, nature of the undertaking did not enhance their motivation to do so. This is quite understandable given that their day-to-day gratifications and livelihoods are based on clinical work. Second, most of these clinicians have had only limited training or experience with the methods of experimental research. Some viewed this type of research as meaningless, that is, as contributing little to their day-to-day practices. Others, who had previously participated in research enterprises, felt the results had distorted or badly misrepresented what psychotherapy had to offer. Third, there was continuing concern over the ownership of the "product." That is, there was a suspicion that the NIMH would use the results of these meetings for some purpose about which they had neither been informed nor over which they had control. Fortunately, these suspicions diminished over time as the groups interacted with, and came to know, the NIMH representatives. Although the circumstances were somewhat different our experiences paralleled some of those described by Graff and Crabtree (1972). Despite its difficulties, we believe the program has made a contribution to the conduct of future research. On the one hand, the program has led us to conclude that it is unreasonable to expect those who are primarily identified as clinicians to be *directly* involved in the design and day-to-day conduct of rigorously designed psychotherapy research. But on the other hand, it has confirmed our belief that clinicians can make critical contributions to psychotherapy research *before* a precise methodology is spelled out. The clinicians' acumen and sensitivity to practical issues are invaluable in designing experiments that are not only methodologically sound but *feasible*. The specification of hypotheses about how changes in patients will occur can only be done by clinicians with extensive experience in the observation of such changes. By consulting with clinicians in designing a psychotherapy research project, the researcher can decrease the likelihood of missing crucial change variables, while at the same time increasing the likelihood that his research will have credibility among clinicians and eventual impact on practice.

New Directions

Of the twelve papers in this section, three are reviews (Chapters 17, 18, and 26). Taken together, the three reviews plus Wexler's short statement (Chapter 27) provide a current perspective on past research in this area. In addition, Chapter 17 outlines six basic requirements for an adequate design to study a psychosocial intervention and gives an example from an ongoing project.

Four papers in the section describe new psychotherapy research that was stimulated by discussions in the Psychotherapy of Schizophrenia program (Chapters 19, 20, 23, and 24). Each addresses a different issue and uses its own methods of study. Two of the studies (Chapters 19 and 23) attempt to elaborate in a systematic way two preconditions for good psychotherapy, i.e., how to select a schizophrenic patient for individual psychotherapy and how to optimize the selection of a psychotherapist to work with such a patient. The patient-selection study (Chapter 19) used a questionnaire to survey the clinical experience of program participants. Though interesting, it has all the limitations of questionnaire studies; that is, the selection of questions asked tends to predetermine the results. The patient-therapist matching study (Chapter 23) grew out of discussions of clinical experiences of members of the Washington group. It represents an effort to translate previously intuitive attempts to match the right patient with the right therapist into an instrument that would allow the systematic assessment of the relevant personality dimensions of both patient and therapist. Because it isolates only one factor of many involved in the determination of outcome, its predictive validity may be limited. Nevertheless, the study is an important step in the process of identifying and translating into measurable variables aspects of the psychotherapeutic process that have heretofore been strictly an intuitive art form.

The other two studies examine the patient's course during treatment. Clarence Schulz's scale (Chapter 20) aims to assess change in self-object differentiation (a critical theoretical construct in many theories of schizophrenia). As such, it meets a frequent objection of therapists that research scales tap patient dimensions irrelevant to the goals of individual psychotherapy. One of the problems of such a scale is that it requires highly sophisticated and therefore potentially idiosyncratic judgments about patients. Therefore, studies of interrater reliability will be very important. Lawrence Kayton's study (Chapter 24) is a retrospective account of thirteen schizophrenics who made good recoveries despite their having initially appeared to be poor prognostic risks. Like a similar retrospective report by Rubenstein (1972), this study attempts to define clinical and treatment course features that allow these patients to be identified prospectively and thereby give them treatment optimizing their changes of recovery. This study is another attempt (like the patient-therapist matching study) to define more precisely characteristics of particular patients that suit them to particular types of treatments or treaters—a critical question if limited resources are to be deployed most efficiently and effectively.

Deficiency, Conflict, and Therapists

A number of issues with research implications not covered in the papers were raised in the group discussions and at the Stockbridge meeting. A major theoretical and technical issue is whether schizophrenia is principally a *deficiency* or a *conflict* disorder. Clearly, whichever theoretical view is adhered to will have implications for both the conduct of treatment and the design of research. If schizophrenia is seen as a deficiency state, the psychotherapeutic process should involve graded structure, with gradually increasing task demands, somewhat like a course of study. In this view, modeling and identification are likely to be vitally important in the therapeutic process. In contrast, a conflict model implies need for only minimal structure, and utilizes interpretation for the resolution of conflict as central to the therapeutic process. In the conflict scheme, change is seen as more likely to occur if split-off or repressed events or affects are reunited with their current counterparts. Although the deficiency and conflict positions have been somewhat oversimplified and the contrasts overdrawn, the differences in treatment technique and critical variables to be studied in each are obvious. For example, in the deficiency model what the therapist *does* would be of central concern, whereas in the conflict model what he *says* would receive greater weight in assessment procedures. Given the difficulties of specifying in measurable terms the ingredients of even these two disparate, oversimplified theories and techniques, it must be concluded that studies of psychotherapy, if they are to be widely credible, should stick very close to the phenomena being examined, with minimal use of inference.

In the Psychotherapy of Schizophrenia program, it was possible to obtain agreement on the description and occurrence of certain circumscribed behaviors and events, but as soon as inferences based on individual theories were drawn, we found it difficult to obtain agreement even within our study groups. In the absence of a generally accepted unifying or unified theory of schizophrenia, any study would be wise to stay grounded in its observations if there were to be any basis for replication by investigators of differing theoretical persuasions.

Several interesting and relatively neglected therapist problems that might affect the design and conduct of research were raised: for example, what about the invasion of the therapist's privacy by the research? Protection of the patient's confidentiality has long been a concern in the very close contact that occurs during individual psychotherapy; however, there must also be safeguards for the therapist's privacy. Will participation in a research protocol with other therapists result in a loss of individuality?

Will patients use the research as leverage for manipulation? What of the therapist's fear of comparison with his peers and potential loss of esteem should his therapeutic efforts prove inefficacious? The difficulties our groups encountered around this issue, even without a formal protocol, lead us to believe that researchers must pay close attention to these therapist problems if a successful study of individual psychotherapy is to be conducted.

Several contextual factors that affect the design and conduct of psychotherapy research were discussed by conference participants. Psychotherapy cannot operate independently of the institution's prevailing value system(s). For example, in a given institution, what place in the hierarchy of importance does individual psychotherapy take? If it is believed to be most important by the therapists, are there discrepancies between their views and those of other staff members? The conduct and interpretation of research results might be very different in an institution where psychotherapy is uniformly valued as compared with one in which it is viewed (except by those involved in the research) as a dying art form to which the coup de grâce will be delivered by the study. Thus, sensitivity to contextual issues was seen as vital to this type of research endeavor.

Narrowing the Perspective

It may be seen that the deceptively simple question "Does individual psychotherapy work with schizophrenic patients?" is really only the tip of an iceberg. The four pilot research efforts reported here are focused on important aspects of the iceberg. Unfortunately, an answer to the most critical question, "How can we say with certainty that psychotherapy is, in fact, occurring?" eludes us. The answer to this question may be a necessary precondition to both the study of whether (outcome) and how (process)

psychotherapy works. To study the outcome of psychotherapy in the absence of assurances that it is actually
occurring would be like investigating the efficacy of a drug
without being certain it had been ingested. Having been
assured that psychotherapy is going on, the researcher
needs assessments of outcome that are fair to the treatment
goals. For example, Schulz would hypothesize that the patient receiving psychotherapy would be better able to tolerate and maintain greater self-object differentiation in the
face of a relationship than would a patient not receiving
individual therapy. Thus, outcome, if defined in terms of
symptom remission or length of stay (two commonly used
criteria), would be tangential, at best, to this hypothesis.
The central therapeutic processes in Schulz's scheme
would be those patient-therapist interactions that fostered
self-object differentiation. Hours of psychotherapy, a common process assessment device, might not reflect this aspect of therapy at all. Other measures of process, while
having more content (e.g., Barrett-Lennard's Relationship
Inventory, 1962) than simple measures of time spent, might
also not tap the dimensions that Schulz believes are important in the therapeutic process.

Although the isolation of a single aspect of a study of
psychotherapy (e.g., outcome, process, etc.) may be artificial and give a very incomplete picture, the field does not
appear to be ready to address the total gestalt of individual
psychotherapy with schizophrenic patients at the present
time. It does, however, appear that the field is now ready to
begin a series of pilot studies designed to develop important new methods and data and lead to larger, more comprehensive projects. As noted above, the early work
should probably concentrate on being able to establish
whether or not psychotherapy is, in fact, going on between
the patient and the therapist. Once this determination is
possible, then attention to sample selection, description of
patient and therapist, therapeutic process, theoretical constructs (and their technical implications), contexts in which

treatment takes place, and finally the assessment of outcome should be undertaken. The need for a total answer (i.e., encompassing the total gestalt) seems to have held the progress of psychotherapy research, especially in schizophrenia, in check. If investigators can give up some of their narcissism and allow themselves to accept and build on partial answers derived from a variety of sources, it will eventually be possible to build, through accretion, a more nearly complete picture. At that point, two long-term studies of individual therapy would seem to be warranted: an in-hospital study of first-admission patients treated intensively by experienced psychotherapists and a study of recently discharged patients treated intensively by experienced psychotherapists in an outpatient setting. Both of these designs could, if the therapy were carried on for a sufficient period of time, maximize the possibility of finding effects from the psychotherapy. The inclusion of drug and placebo conditions would allow hypotheses about interactive and antagonistic effects of drugs with psychotherapy to be tested. The design must take into account the possibility that the effects of therapy may be slow to begin (Hogarty and Goldberg, 1973) but long-lasting, and may intensify after the cessation of treatment. In addition, the design must allow an identification of responders and nonresponders within each experimental condition.

The complexities of research on the psychotherapy of schizophrenia highlighted above will become apparent in the chapters that follow. The formidable difficulties involved in psychotherapy research may frighten away all but the naive or foolhardy, especially at a time when the research context—principally because of the shortage of money—favors simplistic, facile, low-risk research endeavors. Clearly, psychotherapy research is not simple, easy, or low risk. Despite the rather auspicious beginnings made as a result of this program, it remains to be seen whether the long-term, time-consuming, difficult studies that seem to be necessary will be undertaken.

REFERENCES

Barrett-Lennard, G. T. Dimensions of therapist response as causal factors in therapeutic change. *Psychological Monograph: General and Applied.* vol. 76, no. 43 (whole no. 562), 1962.

Graff, H., and Crabtree, L. H., Jr. Vicissitudes in the development of a psychoanalytic research group. *Journal of the American Psychoanalytic Association,* 20(4):820 –830, 1972.

Hogarty, G. E.; Goldberg, S. C.; and the Collaborative Study Group. Drug and sociotherapy in the aftercare of schizophrenic patients: one-year relapse rates. *Archives of General Psychiatry,* 28(1):54–64, 1973.

Rubenstein, R. Mechanisms for Survival after Psychoses and Hospitalization. Presented at the annual meeting of the American Psychological Association, Dallas, 1972.

17
EVALUATION OF
PSYCHOSOCIAL TREATMENTS
Loren R. Mosher, M.D.

A Conundrum

It may be that I am addressing an impossible topic. Perhaps the psychological treatment of schizophrenia will eventually prove unresearchable. Whether the task of studying this process is an impossible or merely an incredibly complex undertaking remains for time to tell. One thing is certain, however: there are at present few adequate studies of psychosocial treatments of schizophrenia.

Why is this so? Schizophrenia is not the only disorder for which the evidence of the effectiveness of various psychosocial treatments is inadequate; this is true of most psychiatric conditions. Nonetheless, fewer efforts have been made to study the nonsomatic treatment of schizophrenia than of the psychoneuroses, for example. This lack of investigative interest may relate to a view of schizophrenia as an "incurable disease," as well as a general disenchantment among analysts (beginning with Freud) with its potential treatability. In addition, some psychological treatments for this disorder—milieu and group therapy, for example—have only recently come into widespread use, perhaps accounting in part for the dearth of evidence for their efficacy in schizophrenia. But why the many long-time adherents of the individual psychotherapy of schizophrenia have never subjected their techniques to systematic scrutiny is more difficult to fathom.

Reprinted by permission from *Hospital and Community Pscyhiatric Conf.*, 23 (8):229–234, 1972.

Before I propound a model for the evaluation of the psychological treatment of schizophrenia, and illustrate it with a study that is presently in progress, I think it worthwhile to set a theoretical context. Without this information, you are left to your own projections about my theoretical position with regard to the conditions we designate as "schizophrenia."

The term "schizophrenia" has no meaning for me. That is, it does not describe a disease or even characterize adequately a group of patients. Indeed, as a clinician, I find this diagnostic label not only meaningless but an actual barrier to therapy. Too often, in my experience, therapists become so involved in diagnosis per se that they lose sight of what should be their real goal—helping patients. You may ask, legitimately, how I can be interested in researching a meaningless, even damaging word. To that question, I can only respond that I am inconsistent—I have a "split personality," if you will. As a researcher, I am capable of adopting attitudes I feel to be contrary to good psychological treatment. I believe it necessary for the researcher to define the population with which he is dealing, even if his definition is a purely arbitrary one. Moreover, in my own defense, I consider it possible, *for research purposes*, to "label" a carefully defined set of behaviors common to a group of patients without adversely affecting the philosophy and conduct of treatment. And, indeed, my main purpose for doing research in the first place is to provide scientifically acceptable data about what kinds of psychological procedures may be *antitherapeutic*. For example, it is my feeling that a traditonal psychoanalytic approach to most of the individuals we call schizophrenics will only reinforce their madness. But I have no firm data upon which to base this assumption. Thus, in many ways my interest is to protect so-called schizophrenics from being driven *further out* by treatment; without systematic research, it will never be possible to set up valid guidelines as to what should or should not be done in the treatment of their disorder.

Strategy

In general, I recognize six major criteria for research on psychological intervention:[1]

1. Theory and technique. The nature of the treatment to be delivered must be adequately defined. Moreover, definition should coincide with reality; that is, the treatment should relate in a coherent and meaningful way to the theory underlying it. As is well known, what we say (and believe) we are doing may be very different from what we really *are* doing.

2. Patient characteristics. The patient group should be adequately defined. Since diagnostic difficulties with schizophrenia are notorious (and it clearly a "wastebasket" term), each researcher's criteria must be made explicit (i.e., based on behavioral items that can be rated reliably) to permit replication and comparison across studies. At the very least, schizophrenic patients should be subdivided according to quality of premorbid adjustment (i.e., insidious vs. acute onset and/or level of social competence) and according to the presence or absence of paranoid symptoms. Such attempts at subclassification have been shown to produce greater homogeneity in patient samples. Moreover, in research designed to identify responders to a particular treatment, the sample should be of sufficient size to allow for an adequate number of patients who are homogeneous for such variables as age, socioeconomic status, and sex. Because of the heterogeneous nature of the diagnostic category, the delimitation of subgroups is especially important

in schizophrenic research. There is no reason to expect that all members of a class of disorders will respond to a single type of intervention. Only by the identification of subgroups of responders will we eventually be able to assign treatment on rational grounds.

3. Therapist characteristics. In studies of psychological intervention, the therapist, as well as his patients, must be the object of study. At a minimum he should be categorized along the A/B dimensions of Whitehorn and Betz (1954) and according to level of experience, theoretical orientation, enthusiasm, and type of patient/therapist relationship that evolves. In studies of group of milieu therapy, his role as a leader should obviously be part of any research evaluation.

4. The process. Research addressing primarily the *result* of interpersonal interactions cannot ignore these processes themselves. Unfortunately, our tools for evaluating a transacting dyad are inadequate. While the individual roles of both patient and therapist have been studied extensively (e.g., Rogers, Gendlin, Kiesler, and Truax, 1967), the transactional flow *between* them has received little attention. This area is vitally in need of new methods.

5. The context. Psychological interventions are very sensitive to the context within which they are delivered. It is therefore crucial to understand the attitudes, belief systems, and demand characteristics of the settings in which treatment is carried out.

6. Outcome. Criteria measuring outcome should be carefully defined and do justice to the treatment beng tested. In assessing individual psychotherapy, for example, measures of personality change and insight are clearly more relevant than mere symptom reduction. These criteria should also allow for a long-range view. Interactional techniques are generally slower than somatic treatments, but their effects may be relatively enduring and may intensify over time.

Soteria: An Example

Alma Menn and I have begun an innovative project on the West Coast. If it is successful, its implications for the psychiatric profession and mental hospitals are great. In the interests of time, I shall not detail the project's adherence to rigorous design in areas other than those mentioned above (e.g., controls, the drug variable, statistical evaluation, etc.).

In brief, the project will test the developmental crisis orientation to an initial episode of schizophrenia. This philosophy will underlie the therapy to be given by indigenous, nonprofessional, specially trained personnel ("guides") to a group of schizophrenic patients living in a home in the community which we call Soteria House. These patients and the members of a comparable control group will be followed, in terms of outcome, for two years after discharge from our facility or, in the case of the controls, the psychiatric ward in the local general hospital. Let me turn now to our attempts to deal with each of the six areas noted in the introduction.

The Phenomenological Stance

To present this approach as a "theory" with a related "technique" is inherently contradictory; that is, the approach is mostly a "not-theory" with an associated "nontechnique." It is predicated on the therapist's assuming a phenomenological stance—i.e., responding to each individual patient according to his unique needs. This approach does, however, have some guiding principles that, if stretched and fleshed out sufficiently, might be called a theory. Our treatment philosophy draws upon crisis theory (Caplan and Lebovici, 1969; Erikson, 1959; and Lindemann, 1944), the writings of David Cooper (1967) and R. D. Laing (1967), and the lore of the psychedelic movement. We have tried to capture this philosophy's essence by calling it a "developmental crisis" approach, a term that suggests both developmental theory and positive growth through learning. We feel the medical disease, deficit, and pathology-based model has too long dictated a set of pessimistic expectations with regard to schizophrenia.

Any attempt to describe the developmental crisis approach is complicated by our objection to the negative connotations of much of the traditional vocabulary of medicine and psychiatry. As usually defined, terms like "schizophrenia," "disease," "treatment," "staff," and "patient" are meaningless when applied to our research setting. Nevertheless, in the absence of any new, universally understood developmental crisis vocabulary, we must fall back upon standard psychiatric terminology when attempting to communicate our techniques. Please bear in mind, however, that these terms are used *analogously* and do not necessarily carry the meanings they have in most medical/psychiatric circles.

A brief quote from a brochure describing Soteria House may illustrate its philosophy:

> It is believed that by allowing and helping the resident to gradually work with and through his crisis in living, or schizophrenia, he will be better able to understand himself and his fears. So rather than ignoring or quelling this altered state, he will explore it, understand it, and finally learn from it. Our House believes that this growth process may leave him with an even stronger sense of identity than before his episode.

At Soteria House, the schizophrenic reaction is viewed as an "altered state of consciousness" in an individual who is experiencing a crisis in living. This crisis is usually one that has developed within the psychosocial matrix of a family or small group. As the psychosis evolves, the entire family or group experiences crisis along with the individual labeled as "deviant," in that they are forced to confront

the strange behaviors related to his altered state of consciousness. Simply put, the altered state involves personality fragmentation, with the loss of a sense of self. In this
state "beyond reason," modalities of experience merge,
the inner and outer worlds become difficult to distinguish,
and mystical sensations are experienced. Often the patient's terror at his altered state is reinforced by the intense
fear he arouses in others, whose own sanity is challenged
by his seemingly inexplicable behavior.

Few clinicians would disagree with a description of the
evolution of psychosis as one of fragmentation-disintegra-
tion. But at Soteria House, the disruptive psychotic experience is also believed to have unique potential for
reintegration-reconstitution if it is not prematurely aborted
or forced into some psychologically straitjacketing compromise. Such a view of schizophrenia implies a number of
therapeutic attitudes. All modalities of the experience are
taken by Soteria House staff members as "real." They
view the experiential and behavioral attributes of the psychosis (clinical symptomatology), including irrationality,
terror, and mystical experiences, as *extremes* of basic human qualities, which are not to be considered nonhuman,
and not to be related to in a depersonalized way. Because
the fragmentation process is seen as having potential for
psychological *growth*, the individual experiencing the schizophrenic reaction is therefore to be tolerated, lived with,
and related to, but not "treated" or used to fulfill staff
needs. Limits are set if the person is clearly a danger to
himself and/or others; they are not set merely because of
an inability of others to tolerate his madness. The psychotic experience is seen as intelligible in terms of the nature,
qualities, and characteristics of the psychosocial matrix in
which it developed—this forms part of the basis for our
orientation to the patients *and their families* and for the
goal of developing sympathetic, understanding relationships in Soteria House. Because even "irrational" behav-

ior and beliefs are regarded as valid and capable of being understood, the staff's major function is to help provide an atmosphere that will facilitate the integration of the psychosis into the continuity of the individual's life. The mystical experiences of psychosis are also accepted as valid and as comprehensible in a metaphorical sense related both to cultural background and the dynamics of the family.

The Soteria House's staff has been specially selected as having the potential ability to tune into the patient's altered state of consciousness. They have been trained to act as a projective screen for the patients and to provide them with reassurance, help in problem solving, support, and protection.[2] During the acute phase of psychosis, staff members form special one-to-one or two-to-one relationships with the disorganized patient, performing a role similar to that of the LSD trip guide; the psychotic experience is shared and reflected, so long as both patient and guide do not experience intolerable levels of fear and anxiety. This intense, dyadic relationship is the program's primary interpersonal unit and source of control. Authority lines and roles are not clearly delineated (e.g., there are no staff meetings), staff members do not wear uniforms, and they are not seen as having "the" answer. There are relatively few *prescribed* expectations to which patients are pressured to conform; the expectations that *are* prescribed relate to avoiding harm to the patients, the staff, the community, and the program. While the residence encourages patients to participate in a variety of activities (aimed at the development of a sense of self, physical and psychological), their need for solitude and safety in a turmoil is also respected. Because it is meant to develop out of the needs of its residents, the Soteria House's program is expected to change as new needs emerge.

Over time, the project's theory and technique will become more closely articulated. We intend eventually to prepare a manual describing a variety of situations and techniques for dealing with them, based on our experiences. The autobiographical accounts of the guides and the guided (obtained during their stay and in a debriefing at discharge) will be used in a critical incident analysis.

Patient Characteristics

At admission all patients will be diagnosed according to explicit reliable criteria by independent diagnosticians. They will also be rated on the Inpatient Multidimensional Psychiatric Rating Scale (Lorr, McNair, Klett, and Lasky, 1962) and the Short Scale for Rating Paranoid Schizophrenia (Venables and O'Connor, 1959) and be characterized as to mode of onset (acute vs. insidious) (Vaillant, 1964). Family ratings will include a social history and the Katz Adjustment Scales (Katz and Lyerly, 1963), which rate symptomatic behavior as reported by the family and the patient. These measures have all been widely used in studies of psychotic patients. Most relevant in terms of the treatment technique, however, are our attempts to characterize changes over time using non-symptom-based measures. For example, because we feel our milieu should aid the patient in integrating the psychotic experience into the continuity of his life, we are attempting to measure, by means of a self-report questionnaire developed by Soskis (1968), changes in the individual's attitude toward his illness. The items may then be scored to place the patient into one of four categories (originally specified by Mayer-Gross, 1920) based on whether he (1) has integrated the psychotic experience into his life, (2) has denied his illness, (3) feels it has left him with no future, or (4) views it as an encapsulated (unintegrated) event. Thus, we hypothesize that our patients will fall into category 1 significantly more often than will controls. We will also study changes in introversion/extroversion by means of the Myers-Briggs Type Indicator (Myers, 1962). We expect that our experimental patients will have larger change scores than controls, although not necessarily only toward increased introversion. Other patient-characteristic measures to be administered include the Barron-Welsh Art Scale (Welsh, 1959), the As Experience Inventory (As, O'Hara, and Munger, 1962), the Fundamental Interpersonal Relations Orientations Test (Schutz, 1958), and the Family Relationship Test (Scott, Ashworth, and Casson, 1970). The relevance of these measures to our theory and technique is partially explained by the title of each.

Therapist Characteristics

The primary therapists in this setting are specially trained "street people" who may have themselves experienced an altered state of consciousness. In addition to the A/B Therapist Scale (Whitehorn and Betz, 1954) and the California Psychological Inventory (Gough, 1956), they will take the same attitudinal measures given the patients (e.g., the Myers-Briggs Type Indicator). They will also write autobiographies at the beginning of their employment and at three intervals corresponding to retesting on the battery of paper-and-pencil measures. These measures will allow us to identify characteristics of persons particularly well suited to working with psychotics in general, or with certain types of patients. They will also enable us to chart changes that occur in staff members as the project progresses.

The Black Box

Most of the evaluation of the therapeutic process, especially the quality of relationships established, must depend upon reports from the parties involved in each therapeutic dyad. While these first-person accounts are probably the most valid indicators of interpersonal transactions, they are subject to unknown distortions, biases, and omissions. We will therefore ask other Soteria House residents, both staff members and patients, to describe the dyadic relationship that they, as comparative outsiders, observed. We will also have an uninvolved social psychologist conduct debriefing sessions (at discharge) with patients and staff. This will allow us to compare reports from a variety of sources for views of important therapeutic events.

Finally, a Ward Atmosphere Scale (Moos, 1968) will be administered to both guides and guided at three monthly intervals. Thus, the perceived characteristics of Soteria House (and also of the control ward) will be systematically evaluated by residents. Because this scale has been used in many settings we will be able to compare and contrast our milieu with those already characterized. This will also help us to gauge the discrepancies between the actual and "ideal" characteristics of our milieu.

The Wider Social Network

This has been described above; briefly, it is imbued with the expectation that an acute psychotic crisis can be a learning experience, resulting in growth, personality development, and enhanced psychological functioning. The treatment context will be evaluated by self-reports, independent consultants, and research instruments. In addition, the patient's family context will be measured by the Katz Adjustment Scales (Katz and Lyerly, 1963) and the Family Relationship Test (Scott et al., 1970), both filled out by patient and family.

Better, as Good, or Worse?

The variety of outcome measures to be used range from fairly standard symptom scales (e.g., IMPS) to the more theoretically relevant attitudinal measures (e.g., Soskis, 1968). All measures will be repeated over time so that change scores can be derived. We will, in addition, use number of hospitalizations, number of days hospitalized, work, interpersonal functioning, and total treatment cost as outcome measures.

Much emphasis is placed in this study on the self-report; our intent is to attempt to obtain from those who *really* know (the psychotic persons) what they consider the nature of their experience, what in that experience they view as of value, and the way they evaluate their current functioning. For example, we anticipate that some of Soteria House's former residents may give up white-collar work to become manual laborers or craftsmen. While mental health professionals would ordinarily consider such occupational changes as a decrease in functioning, it might well be evidence of *enhanced* competence, if viewed this way by the individual himself. We feel that this highly individual view is most important in fairly assessing the developmental crisis model.

This study has many imperfections; I present it only to illustrate our attempt to address the several *classes* of variables that are crucial to any study of outcome of psychosocial treatment. Compromises must be made in research; we've made many. Hopefully, they are not ones that will result in the study's losing meaningfulness for the treatment it hopes to evaluate. Triviality is the bugaboo of all too many studies of psychological intervention. Most importantly, each *area* covered is one that one or another previous study has failed to address. In our study we hope to at least grapple with each class of variable, even if at times unsatisfactorily.

Summary

Six major areas that should be addressed in the conduct of research on the psychosocial treatment of schizophrenia are presented. To illustrate the research model propounded, an ongoing research project is described. Set in a house in the community, this project is designed to test the "developmental crisis" orientation to an initial episode of schizophrenia. Therapy is given by specially trained paraprofessionals who view the psychotic experience as a response to a crisis in living which, if handled properly, may result in psychological growth and enhanced functioning. During the acute phase of psychosis, staff members form special one-to-one relationships with the patient, performing a role similar to that of the LSD trip guide. Unlike the usual psychiatric ward, the treatment setting is not characterized by a plethora of rules, regulations, and prescribed activities. Limits are set only if the patient is clearly a danger to himself or others.

To test the effectiveness of this setting, the experimental patients and members of a control group from a psychiatric ward in a local general hospital will be followed for two years after discharge. Indicators of outcome include number and length of hospitalizations, ability to work, interpersonal functioning, and total treatment cost. In addition, changes in both groups of patients will be measured at intervals during treatment by means of autobiographical written accounts, standard symptom scales (e.g., the IMPS), and attitudinal tests chosen as particularly relevant to the theory and technique (e.g., the Barron-Welsh Art Scale and the Soskis Attitude Toward Illness Questionnaire).

REFERENCES

As, Arvid; O'Hara, J. W.; and Munger, M. P. The measurement of subjective experiences presumably related to hypnotic susceptibility. *Scandinavian Journal of Psychology*, 3:47, 1962.

Caplan, G., and Lebovici, S., eds. *Adolescence: Psychosocial Perspectives*. New York: Basic Books, 1969.

Cooper, D. *Psychiatry and Anti-Psychiatry*. London: Tavistock, 1967.

Erikson, E. H. Identity and the life cycle: Selected papers. *Psychological Issues*, 1: 1, 1959.

Fiske, D. W.; Luborsky, L.; Parloff, M. B.; Hunt, H. F.; Orne, M. T.; and Reiser, M. F. Planning of research on effectiveness of psychotherapy. *American Psychologist*, 25:727, 1970.

Gough, Harrison G. *California Psychological Inventory*. Palo Alto, Calif.: Consulting Psychologists Press, 1956.

Katz, M. M., and Lyerly, S. B. Methods of measuring adjustment and social behavior in the community. I. Rationale, description, descriminative validity, and scale development. *Psychological Reports*, 13:503, 1963.

Laing, R. D. *The Politics of Experience*. New York: Ballantine Books, 1967.

Lindemann, E. Symptomatology and management of acute grief. *American Journal of Psychiatry*, 101:141, 1944.

Lorr, M.; McNair, D. M.; Klett, C. J.; and Lasky, J. J. Evidence of ten psychotic syndromes. *Journal of Consulting Psychology*, 26:185, 1962.

Mayer-Gross, W. A paper dealing with the various ways the acute psychosis may affect the basic values of an individual. *Zeitschrift fur die Gesamte Neurologie und Psychiatrie*, 60:160, 1920.

Moos, R. H. The assessment of the social atmosphere of psychiatric wards. *Journal of Abnormal Psychology*, 73:595, 1968.

Mosher, L. R.; Reifman, Ann; and Menn, A. Characteristics of nonprofessionals serving as primary therapists for acute schizophrenics. *Hospital and Community Psychiatry*, 24(6):391–396, 1973.

Myers, Isabel B. *Manual, The Myers-Briggs Type Indicator.* Princeton, N. J.: Educational Testing Service, 1962.

Rogers, C. R.; Gendlin, E. T.; Kiesler, D. J.; and Truax, C. B., eds. *The Therapeutic Relationship and Its Impact: A Study of Psychotherapy with Schizophrenics.* Madison: University of Wisconsin Press, 1967.

Schutz, W. C. *The Interpersonal Underworld.* Palo Alto, Calif.: Science and Behavior Books, 1958.

Scott, R. D.; Ashworth, P. L.; and Casson, P. D. Violation of parental role structure and outcome in schizophrenia: a scored analysis of features in the patient-parent relationship. *Social Science and Medicine*, 4:41, 1970.

Soskis, D. A. The Schizophrenic experience: a follow-up study of attitude and function. New Haven: Department of Psychiatry, Yale University School of Medicine, 1968.

Strupp, H. H., and Bergin, A. E. Some empirical and conceptual bases for coordinated research in psychotherapy: a critical review of issues, trends, and evidence. *International Journal of Psychiatry*, 7:18, 1969.

Vaillant, G. E. Prospective prediction of schizophrenic remission. *Archives of General Psychiatry*, 11:509, 1964.

Venables, P. H., and O'Connor, N. A short scale for rating paranoid schizophrenia. *Journal of Mental Science*, 105:815, 1959.

Welsh, G. S. *Welsh Figure Preference Test, Preliminary Manual.* Palo Alto, Calif: Consulting Psychologists Press, 1959.

Whitehorn, J. C., and Betz, B. J. A study of psychotherapeutic relationships between physicians and schizophrenic patients. *American Journal of Psychiatry*, 111:321, 1954.

Footnotes

1. These criteria are extensively discussed by Fiske, Luborsky, Parloff, Hunt, Orne, and Reiser (1970) and by Strupp and Bergen (1969).

2. The selection, characteristics, testing and special training of these indigenous paraprofessionals ("street-people") has been completely explicated elsewhere (Mosher, Reifman, and Menn, 1973).

18

EVALUATION OF PSYCHOTHERAPY
Jarl E. Dyrud, M.D.
Philip S. Holzman, Ph.D.

The Psychotherapy of
Schizophrenia:
Does It Work?

Multiple Meanings

Many a difficult question—such as the one posed to us—
has resolved itself into clearer focus by judicious rephrasing. The question as it appears above allows no clear-cut
answer, brings us no nearer to fruitful understanding of the
critical issues before us, and indeed may even be counter-
productive—all for reasons of the ambiguities in the words
"psychotherapy" and "schizophrenia" and in the vague-
ness of the meaning of "Does it work?" For most clinicians, the two key words of schizophrenia and
psychotherapy have stimulated confusion in that one
man's schizophrenia is another man's schizophreniform
psychosis, and in most researchers the "Does it work?"
challenge conjures up kaleidoscopic visions of outcome
criteria merging into outcome criteria. What does "work"
mean?

We therefore choose to begin by restating the question in
a way that permits answers that are less representative of
partisan views and more indicative of the current state of

Reprinted from *American Journal of Psychiatry*, 130(6): 670–673, 1973.

our knowledge. We hope the clarity that will emerge will be regarded as helpful and not merely as obsessional hair-splitting. In this brief paper, then, we will first attempt to clarify the question by considering each of its elements, and then go on to try to answer the challenge from the available data.

Psychotherapy

For the sake of consistency we will confine ourselves here to speaking of one-to-one treatment, but with the clear understanding that this form of psychotherapy is a deliberate and specialized pursuit arising out of the patient's broader supportive milieu in which a variety of other psychosocial events occur. It is well to bear in mind that this milieu has always been with us. It operates on intensive psychotherapy wards just as certainly as on wards labeled drug treatment only. It was the therapeutic agent in "moral therapy" (1) in the last century. It had its burst of enthusiasm as a therapy following the Second World War and was then almost totally eclipsed by the advent of the phenothiazines with the development of more precise measures of effectiveness. No one knew what the central effects of the drugs were, but research design was easy. Control and comparison groups could be marshaled; randomization, double-blind, and cross-over designs added elegance to the evaluative process. Another revival of interest in the milieu is now upon us as behavior-modification techniques make the milieu operate in ways that are more observable and controllable (2). Change indicators in behavior have become easy to specify, although the issues of generalization to the noncontrol and post hospital environment are still to be investigated. All of this is to say that we have hopes now of specifying more of the "nonspecific" therapeutic events in a patient's career.

One of our human characteristics seems to be our need for explanations (3). Our efforts to account for events are usually focused on a single aspect called the "essential ingredient" of a transaction. Much of the disputation in our field is concerned with elevating one or another aspect of the total care of the patient, such as medication or psychotherapy, to this status, with a corresponding neglect of other factors operating in the patient's milieu.

As far as individual psychotherapy is concerned, there seems to be only a small gain from restating a well-known view: psychotherapy is not a unitary process. Yet for the sake of our argument let us repeat that psychotherapy is unlike most other therapeutic procedures, as in surgery, for example, where accurate diagnoses are possible and, on the basis of those diagnoses, rational treatments consisting of clearly defined procedures can be begun. In contrast, psychotherapy does not consist of a definite set of operations and the essence of the procedures is still a matter of personal preference, bias, and lively controversy. There is no "dose" of psychotherapy. The procedures subsumed under the lablel "psychotherapy" include the classical psychoanalytic procedure, those based upon it, those emphasizing only understanding, or affect-expression, or modification of observable behavior by operant techniques, to name only a few of the occupants of this psychosocial Tower of Babel.

The people who present themselves for such treatment, too, comprise a heterogeneous group, obviously not suffering from a single, reliably diagnosed condition. Rather, a range of human problems is presented, including situational crises, neurotic conditions, character difficulties, and psychoses. Further, the people who present themselves for help from psychotherapists differ among themselves in striking ways: intellectually, characterologically, socioeconomically, culturally, in age, and in hosts of life experiences.

We could expand the list of complications in the use of the word "psychotherapy," but we will mention only one more: the enormous range of differences among psychotherapists. Whereas the technical operations of surgical procedures can be taught and variations are a matter of general codification, psychotherapists can rarely be taught the ingredients of most psychotherapies: empathy, compassion, tact, timing, mutative intrusiveness, and interest in the various kinds of human problems that patients present. The therapist himself is therefore a crucial variable in the psychotherapeutic relationship. This is so not only insofar as orientation to psychotherapy is concerned, but also in regard to the kind of person the psychotherapist is.

From these considerations it would seem that the first element of the question should be changed from psychotherapy to "some psychotherapeutic procedures practiced by some psychotherapists."

Schizophrenia

The term "schizophrenia," like "psychotherapy," is an example of what may be called the "fallacy of misplaced singularity." Bleuler (4), of course, spoke of "the group of the schizophrenias," by which he recognized the heterogeneity of conditions subsumed under the label. The conditions include the clear-cut process schizophrenias, insidious in their onset in early adolescence and proceeding ever more malignantly into dementia: the oscillating phasic schizophrenic conditions; the rigid, litigious paranoid schizophrenic processes that appear in the third and fourth decades of life; the acute schizophreniform psychotic episodes, from which some patients recover apparently completely, as Laing (5) and Menninger (6) have described, and from which many more patients never reach a *restitutio ad integrum*. There are nonpsychotic conditions, too, which we label schizophrenic: the so-called latent schizophrenias, iincipient schizophrenias, ambulatory schizophrenias (7), and even remitted schizophrenias.

Much of the research data emerging from family and

genetic studies (e.g., Heston[8], and Rosenthal, Kety, and Wender[9]) point to even broader areas of concerns than that of syndromal descriptions; these studies suggest a spectrum of conditions that include people with severe neurotic symptoms and even those without pathology but who show a distinctive, novel, creative outlook on reality. In some studies it has been found that subtle evidence of thought disorder exists in a setting of normal social, occupational, and family behavior. From these studies perplexing questions about etiology arise: Are the serious schizophrenias to be considered etiologically related to the neuroses? That is, if one accepts a conflict etiology of neurosis such as that presented by Freud, can one fit the schizophrenias into such a psychoanalytic model? Or, if one accepts a thoroughgoing empirical model such as the one Skinner (10) has outlined, in which all behaviors are learned outcomes of their consequences, can one fit the schizophrenias into such an operant model?

It would appear that the second element of the question has resolved itself into "the schizophrenias," and has implicated an etiology that may be far more complex than the conditions for which the usual psychotherapies were developed. This position does not disavow the etiological importance of learning, family strains, and intrapersonal conflicts. Rather, with our expanding knowledge of genetic, biochemical, and quasi-stable personological factors, we prefer to think of all of these factsors as "contributory" or "necessary etiological conditions," rather than specifically or uniquely causal in the schizophrenias. In keeping with Adolph Meyer's psychobiological approach (11), we recognize that a crucial diagnostic task is the assessment of the relative contributions of familial, genetic, conflict, biochemical, psychological, and sociocultural factors in order to be able to aim a treatment program at its proper target. For it would seem that in the severe, disintegrated schizophrenic conditions a plurality of therapeutic

methods would be called for simultaneously or sequential-
ly, rather than reliance on one technique alone. Thus, the
early treatment steps may well be focused on reducing the
ambiguity of the environment in an operant conceptual
framework to be followed by more stress on the therapeutic relationship, perhaps in conjunction with phenothiazine
administration.

Does It Work?

We have already alluded to the ambiguities in this question. The "it" is really "they," and by "work" we need to
specify more precisely the outcomes we expect or hope for
in the various kinds of schizophrenic conditions. If the
expectation is merely discharge from a hospital, the overwhelming weight of evidence presents psychotherapy as
having very little effect (12). The phenothiazines alone
claim clear justification for an ameliorative effect and even
those original generalizations are having to be revised to
take into account the diversity of the schizophrenias. Goldstein (3), for instance, suggests strongly that nonparanoid,
good premorbid schizophrenic patients may be adversely
affected by phenothiazines. Over all, however, research
suggests that psychotherapy either alone or in combination
with the phenothiazines contributes no significant reduction in the hospital stay of schizophrenic patients. We do
not challenge the validity of these findings. A critical issue,
however, is the nature of the criterion of outcome as it
relates to the overall process of treatment. The criterion
for discharge from a mental hospital may have little relation to much else about a patient except his greater man-
ageability. Many other aspects of the patient's condition
may not be considered in this decision. For example, relevant issues should include (*a*) whether he can gainfully
support himself and his family, or, if the patient is a woman, whether she can return to her specific occupation,
whether this be gainful employment or homemaking; (*b*)

reintegration into the community; (c) whether there can be developed self-generating behavior that brings in a significant pleasurable return; this would include for younger patients help with career lines, resuming school, occupational training, and the learning of social skills.

It is obvious, after short reflection, that the criterion of discharge from the hospital is not one that favors the emergence of psychotherapy as a viable therapeutic tool. Not the least of the reasons for its inappropriateness is the fact that psychotherapy hinges on a subtle yet powerful factor of trust, a feeling of respect, expectation, and hope which the patient develops. These attitudes take time to form and more time to nurture. The therapist, whatever his persuasion, attempts to break into the isolation, loneliness, and for many patients the terrifying world of bewildering instability to become a stable figure on whom the patient can rely for advice, direction, interpretation, or mere presence. Therefore, one gets another perspective on the effectiveness of psychotherapy if one uses relapse rates as the criterion of outcome. While we await the follow-up data from the Camarillo study (14), the Hogarty-Goldberg (15) results strongly endorse a psychotherapeutic contact as having a significant effect on holding down rehospitalization rates. The psychotherapy employed in that study was a variant of avuncular guidance called "major role therapy." It was essentially vocational counseling and social casework in the context of firm interpersonal bonds. The statistics are instructive: at the end of twelve months after discharge from hospitals, 72 percent of the placebo-alone group relapsed; 63 percent of the group receiving placebo plus major role therapy relapsed; 33 percent of the phenothiazine group alone relapsed, and 26 percent of the group receiving drugs plus major role therapy relapsed. Clearly major role therapy helped reduce relapse rates over that of drugs alone. But even more striking is the fact that the major effect of the major role therapy begins to show itself only after seven months, particularly in combination with maintenance drug therapy. Individual differences among relapsers and nonrelapsers point to the necessity for further defining groups of patients along relevant demographic, cultural, clinical, and personologic characteristics in order to assess which patients will significantly profit from the particular brand of psychotherapy under study.

Increasing Specificity

The Hogarty-Goldberg study, then, is consistent with the view that psychosis is a phase of a schizophrenic adjustment which requires resolution by the most efficient means possible. Following this phase, a period of habilitation may be profitably introduced for some patients. For which patients the psychotherapeutic phase is required is a matter to be left to systematic research. There are many acutely schizophrenic patients who improve dramatically regardless of what we do; there are those who remain psychotic in spite of what we do; and there is a group of patients for whom it matters very much what we do. The question remains open as to what treatment is appropriate and adequate for which patients. What is missing from our research armamentarium is the use of sensitive instruments to detect the myriad intrapersonal changes that occur with and without psychotherapeutic intervention. There is no *a priori* reason to assume that the fantasy meaning attached by the patient to events in reality can be influenced only by one-to-one psychotherapy. Other clarifying interactions can occur on the ward, medication *can* clear cognition, and direct behavioral intervention as an access route to revamping symbolic processes remains a real and unassessed possibility.

A small number of dedicated psychotherapists devoting many years to the treatment of small numbers of patients have reported sporadic success with their schizophrenic patients (Fromm-Reichmann [16], Searles [17], Wexler

[18], Will [19], Sullivan [20], Ekstein [21]). While no systematic evaluation of the process was attempted by these gifted people, the length of time and the great absorption required for this kind of intensive procedure would make it unfeasible for the vast numbers of people diagnosed as schizophrenic. The theoretical rationale of this approach to psychotherapy assumes that the schizophrenic condition, like a symptom neurosis, is a compromise outcome of unconscious conflicts, resolvable with less pain to the person by psychoanalytic exploration. Without denying the role of internal conflict in schizophrenic disorganization, we would opt for relegating to it a contributory significance, secondary to what Freud called a "narcissistic disturbance" and which we would translate as "structural and developmental deviations in respect to one's self-feeling." Nonpsychological variables, we believe, must be recognized in this context, and to that extent pharmacologic treatment should be considered as part of the treatment program, particularly when psychotic symptoms are manifest. Since the investment of time is so great in this particular kind of psychotherapy, we would endorse it as a research technique into the schizophrenic experience rather than as an efficient therapeutic agent.

In a number of studies evaluating the relative merits of somatic treatment vs. psychotherapy it would seem that a principal reason that nonpsychological treatment such as drugs consistently are superior to psychosocial measures is that the special target of each therapy has not been recognized. Drugs will reduce thought disorganization, quiet an unruly and excited patient, or mobilize a withdrawn patient. It remains for psychosocial interventions to teach and to train, to reassure and to raise self-confidence, to help with skills for living which some patients may never have learned or learned badly. These interventions take time to become effective, but when they do there is some evidence, of which we need more to be certain of it, that less medication is needed to maintain a patient in a stage of remission.

In the early 1960s the field of the biochemistry of schizophrenia received a searching examination by Kety (22), who found many of the studies to be methodologically deficient. Unwarranted conclusions were seriously questioned by Kety. That review had the effect of improving the standards of many of the studies and ushered in a new era of biochemical advances with respect to schizophrenia. The field of the psychotherapy of schizophrenia could well profit from a similar intensive review of studies. That review would surely point to several of the issues raised in this paper. First, the nature of the outcome criteria: what is it that we expect psychosocial interventions to accomplish in which patients, at what stage of the disorder, by what kinds of therapy? Second, what is the role of intrapsychic conflict resolution in the treatment of the schizophrenias, at which stages of the disorder would it seem irrelevant, and at which stages would it seem helpful to introduce such a therapeutic regimen? Third, what is the role of teaching living skills to which patients? And fourth, what qualities of patient and therapist should be matched? This last point, one not developed in this paper, impresses us as having important consequences for effective treatment. The Whitehorn-Betz (23) categories of A-B therapists began the search into this area; we need now to probe further into this question, including the cognitive-stylistic organization (24, 25) of both patient and therapist to study the effect on various outcomes.

REFERENCES

1. Bochoven, J. S. *Moral Treatment in American Psychiatry.* New York: Springer, 1963.
2. Ayllon, T., and Azrin, N. *A Motivating Environment for Therapy and Rehabilitation.* New York: Appleton, 1968.
3. Hunt, H., and Dyrud, J. Perspective on behavior therapy. In *Research in Psychotherapy*, ed. J. M. Schlien. Washington: American Psychological Association, 1968, vol. 3, pp. 140–152.
4. Bleuler, E. *Dementia Praecox or the Group Schizophrenias* (1908), trans. J. Zinkin. New York: International Universities Press, 1950.
5. Laing, R. D. *The Divided Self.* London: Tavistock, 1960.
6. Menninger, K. Hope. *Am. J. Psy.*, 116:481–491, 1959.
7. Zilboorg, G. Ambulatory schizophrenia. *Psychiatry*, 4:149–155, 1941.
8. Heston, L. Foster home reared children of schizophrenic mothers. *Brit. J. Psy.*, 112:819–825. 1966.
9. Kety, S., Rosenthal, D., Wender, P., et al. The types and prevalence of mental illness in the biological and adoptive families of adopted schizophrenics. In *The Transmission of Schizophrenia*, ed. D. Rosenthal and S. Kety. New York: Pergamon, 1968, pp. 345–362.
10. Skinner, B. F. *Cumulative Record.* New York: Mamillan, 1961.
11. Meyer, A. The justification of psychobiology as a topic of the medical curriculm. *Psychol. Bull.*, 12:328, 1915.
12. May, P. R. A. *Treatment of Schizophrenia: A Comparative Study of Five Treatment Methods.* New York: Aronson, 1968.
13. Goldstein, M. J. Premorbid adjustment, paranoid states and patterns of response to phenothiazine in acute schizophrenia. *Schizophrenia Bull.*, Winter, 1970:24–39.

280 Psychotherapy of Schizophrenia

14. Hogarty, G., and Goldberg, S. Drug and sociotherapy in the post-hospital maintenance of schizophrenia. *Arch. Gen. Psy.*, 24:54–64, 1973.

15. Fromm-Reichmann, F. *Principles of Intensive Psychotherapy.* Chicago: University of Chicago Press, 1950.

16. Searles, H. F. *Collected Papers on Schizophrenia and Related Subjects.* New York: International Universities Press, 1965.

17. Wexler M. The structural problem in schizophrenia: therapeutic implications. *Int. J. Psychonal.*, 32:157–166, 1951.

18. Will, O. A., Jr. Schizophrenia, the problem of origins. In *The Origins of Schizophrenia*, ed. J. Romano. New York: Excerpta Medica Foundation, 1967, pp. 214–227.

19. Sullivan, H. S. *Schizophrenia as a Human Process.* New York: Norton, 1962.

20. Ekstein, R. *The Challenge: Despair and Hope in the Conquest of Inner Space.* New York: Brunner, 1971.

21. Kety, S. Biochemical theories and schizophrenia, part 1. *Science* 129:1528–1532, 1959.

22. Kety, S. Biochemical theories and schizophrenia, part 2. *Science*, 129:1590–1596, 1959.

23. Whitehorn, J. C., and Betz, B. J. A study of psychotherapeutic relationships between physicians and schizophrenic patients. *Am. J. Psy.*, 111:321–331, 1954.

24. Witkin, H., Lewis, H. B., and Weil, E. Affective reactions and patient-therapist interactions among more differentiated and less differentiated patients early in therapy. *J. Nerv. Ment. Dis.*, 146:193–208, 1968.

25. Gardner, R. W., Holzman, P. S., Klein, G. S., et al. Cognitive control. Psychol. Issues Mono. 4. New York: International Universities Press, 1959.

19

THERAPIES WITH SCHIZOPHRENICS
Lyman C. Wynne, M.D., Ph.D.

At the beginning of the paper entitled, "The Psychotherapy of Schizophrenia: Does It Work?" Dyrud and Holzman state: "Many a difficult question—such as the one posed here—has resolved itself into clearer focus by judicious rephrasing." They have noted ambiguities in the words "psychotherapy" and "schizophrenia" and the unsatisfactory criteria which have been used in the study of outcome. Although their article is thoughtful and thought-provoking, I believe their misgivings do not go far enough. Not only does there have to be consensus about the key concepts, but additionally this question can become meaningful and possibly answerable only if it is embedded in a context of questions about other therapies. Except with the least disturbed schizophrenics seen in office practice, one-to-one psychotherapy does not, in my view, constitute a viable therapeutic program with schizophrenics. Although individual psychotherapy can be a significant aspect of a therapeutic program, research that evaluates therapy should be oriented to the overall therapeutic effort and not be addressed to this or any other single component.

As a preliminary aside, before discussing the implications for research on this broader contextual problem, I suggest a couple of modifications in the phrasing of the question, "Does the psychotherapy of schizophrenia work?" First, it is preferable to frame questions about

Presented at the Conference on Psychotherapy of Schizophrenia, Stockbridge, Mass., October 13, 1972.

psychiatric treatment so as to acknowledge explicitly the fact that persons, not "diseases," are participants in the therapy. Schizophrenics, not schizophrenia, take part in therapy. Even if one speaks of schizophrenia as a disease for purposes of diagnostic or theoretical discussions, the therapeutic process necessarily involves persons in their total complexity. An adequate treatment program with schizophrenics cannot enduringly focus only upon whatever the therapist regards as the more or less specific symptomatic core of schizophrenia. Dyrud and Holzman have hopes of "specifying more of the 'nonspecific' therapeutic events in a patient's career." When this is achieved, the consequences for research on treatment then can be explored.

Second, as clinicians most of us now accept the notion that schizophrenics retain, or can regain, areas of positive functioning which coexist with whatever deficits are assumed to be present. Therefore, both in our therapies and in our research about these therapies, we should make explicit that we expect to collaborate *with* schizophrenics in understanding and building their strengths. I object to the distancing effect embedded in the notion of therapy *on* or *of* schizophrenia. Such distancing will seriously limit the patient's contribution to goal-setting and lead therapists to underestimate and misunderstand the patient's transactional impact.

More broadly, as I have mentioned, I doubt the wisdom of posing a question about treatment with schizophrenics in terms of *any single* form of therapy, individual psychotherapy, pharmacotherapy, or whatever. Further, I do not agree with the restricted definition of the term "psychotherapy," which Dyrud and Holzman have defined as "one-to-one treatment . . . a deliberate and specialized pursuit arising out of the patient's broader supportive milieu in which a variety of other psychosocial events occur." Given this definition, family and group psychotherapy are thereby set aside as merely supportive in a way which is contrary to current concepts and findings (cf., e.g., Wynne, 1974; O'Brien et al., 1972). I believe that the treatment of schizophrenics, as well as research which evaluates such treatment, will produce unclear and ambiguous results if any treatment modality, including one-to-one psychotherapy, is *enduringly* given priority. Such a restriction may, indeed, lead us to expect too much, at the wrong time, of one-to-one treatment, and actually undermine an adequate evaluation of the merits of this approach in those circumstances when it should be given priority.

The heterogeneity of schizophrenics and the variations over time of the individual patient are widely recognized. Nevertheless, many treatment programs seemingly ignore these differences. Most commonly, phenothiazines are administered as a routine, usually begun before a thorough baseline assessment has been carried out, and their use not altered until there are drug side effects or the patient is uncooperative, rather than because changes in clinical status have occurred. One-to-one psychotherapy, in a few institutions and by relatively few therapists, has been carried out with a comparable persistence, sometimes because of faith in the method or, in two or three programs, because of a research design. I am not aware of other disorders, except various forms of criminality, in which the treatment approach appears to be so slowly modified to suit the current clinical condition.

In individual psychotherapy with schizophrenics, the rationale for continuity is explicit and logical, though frequently challenged. The maintenance of a dedicated, individual psychotherapeutic relationship throughout long periods of negative or uncertain progress is, of course, believed to be essential for the trust and object constancy that may eventually facilitate enduringly positive change. Let us take for granted, for purposes of discussing research strategy, that this rationale constitutes a hypothesis worthy of continued evaluation. I choose not to consider here the profound research difficulties created by the great diversity in the personalities of psychotherapists and the ways in which they work with schizophrenics. Rather, my concern is with the problems as well as the opportunities created by the interweaving of individual psychotherapy with other processes or events.

First, let me give an example of a clinical situation in which the possible merits of individual psychotherapy were difficult, if not impossible, to evaluate. A week ago at Strong Memorial Hospital in Rochester, on a teaching round, I saw a young woman who was in a highly perplexed, acutely psychotic state of a few weeks' duration. She showed the characteristically schizophrenic pattern that Sullivan described as the "spread of meaning" (1940). She imbued commonplace stimuli with personalized meanings, could not sustain or build up any particular meaning, and was tossed and turned by stimuli because of a seeming impairment of her ability to screen out, or filter, what were, for her, fragments of experience. I learned that in her treatment several modalities and programs were being used simultaneously. She was being given phenothiazines, had an individual one-to-one relationship with a psychotherapist, and was participating both in an activities program off the in-patient floor as well as in milieu "community" meetings on the floor. The program approximated what has been called a "total push" intended to activate chronically apathetic schizophrenics. However, this patient was not chronic and overstabilized but acutely disorganized. Her presenting complaint was that she could not stand "all the lights."

Not unpredictably, this young woman had had a very chaotic life that at no point had been fully integrated. Recently, her life became even more complicated because she had just left her family to drive from the Pacific Coast to Rochester, New York, with a young man whom she had met just before the trip. No stable, interpersonal relationships were available to her in Rochester. She had moved to Rochester without really grasping that it was different from Manhattan. She expected to be mugged by Puerto Ricans if she stepped out of her room and, therefore, did not test to find out what this strange city was really like.

The patient and I talked quietly about where she now was and about matters in the hospital setting that might be simplified and clarified. In effect, this seemed to reduce the ambiguity of the environment, a term used by Dyrud and Holzman. Her anxiety level perceptibly dropped and her hallucinatory experience evaporated while we talked. Five days later, when I asked what was going on in the treatment with this patient, I learned that for the following two and a half to three days the patient had been dramatically free of symptoms. However, she then had an equally dramatic relapse and recurrence of psychotic symptoms. Inquiry revealed that the relapse began when she had been brought into a group therapy session on the floor with a number of acutely psychotic patients, none of whom she knew. The group also included six staff members, only one of whom she had seen before. Midway through this group therapy session, she was invited to express all of her thoughts, and she became grossly hallucinatory on the spot.

Meanwhile, the resident who was seeing the patient in one-to-one psychotherapy became very puzzled and discouraged about the effectiveness of his therapy. Until the relapse, he had been ascribing the patient's progress to events in the individual psychotherapy. Now he began to assume that he must be doing something wrong in his therapy with the patient and had formulated a plausible hypothesis. (It was only later that he put together a picture of the other events in the patient's ward experience and their timing.) The point I would like to make is not necessarily that he was inept in his psychotherapy or wrong in his hypothesis. Rather, he may well have been doing very expert one-to-one individual psychotherapy. Also some of the other things that were taking place, such as the group therapy, conceivably could have been quite appropriate and helpful at a *different* stage of this patient's disorder.

From this vantage point, it seems to me that despite the obvious difficulties of trying to look at the multiple types of psychosocial experiences and biologic-pharmacologic processes going on over time, unless we do obtain data about the major events both within the person and in the setting, I despair of our ability to evaluate *any one* of them. We all too readily give special weight to those factors which are most easily identified, such as the drugs which have been administered. Even drug evaluation has difficulties, as in the Hogarty-Goldberg study (1973). These investigators discovered that a high relapse rate was partially explained because only 50 percent of the patients who were given drugs were actually taking them.

Not only do we need to sort out the multiple kinds of events taking place at any given time, but we need to separate them *over* time. Clinically, I believe we all have noted that what is appropriate with the acutely psychotic patient, such as the one I have just described, differs from what is appropriate with, for example, a chronic, fixedly delusional paranoid. In the latter case, the therapist may want to jar the patient loose, and in the former the therapist may want to help the patient restrict and focus his attention.

Such considerations led me to conclude that, while we still should assess long-term outcome, it is often more realistic and appropriate to evaluate *short-term, problem-oriented* issues in relation to therapies that have both a short-term, problem-oriented goal and also pave the way for a later, often different treatment approach. The perplexity and fragmentation of acute schizophrenic psychoses is an example of a problem which could well be examined from this vantage point. The short-term problem of the acute, symptomatic state is usually treated at present with high doses of psychoactive drugs. An alternative, much less commonly attempted in recent years, is to establish an intensive, one-to-one relationship in an environment as simplified and free from ambiguity as possible. I believe that a focus on the here-and-now experience of the patient, without complex dynamic or "genetic" interpretations, is necessary at this stage. Also, collaborative therapy with the family and with staff in the treatment milieu is usually essential because of their involvement with the patient just before or soon after the onset of acute psychosis. Given an adequate support system of this kind, "interpersonal" therapy, as compared with an emphasis on pharmacotherapy during the acute psychosis, needs much more careful research scrutiny than it has yet received. The assessment should go beyond the speed with which the acute symptoms are relieved. It is my clinical impression, which I cannot substantiate with systematic data, that "snowing" an acutely psychotic patient with drugs may leave him more prone to relapse, and/or chronically fearful of relapse. In contrast, if the patient can experience the acute psychotic phase thoroughly but with sufficient support so that he is not enduringly panicked by possible recurrence, then the chances improve for a longer-term, positive result with less frequent relapses.

Thus, each form of treatment needs to be examined both in relation to the immediate problem or clinical state and in relation to its undermining other forms of treatment, then or later. It is often assumed by dynamic psychotherapists that resolution of intrapsychic conflict is necessary before substantial change in "external" behavior can be achieved. On the other hand, by building interpersonal skills through rather simple, nondynamic techniques, such as "role therapy" and behavioral modification therapy, the patient may be better able to structure himself and his experience of the world so that he can become more observant in psychotherapy of some of his intrapsychic processes. Many schizophrenics are so ill-equipped as to ordinary skills of living that such learning needs to be given a high priority in long-term treatment.

In these and other ways, positive effects of psychotherapy may be obscured or undermined by planned or unplanned life events. However, the converse possibility should also be considered: negative or dubious effects of psychotherapy under certain circumstances may be attenuated by benefits from other treatment modalities or from fortuitous changes in the patient's life. Because negative reactions and resistance are regarded as expectable aspects of psychotherapy, these are not bases for quickly interrupting a long-term psychotherapeutic effort. Nevertheless, at such times, recurrent questions are asked in an active clinical and research program: Should other modalities be added; should the individual psychotherapy be interrupted; should the therapist be changed?

If the design of research or therapy calls for stability and minimal change, then the individual psychotherapist may obtain little support and collaboration from others. Major changes may disrupt the research plan. My preference is to propose a more comprehensive research design in which such changes *are expected* and which can use the best clinical judgments that are available in bringing about changes in the treatment program that were not initially anticipated. One-to-one psychotherapy then becomes a component of the clinical program; the therapist is a member of the clinical team and not the primary decision-maker of the therapeutic plan. The head of the clinical team should be in a position to view the overall treatment context, to draw upon resources as needed, and, preferably, to be the primary family therapist.

For certain phases of therapy with schizophrenics, conjoint family therapy is highly facilitatory and is sometimes crucial in order to consolidate and sustain gains that may occur in individual psychotherapy. Usually two co-thera-pists—one oriented primarily to the family as a social unit and the other to the identified patient—make the most effective team. With schizophrenics and borderline patients and their families, who typically have a tenuous hold upon their experience of reality, concomitant individual and family therapy enhances, in my experience, the effectiveness of both, especially when symptoms are at a subacute level. Regardless of the details of such a clinical approach, it seems to me that, nearly always, other modalities besides individual psychotherapy should be introduced at various stages of treatment with schizophrenics. Hence, the research plan should acknowledge the clinical reality and not regard the rest of the program, other than the one-to-one psychotherapy, as a set of background events or "noise."

A collaborative treatment program complicates the research design in one sense, but also simplifies it by bringing more of the potentially significant data and variables into direct view. Often, staff participating in other parts of the clinical aspects can make useful research ratings of change.

The assessment of change should and can be carried out with standard instruments, relevant to multiple dimensions which are consistently studied despite changes in therapies. As examples, I would add to the suggestions of Dyrud and Holzman: the study of psychophysiologic reactivity, the use of the Self-Other Differentiation scale (Schulz), and a systematic assessment of the interpersonal network of family and family-surrogate roles and loyalties. This research approach would go well beyond, but include, gross and sometimes misleading measures such as length of hospitalization.

This is, however, not the appropriate occasion to attempt to elaborate further on many aspects of the evaluation of one-to-one psychotherapy with schizophrenics. Nevertheless, I have attempted to underline a clinical view with research consequences: Individual psychotherapy with schizophrenics should be embedded, and studied, in a context of other therapies. Unless this context is carefully taken into account, both the strengths and limitations of the individual psychotherapy itself cannot be systematically or sensibly assessed.

REFERENCES

1. Dyrud, J. E., and Holzman, P. S. The psychotherapy of schizophrenia: does it work? *Am. J. Psy.*, 130:670–673, 1973.
2. Hogarty, G. E., and Goldberg, S. C. Drug and sociotherapy in the aftercare of schizophrenic patients. *Arch. Gen. Psy.* 28:54–64, 1973.
3. O'Brien, C., Hamm, K., Ray, B., Pierce, J., Luborsky, L., and Mintz, J. Group vs. individual psychotherapy with schizophrenics. *Arch. Gen. Psy.* 27:474–478, 1972.
4. Sullivan, H. S. *Conceptions of Modern Psychiatry.* New York: Norton, 1940.
5. Wynne, L. C. Family and group treatment of schizophrenia: An interim view. In Cancro, R., Fox, N., and Shapiro, L. (eds.), *Strategic Intervention in Schizophrenia.* New York: Behavioral Publications, pp. 79–98, 1974.

20
FACTORS INFLUENCING THE SELECTION OF PATIENTS FOR INDIVIDUAL PSYCHOTHERAPY

John G. Gunderson, M.D.
Robert Hirschfeld, M.D.

Introduction

Individual psychotherapy has always been a relatively rare and expensive resource compared to the overall requirements for service by schizophrenic patients. Moreover, several studies have suggested that individual psychotherapy is not clearly beneficial for treating schizophrenia unless applied by gifted therapists or with optimally selected patients (1). These facts underscore the importance of developing means of maximizing the efficacy of psychotherapy by careful selection of appropriate patients. In this paper we have used the collective experience of eighteen senior and/or gifted therapists to develop guidelines that may be useful in selecting schizophrenic patients for individual therapy.*

Factors Assessed

Twenty-five experienced clinicians have met a number of times for the past two years to discuss various aspects of individual psychotherapy with schizophrenia (2, 3). One of

*Dr. Marvin Adland, Dr. Nathaniel Apter, Dr. Gerald Aronson, Dr. Jarl Dyrud, Dr. Stanley Eldred, Dr. David Feinsilver, Dr. John Fort, Dr. Beatriz Foster, Dr. Roy Grinker, Dr. James Grotstein, Dr. Arthur Malin, Dr. Clarence Schulz, Dr. Daniel Schwartz, Dr. Elvin Semrad, Dr. Helm Stierlin, Dr. Milton Wexler, Dr. Otto Will, Dr. Lyman Wynne.

the questions discussed was: How do you characterize the kinds of schizophrenic patients who will profit from individual psychotherapy in contrast to those who won't? Out of these discussions came a list of thirty-six factors that were grouped into five categories: symptomatic, demographic, historical, interpersonal, and ego function (see Table 1). The participants were then asked to score each of these factors from 1 to 7 in order of importance. A score of 1 indicated that factor was of no use to the clinician while a score of 7 indicated that the factor was always important and by itself a significant predictor of outcome from psychotherapy. We recognized that an important prognostic factor may occur rarely and on balance not be frequently useful. So we then asked the clinicians to review the list of factors and mark those they felt were most generally useful to them (although not necessarily as powerful as others). Because of the rather narrow range of scores given by each individual therapist, the raw scores for each clinician were converted to standard scores (using the mean and standard deviation of the raw scores as a base line for each clinician). Means were calculated from these standard scores. In addition, standard deviations were derived for each of the factors to determine the range of opinion on any given one.

TABLE 1
Prognostic Items

A. *Demographic*
1. pt. <15 y.o.
2. pt. >40 y.o.
3. first overt psychosis (vs. having had previous psychoses)
4. insidious onset
5. acute (vs. long-standing schizo.—i.e., chronic)
6. IQ <90 (subaverage)
7. ethnic-racial background differs from therapist's

B. *Historical*
   8. some academic success
   9. some talent
  10. some employment success
  11. habitual acting out
  12. has lived away from home successfully (i.e., w/o psychosis)
  13. has had heterosexual relationship
  14. has had heterosexual intercourse
  15. has been refractory to previous psychotherapy
  16. has improved on drugs
  17. known precipitating stress

C. *Interpersonal*
  18. interested, cooperative family
  19. family views problem as a disease
  20. interested helpful friends
  21. likeable
  22. interested in becoming "attached"
  23. is "real"
  24. shows disinterest in psychotherapy

D. *Symptomatic*
  25. is distressed by psychosis (ego dystonic)
  26. relates psychosis to life events
  27. displays painful affect
  28. has signs of depression
  29. is predominately paranoid, hebephrenic, catatonic, or simple
  30. is fragmented (vs. organized)

E. *Ego Functioning*
  31. can reality test
  32. can delay (has some self-control)
  33. can observe self
  34. can problem solve
  35. can integrate experience
  36. can tolerate pain

Demography and History

Table 2 shows a rank ordering of the degree of importance assigned to each of the thirty-six factors. No single factor emerged as having great predictive significance. For many therapists this was consistent with the belief that the therapist's personality, skill, and so on are as important or more so in determining the outcome of psychotherapy as is the patient presenting problems (3). We surveyed the range of items to look for natural clusterings that held together clinically regardless of the category (i.e., symptomatic, historical, etc.) of origin. We will discuss the results by category first, then attempt to integrate them.

Almost all categories of factors had considerable scatter which reflected the diversity of opinion about different individual items within a category. This was apparent most dramatically in the demographic category, which included both the most important and the least important factors. The two most important factors were insidious (vs. sudden) onset and acute (vs. chronic) course. This conforms to general clinical impressions as well as previous research evidence. The least important factor was having ethnic/racial background differences with the therapist. The unimportance assigned this factor seems to reflect a devaluation of attitudinal issues at the start of therapy (both the second and third least important items also concerned initial attitudes).

Among the *historical* factors, having a known precipitating stress was considered most important. This is consistent with the great weight given the demographic factors concerning acuteness of onset and duration. Still, the importance attached to knowing a precipitant is a valuable concept in itself. Assessment of this variable is readily obtainable, and it provides a valued means of entree into the patient's "real life." Some advocate this as the primary focus of the initial stage of treatment (4).

Among other historical factors, having displayed some employment success was adjudged much more important than having academic success. There was also a high level of agreement about the importance of these factors among the therapist group (i.e., low standard deviation). Apparently the skills needed for working well at a job are more useful allies for psychotherapy than are those skills needed for school success. This interpretation suggests that a steadily employed factory worker with a history of poor school achievement would be a better psychotherapeutic candidate than a comparably aged schizophrenic graduate student who never held a regular paying job. Similar to the lack of importance of academic success was the low value given having a particular talent (i.e., music, art, etc). These findings suggest that steadiness and reality-focused activities are stronger therapeutic allies than brains or talent. The value given to having lived away from home echos this overall impression that having found some areas of life sufficiently neutral to permit successful social-behavioral functioning is very important. Yet habitual acting out, which would seem to be at odds with employment success, reality oriented activities, and keeping psychotherapy appointments was given paradoxically little significance. It also seems to conflict with the importance some therapists attach to the capacity to delay. No logical interpretation of this confusing result is readily apparent.

The responses to a number of factors dealing with previous therapy and attitude toward treatment were interesting. Having had previous psychotic episodes, having been refractory to prior psychotherapy, having been drug responsive, and being disinterested in therapy were all considered relatively *un*important. Perhaps this is attributable, in part, to the reputation as gifted therapists that many of these clinicians have earned. Some of these therapists are used to dealing with the treatment failures of other therapists.

Ego Functioning

Three *ego function* factors were considered to be highly important. These were: reality testing, integrating experience, and the ability to observe oneself. Yet none of these three factors—nor any other ego function factor—was considered to be a commonly usable assessment criterion. In fact, though ego function factors were highest in overall importance as a group, they were lowest in the frequency with which they were considered useful indicators for prognosis in psychotherapy. This discrepancy may reflect several things. First, the ego function assessments require a degree of knowledge about a patient which may not be readily available during the initial evaluation. This is illustrated by the fact that the ego function "tolerates pain" was among the most controversial items (that is, it had the greatest range of importance attached to it) while the closely related symptom item "displays pain" was among those items that had the least range of controversy—that is, almost everyone scored it uniformly high. Second, some felt these ego functions are seldom present in any true schizophrenic psychosis. Several clinicians felt that being able to "reality test" or observe self were incompatible with being psychotic. Third, the ego functioning items were sometimes ambiguous for a given rater because they were often closely identified with a specific therapist or section of the country. In any event, the infrequency with which these items were thought to be useful, even though important, points to the need for other factors to assume greater predictive significance in selecting patients for psychotherapy.

Interpersonal Relations and Symptoms

Similarly, the *interpersonal* factors failed to emerge as having much usefulness in selecting patients for psychotherapy. Like the ego function factors, many of these items were closely connected with specific people or provincial interests. Unlike the ego function factors, none of these factors were considered to be particularly important. On the other hand, when given the opportunity to make added suggestions for the list of factors, many therapists concentrated their suggestions in this area. Yet even here there was little overlap as the therapists offered suggestions such as "can be empathic with the therapist," "elicits hopefulness in the therapist," "responds positively to interpretations," and "is interested in contact with therapist." Thus, many therapists value idiosyncratic interpersonal factors but none emerges as being of general usefulness.

The final category yielding important items was the *symptom* picture. The factor "patient is distressed by his psychosis" (i.e., he finds it ego dystonic) was not only important prognostically but also very frequently useful. Thus this quality is very powerful in the original assessment. The other important symptom, though not particularly common in its usage, was "displaying painful affect." Showing signs of depression was considered to be more frequently useful than displaying painful affect, but was slightly less important prognostically. The clinicians clearly indicated that catatonic and paranoid patients were better psychotherapy candidates than either hebrephrenic or simple schizophrenics. Yet this breakdown into traditional subtypes was not considered very important in comparison with most other items.

TABLE 2
Rand Ordering of Prognostic Items

1. insidious onset
2. acute (vs. long-standing schizo.—i.e., chronic)
3. can observe self
4. can reality test

5. can integrate experience
6. is distressed by psychosis (ego dystonic)
7. known precipitating stress
8. some employment success
9. displays painful affect
10. IQ <90 (subaverage)
11. has lived away from home successfully (i.e., w/o psychosis)
12. can delay (has some self-control)
13. relates psychosis to life events
14. interested, cooperative family
15. has signs of depression
16. likable
17. can problem solve
18. interested in becoming "attached"
19. can tolerate pain
20. first overt psychosis (vs. having had previous psychoses)
21. has had heterosexual relationship
22. pt. <15 y.o.
23. is "real"
24. is predominately paranoid, hebephrenic, catatonic, or simple
25. some talent
26. interested, helpful friends
27. some academic success
28. pt. >40 y.o.
29. has improved on drugs
30. habitual acting out
31. has had heterosexual intercourse
32. is fragmented (vs. organized)
33. has been refractory to previous psychotherapy
34. family views problem as a disease
35. shows disinterest in psychotherapy
36. ethnic-racial background differs from the therapist's

Conclusions

The general thrust of these results is to confirm previous studies on prognosis on schizophrenia[5,6] and to lend clinical authority to such studies. But these results also suggest a few variations beyond the traditional signs for good prognosis, which may aid selection of patients for individual psychotherapy. Such traditional prognostic signs for schizophrenics as heterosexual relationships, friendships, and likability and traditional motivational factors like attitudes towards illness or therapy were considered unimportant by the clinicians.

The following five factors integrate the results of this survey:
1. sudden (vs. insidious) onset
2. precipitant is known
3. psychosis is ego-dystonic
4. displays pain, depression
5. employment or academic success outside nuclear home

They tap different areas of function (e.g., demographic, historical, and symptomatic) and should have some independence from each other. Moreover, they present no major assessment problem. This is indeed a fortuitous and unpredicted finding. Thus it appears that even the most experienced sophisticated clinicians would be unwilling to trust prognostications for therapy on their early assessments of such subjective qualities such as ego function and interpersonal factors.

Future research is planned to evaluate the actual prognostic significance of these factors for individual psychotherapy. A similar study by Auerbach, Luborsky, and Johnson using clinicians experienced with neurotic patients has been reported (7). For the present, we recommend that

schizophrenic patients being considered for individual psychotherapy should be evaluated on the basis of these five
qualities. We believe that the enormous clinical experience
utilized in deriving these five qualities provides them prima
facie validity as rational guides for selection.

REFERENCES

1. Feinsilver, D. B., and Gunderson, J. G. Psychotherapy of schizophrenia: is it indicated? A review of the relevant literature. *Schizophrenia Bulletin*, Fall (6):11–23, 1972.
2. Friedman, R. J.; Gunderson, J. G.; and Feinsilver, D. B. The psychotherapy of schizophrenia: an NIMH program. *Amer. J. Psychiatry*, 130:674–677, 1973.
3. Gunderson, J. G. Controversies about psychotherapy of schizophrenia. *Amer. J. Psychiatry*, 130:677–681, 1973.
4. Semrad, E. V. A clinical formulation of the psychoses. In *Teaching Psychotherapy of Psychotic Patients*, ed. D. Van Buskirk, pp. 5–17. New York: Grune & Stratton, 1969.
5. Philips, L. Case history data and prognosis in schizophrenia. *J. of Nervous and Mental Disease*, 117 (6):515–525, 1953.
6. Vaillant, G. E. The prediction of recovery in schizophrenia. *J. of Nervous and Mental Disease*, 135:534–543, 1962.
7. Auerbach, A. R.; Luborsky, L.; and Johnson, M. Clinicians' predictions of outcome of psychotherapy: a trial of a prognostic index. *Amer. J. Psychiatry*, 128:830–835, 1972.

21

SELF AND OBJECT DIFFERENTIATION AS A MEASURE OF CHANGE IN PSYCHOTHERAPY

Clarence Schulz, M.D.

Ego Boundaries

The Washington study group on schizophrenia[1] has been focusing on the concept of self-differentiation and object-differentiation as an important aspect of the theory of psychopathology of schizophrenia. In the course of our discussions we have evolved a clinical rating scale to help us assess changes in the patient related to this differentiation of self-representation from object-representation.

The theoretical concept had its earliest formulations in Tausk's use of the phrase "loss of ego boundaries." The metapsychological description has been quite clearly elaborated and formulated by Edith Jacobson.[2]

The baby's wish for oneness with the mother, founded on fantasies of oral incorporation of the love object, will easily bring about refusions between self- and love-object images whenever the child experiences gratifications, physical contact, and closeness with the mother. Evidently, such experiences of merging with the love object are always connected with a temporary weakening of the function of perception— i.e., of the awakening sense of reality—and with a return to the earlier, undifferentiated state.

[1]The group consists of Drs. Marvin Adland, David Feinsilver, John Fort, John Gunderson, Clarence Schulz, Helm Stierlin, and Lyman Wynne.
[2]Edith Jacobson follows the concepts originally proposed by Mahler.

Kernberg has described self-object fusion as the distinctive aspect of psychosis to differentiate it from the borderline states. In Kernberg's descriptions, borderlines and psychotics might both show regressive phenomena and primitive defenses such as splitting, denial, projection.

To review briefly the parallel correlates with normal human development, it is postulated that the postnatal infant shows no awareness of a separateness of itself from its surroundings. Gradually, as the nervous system matures, together with the developmental aspects of the early primitive ego apparatus, the child experiences a fleeting sense of some separateness from its mother. This takes place in a situation of gratification and frustration. There gradually develop repeated fusions and mergings of self with other, alternating with gradually increasing delineation of a separateness. These awarenesses are designated as "self-representations" and "object-representations" (Jacobson). It is important to remember that initially the self is experienced as a body self or "body ego" (Freud). It has also been postulated that there exist separate divisions of "good" and "bad" selves as well as separate "good" and "bad" objects. It seems that schizophrenic patients have never established a clearly delineated differentiation of self from other, or at least they are vulnerable to a greater readiness to the blurring of these distinctions. Our study group decided to see if we could establish a scale for the evaluation of the development of the patient's capacity to retain differentiation while establishing empathic closeness with another during the course of psychotherapy (Table 1).

Fear of Loss of Self: An Example

A brief clinical description will serve to make this theoretical formulation more clinically relevant. The patient showed some other prominent aspects of what we come to find characteristic of the clinical picture in schizophrenia, including fear of hostility and conflicts about expressing this, loneliness, withdrawal, and so forth, but here we will be focusing mainly on the signs and symptoms that seem to have more direct bearing on the self-representation/object-representation question. This is an eighteen-year-old high school graduate who had had several hospitalizations, usually precipitated by suicide attempts. The onset occurred about two years prior to the present treatment experience. There were prominent depressive themes throughout her clinical course. She was dressed in a manner characteristic of her age group: blue jeans, a bulky sweater, her hair combed straight and long. She tended to speak in a very quiet voice and always wore a bit of red, which she considered her trademark. Her presenting problem was her concern that she did not know whether she was dead or alive. She spoke of her fear of others, her reluctance to approach other people for fear that others would control her. She elaborated and said that she was afraid that if she becomes close and the other person leaves and turns out to be untrustworthy she will then hate herself and it was safer to withdraw. A further description of the uncertainty about whether she was alive or dead indicated her fear that she would lose her "self."

During the course of her psychotherapy, a friend who visited her in the hospital told her that just because she told someone her thoughts, it did not mean that these thoughts no longer belong to her. This comment seemed to make a big difference to the patient. We focused on when the sense of feeling swallowed up or engulfed would occur, and she described an occasion when this happened during a visit from her mother. She thought of her mother as a huge amoeba. On further inquiry, it was discovered that it was precisely at the point where they discussed plans for a holiday dinner together that she experienced this fear of being swallowed up. She described a dream of being quite angry at her father and telling an aide about these feelings. Still in the dream, as she told about the feelings she got more and more out of control, and was then thrown in seclusion, as she put it. Then, still continuing in the dream, when her mother visited, the patient was let out of seclusion. She then became more disturbed and was put back in seclusion. In addition to the dream illustrating her concern about her anger getting out of control, I also saw in it that in her anxiety in relation to her mother her anger, lack of control, use of seclusion room, and perhaps her psychiatric illness itself was a way of keeping away from her mother.

At one session she was unable to talk at all. She was unable to divulge her "secret." Finally she decided that since this was a Friday, she might be able to tell her friend first over the weekend and then after this be able to talk with me about it the first of the next week. I think this served as a way of interposing a barrier between us and thereby to reinforce the differentiation. Also, by including this friend, it tended to dilute the intensity of the treatment relationship as well as a way of getting the therapist to inquire and pursue to foster a kind of differentiated relatedness. Eventually, the "secret" turned out to be angry feelings toward the therapist in relation to a sense of distrust that had been displaced from some feelings after receiving a message from her brother. On another occasion, after a session in which I speculated that her creation of a painting may have served as part of its purpose the solution to an aspect of her treatment, much as a dream would do, she felt "robbed." It was as though the picture were not solely created by herself and for herself. When I pointed out that perhaps one thing that is an important characteristic of painting is that it's not done with anyone else, she said she had always had trouble joining others in a project such as a school paper. The solo aspect of painting did appeal to her. In treatment, there were frequent instances of her concern about closeness and involvement with me. When she realized that her sessions were becoming important to her, she would try to push the thought away. Eventually the patient did show greater understanding of her dependent attachment to her mother, and a greater ability to deal more forthrightly with her mother's reciprocal dependency on her.

Development of
the S.O.D. Scale

We began by using the scale on a small sample of seven patients. It had been our intention not to attempt comparison of one patient with another, but rather to compare the same patient with himself over a period of time. We asked the therapist to do the ratings at three points in time. The first two ratings were separated by a period of two months or so, and the third rating was done a week after the second rating. This latter step was suggested by Dr. Michael Sachs of NIMH, with a view to testing the reliability of the person filling out the scale. The person analyzing the data did not know that the third rating followed so closely on the heels of the second, and commented that to all intents and purposes, all of the change came on the second rating, with the third rating having no effect. The seven patients were in treatment with six different therapists. Each patient showed a total score shift to the right, which should reflect improvement, since the higher the score, the more positive the implications. The sample was too small to evaluate the individual items. We did, however, make some changes in the current revision after this pilot sampling. The items have been grouped under four headings and the scale itself is accompanied by the explanation of each item. Our first version of the scale showed a five-point spread. In the total of all scorings the extremes of 1 and 5 accounted for 15 percent of all ratings. By changing to a spread of 1 to 7, we are hoping for a finer discrimination of change. An item in the original scale has been dropped. We had asked the therapist to assess his countertransference on a symbiotic vs. a more differentiated level. The idea behind this was derived from Searles's writings on the phases of treatment, and it seemed appropriate that an assessment of change in the therapist's responses would reflect a change in the patient. In the actual scoring of this item, there was practically no change. It was far below any of the other items. Explanations for this might be found in the difficulty the therapist might have in detecting shifts in countertransference, or it may simply be that two or three months is not long enough to reflect change in this area.

These questions bring up major questions for which we shall be seeking answers. What are we measuring, anyway? Would change on this scale merely parallel changes by already established scales? Is it possible that patients can improve with no change in self-object differentiation, which is, after all, postulated as a fundamental underlying psychopathological fault?

In our opinion, the total score on the scale would not be useful in comparing one patient with another, and therefore it is not a useful prognostic device. Rather, it is the comparison of the same patient at different periods of time that we hope will reflect some direction in the course of treatment.

Our plan now is to try out the scale in its revised form with a large number of patients—schizophrenic and others —with a variety of therapists in different treatment settings.

We are concerned about the bias that exists with therapists who wish to see their patients improve—almost a universal phenomenon—and consequently reflect this in their ratings. In addition to therapists, the scale will be scored by clinical administrators, nurses, chiefs of service, and supervisors to offset therapist bias. Anyone who uses the scale will require some preliminary orientation to these concepts.

We shall also have a group do ratings after observing a one-way-vision interview to check variations among raters. At a later time, the same group will do ratings with the same interviewer-patient combination.

One by-product of our efforts so far has made it easier to pursue this study. The therapists have been enthusiastic in using the scale as a check list in carrying on their psychotherapy. The scale has functioned as a useful teaching device.

TABLE 1
Scale for Self-Representation
Object-Representation Differentiation
(SOD)

Patient ....
Sex..
Age ....
Diagnosis..
DSM No...
Date ....
Weeks of therapy with this therapist...
Person filling out scale ....
Years in psychiatry..
Profession ....

1. Manifestations primarily related to patient-psychotherapist transactions but also ratable by other staff.

   a. Patient oversensitive to intrusive aspects of therapeutic situation.   1 2 3 4 5 6 7   Readily discloses information.

   b. Countertransference fusion of patient and therapist.   1 2 3 4 5 6 7   Clear delineation of patient and therapist.

   c. Accentuation of great gulf of inequality between therapist and patient.   1 2 3 4 5 6 7   Permits closer approximation of patient-therapist status.

d. Inability to agree / disagree 1 2 3 4 5 6 7   Able to agree / disagree
with therapist in a discrimi-   with therapist in a discrim-
natory way.   inatory way.

e. Agreement / consensus / 1 2 3 4 5 6 7   Agreement / consensus /
closeness with therapist as-   closeness with therapist
sociated with engulfment /   enhances sense of self-
being swallowed up / nega-   identity.
tivism.

f. Patient confuses role with 1 2 3 4 5 6 7   Collaborates with thera-
that of therapist.   pist with clear delineation
                                                    of roles.

2. Manifestations apparent in patient's interactions with all staff.

a. Misidentification of self / 1 2 3 4 5 6 7   Clear perception of self /
others.   others.

b. Pre-ambivalent (split) view 1 2 3 4 5 6 7   Fusion of "good" / "bad"
of others / self as "good" /   into ambivalence.
"bad."

c. Gender identity confusion. 1 2 3 4 5 6 7   Stable sense of sexual
                                                    identity.

d. Patient's experience be- 1 2 3 4 5 6 7   Privacy of body and men-
lieved to be the experience   tal experience.
of the other person.

e. Excessive stimulus input 1 2 3 4 5 6 7   Relative freedom from
needed to maintain sense of   physical contact need.
body identity.

f. Overreaction to loss of 1 2 3 4 5 6 7   Acceptance of loss as nat-
body parts.   ural function.

g. Inability to see self as se- 1 2 3 4 5 6 7   Capacity to see self as separate from the surround-   parate from surroundings.
ings.

h. Pretransference (autistic, 1 2 3 4 5 6 7   Transference relationship.
symbiotic) relationship.

i. Confusion / disorganization 1 2 3 4 5 6 7   Feeling (grief / guilt / an-
/ paranoid response to sepa-   ger / tenderness) respon-
ration from others or change   ses to separation from
in patient's situation.   others or change.

j. Patient avoids close / inten- 1 2 3 4 5 6 7   Capacity for intimate rela-
sive relationships or has   tionships.
many superficial relation-
ships.

Explanation for S.O.D. Scale

1. Manifestations primarily related to patient-psychotherapist transaction but also ratable by other staff

   a. Patient oversensitive to in- 1 2 3 4 5 6 7   Readily discloses informa-
   trusive aspects of therapeu-   tion.
   tic situation.

   Patient complains of living in a goldfish bowl or seems to absent himself in the bathroom at the time of the appointments. In the verbal exchange, the patient shows a guardedness to the therapist's questioning and often reverses the questioning. Experiences the session as concern that the therapist will control, use it against him, and often withholds his "secrets." Complete opposition to disclosure would score as 1. Partial disclosure followed by guardedness would score as 4.

   b. Countertransference fusion 1 2 3 4 5 6 7   Clear delineation of pa-
   of patient and therapist.   tient and therapist.

   The therapist shows symbiotic countertransference phase phenomena (Searles). Slips of the tongue mix up therapist and patient. Therapist unable to tell whether quotation is from himself or patient. Staff sees therapist as extremely "overinvolved." This should score as 1. When therapist and patient are seen as alternating between symbiosis and "objectivity," it would score as 4.

   c. Accentuation of great gulf 1 2 3 4 5 6 7   Permits closer approxima-
   of inequality between thera-   tion of patient-therapist
   pist and patient.   status.

   The patient emphasizes the difference between patient and therapist, such as items on religion, value systems, intelligence, competence, gender, approach to treatment, medications. Immediate and consistent emphasis on differences would score as 1. Ambivalent, brief toleration approaching equality would score as 4.

   d. Inability to agree / disagree 1 2 3 4 5 6 7   Able to agree / disagree
   with therapist in a discrimi-   with therapist in a discrim-
   natory way.   inatory way.

   The patient disagrees with almost everything or, in an opposite way, the patient shows an excessive compliance with all of the therapist's statements. In either case, there is a lack of listening, weighing, and giving an independent opinion, and should score as 1. When patient shows a moderate ability to discriminate, it would score as 4.

   e. Agreement / consensus / 1 2 3 4 5 6 7   Agreement / consensus /
   closeness with therapist as-   closeness with therapist
   sociated with engulfment /   enhances sense of self-
   being swallowed up / nega-   identity.
   tivism.

   There will be a repeated sequence whereby the experience of the patient's being understood by the therapist will be experienced as a threat to the patient. Any warmth, expressed concern, or tenderness on the part of the therapist or patient will immediately be followed by an undoing of this out of fear of being engulfed.

Sometimes clarity with a patient who is otherwise confused will bring about the same result. Patients will defend against merging with negativism. Inability to tolerate any closeness would score as 1. Brief, transient, unsustained closeness would be scored as 4.

f. Patient confuses role with   1 2 3 4 5 6 7   Collaborates with thera-
   that of therapist.   pist with clear delineation
                                               of roles.

The patient might insist on occupying the therapist's chair or ask questions in the manner of the therapist. This would score as 1. Patient might occasionally offer to interpret dreams of the personnel or to set up appointments with fellow patients. This would score as 4.

2. Manifestations apparent in patient's interactions with all staff

a. Misidentification of self /   1 2 3 4 5 6 7   Clear perception of self /
   others.   others.

Misperceptions of people, either himself or others, usually in terms of important figures from the past. Patient might say he had known another patient when they went to school together or that he met the therapist in some previous travels. A clear delusional misidentification would score 1. Gross identification with or feeling like being the therapist would be 4.

b. Pre-ambivalent (split) view   1 2 3 4 5 6 7   Fusion of "good" / "bad"
   of others / self as "good" /   into ambivalence.
   "bad."

These patients clearly divide the environment into populations of those who are all good and those who are all bad. Similarly, therapists and other staff are split into good and bad. Patient also has total reactions in his attitudes about himself as being good or bad or rapidly alternating from one to the other. It is the totality that is characteristic and when present in clear dichotomy should be scored as 1. Alternations between ambivalence and splitting into good and bad should score as 4.

c. Gender identity confusion.   1 2 3 4 5 6 7   Stable sense of sexual
                                               identity.

A patient uncertain as to what sex he is or indicates that the one side of his body is male and the other side female would score as 1. A patient frequently referring to himself as herself as though he or she were of the opposite sex would score as 4.

d. Patient's experience be-   1 2 3 4 5 6 7   Privacy of body and men-
   lieved to be the experience   tal experience.
   of the other person.

The patient talks about reading the therapist's mind or the therapist's reading the patient's mind. If the patient has a headache, the other person also has a headache. There is a sense of a lack of privacy and delineation, such as thoughts being broadcast on radio or TV. As soon as the patient thinks something, the therapist knows this without the patient having to tell the therapist. If of delusional proportions, score a 1. Attitudes reflecting the notion that therapist ought to know patient's thoughts would score as 4.

e. Excessive stimulus input 1 2 3 4 5 6 7   Relative freedom from
   needed to maintain sense of   physical contact need.
   body identity.

The patient will be involved in activities that provide an afferent input, such as rocking, self-injury, gorging, starving, smoking, shouting until hoarse, self-mutilation, head banging. When almost continuously present should be scored as 1. If able to have periods of only moderate physical input should be scored as 4.

f. Overreaction to loss of 1 2 3 4 5 6 7   Acceptance of loss as nat-
   body parts.   ural function.

Patients will show anxiety and opposition over routine clinical care items, such as blood samples, fingernails, haircut, feces, and urine. Often these things might be retained, causing severe discomfort. This, in turn, helps the patient experience a sense of body self. Absolute refusal by patient scores as 1. Reluctance or apprehension scores as 4.

g. Inability to see self as se- 1 2 3 4 5 6 7   Capacity to see self as separate from the surround-   parate from surroundings.
   ings.

The patient personalizes ordinary environmental stimuli and shows hyperacuity toward such stimuli. The airplane flying overhead has a message. A delusional idea of reference scores as 1. If patient pays attention to these stimuli but knows there is no connection with him, it would score 4.

h. Pretransference (autistic 1 2 3 4 5 6 7   Transference relationship.
   symbiotic) relationship.

The patient projects feelings of himself onto the therapist or others. The patient will express instant global reactions to the therapist, such as panic, aggression, complete withdrawal, overwhelming love, rather than more selective "transference" responses. This would score 1. If patient sometimes projects and sometimes transfers, it would score 4.

i. Confusion / disorganization 1 2 3 4 5 6 7   Feeling (grief / guilt / an-
   / paranoid response to sepa-   ger / tenderness) respon-
   ration from others or change   ses to separation from
   in patient's situation.   others or change.

The patient shows regressive or psychotic defense and symptomatology, especially in response to separation experiences, such as the end of the session, at weekends, or at vacations, or if the therapist is sick. With some patients, the separation may be as minor as the therapist's not hearing a remark or daydreaming briefly or even losing eye contact with the patient for a moment. Extreme intolerance would score as 1. Patients also show these symptoms upon any move of closeness toward the therapist when such is especially highlighted around making the patient aware of the closeness and attachment at the time of separation. Mixtures of affective experience together with resorting to regressive defense would score as 4.

j. Patient avoids close / inten- 1 2 3 4 5 6 7   Capacity for intimate rela-
   sive relationships or has   tionships.
   many superficial relation-
   ships.

Patient may avoid all relationships or frequently will show relationships with several people. If dating, will have several girl friends and will be threatened if it becomes serious at any point. Patient diversifies his investment like a mutual fund. Such patients often request a change in assignment of therapist if situation gets to be too close. Inability to tolerate any close relationship scores a 1. Ability to have a brief intensive relationship followed by withdrawal would score as 4.

22

SCHIZOPHRENIC CORE DISTURBANCES
Helm Stierlin, M.D., Ph.D.

The preceding presentation relied on a theoretical perspective on schizophrenia to which E. Jacobson, M. Mahler, A. Modell, O. Kernberg, H. Searles, and L. C. Wynne, among others, have contributed. Here I want to focus on the concept of a "schizophrenic core disturbance" which the above perspective suggests. This concept, as I shall try to show, may order and link various forms of the schizophrenic disorder and may permit a more natural clarification of subtypes of schizophrenia than seems feasible within existing frames of reference.

A Comparison with Bleuler's Concept of Schizophrenia

The core disturbance under discussion can be called the disturbance in self-differentiation or, more briefly, the schizophrenic "differentiation disturbance." E. Bleuler introduced a similarly pivotal concept when he focused on the schizophrenic's "loosening of associations." Equipped with this concept, Bleuler explained schizophrenic symptoms as either direct manifestations of a loosening of associations (reflecting a breakdown of the hierarchic structure of our thought processes) or as secondary, substitutive phenomena. He used Freud's earlier psychoanalytic ideas to make this theory convincing. To underpin it, he adduced genetic, developmental, and transactional viewpoints.

The concept of a differentiation disturbance, as here presented, is both like and unlike Bleuler's core concept. Space does not permit me to trace the similarities and differences in detail. Suffice it to say that the concept of a differentiation disturbance zeroes in on what we believe is most specific and salient in schizophrenia while it yet allows us to see schizophrenic phenomena on a continuum with "normal" phenomena. (The comparison with essential hypertension, introduced some time ago by L. C. Wynne, seems useful here: at the one extreme, we can speak of a hypertensive core disturbance when hypertension, enduringly established, can be measured by all willing and equipped to do so; at the other extreme of the continuum, we find normal blood pressure notwithstanding its fluctuations in response to stresses, different life situations, time of the day, etc. In between, linking the two extremes, is a gray, transitional zone where some observers see essential hypertension and others not, depending on their vantage points, measurements, time of observations, etc.)

Like Bleuler's concept of a core disturbance, our concept of a differentiation disturbance opens up, as well as implies, a supportive genetic, developmental, and transactional perspective. Here we shall mainly focus on the developmental perspective, yet try also to do some justice to the transactional perspective.

Two Varieties of "Differentiation Disturbance"

To grasp the developmental perspective, we must now return to the earlier presented clinical case (see Chapter 5) and the S.O.D. rating scale (see Chapter 20). We note here that the "differentiation disturbance" can reflect either of two trends: one toward symbiotic fusion, and another toward autistic isolation. Symbiotic fusion, for example, looms when the self, its boundaries permeable, cannot be differentiated from other objects. In contrast, autistic isolation threatens when this self, inflexibly and insensitively, walls itself off in autism or exaggerated separateness. Either of these defensive trends may harden into a relatively enduring adaptive or, better, nonadaptive life style, or may transiently blend into, or alternate with, the other trend.

The "Differentiation Disturbance" in Wider Developmental Perspective

The meaning of these two trends becomes clearer when we consider self-differentiation, as earlier described, within the larger process of human differentiation-integration. This larger process unfolds in accord with a widely accepted developmental principle that H. Werner stated as follows: "Wherever development occurs, it proceeds from a state of relative globality and lack of differentiation to a state of increasing differentiation, articulation, and hierarchic integration."

Within this larger process, differentiation precedes integration. Only after bodily or psychologic processes and capacities have become at least partially differentiated can they become hierarchically integrated, organized, and related to one another. Thus, "part and whole, event and context, self and non-self, become articulated" (Wynne and Singer). Once the developmental process has come under way, any gain in integration tends to promote further differentiation. And so on. The relation between differentiation-integration is thus reciprocal and the development expands spirally—that is, leads to ever new levels of intrapsychic and interpersonal complexity.

A failure in self-differentiation, as sketched out earlier, crucially interferes with the achievement of such intrapsychic and interpersonal complexity. The nature and timing of such interference seems here central. The earlier and the more massive the interference, the more will later processes of differentiation-integration be blocked or thrown off track. The ego, the chief agent as well as object of differentiation-integration, will then be deformed or damaged. From this vantage point, the schizophrenic differentiation disturbance reflects primarily a failure and derangement of ego development.

A Theoretical Framework for Classifying Types of Schizophrenia

Within the above developmental model we can distinguish, first, *arrests of differentiation*; second, *regressive or defensive dedifferentiations*; and, third, *uneven, dysfunctional differentiations*.

Each disturbance in differentiation characterizes one type of schizophrenia. In each case the spiraling development toward increasing differentiation and integration is hampered, but in differing ways and with differing implications for growth and therapy. Given the complexity of life processes, none of these types is likely to occur in pure culture. Rather, most adult schizophrenias will reflect a blend of the above three possible disturbances, with one usually being dominant. It is this relative dominance of one type of "differentiation disturbance" which allows us to classify schizophrenic disorders.

Schizophrenic Disturbances Characterized Chiefly by Arrest of Differentiation

Here belong two varieties of so-called process schizophrenia, both of which reflect rather enduring characteristics or life styles: (*a*) an amorphous, undifferentiated, seemingly symbiotic variety, and (*b*) an "autistic" variety, which may consolidate into a paranoid state. In the first variety, self-object boundaries appear excessively fluid and permeable; in the second, they are rigidly sealed off, the individual seeking his salvation in a precocious pseudo-autonomy.

Schizophrenic Disturbances Characterized Chiefly by a Predominance of Regressive (or Defensive) Dedifferentiation

Here belong many of those acute schizophrenic disturbances in which reactive and defensive aspects stand out. The individual's previously achieved level of self-object differentiation is likely to return (or even to improve) once he has worked through critical problems in living (e.g., threats of intimacy or conflicts over separation from parents).

Schizophrenic Disturbances Characterized Chiefly by the Dominance of Uneven, Dysfunctional Differentiation

Again, two major varieties are possible, both of which reflect relatively enduring schizophrenic characteristics or life styles: (*a*) a (relatively) underdifferentiated variety with (relatively) "soft" self-object boundaries, strong field dependence (á la Witkin), proneness to shame, hallucinations, and an anaclitic, symbiotic cast; and (*b*) a (relatively) overdifferentiated, field-independent, paranoid, delusional, and/or autistic variety where a rigid pseudo-autonomy is (overtly) sought and defended.

The Implied Transactional Perspective

In the foregoing I have outlined a developmental perspective that allows us to classify certain types of schizophrenia. This developmental perspective, though, is not enough. It must be made multidimensional, as it were, by integrating it with a transactional perspective (and with a genetic perspective that here is totally omitted). This point is crucial. From the beginning, such transactional perspective was implied in the above developmental perspective, as our definition of the schizophrenic core disturbance linked this disturbance expressly to the achievement of, or failure to achieve, closeness or empathy with another person. Closeness and empathy are transactional dimensions. This means that any disturbance of self-differentiation, in order to be experienced, assessed, or corrected, must include reference to the relevant transactional context. This holds particularly true for all relationships intended to be therapeutic. The other (or others) with whom one seeks or fears closeness or empathy must always be kept in the picture. This applies typically to the clinical phenomena summarized in the differentiation scale. But this theme— i.e., the needed reconciliation of a transactional with the above developmental perspective—although crucial to our concept of a schizophrenic core disturbance, cannot here be elaborated.

23

ALTERNATIVE
MEANS OF MEASURING CHANGE
Elvin V. Semrad, M.D.

Ego Profile Scale

The Washington study group on schizophrenia has been focusing on the concept of self-differentiation and object differentiation as an important aspect of the theory of psychopathology of schizophrenia ("the differentiation disturbance"). In the course of their discussions, a clinical rating scale evolved to help assess change in the patients related to this differentiation of self-representation from object representation. Although we are of the same theoretical persuasion (1), differences of language that grow from efforts to capture common clinical experience have made it necessary for me to translate, I hope correctly, some of the items that the group had selected to rate. The authors centered their attention around the self-object axis and illustrated this in their clinical vignettes in order to capture the series of "stopways" on the route from the more immature to the more mature state in the course of therapy. Their focus on the differentiation of self from object representation implies that "the schizophrenic core disturbance is a disturbance in self-differentiation." They link this disturbance developmentally to the achievement of, or failure to achieve, closeness and empathy with another person. I agree that any disturbance of self-differentiation, in order to be experienced, assessed, or corrected, must include reference to the relevant transactional context and agree this is particularly true for all relationships intended to be therapeutic.

I share with the authors a hope that the development of a clinical rating scale to measure change during therapy will allow more meaningful understanding of clinical states (27, 28, 31) in the schizophrenias than do such concepts as diagnosis and symptom clusters, as they are observed during states of regression and return to more optimal ego functioning as the result of therapeutic interventions.[1]

The Ego Profile Scale (18) represents our effort to devise an instrument that would be useful in making more precise statements about progress and prognosis. I like to think in terms of purpose, and for that reason our Ego Profile Scale uses statements of behavioral manifestations for simpler rating and assessment than is used in the S.O.D. Scale.

Object Relations Patterns

The assumptions upon which the scale (18) is built are derived from years of clinical experience with schizophrenic patients. They are:

---

[1]A comprehensive clinical approach (2, 3, 4, 5) to assist the schizophrenic person in his improvement, rehabilitation, and possible recovery is a general objective—the development of his capacity to love, live, and work in a reasonable degree of subjective comfort. The approach is primarily psychotherapeutic. This includes the personal diagnostic processes, prescription and use of impersonal processes, the ego compensation processes, the ego maintenance processes, and finally the analysis of the psychosis-vulnerable ego (intensive-dynamic psychotherapy). We emphasize the need to differentiate psychosis vulnerability from psychosis proper (7, 8) and view the psychosis proper essentially as a regressive phenomenon, a decompensation, with the compensation process structured (9) to enable the patient to return from regression to optimum ego functioning for himself. We have observed that after recompensation there follows a period of nine to twelve months during which the patient works to reestablish relationships with his own objects, aided by the patterns of his experience with his therapist. He is helped to recognize his own contributions to his maladjustment by analysis or his ego functioning in relation to his life issues. This nine-to-twelve-month period is also referred to as the ego maintenance processes. By mutual agreement, therapist and patient often agree to terminate official visits at this point. Availability for maintenance support must remain a possibility. The sustenance, support, and gratification of a patient in therapeutic alliance provides a corrective ego experience (6) crucial for ego compensation and capacity to forge into a transference relationship and intensive psychotherapy to study psychosis vulnerability in a manner that we know in psychoanalysis.

(*a*) The manner in which a patient negotiates his relationships with a meaningful object, including, of course, therapists, is habitual with him and is dependent on longstanding ego executant patterns of behavior which can be identified as they are revealed to the therapist (29). Statements for our scale were based on these patterns of behavior and follow very closely the personality trends of Whitehorn (12).

(*b*) These ego executant acts can be classified into patterns (clusters) of repetitive behavior (19, 20). Behavior patterns imply object need, as well as suggest to the therapist the appropriate course of action.

(*c*) These patterns are observed in everyday life (12) and are within normal limits for certain phases of child development (13). Their pathology arises only in their perseverence at the wrong time in the wrong place or with the wrong person. Place and person are very important and the scale assumes that they are constant as the patient is rated over time.

(*d*) These patterns of behavior are best observed by one involved in relationship with the patient, as in a therapeutic relationship. This scale assumes that to a greater or lesser extent the observations are derived from the experience of changing impact of an ongoing relationship upon the observer.

(*e*) These executant patterns of behavior can be ordered into a hierarchy and may be observed both in ego ontogeny and in regression and progression to and from optimal functioning.

Basically, we believe the ego manifests behaviors that can be classified into three main categories in order of ontogenetic maturity, as follows: (*a*) The ego functions to preserve itself. The behavioral manifestations of this most primitive function of the ego are seen as patterns of denial, projection, and distortion. They are observed in proportion to the extent that the ego is overwhelmed whether the process is in progression or regression. (*b*) The ego develops capacities to get other people's support, encouragement, and help. Almost as though in payment for such services, it learns to do something for itself in return. The patterns of the behavior involved in the "getting help" function of the ego are the compulsive obsessive patterns, the hypochondriacal patterns, and the neurasthenic patterns. (*c*) Finally the ego develops capacities to ask nothing of its objects other than mutual gratification for which it is willing to make self-sacrifices, not only in the interest of preservation of inner constancy but as well to maintain constancy in interpersonal relationships. These behavior constellations consist of dissociation patterns (hysterical behaviors), somatization (internal) visceral ego discharge, and the anxiety-alerting patterns.

In order of ontogenetic development, these patterns may be summarized as follows:

1. The denial patterns
2. The projection patterns
3. The distortion patterns
4. The compulsive-obsessive patterns
5. The hypochondriacal patterns
6. The neurasthenic patterns
7. Escape through narcosis patterns
8. Dissociation patterns
9. Psychosomatic patterns
10. Sublimation patterns
11. Combinations of above patterns—for example, so-called constitutional inadequacy cases are combinations of obsessive patterns, neurasthenic patterns, and hypochondriacal patterns.

For the portion of our scale dealing with psychosis we selected items of behavior that we felt indicated denial patterns, projective patterns, and distortion patterns (i.e., they can't think straight) of behavior. For example, there is

a whole group of very chronic patients (26) who have remained in a state of denial for years and are sometimes
thought of as basically organic problems (22, 23).

Shifting Defenses During
Regression/Recovery

In schizophrenia, we have conceptualized the regression-
recovery process as involving a shift in defenses along a
pathological continuum (11, 12, 13, 14, 15, 16, 17, 18, 19,
24). During convalescence a patient employs progressively
less pathological defenses to the point of recovery of the
capacity to experience relatively unmodified sadness and
anxiety. Some defenses are more mature than others, and
immature defenses in the course of recovery give way to
more mature defenses. The ego, in warding off the dis-
quieting elements, whether from within or without, gener-
ates a behavioral signal that demands that the caring
objects actively demonstrate care, that they exhibit the
feeling expression of eros, the instinct that accepts, constructs, and integrates. The need of love from someone is
an ever present need common to all people. At the same
time its denial in fantasy, word, or act is equally omnipre-
sent. Projection serves to force the object to care and distortion exploits the imagination to relieve the life
dissatisfactions creatively. We believe it is crucial to many
diagnostic, therapeutic, and research tasks to specify the
level at which the patient's ego is functioning in terms of
these patterns.

When I examined the S.O.D. Scale categories it seemed
to me these categories reflected different levels of ego
functioning that might well be classified as involving a shift
in defenses, along a pathological continuum as part of the
regression-recovery process. This ego-function view allows indices of progression or regression to be rated more

clearly. Of course, one must always acknowledge that the rater himself will make a contribution to the assessment. Its magnitude will always be difficult to measure.

I have made an attempt to translate and compare, I hope correctly, some of the items the Washington group has selected to rate in the S.O.D. scale with those found in our ego profile hierarchy (18) and Erikson's (11, 21) blueprint of essential strengths that evolution has built into the ground plan of the life stages. (See Figure 1.)

As I would see it, the items on the S.O.D. scale might be expected to change in an evolving sequence paralleling the patient's growth. They do not, in my opinion, all tap one basic phenomenon about schizophrenia such that they should be expected to move in concert and parallel only the self-object differentiation changes. Thus, I would arrange them heirarchically and expect items having to do with negativism-agreement to change before exaggerated responses to bodily parts or ego boundaries would.

Reconstitution and Change
in Defenses

Following the Course of an Acute Patient

A seventeen-year-old unmarried Jewish girl was admitted with the diagnosis of acute schizophrenia. She was withdrawn, hallucinated, dissociated in affect, inappropriate, and unpredictable, and after a week became denudative. She was treated with Thioridazine and psychotherapy by a first-year resident. Her thoughts were concrete and therapeutic contact was difficult, but she did on occasion share her delusion. By the end of the month she had achieved considerable recompensation. Her Ego Profile Scores in the first week revealed major reliance on the Narcissistic Triad of Defenses (Figure 2). Her helplessness was revealed in the Neurasthenic curve of the Affective Triad, and in the Neurotic Triad her severe anxiety was recorded. The Ego Profile Scores as well as clinical observation demonstrated that the preservation of psychic constancy had a very high priority, greater than that of exhibiting less disturbed behavior. As the Narcissistic Scores of this patient became less intense over time, the Affective Triad became relatively more prominent, especially with regard to neurasthenic helplessness and hypochondriasis during the second to sixth week. During this period the demands on caring objects were intense, as revealed by her attempts to stimulate responses in and be stimulated by the caring objects. Active appeasement is a means toward the achievement of this goal, and is revealed by her being good or being bad and particularly by her being sick (hypochondriacal patterns) or studiously inept (neurasthenic patterns). In her psychotherapy, object compliance solved a major issue for her at this time as absence of such compliance would have brought on pain, sadness, and defensive acts known as depression and/or anger, or a regressive retreat through an ego sacrifice to a more narcissistic level. It is to be noted that during the eighth month, as the Narcissistic Triad of defenses become less prominent, the affective distress still persisted but was accompanied by a marked rise in the neurotic defenses, especially dissociation and somatization. However, anxiety diminished. The overall clinical improvement was extensive as the Neurotic Triad of Defenses became more prominent. While this triad bespeaks self-sacrificing behaviors, from a functional point of view it serves mainly to modify and mitigate unconscious conflict over instinctual expression and thereby always serves to allow for involvement with other people in the service of more equitable personal relationships. The overuse of the anxiety pattern is often highlighted in situations of crisis. This patient's anxiety decreased over the course of fourteen weeks, by which time she was sufficiently improved to leave the hospital.

The narcissistic patterns indicated to the therapist her need to have him demonstrate caring, allowing the patient to feel that she mattered to him. The Affective Triad alerted him to an awareness of the need for supportive measures, that is, doing something to enable the patient to help herself through her own efforts and at a level above and beyond self-preservation. And the Neurotic Triad guided him to participation and gratification in considerable measure as a present, nonpunitive, nonseductive psychotherapist.

Recovery Patterns of Patients 15+Years After Psychosis

Figure 3 shows the way the patients look fifteen years after an acute schizophrenia episode and hospitalization. The details here will be subjugated to illustrate the Ego Profile Ratings indicating ego functioning. I shall discuss only the best and worst functioning groups, I and IV, to highlight the contrasts.

The striking feature of Group I is their chronic dependency on hospitals. Six persons account for 21 admissions and 1,000 patient months in hospital. Only one received psychotherapy of significant duration at the time of first admission. The treatment of Group I patients has been primarily somatic, including electric and insulin shock, lobotomy, and phenathiazine drugs. At follow-up all six patients were attended, looked thin, drab, and odd. Although they went through the motions of an interview, meaning and emotion were missing with one exception. Adaptive capacity was minimal. The Ego Profile of this group shows high levels of denial, projection, distortion (the Narcissistic Triad), and surprisingly a high reading on the neurasthenia factors (Figure 4).

Throughout their careers, the common theme is a failure to form stable relationships with people, including their physicians. These patients did not appeal to anybody.

Group IV demonstrated recovery with resolution of psychotic crisis. Before their acute illness, they were well educated and working; all but one was married. They had a fairly rich array of talents. Two of the patients in this group of nine were admitted with the diagnosis of schizophrenia and discharged with the diagnosis of psychotic depression. For most of the patients, one hospitalization was benign, meaningful, and sufficient. Several had stormy courses until things seemed to click during one specific hospitalization. Six of the nine received ECT; insulin and drugs were used less frequently. Two received no psychotherapy beyond initial workup, but six received 40 to 250 interviews, and one still sees her therapist occasionally. The patients remember specific exchanges and general attitudes from their therapy, whose brevity is to be noted. At follow-up the persons in the fully recovered group were cooperative and wished to contribute and to be praised. In our interviews this was a trusting and unpeculiar group; some plodded, some lectured, some seduced, some suffered. In addition to being nonpsychotic, each person possessed a distinctive style of living, reacting, and achieving gratification. The health of this group is documented by the high rating they received on work and on affective and interpersonal capacities (Figure 3). Eight people in the group had twenty-two children compared with four children among the other three groups combined. The Ego Profile of Group IV shows high scores on compulsivity and anxiety and *low* scores on the other scales (Figure 4). Their profile is not too dissimilar to that of a group of psychiatric residents—anxious but functioning very well.

While our methods do not permit definite statements about the whole population of acute schizophrenics, there seems little doubt that different outcome patterns do exist (10). The significance of these patterns extends beyond the idea that one third got better, one third got worse, and one third stayed the same. We interpret our findings to show that patterns in the life histories of schizophrenic persons may be distinguished in terms of specific constellations of affect, ego capacity, and a level of object relationships. Group I emphasized here are "empty," lonely people who have failed to maintain contact with people beyond adolescence; their failure includes parents, friends, mates, and caretakers. The notable thing about Group IV, the fully recovered group, is their high rate of marriage and child-rearing—these people have risked intimacy and made an effort at their jobs as well as in their parental roles to give to the next generation.

Summary

Four life issues which best differentiate the four outcome groups are:
1. Object attachment
2. Loss of dependency
3. Intimacy
4. Child-rearing

The Ego Profiles associated with the resolution of these issues are illustrated in Figure 4. Thus, Group I patients, who use narcissistic defenses predominantly, have not been able to attach themselves to objects, whereas Group IV, with its use of neurotic defensive patterns, has usually been able to be intimate and have children.

In closing I would like to commend the Washington group's efforts and hope that a continuing dialogue will allow us to use the S.O.D. and our Ego Profile Scale in complementary ways.

REFERENCES

1. Gitelson, M. Psychoanalysis and dynamic psychiatry. *Archives of Neurology and Psychiatry*, 666:280–288, 1951.
2. Semrad, E. V. *Comprehensive Therapy of Schizophrenia. In Current Psychiatric Therapies*, ed. J. N. Masserman, vol. 7, pp. 77–87. New York: Grune & Stratton, 1967.
3. Semrad, E. V. Long-term therapy of schizophrenia (formulation of the clinical approach). In *Psychoneurosis and Schizophrenia*, ed. G. L. Usdin, pp. 155–173. PPhiladelphia: Lippincott, 1966.
4. Semrad, E. V., and Van Buskirk, D. *Teaching Psychotherapy of Psychotic Patients*. New York & London: Grune & Stratton, 1969.
5. Semrad, E. V.; Binstock, W. A.; and White, B. Brief psychotherapy. *American Journal of Psychotherapy*, 20(4):576–599, October 1966.
6. Freud, Anna, and Aichhorn, A. An obituary. *International Journal of Psychoanalysis*, 32:51–56, 1951.
7. Ewalt, J. R. *Psychotherapy of Schizophrenic Reactions. In Current Psychiatric Therapy*, ed. J. N. Masserman, vol. 3, pp. 150–170. New York: Grune & Stratton, 1963.
8. Mann, J., and Semrad, E. V. Conversion as process in conversion as symptom in psychosis. In *The Mysterious Leap from Mind to the Body*, ed. F. Deutsch, pp. 11–26. New York: International Universities Press, 1959.
9. Semrad, E. V., and Day, M. Techniques and procedures used in the treatment and activity programs for psychiatric patients in changing concepts and procedures. In *Psychiatric Occupational Therapy*, published by the American Occupational Therapy Association. Dubuque, Iowa: William I. Brown Co., 1959.
10. Merifield, J.; Carmichael, W. G.; and Semrad, E. V. Recovery Patterns 15 Years After Acute Psychosis.

Read before the APA Annual Meeting 1971 at Washington, D.C.

11. Erikson, E. H. Childhood and Society, in *Eight Stages of Man*, pp. 229–234. New York: Norton, 1964.
12. Whitehorn, J. C. Guides to interviewing and personality study. *Archives of Neurology and Psychiatry*, 52:197–216, 1944.
13. Freud, Anna. *The Ego and the Mechanisms of Defense.* New York: International Universities Press, 1946.
14. Vailliant, G. Theoretical hierarchy of adaptive ego mechanisms. *Archives of General Psychiatry*, 24:107–118, 1971.
15. Engle, G. L. *Psychological Development in Health and Disease.* Philadelphia: Saunders, 1962.
16. Menninger, K. *The Vital Balance.* New York: Viking Press, 1963.
17. Schaefer, R. Mechanisms of defense. *International Journal of Psychoanalysis*, 49:49–62, 1968.
18. Semrad, E. V.; Grinspoon, L.; and Feinberg, S. E. Toward the development of the ego profile scale. *Archives of General Psychiatry*, 28:70–77, January 1973.
19. Semrad, E. V. The organization of ego defenses and object loss. In *The Loss of Loved Ones*, ed. D. M. Moriarity. Springfield, Ill. Charles C. Thomas, 1967.
20. Semrad, E. V. On the need for specificity in the description of clinical function and somatic studies of psychosis. In *Future of the Brain Sciences*, ed. S. Bogoch, pp. 562–567. New York: Plenum Press, 1969.
21. Erikson, E. H. The roots of virtue. In *The Humanist Frame*, ed. J. Huxley. New York: Harper & Row, 1961.
22. Semrad, E. V., and Finely, K. Note on the pneumoencephalogram and electroencephalogram: findings in chronic mental patients. *Psychiatric Quarterly*, 17:76–80, 1943.
23. Sachar, E. J.; Mason, J. W.; Holmes, H. B., Jr.; and

Artiss, K. L. Psychoendocrine aspects of acute schizophrenia reaction. *Psychosomatic Medicine*, 25:510–537, 1963.

24. Semrad, E. V. Hierarchy of psychotic defenses. Unpublished paper.
25. Stierlin, H., and Schulz, C. An attempt to measure change during psychotherapy with a psychotic patient. S.O.D. scale and addendum. Unpublished paper.
26. Beuscher, W.; Carmichael, W.; Hasonbush, L.; Mackenzie, J.; and Semrad, E. V. The psychotherapeutic experience in chronic schizophrenics. In Grinspoon, L.; Ewalt, J.; and Shader, R., eds. *Schizophrenia: Pharmapsychotherapy and Psychotherapy*, ed. L. Grinspoon, J. Ewalt, and R. Shader, chap. 9. Baltimore: Williams and Wilkins, 1972.
27. Campbell, C. M. *Destiny and Disease in Mental Disease and Mental Disorder*. New York: Norton, 1935.
28. Kraepelin, E. *Dementia Praecox Paraphrenia*, ed. R. M. Barclay. Edinburgh: Livingston, 1919.
29. Arsenian, H., and Semrad, E. V. Schizophrenia and language. *Psychiatric Quarterly*, 40:449–458, July 1966.
30. Freud, S. New introductory lecture. In *The Complete Psychological Works of Sigmund Freud*, vol. 16. London: Hogarth Press, 1963.
31. Bleuler, E. *Dementia Praecox in the Group of Schizophrenias*, trans. J. Zenkin. New York: International Universities Press, 1950.

FIGURE 1

An Attempt to Compare Ego Profile Hierarchy with Items on the Washington S.O.D. Scale and Erikson's Eight Stages of Man

THE EGO'S DEFENSIVE PURPOSE IS TO PRESERVE ITSELF

A Ego patterns (strengths)	B Signal to therapist of patient's need	C Erikson—growth & crises (as alternative basic attitudes)	D Erikson (person's strength)	E Clinical observation (Washington)	F Therapy implications
Denial patterns	Caring & love	Basic trust vs. basic mistrust	Drive & hope	(K) Negativism (oppositional, provocative relationships or warmth "by friction") (B) Pretransference (autistic / symbiotic) relationship	(K) Capacity for empathic closeness (B) Transference relationship
Projective patterns	Sharing of responsibility	Autonomy vs. shame & doubt	Self-control, will power	(I) Agreement / consensus / closeness associated with engulfment / swallowed up / merging (L) Accentuation of great gulf of inequality between therapist & patient	(I) Agreement / consensus with therapist enhances sense of self-identity (L) Permits close approximation of patient-therapist status
Distortion patterns	Therapist's pursuit of reality detail	Initiative vs. guilt	Direction & purpose	(A) Clear perception of self / others. (O) Preambivalent View of others / self as "good" / "bad"	(A) Clear perception of self / others. (O) Fusion of "good" / "bad" into ambivalence

THE EGO'S EFFORTS TO GET SUPPORT FROM OTHER PEOPLE AS A FOLLOW-THROUGH ON THE ABOVE WHICH SET THE STAGE FOR ENTRANCE INTO LIFE

Compulsive obsessive patterns	Substitute goodness patterns	Industry vs. inferiority	Method & competence	(G) Inability to agree / disagree with therapist in a discriminatory way	(G) Able to agree / disagree, etc.
				(M) Confusion / disorganization / paranoid in response to separation from others or change in patient situation	(M) Affective experience (grief / anger / tenderness) in response to separation from others or change
Hypochondriacal	Patterns-purpose: excused from performance through sickness	Identity vs. role diffusion	Devotion & fidelity	(C) Inability to see self as separate from the surroundings	(C) Capacity for self observation
				(D) Gender identity confusion	(D) Stable sense of sexual identity
Neurasthenic patterns	Inepitude excuses for performances	Intimacy vs. isolation	Affiliation & love	(H) Patient oversensitive to intrusiveness of therapeutic situation	(H) Readily discloses information
				(P) Excessive stimulus input—maintain sense of body identity	(P) Relative freedom from physical contact need

EGO SACIFICES FOR INTERPERSONAL OBJECT MAINTENANCE AND GRATIFICATION

Dissociative patterns	Adult sexual responsibility	Generativity vs. stagnation	Production & care	(J) Patient avoids close / intensive relationships / intensive relationships or has many superficial relationships. (E) Patient confuses role of that with therapist	(J) Single or few intimate relationships (E) Collaborates with therapist
Somatization patterns	Conversion of interpersonal conflict into internal visceral activity	Ego integrity & despair	Renunciation & wisdom	(F) Permeable ego (self) boundaries (N) Overreaction to los· of body parts	(F) Well-Delineated ego (self) boundaries. (N) Acceptance of loss as a natural function
Anxiety alert patterns	Maintenance of object & self balance; use of anxiety as a signal	(EVS) Awareness for synthesis vs. ignorance, equanimitas vs. object anxiey avoidance	(EVS) Adaptation	(EVS) Adaptation: appropriate alertness and considerate response with work / interpersonal relationship (love) / and subjective comfort	Equanimitas

figure 2

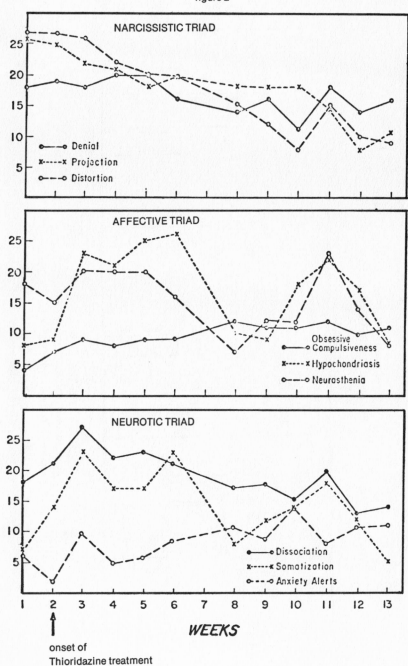

NARCISSISTIC TRIAD

o——o Denial
x-----x Projection
o---o Distortion

AFFECTIVE TRIAD

Obsessive
o—o Compulsiveness
x-----x Hypochondriasis
o——o Neurasthenia

NEUROTIC TRIAD

•——o Dissociation
x-----x Somatization
o---o Anxiety Alerts

WEEKS

onset of
Thioridazine treatment

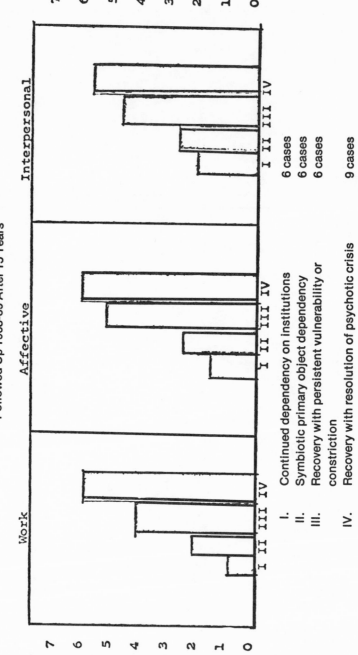

figure 3

Current Adaptive Capacity of 27 Schizophrenic Patients
Followed Up 1968-69 After 15 Years

I. Continued dependency on institutions — 6 cases
II. Symbiotic primary object dependency — 6 cases
III. Recovery with persistent vulnerability or constriction — 6 cases
IV. Recovery with resolution of psychotic crisis — 9 cases

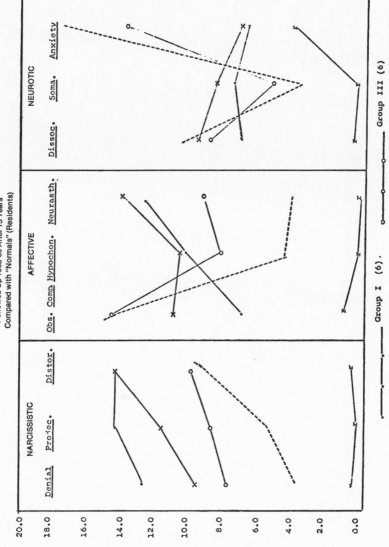

figure 4
Ego Profiles (Mean) of 27 Schizophrenic Patients
Followed Up 1968-69 After 15 Years
Compared with "Normals" (Residents)

24

MATCHING THERAPISTS WITH SCHIZOPHRENIC PATIENTS

John G. Gunderson, M.D.
Clarence G. Schulz, M.D.
David B. Feinsilver, M.D.

Fit and Misfit

In 1950 Dr. Freida Fromm-Reichmann (1) pleaded that "it should be one of the goals of the science of psychotherapy to increase our ability to determine the types of personality [of therapist] and the types of mental patients who are best suited to engage in psychotherapeutic work with each other." Our interest in this subject arose from the early discussions of the Washington study group on psychotherapy of schizophrenia about the qualities of a good psychotherapist. It was soon apparent that it was impossible to delineate characteristics of a good therapist without relating these to the particular characteristics of the schizophrenic patient the therapist was to work with. We thus moved into the problem of matching patient with therapist and trying to determine the characteristics that make for a suitable fit or mismatch. As a practical matter, matching a therapist and patient often depends on the therapist's availablilty and his willingness to work with the patient. However, in many other instances, administrative decisions are reached on an empirical basis from what is known or thought to be known about the available therapists. Beginning from an anecdotal collection of such clinical impressions, we have organized these hypotheses into categories which might be

Other participants in the study group involved in this work are Marvin Adland, M.D.; John Fort, M.D.; Loren Mosher, M.D.; Helm Stierlin, M.D.; and Lyman Wynne, M.D.

validated. The project described here represents an effort to specify, systematize, and evaluate the validity of these empirically derived clinical hypotheses about the qualities of therapists which match well with particular personality dimensions in the schizophrenic patients.

Despite the common clinical impression and supporting research evidence that factors such as the sex (2) and the initial likability (3) of patient and therapist may be important, we believe these are secondary qualities that are clinically important only—or mainly—insofar as they are reflective of basic personality qualities. These factors often serve as convenient rationalization for selecting or changing patient-therapist matches. We believe therapists and patients assigned to each other probably do better than matches based on initial attraction. As a generalization, we concluded that differences between patients and therapists often cause curiosity and initial attraction, but the similarities provide more enduring bonds. Quantitative research has tended to support this conclusion (3).

Personality Dimensions

The hypotheses which we have developed about patient-therapist matching concern personality dimensions. We recognize that schizophrenia encompasses a broad range of clinical phenomena and personality types. In clinical practice the subcategorization of schizophrenics used by us is based more on personality characteristics or symptoms (for example, depression, aggression, hysterical, hopeless) than the traditional subcategories of catatonic, hebephrenic, paranoid, etc. Likewise, we felt that the personality of the therapist looms as especially important for matching with schizophrenic patients because of the relative importance of the "real" relationship (4), especially during the critical initial phases of therapy. Rogers et al. (5) have also noted that the relationship looms as particularly important with schizophrenic patients compared with other types of patients in psychotherapy.

The best-known effort to distinguish the characteristics of good therapists for schizophrenics was the original Whitehorn-Betz study in 1954 (6). Their study attempted to correlate the effectiveness of treatment with the therapist's scoring on a vocational preference test. The therapists were divided into the well-known *A/B* types. On the Strong Vocational Interest Blank the *A* therapists scored higher on lawyer and CPA vocations and were more successful with patients, while the *B* therapists scored higher on printer and mathematics–science teacher vocations and did poorly with patients. This work and the subsequent studies that have come out of it are well summarized in a recent review by Razin (7). The meaning of the *A* and *B* types has always remained elusive. Our approach, with its emphasis on personality dimensions, has more promise of providing clinically meaningful results and may help explain the *A/B* types.

The following were some of the more clearly emerging specific patient-therapist matching variables: (*a*) tacit, withdrawn patients need active, intense therapists, not analytic caricatures. (*b*) Fragile, shaky patients do better with more passive therapists and do not do well with active, intense therapists. (*c*) Acting-out patients need a therapist who is himself something of an "actor out," not someone who tends to be moralistic and hyperconventional. (*d*) Aggressive paranoid patients do well with either a woman or a man comfortable with passivity or a somewhat "paranoid" therapist who is empathic with a world view of "everybody is against me," so long as this does not lead to an overinvolvement or *folie â deux*. They do not do well with a male having a need to assert his masculinity. (*e*) Hysterical, seductive females tend to do well with grandfatherly types who enjoy seductive stimulation but would not do well with a young, single male having savior fantasies and needs for love. (*f*) Depressive patients need someone who is comfortable with all the various aspects of depression within himself (demandingness, emptiness, rage). (*g*) Hopeless, giving-up patients need a charismatic therapist, one who is able to follow through for the long term.

The Initial Study

Our initial effort to study these clinical hypotheses of patient-therapist matching generated in the study group began when two of us studied matches as presented during weekly case conferences at Chestnut Lodge. Objectives in this phase of the study were fourfold: (*a*) to evaluate the feasibility of rating reliably the above personality dimensions of patient and therapist; (*b*) to refine these hypotheses and identify other possible major determinants within the patient-therapist dyad; (*c*) to explore how well the matching dimensions seemed to correlate with the working therapeutic relationship; and (*d*) to explore the potential for a future, more rigorous predictive study. We observed more than thirty matches, half of which involved chronic schizophrenics. A preliminary report was made on these (8).

We had surprising success for our first two objectives. We found that, at least among ourselves, we could achieve reliability on a five-point scale in a consistent manner while rating the patients and therapists independently. At the same time we became aware of the need for further reliability studies which included raters who were not aware of the hypotheses and who had not been involved in development of the rating scale.

We were able to refine our hypotheses greatly and to identify several other possible variables. For example, we cleaved the hypothesis about aggressive paranoid patients into two separate issues. Aggressive schizophrenic patients do well with therapists who are comfortable and unafraid with such hostility. This comfort could be in the form of unconcerned physically unthreatening types (such as Frieda Fromm-Reichman) or by being rather authoritarian and physically prepossessing. For paranoid patients we refined the concept about a proper therapist into the dimension of "externalizing." Externalizing therapists often are very social- conscious, are somewhat self-referential, and favor underdogs. To our original list of hypotheses we added the concept that the anxious schizophrenic would do well with a composed, stable therapist but would do poorly with a frenzied, disorganized one. We also felt that the dependent patient would do well with a therapist who is comfortable being dependent but not one who is counterdependent. These and the original hypotheses were then translated onto separate rating forms for patients and for therapists (see Appendix). We hoped these new and more fully explained rating forms would allow ratings to be made by untrained but sophisticated clinicians who were uninformed of the research. By putting the ratings of patients and therapists on separate forms it becomes possible to make predictions of differential effectiveness for a given therapist who is working with a number of patients. It is also possible to use different raters for the patients and their therapists.

With respect to our third objective, it seemed quite clear from our retrospective evidence that the personality matching was an important factor in determining whether the relationship was progressing favorably or not. Parenthetically this seemed just as true for patients of diagnostic categories other than schizophrenia. Two personality dimensions struck us as consistently powerful; that is, when there was a strong favorable match along these dimensions, a good therapeutic relationship resulted, and when there was a strongly unfavorable match, a poor therapeutic relationship developed. The first of these was that patients with depressive qualities would do well when matched with therapists who are comfortable with depression. While occasionally the patient emerged as the rate-limiting partner in dealing with depressive issues, at least as often therapists found ways of avoiding these issues. In several instances this was evident in the therapist's initial interest in the patient's naughtiness, misbehavior, or psychotic productions. Most frequently, though, therapists avoid depressive issues by passivity. A woman admitted two months after losing her child remained psychotic for several years while her therapist patiently attempted to follow her lead in interviews. She eventually improved after a symbolic burial of her child in which she wept with an aide. We felt that not only should therapists who work with schizophrenic patients who are dealing with depressive issues be tolerant of depression, they need to recognize their importance and actively help patients look at them. Yet such active therapists may try to impose a depressive set on patients before the patient is ready to deal with this. For example, a disorganized fragile patient was matched with a therapist who expected the patient to change greatly and who wanted the patient to look at his long history of failures and disappointments. The patient would respond to the interactional stress with the therapist by fragmenting. In this instance the patient wasn't ready to deal with depression and the therapist's activity was threatening. The second dimension that emerged as extremely important involved our hypothesis that schizophrenic patients who were hysterical would do well with therapists who were grandfatherly. This dimension was most important when there was a mismatch. We noted that the relationship failed if a seductive patient was matched with a therapist who found it difficult to remain involved with the drive-related material while still remaining comfortably objective. When, in contrast, "comfortably attached" therapists were able to respond appropriately to the seductive needs of their patients, this failed to be a serious deterrent. A striking example of this occurred when a therapist's difficulty in the therapeutic relationship with a seductive patient subsided shortly after he married. These observations thus expand on Freud's statement that for seductive women, "younger men . . . not yet bound by a permanent tie may find it a hard task" (9).

Our fourth objective was to explore the potential for a more rigorous predictive study. We felt that it would be possible to utilize our more defined and refined hypotheses to rate patients and therapists in a reliable manner and to make predictions from these. Nevertheless, while the personality matching seemed to be a major determinant of the outcome, it was apparent that many other factors also needed to be taken into account. We were impressed, as others have been (10, 11), with the importance of other matching factors such as the fortuitous coincidence of the therapist's or patient's resembling an important person from the other's past history. For example, a very chronic patient with repeated treatment failures was making progress with a swarthy, bearded Latvian therapist. In her family history was a romantic Latvian man who had taken the patient's mother away from an unhappy home and had been an oft-cherished memory as the happiest event in the mother's life. The point is that it is very difficult to know beforehand which factors might loom forward and "carry the day." It remains unclear how we might best assess the predictive value for our dimensions except in regard to the way the therapeutic relationship proceeds. It would seem to require a much more exhaustive and very difficult study to assess reliably the progress of the therapeutic relationship and relate this to the patient's progress in other realms of his living (e.g., work, symptoms, discharge, etc.).

Reliability and Predictive Validity

We discovered that it is an extremely sensitive problem to study the therapist's personality characteristics which influence psychotherapy. Such a study is resisted and resented insofar as it implies that a therapist may be a poor match with a given patient or insofar as a therapist feels that his technical skills are more important than personality dimensions. Issues of confidentiality between researchers and therapists and issues of support between researchers and hospital administrators become of paramount importance under these circumstances. Our initial lack of attention to the effect of such research on the field of study led to difficulties that were anticipated and corrected when the project was shifted to another setting. In 1973 we decided to continue the second phase of this project at the Sheppard-Pratt Hospital because of the greater administrative support provided for the study and the greater availability of a large number of new matches.

As our first goal we attempted to assess the reliability of our forms in a more rigorous manner. We were particularly interested in assessing the reliability of the therapist rating form because it involved more subtle judgments and more sensitive clinical issues than the ratings of the patients. On the basis of results from having either two or usually three independent raters evaluate fifteen therapists, we found an overall interrater reliability using the Pearson product-moment correlation coefficient to be 0.6 when judgements were compared between two independent outside raters. When the mean score from these two outside ratings was compared with ratings made by the therapists themselves, the correlation coefficient sank to 0.5. We formed a clinical impression that the better self-knowledge among therapists, the closer their ratings correlated with those of the outside observers. We feel these results mean that the outside raters were more objective in their evaluations, and this suggests that self-ratings by therapists are less valuable than the ratings made by others. The outside raters were either chiefs of service or psychotherapy supervisors who had some knowledge of therapists personally as well as professionally. This personal knowledge we feel is a prerequisite for making such personality judgments.

Although our data on the patient evaluation form are not so extensive, the correlation between raters seems to be higher on this form. This is expected because of the relatively gross nature of the pathology in the patients compared with therapists, the relative ease and sophistication with which raters make such judgments about patients compared with colleagues, and the relatively greater familiarity with the personality dimensions used on the patient form compared with the therapist form.

The second goal of our current project has aimed at developing a means of assessing the validity of predictions made from our matching hypotheses. We collected data on twelve patient-therapist matches. A serious practical problem quickly became apparent for the majority of the twelve matches: Neither clear-cut suggestions of mismatch nor particularly good matching were found. In part this might be due to the rather conservative (i.e., reluctance to polarize) ratings made of the therapists. It may also mean that a relatively carefully selected group of therapists will rarely possess polar tendencies on any of the personality dimensions on our scale. This suggested two means by which the amount of variance might be increased in ratings. The first would be to increase the range of ratings from a five-point scale to a seven-point scale. The second is to apply these rating scales to a population of people engaged as therapists who might be expected to exhibit more polarized or, at least, less homogeneous personality characteristics. We are thus engaged in utilizing these forms to assess matching with nonprofessional therapists in other clinical settings. With respect to those four matches where more clear-cut predictions could be made, we asked the supervisors to make overall clinical judgments on how the therapeutic relationship was progressing and what types of problems existed approximately three to six months after the initiation of therapy. While the number of cases is too small to permit generalization, the results confirmed our predictions toward either a good or a poor match. This phase of our study impressed us once again with the difficulty in culling out a reliable means of assessing the validity of our predictions.

Summary

This paper has presented a description of an effort to move from sophisticated clinical observations toward testable hypotheses with regard to matching therapists with schizophrenic patients. We have defined ten hypotheses about personality factors in therapists which will match well or poorly with personality factors in schizophrenic patients and have developed a means for quantitatively and reliably assessing these personality dimensions. From retrospective evidence the validity of these hypotheses has been impressive, but in moving toward evaluation of predictions in a prospective study we have encountered and have here attempted to enumerate many difficulties. More impressive than the research itself has been the value of looking at the meaning issues systematically. In so doing we expanded our awareness of this complicated area while acquiring valuable guidelines that can be useful in clinical work. It is hoped that this preliminary communication will encourage other clinicians and researchers to think carefully about these issues.

APPENDIX

Patient-Therapist Matching

Form A.   Evaluating Patients

This form is intended for the evaluation of patients at the time they are being assigned to a psychotherapist. The frame of reference (i.e., for comparison) is other psychiatric patients. This form can be filled out by ward administrators, an evaluating or consulting clinician, or the therapist him(her)self.

Scoring: 1. absent or minimally present
2. present
3. average
4. a dominant feature
5. predominating

Evaluator's: Name .... Relationship to patient ....
Patient's: Name .... Diagnosis .... Date ....
           Sex .... Age ....
Therapist's: Name .... Sex ....

Patient Dimension   *Score (1-5)*

1. Passivity
   1. aggressive, active, self-assertive
   2.
   3.
   4.
   5. submissive, passive, compliant

2. Hostility
   1. timid, retiring
   2. sometimes irritable
   3. sometimes hostile
   4. belligerent, has angry outbursts
   5. assaultive, may be "dangerous"

3. Paranoia
    1. not paranoid
    2. suspicious
    3. occasional ideas of reference
    4. paranoid characters, use projection, episodically paranoid
    5. systematized paranoid delusions

4. Sociopathy (consider past history)
    1. not sociopathic
    2.
    3. tendency to manipulate, act out, be impulsive
    4. repetitive acting-out episodes
    5. habitual or addictive acting out

5. Fragility (of defensive structure)
    1. stable, unyielding defensive armor
    2.
    3. sensitive to change, excitable
    4.
    5. extremely sensitive, regression-prone, tendency to fragment

6. Seductiveness (as used here, this includes general involvement and concern with sexual-id matters. Particularly it refers to the degree to which the patient's verbalizations and manner are body-oriented and evocative and doesn't necessarily depend on the usual signs of neurotic hysteria)
    1. cold, distant, businesslike
    2.
    3. appealing (may be via helplessness or masochism as readily as sex)
    4.
    5. id preoccupations, clearly seductive

7. Depression
    1. not depressed
    2. some depressive issues apparent on probing
    3. sad, irritable, cries readily, shows depressive affect
    4. clinically depressed
    5. severe depression: feels helpless, hopeless, suicidal, self-depriciative

8. Assigned hopelessness (the patient's prognosis as evaluated)
   1. good prognosis
   2.
   3. uncertain prognosis
   4.
   5. patient seen as chronic, irreversible

9. Anxiety
   1. controlled, no overanxiety
   2.
   3. becomes anxious in some situations
   4. anxiety complaints
   5. clinically anxious, panicky

10. Dependency
    1. Independent
    2.
    3. Covertly dependent
    4.
    5. clinging, ready dependency

Form B.   Evaluating Therapists

This form is intended for the evaluation of psychotherapists working
with inpatients. The frame of reference (i.e., for comparison) is
other psychotherapists. This form can be filled out by a clinician who
knows the therapist personally.

Scoring: 1. absent or minimally present
           2. present
           3. average
           4. a dominant feature
           5. predominating

Therapist's: Name ....Age ....Sex ....
Evaluator's: Name................ Relationship to therapist...............

Therapist Dimension   *Score (1-5)*

1. Activity
   "Activity refers to the degree to which a therapist is
   active, energetic, alert, engages in many activities (in
   therapy and in personal life), tends to exhort, be playful, interprets readily, may be somewhat intrusive. This
   refers to ongoing life style more than just treatment
   technique.
   1. an analytic caricature; impassive, passive, unstruc-
      turing, etc.

   5. extremely active

2. Comfort with aggression
   May take several forms, e.g., being athletic, authoritarian, takes command, heroic and somewhat argumenta-
   tive or being soft, unconcerned. In either case therapist
   is nonthreatening to aggressive patient and is not threatened by the patient's aggression.
   1. severely anxious with aggression, "chicken"

   5. composed in the presence of aggression (either as
      Napoleon or Grandma Moses)

3. Externalizing
   "Externalizing" refers to the degree to which a therapist tends to blame, see problems as external, sympa-
   thize with underdogs, identify with minority groups,
   believe in victims, be self-referential, feel overly responsible for others (especially patients) and be
   antiauthoritarian.
   1. naive, ready trust

   5. epitomizes externalizing (above), is suspicious

4. "Sociopathic"
   "Sociopathic" is used to define the therapist who has
   experienced life's "seamier" side, has acted out impulses and learned to master them. Such therapists tend to
   be adventurous, pragmatic, pleasure seeking, flexible,
   political.

1. prudish, hyperconventional, principled, rigid

   ↕

5. as above, somewhat unreliable, uses seduction and manipulation

5. Gentleness
   This refers to the degree to which a therapist is low key, soft-spoken, easygoing, and nonintense. This refers to his stable personality traits rather than his manner in a particular situation.
   1. intense, self-assertive, aggressive

   ↕

   5. very gentle

6. Grandfatherliness
   "Grandfatherliness" is meant to reflect the degree to which a therapist retains an interest and pleasure in sexual subjects and other id material without being judgmental or seductive.
   1. puritanical or seductive

   ↕

   3. accepts seduction with pleasure

   ↕

   5.accepts id material with comfort

7. Comfort with depression
   This refers to the degree to which a therapist under-stands his own depressive issues, can tolerate demands without hostility or sympathy, has experienced grief.
   1. depressed, has trouble sitting with depressed patients

   ↕

   3. becomes angry or sympathetic to patient's neediness

   ↕

   5. tolerates the overt or covert demands of a depressed patient with patience and empathy

8. Optimism
   Refers to the degree to which a therapist is optimistic and enthusiastic about patients. Such therapists tend to like challenges, have strong belief in their ability to help —either due to their own omnipotence or by making patients very "special." Therapists may be known for tenacity or charisma.

1. pessimistic, scientific, choosy about patients

5. has contagious optimism

9. Composure
This is the degree to which the therapist is self-contained. Such a therapist is reasonable, stable, steady, and controlled. He is not busy, wordy, frenetic, or disorganized.
1. frenzied

5. composed

10. Comfort with dependency
Can act independently, is comfortable being alone, has full personal life, little conflict over separation, vacations, discharge. Is not overconscientiously concerned or solicitous, doesn't give object or food substitutes to patients.
1. dependent, lonely

5. independent

REFERENCES

1. Fromm-Reichmann, F. Some aspects of psychoanalytic psychotherapy. In *Psychotherapy and Schizophrenia*, ed. E. B. Brody and F. C. Redlick, p. 94. New York: International Universities Press, 1952.
2. Harris, S. The influence of patient and therapist sex in psychotherapy *J. Consult. Clin. Psychol.*
3. Luborsky, L.; Chandler, M.; Auerbach, A. H.; Cohen, J.; and Bachrach, H. Factors influencing the outcome of psychotherapy: a review of quantitative research. *Psychological Bulletin*, 75:145–185, 1970.
4. Gunderson, J. Controversies about psychotherapy of schizophrenia. *Am. J. Psychiat.* 130:677–681, 1973.
5. Rogers, C. R.; Gendlin, E. G.; Kiesler, D. J.; and Truax, C. D., eds. *The Therapeutic Relationship and Its Impact: A Study of Psychotherapy with Schizophrenics.* Madison: University of Wisconsin Press, 1967, p. 296.
6. Whitehorn, J. G., and Betz, B. J. A study of psychotherapeutic relationships between physicians and schizophrenic patients. *Am. J. Psychiat.* 111:321–331, 1954.
7. Razin, A. M. The "A-B" variable in psychotherapy: a critical review. *Psychological Bulletin*, 75 (1):1–21, January 1971.
8. Schulz, C. B.; Feinsilver, D. B.; and Gunderson, J. G. Patient-therapist matching. Presented at the 125th annual meeting of the APA, Dallas, May 1–5, 1972.
9. Freud, S. Observations on transference love. *Standard Edition*, 12:169. London: Hogarth Press, 1956.
10. Stone, M. H. Therapists' personalities and unexpected success with schizophrenic patients. *Am. J. Psychotherapy* 25(4):543–552, 1971.
11. Burton, A. The adoration of the patient and its disillusionment. *Am. J. Psychoanalysis*, 29:194–204, 1969.

25

CLINICAL FEATURES OF IMPROVED SCHIZOPHRENICS
Lawrence Kayton, M.D.

Schizophrenia is perhaps the most dreaded and pernicious of mental disorders. The risk of developing a schizophrenic psychosis in a lifetime has been estimated to be as high as 3 percent (41). Despite the high incidence in the general population, the treatment of schizophrenia remains fraught with difficulties. Ideologies often rule treatment techniques rather than subjecting the ideologies to systematic outcome studies. The gamut of treatment techniques for schizophrenia is staggering, and each camp boasts of its purported successful outcomes. There is, however, good reason for this. Research into the treatment of schizophrenia has been hampered by many factors, such as ambiguity over definition, theoretical and treatment bias of the reporting group, factors of patient selection, and the myriad variables involved in any research of psychotherapy (27, 38).

Weller and Weller

Treatment of the schizophrenic psychosis has advanced considerably since the advent of the major tranquilizers, milieu therapy, and better aftercare programs. However, it is most difficult to assess the effect of different treatments on the basic schizophrenic disorder, which may remain after restitution from a schizophrenic psychosis. Since

This paper was originally presented at the NIMH Conference on the Psychotherapy of Schizophrenia at the Austen Riggs Center in Stockbridge, Massachusetts, October 14, 1972. Another version of this work will appear in the *Archives of General Psychiatry*.

Bleuler (4), many theorists (1, 25, 14) have noted that the schizophrenic disorder can still be discerned after recovery from an acute disorganization. Therefore, one cannot speak of a cured schizophrenic. Yet some schizophrenics show a distinct improvement over their premorbid state at the termination of their psychological disorganization. Not only may these salutory changes endure, but continued psychological growth may ensue. The end result may be a person whose total life condition compares favorably with that of his nonschizophrenic peers.

The purpose of this study is a better understanding of the clinical features of those schizophrenics who manifest substantial and enduring improvement over several years. It was hoped that the delineation of these features might contribute to a more systematic approach to therapy and management. In this study, improvement will include not only better social and vocational functioning, but also a greatly improved self-appraisal and a marked diminution in the intensity of schizophrenic symptoms.

In past investigations, factors influencing outcome have included (*a*) the characteristics of the therapist (2, 3), (*b*) type of therapy, (*c*) nature of the illness, such as in the schizophrenic-schizophreniform dichotomy of Langfeldt (23) and (*d*) the social development of the person prior to his psychosis, exemplified by concepts of the process and reactive schizophrenics (13, 18). This study focused on the nature of the illness, the social development of the person prior to the disorganization, and the clinical course. In order to explore these clinical perspectives, an intensive retrospective analysis was undertaken on thirteen cases of improved young adult schizophrenics.

Selection of Patients

The young adult program at the Psychosomatic and Psychiatric Institute was asked to submit a list of all young adults who had had a substained improvement for at least one year after hospitalization. Initial criteria for improvement were in the spheres of social and vocational functioning. The social criteria included significant same-sexed and opposite-sexed relationships, while the vocational criteria included either work commensurate with level of intelligence and training or full-time attendance at school. A total of forty-two names were collected. Of the forty-two charts reviewed, only thirteen were finally selected. Many of the forty-two patients were nonschizophrenic or there was a serious diagnostic question. Others had inadequate nursing notes or artificially shortened hospitalization due to insurance termination, signing out against medical advice, etc. A follow-up questionnaire designed for a larger prospective study of schizophrenia was sent to each patient. Ten subjects returned the questionnaires, while questionnaire data were collected by phone for three patients. Maintenance of excellent functioning (better than premorbid functioning) was confirmed by the questionnaire data.

Nursing notes were charted on each patient for each of the three eight-hour shifts. These were fairly complete and included behavioral descriptions as well as meaningful verbal content expressed during a shift. The nursing notes were abstracted for each day throughout the hospitalization. Each abstract was accompanied by a complete diagnostic history, the admission note, the discharge summary, and the psychiatric progress notes written by the therapist. Each case was then analyzed for good and poor prognosis features, special historical elements, premorbid character type, special content of hallucinations, delusions, fantasies, and preoccupations, and the pathway toward recovery.

The Setting

In order to develop a perspective into the clinical course of a psychological illness, the setting must be understood. Others who wish to replicate a study must see if similar behaviors and subjective feelings exist in a variety of milieux; therefore, a short description of this hospital follows:

The P&PI, a facility of the 960-bed Michael Reese Hospital in Chicago, is an eighty-bed psychiatric hospital erected in 1951. The P&PI is primarily a private psychiatric hospital, but approximately 20 percent of the beds are occupied by patients treated by resident physicians. Adolescents, young adults, adults, and geriatric patients representing the entire range of psychopathology are treated. The P&PI is designed for a relatively rapid turnover: during 1971, the average length of stay was forty days.

The edifice consists of two patient floors, second and third, which house five wards, three on the second floor and two on the third. The hospital has a system by which severely ill patients progressively transfer to more open wards as they improve. Each ward has a resident physician called a "coordinator," who together with an attending supervisor regulates the milieu of each ward. The formal weekly meetings on each ward consist of one or two patient-staff meetings and one interstaff meeting. The therapeutic emphasis at P&PI remains in the sphere of individual psychotherapy, though there is an active minority of somatotherapists. The value system of the hospital espouses a psychoanalytically oriented theoretical model for psychiatric treatment.

Patient Characteristics

The average age of the thirteen patients was 20.4 years, with a range between 16 and 25. Eleven of the patients were female and only two were male.

The Phillips Prognostic Scale was applied to each patient, utilizing the record of the complete psychiatric history. Though the Phillips scale is a generally more accurate predictor in males, it still provides a useful measure of premorbid social adjustment for the purposes of this study.

It is generally accepted that a score of 18 or more signifies a poor prognosis schizophrenic. The range on the Phillips was 15 to 25. Only four of the thirteen had Phillips scores below 18. The average score was 19.7 for twelve patients. One girl who was sixteen years old upon admission was not rated because the Phillips is not applicable to adolescents. This girl would have been assessed as a poor prognosis schizophrenic, for she had been symptomatic for at least three years prior to hospitalization.

Histories

Psychophysiological disorders were present in the past histories of three female patients. One girl had a four-year history of *grand mal* epilepsy, though a prominent consultant felt the seizures may have been hysterical. Another girl had thyrotoxicosis several years prior to her hospitalization, while still another had a duodenal ulcer at age fourteen.

Congenital physical disorders were present in another three. One girl had a hypoplastic eye and no fingernails, which was the result of a rare ectodermal dysplasia. Another girl had atavistic facial features with hypertelorism. This girl did not develop coherent speech until age seven. Finally, a third girl was born prematurely after her mother had failed to deliver a viable baby after five pregnancies. This girl developed retinitis proliferans from the hyperoxia of an incubator, which resulted in her being only partly sighted.

Childhood disturbances were present in all. Pathological lying combined with other delinquency was present in two, delayed speech was present in three (speech not developing until three or later), a grammar school phobia in one, physical manifestations including hysterical paraplegia were present in two cases, and excessive daydreaming in nine. This was daydreaming that was severe enough to warrant consultations with teachers or sufficient to produce frequent reprimand at home.

Hospitalization ranged between 4 and 18 months, with an average of 9.6 months. Longer hospitalized patients were intentionally chosen so that the record of the illness could be more complete.

Nature of the Psychosis

The schizophrenic psychosis of all thirteen developed over a period of days to weeks, though severe psychopathology had long been present. Certain events preceded the psychosis and also appeared in the speech content so that precipitants could be delineated.

Beginning college preceded the symptomatic disorganization in three, while the stress of a heterosexual relationship seemed to trigger the disorganization in eight. One girl exhibited chronic delinquency over several years, which included drug abuse, promiscuity, and truancy. This delinquency masked a very severe schizophrenic disorder. A paternal death precipitated the schizophrenic fragmentation in two subjects. In one girl, the paternal death ensued only one week before she began college, and thus her psychosis was considered precipitated by the combined stresses of paternal death and beginning college.

There was a strong depressive component in the psychosis of one patient which warranted a diagnosis of schizo-affective schizophrenia. The remainder had occasional to consistent bizarre behavior with occasional auditory or visual hallucinations. All had clearly evidenced thought disorder. Pronounced suspiciousness, negativism, and outright persecutory delusions were present in two. Somatic complaints, many of which could not be distinguished from an actual psychophysiologic disturbance, were prominent in seven of the female patients. Catatonic features were present in six, four of whom also had hysterical features such as sexual seductiveness, engaging charm, and much Oedipal material in the psychotic content of their speech and in their past histories. One patient had hebephrenic elements, though she always seemed to preserve her appearance. Four exhibited an undifferentiated picture.

Out of the thirteen, nine were initially very verbal and four were almost mute. These nonverbal schizophrenics were seclusive and would quietly hallucinate and at other times stare blankly into space. Prominent sexual content was present in three. In two others there was a reversal of fantasy and reality so that an inner fantasy world was created and reacted to as if it were real while the external world was ignored. This process had extended over many years. It is interesting that these two females also had catatonic and hysterical features. Patterns of interaction were quite variable. Upon admission, object-seeking behavior was evident in ten, avoidant behavior in two, and total indifference in one. Of those who were object-seeking, none was clinging.

The disorganization was of varying degrees of severity. In most there was severe disorganization with almost a complete disregard of reality awareness. In others the disorganized states immobilized the person from social interactions and from formulating and initiating plans of purposeful action. These people had subjective feelings of thought scattering, fears of social blundering, and inner emotional confusion or emotional blockage. In six patients, the disorganization had been chronic over two to three years, yet these people were able to maintain a social facade which protected them from being labeled deviant though they were indeed fragmented within.

Despite the disparities in the presenting picture and in the premorbid history, there was a marked homogeneity in the clinical course toward good outcome. The following is a presentation of the clinical observations. These observations have been divided into phases so that the observations may be more easily followed.

Course

Phase I, Internal Disorganization
(may or may not be associated with manifest behavioral disorganization)

In this phase there was a preoccupation with good and bad objects. These objects ranged from ill-defined ones such as inexplicable sinister forces to more personified evil objects such as devils or hallucinatory accusers, to even more definable persons exemplified in persecutory delusions. In those schizophrenics less out of contact with reality, the bad object seemed less persecuting and more coldly rejecting.

There was also a preoccupation with good objects. These also might be ill defined, such as a cosmic godly force, or more definable persons such as Jesus and hallucinatory protecting voices. Some patients temporarily felt themselves to be good and powerful objects with delusions of grandeur or a grandiose sense of self. When the good, powerful object was seen to be the therapist or a staff member, there was a quieting of the concern over the bad objects. During these times, the patient seemed to feel temporarily attached, secure, and protected. Increasing emotional investment was now directed toward the therapist or staff member. Periods of severe disorganization began to wane. If the good, powerful object remained a delusional figure such as Jesus or there were delusions of grandeur, there was also a quieting and temporary absence of bad objects; however, these periods were always short-lived.

With the beginning emotional investment in a more real, external good object there was an increasing vulnerability to disappointment and rejection. With a perceived rejection or anger at the therapist or staff member there was a fairly predictable sequence of events that could be discerned. First, there was a feeling of being totally deserted and alone. This was followed by intense self-abomination with feelings of worthlessness and being completely unlovable. In many instances, this in turn was followed by a temporary return of the bad objects. With the reestablishment of the contact there would again be a disappearance of the bad object.

In addition to concern over good and bad objects, there were other themes. Excessive concern about food intake with fears and delusions about obesity was also seen. Refusal to eat meat was not uncommon. Other psychotic behaviors included curling into fetal positions, huddling in corners, and being mute, blank, and out of contact with reality. These behaviors coincided with verbalized fears of annihilation, plunging into endless water, being suffocated, fears of dying and destruction of the world. An example of this follows; from the psychiatric history of Mary M.:

> The patient has recurrent dreams and vivid waking fantasies of a hallucinatory nature about World War III involving the United States, Russia, or China. One dream begins with Chicago being on fire. She is in a tenement and going through a series of stairs and alleyways to get a fire hose to put out the fire, which is destroying countless thousands. The Russians are planning to take advantage of the fire and bomb Chicago; she must therefore get back to her room, which she does by following the fire hose. In her room a sinister girl has a grenade and suggests that she blow up Mary M. so she can die now and not have to wait. At this point she sees the planes coming overhead and everything becomes red from the fire. The sinister girl throws the grenade as Mary M. runs down the stairs thinking that she doesn't want to die now.
>
> This is often followed by another series of waking dreams that has to do with water. In some of these vivid fantasies there is a sensation of being submerged or being washed back and forth by waves. In one recurrent dream, she is on

a terrace over a body of water which seems suspended over a larger body of water which is probably an ocean. The smaller body of water is frozen and begins to melt. Mother tells her not to come off the terrace, which Mary M. disregards. She jumps into the water. There is a gap in the water which drops into the other larger body of water. She has the sensation that she is making a major decision as she comes into the gap but does not go through. Then she decides to go through it and belatedly realizes she went through the gap into the salt water. She is unable to swim to the beach and feels uncontrollable panic.

Once Mary M. felt safe within the hospital, under the treatment of her therapist, with whom she had been working for several months, she shortly had a clear psychotic episode.

The patient's behaviors and fears became less intense with the use of neuroleptics. The neuroleptics often seemed to enhance the establishment of a trusting contact. However, a trusting contact was made with several patients, although there was no regular use of neuroleptics.

As the positive emotional investment in external objects grew there was either a gradual or a very abrupt waning of the severely disorganized state. Then new behaviors were exhibited which can be described as the phase of postpsychotic regression.

Phase II, Postpsychotic
Regression, Early

Once this phase began it lasted for a period of three weeks to sixteen months. It was usually a stable phase that moved smoothly into Phase III. However, in four patients there were further disorganized states which ensued after the postpsychotic regression began. These further disorganizations were occasioned by separations from the therapist such as vacations, separations from family members, acting out of family psychopathology, attempts to dislodge the patient from his regression, and sometimes the patients seemed to experience great shame in being regressed and could not permit themselves to remain regressed without justification.

In this phase, the person was still disorganized with thought scattering or clogging. The concern with sinister forces occurred sporadically but was muted in emotional intensity. The subjective feeling was one of badness, weakness, aloneness, and frustrating and pervasive sadness. There was an additional feeling of badness which seemed less primitive and more under the sway of reality factors. This seemed to be a sense of worthlessness associated with the shame over being regressed. There was a feeling of great emptiness which was sometimes experienced quite literally. For example, one patient complained of hollowness in the stomach area. There was a passivity that felt imposed upon the person so he was unable to move—as sense of "energylessness' which he could not surmount. In additition, there was a reversal of diurnal rhythm with insomnia during the night and sleeping until ten A.M. to noon with almost uncontrollable urges to nap during the early afternoon. Psychophysiologic disturbances were quite common during this period and were sometimes difficult to distinguish from hypochondriasis. Typical psychophysiologic disturbances were nausea, lightheadedness, ataxia, and painful muscular rigidity. Some of these may have ensued from the phenothiazines, but the symptoms often did not subside with reduction in dosage, changing of medication, or adding an antiparkinsonian agent. There were, however, patients on no regular phenothiazines who did take minor tranquilizers and only occasionally required phenothiazines. These patients also experienced psychophysiological and/or hypochrondriacal distress.

Concentration was markedly impaired so that reading was almost impossible. When reading was attempted there was a feeling of great strain, sudden tiredness, and an inability to comprehend. The words tended to be unorganized so that the person was just "reading" configurations and at best individual words. Periods of staring blankly into space were always reported. Clogging of thoughts or total emptiness was experienced during these blanking episodes. A notable feature of the staring, in some patients, was the diminished frequency of blinking and the staggered frequency of blinking. A widened palpebral fissure was also seen. Though attention could be directed toward other people, it seemed forced. Though there was a strong dyadic wish almost always directed toward the therapist, there was still blank, hollow staring in the therapy sessions. There was a strong desire to be alone, exemplified by eating apart from others. Enforced transactions such as the nurse encouraging the patient to speak about his feelings were very painful and were resisted by the patient. There was, however, an appreciation when staff or other patients would sit with them silently for periods of time. Moderate to severe depression was present and was ostensibly a reaction to the helplessness.

In four patients, gross oral movements were present during this phase, with lip pursing, tongue movements over the lips or between the teeth, and aborted sucking movements. Though these movements could have been oral-buccal dyskinesias on phenothiazines, they lacked the spasmodic and repetitive quality usually due to these dyskinesias. Significant weight gain began toward the latter part of this phase, though a preoccupation with food, body image distortions of largeness, and a feeling of disgusting piggishness had begun in some prior to the clear disorganization.

Phase III, Postpsychotic
Regression, Middle

There was still a continuation of the behavior and experiences of Phase II; however, certain changes became manifest. There was a disappearance of the dirunal reversal with more satisfying sleep at night. There also began to be more concern about appearance, evidenced by dieting, the buying of new clothes, or better grooming. Concentration began to improve and the patient began reading articles in the newspaper or even completed a short novel. Memories became more distinct and there were often beginning discussions of the uncanny experiences of the acutely disorganized state. The psychophysiologic disturbances also subsided. Awakening from seven-thirty to eight in the morning instead of sleeping until late morning began rather abruptly, and the afternoon naps either disappeared or became less frequent. Social relationships began, and the person began spontaneously to sit with others when he ate or came out of his room to sit with others in the lounge. Nonverbal interaction such as playing cards or Ping-Pong with others became noted, though verbal transactions were limited.

It is very interesting that no progress seemed evident to the patient, who now seemed quite comfortable. There was even sometimes denial of progress despite clear evidence to the contrary. An exacerbation of florid psychotic symptoms that would appear in this phase seemed to melt away when interpreted. Once this phase began, the firm but gentle prodding of the patient to action was quite effective in terminating elements of the regression. The therapist had to force three of the patients out of their regressed states by setting immutable discharge dates or placing the reluctant patients on a day-care night hospital program. Eight other patients asked to be discharged when they reached this point, and the therapist discharged them. Some of these people continued to be partially regressed at home for up to one year after discharge.

If there was reinforcement of the illness unwittingly by staff, therapist, or parents at this phase, the symptoms seemed to remain. When consultation with another psychiatrist or a staff conference recommended that the regression terminate, then treatment plans geared toward terminating the regression were successful.

Phase IV, Termination of Regression

In this phase, there was a feeling of being strengthened. There was an ability to effectively initiate activity without external prodding. Diurnal cycle and eating habits normalized. A sense of confidence and security was observed. Ambition was restored though goals were often scaled down. There was still some occasional depression and even a rare perceptual aberration such as depersonalization; but it was reacted to with knowledge that it was transitory. There was often reported an internalized image of the therapist to which the patient related during troubled times. It is of great interest that the termination of the regression was usually very abrupt, sometimes occurring within a day or two. One patient said it was as if "there was some toxin in my blood that suddenly went out of my system overnight."

V. Follow-up

On a 2.5- to 5.5 year follow-up, all thirteen were gainfully employed in an occupation commensurate with their intelligence or were going to school. All had significant to almost complete disappearance of psychotic symptoms. Those two who still had occasional symptoms were not alarmed by such psychotic symptoms as derealization, knowing they would pass. Five still had some dysphoria on occasion.

Ten of the thirteen are now living alone. Initially, after leaving the hospital, six of the ten now living alone lived with their families for a time and later opted to live alone. One male lives with a girl in a thus far successful hetero-

figure 1

Phases Toward Good Outcome

I. Phase of Internal Disorganization (may also be behavioral disorganization manifested)
   A. Preoccupation with good and bad objects.
   B. Feelings of abominable badness, grandiosity, total aloneness, and persecution which may vacillate, or become temporarily fixed.
   C. Fear of regression with fears of total and permanent loss of self.

II. Phase of Postpsychotic Regression
   A. Some continuing internal disorganization with relative stabilization.
   B. Reversal of diurnal rhythm with excessive sleeping during the day.
   C. Eating problems and sometimes oral movements.
   D. Staring and thought clogging
   E. Psychophysiologic disturbances.
   F. Desire to be alone.
   G. Profound passivity.
   H. Feelings of emptiness and being totally alone and unloved.
   I. Depression
   J. Dyadic preoccupation.
   K. Severe but transient exacerbations of disorganization in some patients.

III. Middle Phase of Postpsychotic Regression
   A. Better grooming.
   B. Begins to read.
   C. Memories more distinct.
   D. Wakes up early in the morning about 7 or 8 A.M.
   E. Begins to be with people but little verbal interaction.
   F. Exacerbation now of psychotic symptoms often can be abolished by interpretation or by merely nonreinforcement.

IV. Termination of Postpsychotic Regression (can occur within 1 or 2 days)
   A. Feeling of being strengthened.
   B. Loss of passivity.
   C. Restoration of ambition with often a realistic scaling down of future expectations.

FIGURE 2

Characteristics of Improved Schizophrenics

	Gender	Age At Time of Admission	Phillips Prognostic Scale	Precipitant	Psychosis	Therapist	Clinical Course	Regular Use of Neuroleptics	Length of Stay (Hospital) Months	Childhood Disturbances	Present Living Arrangements	Psychotherapy Status
J.J.	M	22	18	Heterosexual relationship	Hebephrenic features	Resident male	Usual	Yes	18	Excessive daydreaming	With girl	Once every 6 months
W.M.	F	22	20	Beginning college & paternal death	Catatonic features	Jr. psych. female	Usual	Yes	5.5	1)Excessive daydreaming 2)Thyrotoxicosis	Alone	Terminated
F.K.	F	25	16	Heterosexual relationship (marriage)	Schizo-affec. Marked depression	Sr. psych. male	Undulating	No	12	Excessive daydreaming	Alone, now divorced	Psychoanalysis
W.L.	F	20	20	Heterosexual relationship, college finals	1)Catatonic features 2)Oedipal contents	Sr. psych. male	Usual	Yes	12	Excessive daydreaming	Alone	Terminated
L.D.	M	20	23	College finals	1)Mild paranoid 2)Obsessional features	Jr. psych. male	Undulating	Yes	9	Bullying	Alone	Intensive psychotherapy
M.C.	F	18	24	Beginning college	1)Catatonic features 2)Oedipal content	Jr. psych. male	Usual	Yes	7	1)Excessive daydreaming 2)Delayed speech	Alone	Terminated

C.J.	F	22	25	Heterosexual relationship	Catatonic features	Sr. psych. male	Usual	Yes	12	1)Epilepsy 2)Daydreaming 3)Somatizing	Parents	Frequent supportive psychotherapy
H.B.	F	16	Not rated	Chronic delinquency No definable free.	Catatonic features	Resident male	Usual	Yes	12	1)Somatizing 2)Pathological lying 3)Chronic delinquent acts	Alone	Terminated
M.M.	F	18	16	Beginning college	1)Catatonic features 2)Strong sexual content	Sr. psych. male	Usual	No	12	1)Duodenal ulcer (age 14) 2)Excessive daydreaming	Alone	Less than once a week
M.D.	F	20	15	Beginning college	Paranoid delusions	Jr. psych. male	Usual	No	6	1)Congenital facial atavism 2)Delayed speech 3)Pathological lying	Parents	Less than once a week
W.A.	F	20	25	Heterosexual relationship	Mixed with paranoid, catatonic & hysterical features	Sr. psych. male	Undulating	Yes	12	1)Retinitis proliferans 2)Excessive daydreaming	Alone	Frequent supportive psychotherapy
W.B.	F	18	19	Heterosexual relationship	1)Catatonic features 2)Oedipal content	Jr. psych. male	Usual	Yes	4	1)Hypoplastic eye & absence of fingernails 2)Delayed speech	Alone	Terminated
E.R.	F	18	16	Heterosexual relationship (marriage)	Seclusive, empty, depressed	Sr. psych. male	Usual	No	15	1)Excessive daydreaming 2)School phobia	Alone, now divorced	Terminated

sexual relationship. Two of the females who were married later divorced and are now living alone. The two others who do not live alone live with their families. These are families in which the parental relationship shows skew, and where the patient returned home with an identity as passive, impaired, and immature. This identity was mutually acceptable to the parents and the patient.

One year after the symptoms subsided, only four were in regular psychotherapy. Of the four, one was undergoing "modified psychoanalysis," one was in "intensive depth psychotherapy," while two others were in a frequent, supportive type of psychotherapy. Seven subjects had either terminated therapy or saw their psychiatrists less than twice a year. Two subjects saw their therapists less than once a week but more frequently than twice a year. It is interesting that those who terminated or were not in regular therapy seemed to have made the most substantial gains.

The schizophrenics in the study were young adults with a marked predominance of females. This feature is partly an artifact in the selection of the original forty-two names given this investigator, of which the vast majority were female. The young adult program in our institute has an aftercare program in which females predominate because such prolonged dependency is more socially acceptable in women. In addition, there is a tendency in our hospital for young adult males to remain in the hospital for either a shorter time because of the greater shame in being helpless or to be so ill that prolonged hospitalization does not seem to result in the same degree of salutory shift as in the females. Preliminary follow-up data on a larger prospective study of outcome indicate that gender disparity is not nearly as large as in this study.

The Phillips Prognostic Scale indicated that a significant majority of these patients had features associated with poor prognosis. In addition, most of these young adults had strong evidence of moderate to severe psychopathology from childhood. Yet all these patients have had a sustained improvement. Therefore, something must have ensued in their illness which effected this salutory result.

Traversing the Four Phases and Good Outcome

The most likely feature in the illness contributing to successful outcome is the clinical course, for despite the great variation in clinical picture, experience of the therapist, duration of the illness, and past history, there was a striking homogeneity in the clinical course. In each schizophrenic there was pronounced postpsychotic regression following the phase of internal disorganization. This does not say that there aren't other pathways to successful outcome. Sachar et al. (29) have described a parasitic and compliant pathway toward ego reintegration in addition to a postpsychotic regression which they called an anaclitic depressive pathway toward recovery. Their criterion of recovery was a resolution of the psychosis. It would certainly be interesting to have a follow-up report to see if these different pathways were also associated with successful enduring outcomes.

As a corollary to the possibility of different pathways leading to enduring good outcome, this study does not explore the possibility that prevention of a prolonged postpsychotic regression might produce the same good outcome. A very influential and current point of view is that brief hospitalization geared toward aborting the psychosis will prevent the patient from becoming institutionalized or from learning behaviors that will make him label himself, and have others label him, as deviant (30, 24). There is a developing literature that demonstrates that brief crisis-intervention treatment of acute schizophrenic psychosis is more effective than prolonged hospitalization with intensive treatment (7, 8). These studies, however, have used outcome measures that have ignored the experiential aspects of these patients such as continuing symptoms, sense of self, the sense of relatedness toward other people, etc. They have used mostly indices of vocational adjustment and absence of readmission to a hospital. Rogers et al. (26) in their study of the intensive psychotherapy of schizophrenics have demonstrated a significant salutory change in the subjective experiencing of those schizophrenics who developed a feeling of relatedness toward their therapists. Despite the apparent success of the crisis intervention, brief therapy, community approaches, we still do not know if these approaches produce enduring improvement and whether they are as satisfying and useful to the patient as skillfully managed intensive treatment.

In addition, this study cannot ignore the fact that a certain expectation of the milieu as well as the local psychotherapeutic philosophy might certainly affect the clinical course. It can be argued that in a different setting, the course might be very different. Perhaps the reason for the homogeneity in clinical course in various institutions in the country reflects more a similarity of milieu and selection of patients than the actual clinical course.

However, despite the aforementioned reservations, there is a convincing literature that certainly buttresses the findings of this paper. Sachar, et al. (28, 29) and Steinberg et al. (37) have detailed an anaclitic depressive phase interposed between the acute psychotic episode and the final ego reintegration. On an individual therapy basis the phase of internal disorganization corresponds to Searles's phases (32) of "out of contact" and "ambivalent symbiosis," while the postpsychotic regression corresponds to his phase of "full or preambivalent symbiosis." Well-documented treatment cases that have included behavioral observations like that of Odile (21) and the case described by

Schulz and Kilgalen (31) have also demonstrated the traversing of the described phases.

Prognosis studies such as the excellent studies of Vaillant (39) and Huston and Pepernik(17) also add to the validity of the findings of this study. In Vaillant's study of thirty cases of recovered schizophrenics who had maintained their recovery from one to four years, he found symptoms of psychotic depression and a family history of psychotic depression as the most important indicators of eventual recovery. The psychotic depression symptoms in Vaillant's schizophrenics correspond to the phase of postpsychotic regression. Huston and Pepernik (17) delineated overt tension, anxiety, depression, and self-reproaching delusions as some clinical indicators of good prognosis. These features were also found in the successful outcome schizophrenics in this study.

With this evidence, it appears that the traversing of the phases outlined in this study constitutes certain necessary elements in producing substantial and enduring change in schizophrenics. All these elements can be organized to provide a theoretical framework for understanding the changes brought about by traversing the four phases. The ensuing explanation will not consider genetic or other biological contributions to schizophrenia, but will focus on the psychological manifestations of the schizophrenic disorder.

A Kleinian View

A good starting point for this theoretical discussion will be the views of Melanie Klein (19, 20), with important modifications in her theories by Fairbairn (9) and Guntrip (15, 16). First let us have a brief explanation of those Kleinian views of schizophrenia applicable to this investigation. Following this abbreviated presentation, modifications of these Kleinian views will be presented in accordance with data from this investigation.

According to Klein and Fairbairn, the infant's early experiences with the mother are crucial for the development of a secure sense of self. Development is enhanced by satisfying experiences with minimal frustration by the mother and is hampered by excessive frustration of basic needs. With excessive need frustration the infant engages in primitive defensive operations involving splitting the mothering figure into a persecutor and an ideal object which become internalized. These structures then form the nidus of the later superego. Another defensive operation is "ego splitting." One form of ego splitting consists of projecting bad feelings upon the indistinctly perceived mothering figure. This projective identification temporarily frees the infant from feelings of internal badness. Thus excessive frustration results in the eventual introjection of a bad part object. The rage engendered by frustrating experiences is thus perceived in its projected form in the visage or the less differentiated form of the need-satisfying object. If the persecutory anxiety resulting from the frustrating experiences of this paranoid-schizoid position can be surmounted, the infant then enters the depressive position. In this phase, the whole good and bad objects are perceived. In this stage, hostility toward the bad object threatens to destroy the good object, producing separation anxiety. If this stage goes unresolved, it predisposes to later depression. The Klein and Fairbairn formulations thus explain not only the formation of primary introjects evidenced in paranoid and schizophrenic stages but also the link between depression, paranoia, and schizophrenia.

These formulations were carefully reviewed by Guntrip (15) and then taken one step further (16). When there is excessive frustration of basic oral needs, the infant dissociates these unsatisfied needs for love and contact. These longings grow in this unconsciously dissociated portion of the self as the need for love mounts. The infant has in effect consciously surrendered his desire for good mothering, but a portion of the self still contains these very primitive longings. This so-called regressed ego is also called the "schizoid citadel," which can be returned to during periods of excessive stress. That these dissociated needs exist is evidenced by such manifestations as claustrophobic anxiety, fears of closeness, curling up into fetal positions, and difficulties in modulating the intake of food.

There are several theoretical formulations from the Kleinian school which are helpful in understanding the clinical features in this investigation: (*a*) excessive frustration of the basic needs of the infant produces a powerful and enduring memory of a sinister other, (*b*) having sensitive mothering most of the time balances those memories of the sinister other, and (*c*) when an infant is finally unable to have a sensitive mothering experience, he dissociates these needs. Though there is surrender of these wishes overtly, they endure and grow in a dissociated portion of the self. Using this information, we can speculate further utilizing portions of these Kleinian notions.

A Psychogenetic Scheme for Understanding the Schizophrenic Illness

A primary psychological manifestation of the schizophrenic disorder is the failure to internalize a sensitive mothering experience solidly at a crucial, early developmental phase. This hampered internalization causes difficulties in (*a*) the ability to be alone and yet feel secure, as has been described by Winnicott; (*b*) having a solid sense of self relatively separate from the vicissitudes of other people; (*c*) proper tension and affect modulation; and (*d*) the development of basic psychological functions such as volition, perception, thought, and empathy. The failure to solidly internalize sensitive mothering experience may be primarily due to the mother, the infant, or an accidental faulty pairing.

The mothering figure might respond to the infant by her own wants rather than a genuine sensitivity to the infant's needs, or the mother may oversatiate before the infant experiences the tension. This could eventually create a disturbance in tension modulation, and in recognizing internal need states, as has been described by Bruch (6). Sobel (35) systematically observed the schizophrenic mother's interaction with her infant. These infants expressed signs of early disturbance such as depression, apathy, and irritability. Infants born to schizophrenic mothers and fathers who were adopted out did not show nearly the same degree of perturbation. This study indicates that insensitive early mothering produces early signs of disturbance. The privation of a sensitive mothering experience may also be a function of infantile unresponsiveness or erratic responsiveness, as seen in the studies of Fish and Alpert (10). They observed abnormal states of consciousness and muscle tone in infants born to schizophrenic mothers. In a prospective study by Fish et al. (11) the infant Peter, who exhibited maturational inconsistencies, later developed childhood schizophrenia.

Whatever the source of the failure in a sensitive mothering experience, what is finally internalized are the object representations of need frustration, that is, primitive images of sinister, persecuting forces unbalanced by the images of sensitive mothering good object. Without an internalized good object, the child will not have a feeling of being good and secure within himself. Valued persons or institutions in the external world are thus substituted which provide the future schizophrenic with a sense of being acceptable and attached. However, this feeling is dependent upon the continued external presence of these valued objects and there is a continuous need to internalize a good object.

Because of the great excess of frustrating experiences, the infant finally adaptively dissociates his early infantile needs. Concomitant with the adaptive dissociation, there is a halt in those behaviors which would elicit sensitive mothering. There is thus a neurophysiological as well as psychological arrest in this early infant development. Organismic equilibrium is thus very tenuous. Satisfaction of early infantile needs such as for love, contact, predictable need satisfaction, must either be constantly maintained through actual or fantasied transactions with the external valued object or must entirely be suppressed by schizoid indifference. Many precipitants can thus unleash the entire complex or any of its parts. Stimulation of the basic infantile needs, loss of a valued object, activation of potential or actual persecutory experiences, and situation requiring greater autonomy are some of the precipitants seen in this investigation.

The Sequence of Events

With the observations from this study, I would like to postulate the following series of events in a schizophrenic disorganization. With loss or absence of an external valued object there is first a feeling of aloneness, abandonment, and potential annihilation. Next, the feeling of being bad, unloved, and worthless is activated, which explains the terrible aloneness, resurrects hope for a valued other, and protects against the fear of annihilation. If this continues, the images of the frustrating mothering are activated, producing persecutory voices, delusions, or the sense of a sinister presence coming either from within or from the outside. There is then a search for a good object which will protect against the persecutory images and perhaps eventually supply the sensitive mothering experience that had been lacking. Thus either good objects created by delusions and hallucinations or else external objects are imbued with good and powerful characteristics. In this state, the schizophrenic may fixate any of the vacillating positions of self-abomination, persecution, or self-aggrandizement, or communion with a good object. This may be the nidus for more chronically psychotic schizophrenic states.

However, if the schizophrenic begins to feel some attachment and trust in his therapist or a staff member, there is then a waning of good and bad object dilemma. As a sustained, trusting contact begins to develop there is an activation of the dissociated early infantile needs. This activation is signaled by fears of dying, objectless dread, disturbance in body boundaries, destruction of people, dreams of submerging into water, claustrophobic anxiety, adopting fetal positions, and perceptual aberrations. With a continued feeling of inchoate security a neurophysiological and psychological state that had never been successfully traversed as an infant now begins. This corresponds to Phase II or the postpsychotic regressive phase. This is the phase that permits a unique second chance to experience the sensitive mothering necessary to develop (*a*) the capacity to be alone, (*b*) a solid sense of a good self, (*c*) a proper tension and affect modulation, and (*d*) the maturation of incompletely developed psychological functions.

In this phase, there are feelings of intensive passivity, staring and blankness, a feeling of emptiness, a desire to be alone, dyadic preoccupation, concern for food, and even sometimes oral movements. These clinical observations suggest that the schizophrenic in this phase is searching for those experiences that might satisfy unfulfilled primitive gestalts. This entire phase suggests that if there is proper environmental fit with neurophysiological and psychological readiness, there can be the formation of new structures with abolition of intense primitive needs. This can strengthen the organism and partially correct those deficiencies that have caused many of the signs and symptoms called schizophrenia. Phase II is thus seen as the phase of maximum therapeutic value. This is borne out by the previously cited studies by Vaillant (39), Huston and Pepernik (17) and Sachar et al. (28, 29), as well as this study, in which the postpsychotic regression preceded a good outcome. If this contention is correct, it thus is crucial that this phase be reached, not prematurely stifled when reached, and used to provide a therapeutic experience, by making constellations of experience available to be assimilated. This means that the staff and/or the therapist must be able to (a) make a trusting contact with the patient, (b) permit the regression and assuage shame over the regression while assuaging guilt over the neediness which is released, (c) provide relatively unambivalent sensitive mothering. This includes not intruding on the patient, yet being sensitive to when he needs the nonverbal presence of a valued person. In addition, the staff and/or therapist must sensitively, confidently, and kindly assist patient during periods of behavioral dyscontrol and emotional upset. Other aspects of the milieu can also be arranged to provide partial fulfillment of these experiential needs. A beneficial therapeutic regression can also occur out of the hospital if a sensitive and secure milieu can be arranged.

If these experiential needs are satisfied, the schizophrenic moves to Phase III, the middle phase of the postpsychotic regression. This indicates that the regression need not totally continue and that, if reinforced, could become learned behavior which could unnecessarily prolong the illness or even contribute to the eventual institutionalization of the patient. When concentration improves, daytime sleeping diminishes, socialization with others begins, a kind yet firm enforced movement into the outside world is relatively safe, and even an exacerbation of psychotic symptoms will evaporate if it is not reinforced. If proper management is exerted at this phase, then the entire episode terminates in four to eighteen months, with the person able to resume life at a significantly improved level of functioning.

Alternative Explanations of the Postpsychotic Regression

Of the four phases described, the pivotal phase is the postpsychotic regression. The foregoing was a psychogenetic explanation of the way a well-managed postpsychotic regression contributes to eventual improvement. There are, of course, other ways of legitimately explaining why Phase II, the postpsychotic regression, is associated with good outcome. One view is that the postpsychotic regression is akin to the biological response of the blister. In this reaction, trauma is reacted to by the growth of a protective structure that covers over the denuded area to protect it from external stimuli. This structure permits a healing below its surface, and when its sloughs the surface is mostly healed. Thus the postpsychotic regression can be seen to represent a defensive response to stimuli flooding which remains until stimulus modulation can be reinstituted. These theories have been reviewed by Lang and Buss (22) and incorporated into a more comprehensive theoretical framework by Silverman (34).

The traditional view of schizophrenia is based on the medical model. This views schizophrenia as a disease in which the psychosis is the disease which is followed by a convalescence which in this case is the postpsychotic regression. Convalescence is a time where there is no active treatment; however, the patient is observed to ensure that he doesn't become ill (psychotic) again.

Another view of the postpsychotic regression is represented in the work of Fowler et al. (12). In their study, schizophrenics with affect disorders had significantly more relatives with histories of severe depression. It was thus postulated that certain persons who appeared to be schizophrenics were in reality suffering from a variant of affect disorder with its inherently better prognosis. This might suggest that the patients in this study may have had a manic-depressive variant.

A prominent view of this regressive phase has been expressed by Semrad (33). In his formulation, the hypochondriasis and neurasthenia evident at this phase represent defensive maneuvers on the part of the patient. On the basis of this theoretical formulation, a postpsychotic state with pronounced neurasthenia and hypochondriasis bodes a poorer prognosis than a postpsychotic state characterized by obsessive-compulsive defenses.

Finally, it has been argued that postpsychotic regression is an iatrogenic phenomena. Sonnenberg and Miller (36) feel it is the result of the symbiotic opportunity offered in intensive psychotherapy. However, they do speculate that once it begins, it is associated with a good outcome if it is successfully worked through. Others would centend that this phase is an unfortunate result of institutional ideologies that permit regression. All these explanations are cogent and certainly require further study. However, the schizophrenics in this sample were mostly people who would be predicted to have poor outcomes. The observations of this study strongly suggest that a well-traversed postpsychotic regression may be instrumental in *producing* a good outcome in schizophrenia. The model suggested in this paper also provides the therapist with guidelines for management.

Other Observations

Follow-up data suggest that successful verbal psychotherapy in the more traditional sense is best begun after the termination of the postpsychotic regression if the patient wishes to continue. These data also suggest that often a well-treated schizophrenic episode permits the person to individuate without the need for continued intensive psychotherapy. In fact, the best outcomes were associated with those who spontaneously terminated therapy within a year after hospital discharge.

Another interesting finding in this study is the tendency for successful-outcome schizophrenics to live by themselves. This same result has been obtained by Brown, Carstairs, and Topping (5) in their studies of schizophrenics in the community. Living alone indicates that the successful-outcome schizophrenic is now able to be alone without the necessity of maintaining continuous and actual contact with a valued other. The internalization of the good part object can thus be assumed. However, the choosing to live alone also suggests that difficulties in interpersonal intimacy may still exist, so that living alone is preferred. Those who do live alone, however, report relishing their privacy, and have a sense of continuing pride in their new-found autonomy.

Further studies are certainly necessary to test the validity of these observations. The theoretical formulations are closely tied to the data and to existing psychogenetic explanations. These formulations are thus in need of refinement as other data are gathered. In addition, there are numerous facets of schizophrenia to consider and this study does not imply that what has been presented has been exhaustive. However, what was presented is a practical paradigm that can greatly aid in the understanding and treatment of some patients with this elusive and enigmatic disorder psychiatry has named schizophrenia.

Summary

A retrospective analysis was made of thirteen young adult schizophrenics who had improved beyond their premorbid functioning. This marked improvement had been maintained from 2.5 to 5.5 years. The analysis included the psychiatric history, discharge summary, psychiatric progress notes written by the therapist, and the nursing notes. A follow-up questionnaire was completed for each patient. From these data sources, information was compiled on characteristics of the patients, signs of early psychopathology, the nature of the psychosis, the clinical course, and the follow-up. Most of the patients had social functioning indicative of a poor prognosis. All had signs in their childhood of early psychopathology such as excessive daydreaming, delinquent behaviors, and psychophysiological disorders. The psychotic symptoms were quite varied. Of greatest interest was the clinical course. This clinical course was fairly homogeneous despite the different symptom pictures and duration of the illness. There were four phases: (*a*) phase of internal disorganization, (*b*) phase of postpsychotic regression, (*c*) middle phase of the postpsychotic regression, and (*d*) termination of the regression. Features of the clinical course were described and a theoretical scheme was outlined to explain how this type of clinical course, coupled with appropriate management and therapy, could produce a good outcome. Follow-up data indicated that all were able to sustain their improvement in social and vocational spheres and all had subjective improvement in their self-esteem, interpersonal relationships, and general functioning. Most of them presently live alone and only a few have continued in intensive psychotherapy.

REFERENCES

1. Beck, S. J. *Psychological Processes in the Schizophrenic Adaptation.* New York: Grune & Stratton, 1965.
2. Betz, B. J., and Whitehorn, J. C. The relationship of the therapist to the outcome of therapy in schizophrenia. In *Research Techniques in Schizophrenia.* Washington D.C.: American Psychiatric Association Psychiatric Research Report no. 5, 1956.
3. Betz, B. J. Studies of the therpist's role in the treatment of the schizophrenic patient. *Amer. J. Psychiat.,* 123:963–971, 1967.
4. Bleuler, E. *Dementia Praecox or the Group of Schizophrenics.* New York: International Universities Press, 1950.
5. Brown, G. W.; Carstairs, G. M.; and Topping, G. C. Post-hospital adjustment of chronic mental patients. *Lancet,* 2:685–688, 1958.
6. Bruch, H. Falsification of bodily needs and body concept in schizophrenia *Arch. Gen. Psychiat.,* 6:34–40, 1962.
7. Caffey, E. M.; Galbrecht, C. R.; and Klett, C. J. Brief hospitalization and aftercare in the treatment of schizophrenia. *Arch. Gen Psychiat.,* 24:81–86, 1971.
8. Deiter, J. B.; Hanford, D. B.; Hummel R. T.; et al. Brief inpatient treatment: A pilot study. *Ment. Hosp.* 16:95–98, 1965.
9. Fairbairn, W. R. D. Schizoid factors in the personality. In *Psychoanalytic Studies of the Personality,* pp. 3–27. New York: Basic Books, 1952.
10. Fish, B., and Alpert, M. Abnormal states of consciousness and muscle tone in infants born to schizophrenic mothers. *Amer. J. Psychiat.,* 119:439–445, 1962.
11. Fish, B.; Shapiro, T.; Halpern, F.; and Wile, R. The prediction of schizophrenia in infancy: III. A ten-year

follow-up report of neurological and psychological development. *Amer. J. Psychiat.*, 121:768–775, 1965.

12. Fowler, R. C.; McCable, M. S.; Cadoret, R. J.; and Winokur, G. The Validity of Good Prognosis Schizophrenia. *Arch. Gen. Psychiat.*, 26:182–186, 1972.

13. Garmezy, N. Process and reactive schizophrenia: Some conceptions and issues. In *The Role and Methodology of Classification in Psychiatry and Psychopathology*, ed. M. M. Katz, J. O. Cole, and W. E. Barton, pp. 419–466. Washington, D.C., 1968.

14. Grinker, R. R. An essay on schizophrenia and science. *Arch. Gen. Psychiat.*, 20:1–24, 1969.

15. Guntrip, H. *Personality Structure and Human Interaction.* New York: International Universities Press, 1964.

16. Guntrip, H. *Schizoid Phenomena, Object Relations, and the Self.* New York: International Universities Press, 1969.

17. Huston, P. E., and Pepernik, M. C. Prognosis in schizophrenia. In *Schizophrenia: A Review of the Syndrome*, ed. L. Bellak, pp. 531–554. New York: Lagos Press, 1958.

18. Kantor, R. E.; Wallner, J. M.; and Winder, C. L. Process and reactive schizophrenia. *J. of Consulting Psychol.*, 17:157–162, 1953.

19. Klein, M. *The Psychoanalysis of Children.* London: Hogarth Press, 1932.

20. Klein, M. Notes on some schizoid mechanisms. *Int. J. Psychoanal.*, 27:99–110, 1946.

21. Laforgue, R. Contribution l'étude de la schizophrenia. *Evolution Psychiatrique*, 3, 81–96, 1935.

22. Lang, P. J., and Buss, A. H. Psychological deficit in schizophrenia: II. interference and activation. *J. Abn. Psychol.*, 70:77–106, 1965.

23. Langfeldt, G. The prognosis in schizophrenia and factors influencing the course of the disease. *Acta Psychiat. Neurol. Suppl.*, 13, 1937.

24. Levene, H. I. Acute schizophrenia. *Arch. Gen. Psychiat.*, 25:215–222, 1971.
25. Meehl, P. E.: Schizotaxia, schizotypy, schizophrenia. In *Theories of Schizophrenia*, ed. A. H. Buss and E. H. Buss, pp. 21–46. New York: Atherton Press, 1969.
26. Rogers, C. R.; Gendlin, E. G.; Kiesler, D. J.; and Truax, C.B. *The Therapeutic Relationship and Its Impact.* Madison: University of Wisconsin Press, 1967.
27. Rubinstein, E. A., and Porloff, M. B. *Research in Psychotherapy*, vol. 1. Washington, D.C.: American Psychological Association, 1959.
28. Sachar, E.; Mason, J.; Kolmer, H.; and Artiss, K. Psychoendocrine aspects of acute schizophrenic reactions. *Psychosom. Med.*, 25:510–537, 1963.
29. Sachar, E.; Kanter, S. S.; Buie, D.; Engle, R.; and Mehlman, R. Psychoendocrinology of ego disintegration. *Amer. J. of Psychiat.* 126:1067–1078, 1970.
30. Scheff, T. J. Schizophrenia as ideology. *Schiz. Bull.*, 2:15–19, 1970.
31. Schulz, C. G., and Kilgalen, R. K. The treatment course of a disturbed patient. In *Case Studies in Schizophrenia*, pp. 14–60. New York: Basic Books, 1969.
32. Searles, H. F. Phase of patient-therapist interaction in the psychotherapy of chronic schizophrenia. In *Collected Papers on Schizophrenia and Related Subjects*, pp. 521–559. New York: International Universities Press, 1965.
33. Semrad, E. V. Long-term therapy of schizophrenia. In *Psychoneurosis and Schizophrenia*, ed. G. L. Usdin, pp. 55–173. Philadelphia: Lippincott, 1966.
34. Silverman, J. Stimulus intensity modulation and psychological disease. *Psychopharmacologia.* 24:42–80, 1972.
35. Sobel, D. Children of schizophrenic patients: preliminary observations on early development. *Amer. J. Psychiat.*, 181:512–517, 1961.

36. Sonnenberg, S. M., and Miller, J. B. Depression in resolving schizophrenia. *Psychotherapy*, 7:111–117, 1970.

37. Steinberg, H.; Green, R.; and Durell, J. Depression occurring during the course of recovery from schizophrenic symptoms. *Amer. J. Psychiat.*, 124:699–705, 1967.

38. Strupp, H. H., and Luborsky, L. *Research in Psychotherapy*, vol. 2. Washington, D.C.: American Psychological Association, 1962.

39. Vaillant, G. E. The prediction of recovery in schizophrenia. *Int. J. Psychiat.*, 2:617–629, 1966.

40. Winnicott, D. W. The capacity to be alone. *Int. J. Psychoanal.*, 39:416–420, 1958.

41. Yolles, S. F., and Kramer, M. Vital Statistics. In *Schizophrenia Syndrome*, ed. L. Bellak and L. Loeb, pp. 66–113. New York: Grune & Stratton, 1969.

26

RESEARCH IMPLICATIONS
OF THE FOUR RECOVERY PHASES
Nathaniel S. Apter, M.D.

The system we call "schizophrenia" may be regarded as a family of systems capable of great variations in clinical signs, symptoms, and courses, and in responsiveness to various therapeutic modalities. From this standpoint, I shall discuss four research areas to which Dr. Kayton's paper contributes: nosologic problems; psychotherapeutic and psychopharmacological managements of the acute phases; and comparison with chronic schizophrenia.

Nosologic Problems

A paradigm for unique membership in the family of systems is the rare syndrome periodic relapsing catatonia. In 1938 Gjessing identified its clinical features and concomitant metabolic deficiency as well as the hormonal therapy capable of reversing the disorder. While it is premature to infer that young adult schizophrenic patients with good outcome constitute a single membership in the family, Kayton has demonstrated a constructive method for resolving a portion of our nosological problems. His behavioral analyses have disclosed four separate clinical phases that are functionally connected sequences in the course of the illness. He has identified some of the "behavioral structures" of young schizophrenics who not only recover but utilize the psychotic experience for reintegrating personality functions at higher adaptive levels.

Psychotherapy and Pharmacotherapy

Kayton's delineation of four stages toward good outcome supplies behavioral bases for developing more appropriate plans for the phasic treatments of some schizophrenic patients, and suggests new opportunities for evaluating psychotherapeutic and psychopharmacologic effects and their interpenetrations. In Phase I the psychotherapist's goal may be to establish a presence as an object for identification by demonstrating to the patient, through empathic and noncritical observing attitudes, that a firm stand as designated caretaker has been taken. The phenothiazines and related compounds have surely facilitated the management of acutely psychotic states. Questions involving selection of patients for which drugs, their dosages, and for how long, and from whom to withhold neuroleptics, are still open. During Phase II the patient, although severely withdrawn and in poor control of impulses, may employ the therapist as an auxiliary perceptual apparatus for reality testing. The profound passivity that characterizes this phase suggests that the positive aspects of the patient's ambivalence are being reactivated. The psychotherapist may be utilized as the patient's agent for regenerating the hope and trustfulness required for tentative reentry into human relationships. "Do neuroleptics activate the willingness to accept dependency in some patients and reinforce the negative side of ambivalence in others?" is a question that may now be raised with a higher degree of legitimacy. In Phase III psychotherapeutic efforts may be expanded to include some interpretive comments on the patient's interpersonal relationships and their effects. When greater control over impulses is achieved, confidence in interpersonal relationships is enhanced. Continued administration of neuroleptics during this phase may inhibit progress in patients who are struggling to reestablish independent strivings. When Dr. Kayton's young schizophrenics achieved a Phase IV clinical status, some required additional psychotherapeutic assistance and some were maintained on the psychopharmacologic agents. It will be interesting to analyze the differences between these two groups. In this connection, the report of French and Kasanin is recalled. They presented a retrospective study of two patients very similar to the ones under discussion. Neither had the benefits of contemporary psychotherapy or psychopharmacology and recovered at higher levels of integration than prior to the onset of their illness.

Comparison with Recovery in Chronic Patients

Some years ago I described the behavioral changes which take place in chronic schizophrenic patients from the deepest regressive states to remission, of longer or shorter duration, of the psychosis. These findings are now summarized as a source of comparison with the phasic changes that Kayton has described in acute psychoses. Patients who achieve Grade I and II levels are regarded as "irreversible." Attainment of clinical states from Grade III to Grade VI warrants a classification as "reversible."

Grade I: The first shift in behavior occurs as a change in motility patterns. Peculiar posturing, fixed facial expressions, and bizarre automatic associated movements disappear. Relaxation of the facial musculature and loosening of motor activity in large and small joints are the initial signs of remission.

Grade 2: Spontaneous activity increases and is associated with continued flexibility of motor patterns. Previously untidy and incontinent patients begin to take care of their own housekeeping functions.

Grade 3: The spontaneous activity is extended to meet some of the socializing goals of the ward. Verbal communication is at a minimum or absent. In this phase, the predominantly catatonic patients remain nonverbal but volunteer to participate in group functions and give evidence of a feeling of belonging by assuming responsibilities for the group.

Grade 4: Freer communication on both motor and verbal levels with some willingness to reach out for interpersonal contacts appear. Inquiries concerning relatives are made. Letter writing occasionally occurs. Affective discharges are more common. The previously passive, docile patient may give expression to aggressive behavior. Patients with predominantly paranoid features begin to exhibit aspects of their premorbid personality. In them, hostility, suspiciousness, and combative attitudes are replaced by oversolicitousness, docility, submissiveness, and superficial cooperativeness. The greater majority of chronic schizophrenic patients do not progress beyond this stage.

Grade 5: An improvement in the clinical picture appears in terms of ability to socialize, communicate past and current feelings, recall important relationships, meet with relatives and display more or less appropriate affective responses. There remains, however, marked fragility of relationships, feelings of confusion, lack of identity, and evasiveness about leading emotional conflicts.

Grade 6: This appears as a temporary remission. There is a dissolution of the bizarre symptomatology with generalized planning for resumption of life outside the hospital. In one instance a willingness to deal with major emotional conflicts and the events leading up to the world catastrophic reaction appeared. This patient communicated his deep insights into the precipitating events and their meanings in relation to his illness.

Follow-up studies on Dr. Kayton's cohort may eventually yield data either for supporting unitary membership or for assigning some of the patients to other branches in the family schizophrenia.

REFERENCES

Apter, N. S. Alterations of ego functions in chronic schizophrenia. *A. M. A. Archives General Psychiatry*, 1:622–629, December 1959.

French, T. M., and Kasanin, J. A psychodynamic study of the recovery of two schizophrenic cases. *Psychoanalytic Quarterly*, 10:1–21, January 1941.

Gjessing, R. Disturbances of somatic function in catatonia with a periodic course and their compensation. *Journal of Mental Science*, 84:608–622, April 1938.

27

PSYCHOTHERAPY FOR SCHIZOPHRENICS: IS IT INDICATED?

David B. Feinsilver, M.D.
John G. Gunderson, M.D.

With the introduction of many new treatment modalities for schizophrenia in the past two decades and the concomitant increase in psychiatric research interest, a number of investigators set out to evaluate systematically the role of psychotherapy in treating this disorder. Five efforts to compare schizophrenic patients treated with psychotherapy to those treated by other methods were conceived and carried out in the early 1960s. It is interesting to note that, in 1960, when one of these projects was being designed, it was considered unethical to have a control group not receiving psychotherapy. But in 1968, at the conclusion of another study, Jonathan Cole stated that it would now seem unethical to have a control group receiving only psychotherapy. Such a turnabout would certainly suggest that an erosion of confidence in the value of psychotherapy with schizophrenic patients had taken place in the eight-year interim.

This paper, in reevaluating the relevant controlled studies of psychotherapy with schizophrenics, attempts to determine whether such a reversal is, in fact, justified. Is our knowledge of schizophrenia sufficiently advanced to support generalizations about the efficacy of psychotherapy with schizophrenic patients? Would the widespread dismissal of this approach be less certain if its effects on subgroups of patients were examined? Or if the various types of psychotherapy or differences in therapists received greater consideration? Has there been agreement between studies on some of these questions, while other areas remain confused and conflicted? If so, why? It is our hope that this review will identify areas needing further research and highlight the methodological issues which must be considered if future investigators are to achieve more definitive answers than their predecessors.

Selection of Studies

We have limited our review to those studies which are potentially reproducible and which assessed the effectiveness of psychotherapy by comparing psychotherapeutically treated schizophrenic patients with appropriate control groups. To date, only five such studies have been published.

A recent NIMH workshop set forth criteria for methodological rigor which were published (Fiske et al., 1970) in an effort to establish high standards for psychotherapy research. Using these criteria as a guide, we have attempted to evaluate the five studies reviewed here according to sample and therapist characteristics, control groups, type of psychotherapy, outcome measures, and statistical handling. Although the studies are each concerned with somewhat different aspects of the psychotherapy of schizophrenia, their research designs have taken into account at least some of these factors. It is understood that the research criteria which make it possible to assign specific causes to results are especially difficult to satisfy when dealing with human subjects and that studies such as the five evaluated here are necessarily fraught with difficulties and imperfections. We recognize, further, that some of the objections raised in this review may be answered by further reports which are expected to be forthcoming.

The studies are presented here in the order in which the major report of their results appeared in the literature.

Direct Analysis

Direct analysis, a dramatic technique developed by John Rosen (1947 and 1953), has been reported to be highly successful with schizophrenic patients. This intense and extremely active verbal approach involves deep, immediate interpretations of the patient's primary process, psychotic productions, or id content and is accompanied, if need be, by direct authority struggles and physical activity. The patient is generally seen for a number of hours each day during the acute period.

In an effort to evaluate this approach systematically (Bookhammer et al., 1966), fourteen first-break schizophrenic patients (aged 15–35) were selected from consecutive admissions to the Psychiatric Reception Center of the Philadelphia General Hospital to be treated by direct analysis. Eighteen comparable patients were designated as controls and sent to cooperating hospitals, where they received "usual treatment." After the study had been in progress for two and one-half years, nineteen additional control subjects were randomly selected from among those who had passed through the Reception Center during the same time period as those initially studied. At the end of a 5 –5½-year-follow-up period, members of the investigative team rated each patient as "improved" or "unimproved" according to changes in signs and symptoms, work status, attitude toward himself and others, thought processes, and time out of the hospital. No significant differences were found between patients receiving direct analysis (57 percent improved) and either the designated controls (67 percent improved) or the random controls (58 percent improved.

Unfortunately, it is difficult to draw generalizable conclusions about the efficacy of psychotherapy from this study of Rosen's controversial technique. Among the study's deficiencies is its failure to describe the type of treatment received by control patients, who the therapists were, and precisely what the direct analytic therapy consisted of (i.e., its frequency or duration). Moreover, no independent or standardized measures of outcome were used, and no baseline or intermediate assessments were made prior to the five-year follow-up. The absence of early evaluations during treatment or at its conclusion is particularly regrettable, since, according to Frieda Fromm-Reichmann (1952), the primary virtue of the direct analytic method is not its ability to cure schizophrenics, but rather to "help them to emerge quickly from acute psychotic episodes."

Client-Centered Therapy

The results of a study designed to test the effectiveness of Carl Rogers's "client-centered" therapy were reported in *The Therapeutic Relationship and Its Impact: A Study of Psychotherapy with Schizophrenics* (Rogers et al., 1967). In describing client-centered therapy, Rogers (1942) originally emphasized the therapist's ability to perceive and clarify his patient's unrecognized feelings, state, or intended message; but he eventually came to see the efficacy of this nondirective, noninterpretive technique as dependent on the following characteristics of the therapeutic relationship:

• *congruence-genuineness*—the therapist responds as a "real person";

• *empathy*—the therapist senses and expresses the client's felt needs;

• *unconditional positive regard*—the therapist expresses a warm and positive acceptance toward his client.

Rogers hypothesized that any therapy would be effective to the extent that therapists could communicate these crucial attitudes to their clients. Accordingly, the focus of the study to be reviewed here was on the nature of the therapeutic relationship and the variables that affect it.

Conducted under Rogers's direction at the Mendota State Hospital, the project involved the random selection of eight "more chronic" (hospitalized over eight months) schizophrenics, eight "more acute" (hospitalized less than eight months) schizophrenics, and eight normal volunteers to receive client-oriented psychotherapy from eight therapists, each of whom treated one subject from each category. The twenty-four subjects were matched according to chronicity, socioeconomic status, age, and sex to an equal number of controls, who received the same tests but only hospital "milieu therapy." The experimental subjects were seen twice a week in fifty-minute sessions until the termination of treatment (from several months to two and one-half years). Ratings of behavior, symptomatic improvement, and other variables were made by trained, nonprofessional, "blind" raters before beginning, every three months during, immediately after terminating, and one year following treatment. Among the evaluating instruments used were the Minnesota Multiphasic Personality Inventory (MMPI), the Thematic Apperception Test (TAT), the Rorschach Test, the Barrett-Lennard Relationship Inventory, the Wittenborn Psychiatric Rating Scales, and a number of specially designed "process" scales which measured congruence-genuineness, empathy, and unconditional positive regard in the therapists.

Some of the major findings of this study were: (1) Schizophrenic patients receiving psychotherapy demonstrated a decreased need to deny their own experience and greater appropriateness in emotional expression on the TAT. They also showed "a slightly better rate of release from the hospital, and this differential was maintained a year after termination of therapy" (Rogers et al., 1967). The experimental subjects spent 68 percent of their time outside hospitals the year after release, as compared to 40 percent for their controls (*P*<.10). None of the many other outcome measures, including the MMPI, showed a significant difference from the controls. (2) Those schizophrenic patients (as well as normals) who perceived a high degree of empathy and congruence ("process attitudes") in their therapist showed the most change on the MMPI and had better outcomes. (3) The "process attitudes" tended to reach a certain level and stabilize in both schizophrenics and normals. (4) If therapists viewed a relationship positively, but patients viewed it negatively, the outcome was generally negative. The patient's view of the relationship correlated with outcome and agreed with the outside rater's view, whereas the therapist's view often did not.

This study is particularly noteworthy because it was the first to state that psychotherapy for schizophrenic patients can produce measurable differences from control patients and that its effectiveness seems to be related to the establishment of a therapeutic relationship characterized by empathy and congruence. No other study has attempted to sift out the critical determinants within a psychotherapeutic relationship which can affect outcome in schizophrenic patients. Rogers et al. have not treated the patient and the therapist as independent variables, but rather have focused upon their *relationship*—the interaction and process of therapy.

Despite this ambitious study's undeniable merits, it is by no means free of problems. Ironically, the investigators' painstaking attention to methodological issues resulted, by their own admission, in a complicated, unwieldy research design, difficult to implement but still open to criticism from many aspects. A major contaminating factor is the fact that the schizophrenic controls received drugs as a regular part of their "usual hospital" treatment, while the psychotherapy patients received medication "only in emergencies"—i.e., in a completely uncontrolled, irregular, and unknown fashion. This is unfortunate because it is difficult to be sure, in retrospect, how drugs affected the study's ultimate findings. One might speculate that, since the controls probably received more drugs than the experimental group, the effectiveness of psychotherapy reported might be more impressive than it at first appears. Another flaw in the study is the lack of a matched "psychotherapy" control group. Since only "client-centered" psychotherapy was tried, it is impossible to judge the particular merits of this approach or even whether the elements of empathy and congruence might be more evident in other psychotherapeutic techniques, as was suggested by several discussants in the book reporting this study's results. Moreover, reviewers have criticized the rating instruments used to evaluate the psychotherapeutic relationship as being too idiosyncratic (Vaccaro, 1967) and the outcome measures for neglecting basic ward, social, occupational, and home adaptations (Ludwig, 1967, and Shlien, 1967).

Five Treatment Methods

The study which most closely approached optimal methodological rigor was the Schizophrenia Research Project, conducted at the Camarillo State Hospital under the direction of Philip R. A. May. Its major findings were presented in May's influential book *Treatment of Schizophrenia: A Comparative Study of Five Treatment Methods* (1968).

In selecting experimental subjects from among 6,900 "possibly schizophrenic" patients seen at the hospital, May and his co-workers used the following criteria: (1) clinical diagnosis of schizophrenia, (2) first admission *or* no history of previous somatic therapy, (3) no evidence of brain damage, epilepsy, or addiction, (4) aged 16 to 45, and (5) having an "average prognosis." Two hundred and twenty-eight subjects who met these criteria were randomly assigned to five twenty-bed wards, where they received one of the following treatments: (1) psychotherapy, (2) psychotherapy plus drugs, (3) drugs, (4) electroconvulsive therapy (ETC), and (5) milieu alone. The wards were similarly staffed, and each treatment program was supervised by people who believed in the efficacy of their particular approach. Forty-one psychiatric residents and psychiatrists with between six months and six years of experience administered psychotherapy which could be described, in theoretical terms, as psychoanalytically oriented, ego supportive, and reality defining, with a minimum of depth interpretation. On the average, psychotherapy patients were seen two hours per week until they were either released or declared treatment failures at the end of a year. Total time in psychotherapy for each patient ranged from 7 to 87 hours, with a mean of 49 hours.

Ratings of improvement in the five patient groups were made by the patients themselves, by their doctors and nurses, and by an independent team of psychoanalysts who had no connection with their treatment. Among the psychological instruments used to evaluate outcome were the MMPI, the Menninger Health-Sickness Rating Scale, the Camarillo Dynamic Assessment Scales, the Shipley Scale, the Psychotic Confusion Scale, and Barron's Ego Strength Scale. Based on these and other measures, *psychotherapy plus drugs* and *drugs alone* were shown to be approximately equally most effective, while *psychotherapy alone* and *milieu alone* were approximately equally least effective, and *ECT* was intermediate in effectiveness.

In view of the unimpressive showing of *psychotherapy alone*, even the most conservative reviewer must conclude from this study that, for first-admission schizophrenics in the middle prognostic range, individual psychotherapy of an "ego supportive, reality defining" type, administered twice weekly by relatively inexperienced supervised therapists for up to 87 hours, is, by itself, a relatively ineffective treatment when compared to ataractic drugs. Given the finding that *psychotherapy alone* is not the treatment of choice, it remained for May's group to test the value of psychotherapy even as an *adjunct* to drugs by a comparison between the groups receiving *drugs alone* and *psychotherapy plus drugs*. Because trends indicating a superiority for the latter treatment (e.g., patients who received both psychotherapy and drugs showed more "insight" and a greater capacity to think abstractly) were slight, May and his associates concluded that, on a cost-efficiency basis, treatment with *drugs alone* is the most reasonable approach to meeting the needs of the majority of schizophrenics and that psychotherapy is not indicated (with or without drugs) for the hospitalized schizophrenic.

While this conclusion may be valid, one should recognize its limitations and that other conclusions are also possible. By most standards, May's study has only covered the initial phase of psychotherapy, and therefore cannot be used to assess the efficacy of long-term psychotherapy. Moreover, May's cost-efficiency orientation, for all its public health value, overlooks what might be most valuable to individuals who can undertake the expense of prolonged psychotherapy and hospitalization.

May's conclusion is also open to criticism on the grounds that not all of his data have yet been published. For example, one cannot rule out the possibility that statistically insignificant differences noted in the five treatment groups on discharge have become more pronounced with time and that psychotherapy fostered assets not tapped by May's test battery which have proved more lasting than gains accomplished by drugs alone. Also unpublished are May's findings about the therapists who participated in his study. In recognition of the role that such therapist characteristics as "social and ethnic background, attitudes, interests and other personality features" may play in the "outcome of treatment," May's research design included psychological testing of the therapists, division of therapists into "A" and "B" types, and supervisors' ratings of therapeutic effectiveness. Unfortunately, May's findings in this area have yet to be presented. Therefore, one can only speculate that May's statistical handling of psychotherapy as a "homogeneous" treatment may have masked significant differences among therapists. Certainly, this is suggested by the very different recommendations of the various supervisors (compare, for example, Fine, 1968, and Wexler, 1968) and by May's maintaining a role for the "gifted specialist." It is possible that no study can truly assess psychotherapy if it ignores differences in effectiveness among therapists and subgroups of "responders" to psychotherapy among patients. Among the other criticisms leveled at the type of psychotherapy given in May's project were that it was too brief (Grinspoon, 1969; Leavitt, 1968; and Michels, 1969), too nonintensive (Hamilton, 1969, and Wexler, 1968), and that the therapists were lacking in skill (Leavitt, 1968, and Rosen, 1969) or enthusiasm (Fleiss, 1969).

Long-Term Psychotherapy
with Chronic
Schizophrenics

In a project at the Massachusetts Mental Health Center (MMHC), Grinspoon, Ewalt, and Shader (1967) attempted to investigate the effects of long-term, psychoanalytically oriented psychotherapy on chronic schizophrenic patients, with and without drugs. Twenty experimental subjects were selected from among a group of forty-one single males (aged 16–35) who had been hospitalized at the Boston State Hospital for over three years; the remaining twenty-one patients served as controls. Although the investigators attempted to assign patients to experimental and control groups on a random basis, this effort was frustrated because some patients either refused or were not permitted by their families to transfer to the experimental "active milieu" ward at the MMHC, and thus were relegated by default to the control group treated at Boston State Hospital.

Upon their admission to the MMHC, all of the subjects were placed upon a placebo regimen. Thirteen weeks later half of the patients were given thioridazine, while the rest continued to receive placebo. Both placebo and thioridazine groups received individual psychotherapy at least twice a week for two or more years. The participating therapists were eighteen analytically oriented senior staff members whose attitude toward psychotherapy with schizophrenic patients was positive. Patients in the Boston State Hospital control group received "usual treatment," consisting mainly of high doses of various phenothiazines.

During the course of treatment, behavioral ratings were made by nurses using a standard scale, by the patient's family as reported to a social worker, by the patient's therapist, and by senior residents on the ward. In addition, each patient was asked to keep a diary in which he daily recorded comments about his behavior. Based on these measures, the placebo group remained virtually unchanged over two years of therapy, whereas those patients receiving psychotherapy plus drugs showed slight but significantly greater improvement; the latter group tended, in particular, to be more responsive, communicative, and aware of their surroundings than patients on placebo. Differences between the two groups tended to disappear when placebo was substituted for thioridazine during a three-month period at the end of the study.

The comparison of the MMHC experimental subjects with their controls at the Boston State Hospital was based upon follow-up assessments which showed no significant difference between the two groups. While a greater proportion of the MMHC patients were living outside the hospital at follow-up (68 percent as compared to 37 percent of the controls), this finding's significance was lessened by the investigators' clinical judgment that the discharged patients were actually leading more impoverished lives than their hospitalized counterparts. On a more positive note, six of the MMHC patients who remained in psychotherapy beyond three years and who were followed informally continued to show some improvement. The three patients on drugs plus psychotherapy are able to function outside a hospital; all work and show a greater degree of progress than those treated in psychotherapy without drugs. By and large, however, one must conclude from the above findings that the addition of psychotherapy, active milieu, and other modern treatment approaches of the MMHC did not, in a two-year period, significantly improve or even alter the outcome of usual state hospital treatment for chronic schizophrenics.

This conclusion is confused, however, by methodological problems—namely the failure to provide optimal controls. It is important to note that comparisons of outcome were based on the effects of the *entire* MMHC treatment program and that conclusions specific to the value of psychotherapy itself cannot be drawn because the study lacked a control group in the same setting which did *not* receive psychotherapy. The study's design has been further criticized because (1) pairs of patients were not "matched" before the study and then randomly assigned to the treatment group (Cole, 1967) and (2) the Boston State Hospital control group did not include either a placebo group or drug dosages matched to those given the MMHC patients. With regard to the psychotherapy program itself, some have questioned the therapists' motivation for participating in this study (Strupp, 1967) and whether, when dealing with chronic patients (who are notoriously unresponsive to treatment), "any measurable responses to psychotherapy could have been obtained within the period of time included in this study under the most optimal conditions" (Zetzel, 1967). Despite these criticisms, however, it is difficult to dispel the evidence that, for these patients, in the time period studied, psychotherapy compared poorly to drug treatment and was of relatively little value as an adjunct to drugs.

Direct or Ego Analytic Psychotherapy

The value of experience in psychotherapy with schizophrenics was examined in a project headed by Karon (Karon and O'Grady, 1969, and Karon and VandenBos, 1970) at the Detroit Psychiatric Institute. Three groups of first-admission, "clearly schizophrenic" patients from a lower-class Negro population were randomly assigned to receive (*a*) direct analytic psychotherapy, (*b*) ego analytic psychotherapy supplemented, if need be, by drugs, or (*c*) drugs plus supportive psychotherapy in the usual public hospital milieu. One-third of the patients in groups *a* and *b* were seen by an experienced senior therapist, and the remainder were treated by psychiatric residents and graduate psychology students under his supervision. Patients in group *a* were seen five times a week for eight weeks and then once a week thereafter, while those in group *b* were seen three times a week for twenty sessions and then pushed toward once-a-week sessions. Patients in group *c* who did not show improvement after two weeks on the research unit were transferred to a state hospital.

Karon and his associates have reported: (1) Patients receiving psychotherapy (groups *a* and *b*) spent significantly less time in the hospital after one year than drug-treated controls (group *c*). They also showed significantly more improvement on the Visual-Verbal Test (a measure of schizophrenic thought disorder) and on several measures of overall functioning derived by independent observers from a clinical status interview given before and six and twelve months after the initiation of treatment. (2) No differences were found between the two psychotherapeutic approaches (group *a* vs. group *b*). (3) Regardless of whether they received drugs, patients treated by experienced therapists did better overall than those treated by inexperienced therapists. (4) As compared to results achieved in group *c*, inexperienced therapists using supplemental drugs produced shorter hospital stays but did not affect thought disorder, whereas inexperienced therapists who did not use drugs produced striking effects on thought disorder but failed to reduce length of hospitalization.

Unpublished two-year follow-up data* tend to confirm the first three findings above and shed new light on the fourth. After two years, the patients treated by inexperienced therapists who used drugs showed no improvement over group *c*, while those treated by inexperienced therapists who didn't use drugs had spent less time in the hospital than controls. Karon concludes from this that, although drugs help the inexperienced therapist to get a patient out of the hospital sooner, they do not enable him to diminish the patient's thought disorder or his relapse rate.

The above findings are of considerable interest, but unfortunately, as May and Tuma (1970) point out, there are many serious methodological problems in research design which raise questions about their validity. First, the transfer of control patients who did not show rapid improvement from the research unit to a state hospital might, in itself, prolong hospital stay and/or have a negative psychological effect upon patients; therefore, data on these patients may be severely biased. Moreover, as in the MMHC study, it is impossible to isolate the effects of psychotherapy from those of other aspects of treatment, since patients were treated in very different milieus (i.e., the research

---

*Personal communication from Karon.

unit and the state hospital). Secondly, the comparison between the effectiveness of experienced and inexperienced
therapists, when controlled for absence of drugs, is based
on exceedingly small numbers. It is further confounded by
the "professor-student" attitudes inherent in the experienced therapists' supervision of the inexperienced ones.
Finally the effects of drugs cannot be isolated in this experiment; patients who received "supplementary" drugs (at
their therapist's discretion) may have been a more disturbed group, and, in any event, dosages given these patients or the control patients are not recorded. In summary,
this study has serious uncontrolled variables (drugs, hospital setting, and transfer) which seriously weaken its pro-
vocative conclusions. It would seem that this study lends
credibility to the idea of "gifted specialists" and casts
doubt upon the positive interaction of drugs and
psychotherapy.

The Therapist Variable: Correlational Results

While primarily concerned with comparative studies of
psychotherapy's effectiveness with schizophrenics, we do
not wish to ignore totally the considerable literature which
has accumulated over the years on correlative studies. In
particular, since Whitehorn and Betz (1954) first noted in a
retrospective study that some psychiatrists consistently do
well with schizophrenic patients, while others consistently
do poorly, it has been recognized that the therapist's personality, style, or approach may be as important as the
patient himself in determining outcome. Whitehorn and
Betz's observations eventually led to the categorization
(using the Strong Vocational Interest Blank) of therapists
into *A* and *B* types (1960). Therapists whose vocational
interests resembled those of lawyers (type *A*) seemed to do

better with schizophrenic patients than those whose interests more closely resembled those of painters and mathematics–physical science teachers (type *B*). Such studies of
the therapist variable are open to methodological criticism,
but they do draw attention to the danger of treating psychotherapists as a homogeneous sample in studies such as
those reviewed here.

Three of the five studies covered in this review did attempt to explore the "therapist variable." Based on Campbell's revision of the Strong Vocational Interest Blank,
eight therapists in the MMHC study of chronic patients were
classified as *A* and four as *B* types. Although an analysis of
the effect of *A/B* typing in this study did not show significant differences between the patients treated by type *A* or
type *B* therapists, the investigators noted that the two most
improved patients had received phenothiazines and been
treated by type *B* therapists, while the two least improved
patients had received placebo and been treated by type *B*
therapists. Shader et al. (1971) attempted to follow up this
suggestive finding in a study of acute patients treated by
first-year residents. Within the drug-treated group in this
study, significantly more improvement was found in patients whose therapists had high *A* scores ($P<.05$) while
patients in the placebo group tended to show greater improvement when treated by type *B* therapists. One interesting finding of the earlier MMHC study, that the experienced
therapists who encouraged chronic patients to discuss their
anger did significantly better ($P<.05$) than those who did
not, was not true in the later study of acute patients treated
by MMHC residents.

Rogers et al. also divided their eight therapists into *A* and
B types, and were unable to correlate *A/B* status with either outcome or the therapist's capacity for empathy, congruence, and unconditional positive regard. Although May
has not yet reported the results of *A/B* ratings made in his
study, he has noted that the therapeutic results obtained by

residents could not be differentiated from those of junior staff psychiatrists. But obviously the difference in experience between residents and junior staff was not nearly so great as that in the Karon studies, where senior therapists were found to be more effective than psychological interns and psychiatric residents.

While these studies represent only a small portion of the total literature correlating certain variables with outcome, they suggest how confusing and difficult to interpret the results of such research can be. They also underscore the importance of defining the therapy given in a study and of not generalizing its results to other forms of therapy.

Therapist characteristics are an undeniably important and all too often neglected variable in research on psychotherapy. It is important to recall, however, the ironic conclusion of Rogers et al. that one can study the therapist intensively, only then to rediscover that the *patient's* contribution to outcome is also very important and in danger of being overlooked.

Discussion: Results and Implications

Looking at the results of these five studies, what can we conclude about the efficacy of psychotherapy with patients diagnosed as schizophrenic? Because of the marked differences in types of patients, therapy, therapists, comparison groups, and assessment procedures, as well as the many methodological problems pointed out in each study, it is apparent that overall conclusions about the efficacy of psychotherapy with schizophrenic patients can, at the present time, only be stated in a highly qualified and restricted manner. With this in mind, however, it would seem safe to say that the results of the May study warrant acceptance. That is, for acute schizophrenic patients, psychotherapy of an "ego-supportive, reality-defining" type, given once or twice weekly, for less than one year, by relatively inexperienced therapists, either with or without drugs, seems to offer little advantage over the usual "drugs alone" state hospital treatment. Similarly, it would seem reasonable to tentatively accept the conclusion derived from the MMHC study: that is, for chronic schizophrenics, psychoanalytic psychotherapy, given by senior analysts, at least twice a week for two years, with or without drugs, adds little to the drug-oriented treatment afforded in a state hospital. Thus, these studies offer persuasive evidence that drugs alone are the single most powerful and economical treatment for schizophrenic patients *within* one- and two-year time limits. It would be a mistake, however, to go beyond the limited specified conditions of these studies and conclude that psychotherapy has no, or even limited, value for acute or chronic schizophrenics. Nor should we dismiss as idle speculation the possibility that adequate long-term follow-up data—had these been provided—might have radically altered the conclusions summarized above. Certainly, a number of findings suggest that future, more careful investigations, emphasizing other aspects of psychotherapy with schizophrenia, could yield data which will contradict the conclusions of these five pioneering studies. One example is the indication in the methodologically flawed Karon study that, for acute schizophrenics, "direct analytic" and "ego analytic" psychotherapy might have advantages over supportive drug treatment, particularly if the therapist is highly experienced. With regard to chronic patients, Rogers et al.'s study, although not adequately designed to account for drug effects, suggests that psychotherapy will be successful to the extent that the therapist can establish a relationship with his patient that is characterized by "empathy" and "congruence" (responding as a "real person"). These studies indicate, therefore, that the effectiveness of psychotherapy with schizophrenic patients may vary considerably.

Only May's study was designed to test the value of psychotherapy as an adjunct to drugs. But his finding of the seeming equivalence of drugs alone and drugs plus psychotherapy is difficult to interpret since the quality of the therapy given is in doubt. Moreover, until follow-up data to the contrary are published, the possibility remains that favorable trends noted in the drugs plus psychotherapy group have intensified in the years since the study's completion. In the MMHC study, some measures suggested enhanced functioning when psychotherapy was combined with drugs, but this result is confused by the fact that the "drugs only" and "psychotherapy plus drugs" groups were treated in different settings.

Perhaps the most impressive evidence of psychotherapy's possible efficacy comes from correlational data in the studies by Rogers and by Shader et al., which demonstrated that certain qualities in the therapist and his relationship to the patient improve prognosis. But despite the apparent importance of therapist characteristics, evidence in this area—as in so many others—is beset by contradictions. May found no effect secondary to the experience of the therapists, while Karon reported that this factor is extremely important. Shader et al. confirmed the importance of *A/B* typing, yet the qualities demonstrated by Rogers et al. to be important facilitators did not correlate with type *A* therapists in his study. Thus, psychotherapy emerges as consisting of many elements which are, themselves, critical independent variables affecting outcome in an unknown and hence uncontrolled-for manner. This suggests that the failure of controlled studies to demonstrate psychotherapy's effectiveness may stem from an insufficient knowledge of the critical variables in the psychotherapeutic process.

Taken together, the five studies reviewed here have neither proved psychotherapy ineffective nor provided any strong evidence of its helpfulness. While this equivocal conclusion seems a very small reward for the tremendous effort and expense expended in these studies, they have had an influence which is not to be belittled—substantial advances in methodology have been brought about by their experience. It is no accident that the criteria for studies of psychotherapy recommended in 1970 reflect the problems encountered in these studies of the 1960s. For example, the study of Bookhammer et al. demonstrated the need to make assessments of patient's progress at intervals during the course of therapy and also to specify the type, amount, and duration of therapy received by both treatment and control groups—a need which was evident in the Rogers et al., MMHC, and Karon studies as well. Another important lesson learned from the MMHC and Karon projects is the inadvisability of treating experimental and control groups in different institutional settings, thereby making it impossible to isolate psychotherapy as the critical variable in any differences noted between groups.

But in addition to encountering "instructive" problems, each of these studies made positive innovations in research design. The Bookhammer group used long-term follow-up and made an effort to evaluate outcome with a variety of patient variables. Rogers et al. focused on the therapist's technique and relationship to the patient as critical variables in determining outcome. Their use of video tapes and newly developed scales measuring empathy, congruence, and experience of self represents a major effort to quantify the process of therapy. Moreover, by using carefully matched pairs of subjects, randomly assigned to treatment and control groups, Rogers et al. showed that a good study can be designed which does not depend on large numbers of patients. They also demonstrated that the patient may be able to predict outcome more accurately than his therapist can. Contributions made by the MMHC study include the use of staff ratings and diaries and the discovery of the family's effectiveness in rating outcome. The long-term commitment of experienced therapists to this study is an ideal which will be difficult to duplicate in future studies.

The MMHC study also placed the use of discharge as a criterion of outcome into needed clinical perspective. In tentatively identifying the therapist's experience as an important variable, Karon and his associates have provided stimulation for further research. Theirs was also the only study which sought to make therapy more homogeneous by having one supervisor for a whole group of therapists. And, finally, May's study is notable for its attention to cost data and randomization, for its use of supervisors as a "window" to the therapist, concentration on patients with an "average" prognosis, and development of the Camarillo Dynamic Assessment Scale, which assesses relatively subtle aspects of psychological change.

Recommendations

It is unfortunate that the three most ambitious and best-controlled studies (May, Rogers, et al., and MMHC) were carried out concurrently, thus making it impossible for these investigators to benefit from each other's problems and advances. Nonetheless, their efforts now provide a bountiful legacy for future investigators attempting to frame comprehensive comparative studies, which will include, at a minimum, the following features:

• a well-defined patient population;
• matched control groups, in comparable milieus, including a group receiving drugs plus psychotherapy;
• a well-defined, relatively homogeneous, and nonidiosyncratic therapeutic approach;
• a carefully defined and selected group of therapists;
• measures of outcome evaluating behavior in a number of settings and taking into account the patient's own subjective experience of himself;
• long-term treatment and follow-up.

Although it may be said that the studies reviewed here confirm the drug literature in demonstrating the efficacy of drugs in schizophrenia, it is also clear that no definitive answer can yet be given to the more global question of the value of psychotherapy. Psychotherapy, in contrast to drug therapy, consists of many elements which can themselves be viewed as independent variables worthy of investigation. As illuminated in this review, these variables sort into the following three major groupings:

• patient variables;
• therapist variables;
• process variables which define the therapy.

Certainly, these areas will require more careful attention in future comprehensive studies of psychotherapy. Indeed, considering how little we know about these elements, their interactions, and their effects on outcome, we might be well advised to concentrate on correlational studies aimed at enhancing our understanding of these composite variables *prior* to launching large-scale comparative studies. By correlating these variables with outcome, we might arrive at useful guidelines as to what type of therapy is or is not effective with what type of patient—guidelines which ultimately could form the foundation for more ambitious, and more fruitful, comparative studies.

Perhaps because of the pessimism generated by past studies, research on psychotherapy with schizophrenics has, for some time, been in a state of semiparalysis. This is regrettable, since practicing psychotherapists clearly still believe in the efficacy of their approach and have, one would think, a personal stake in demonstrating that their confidence is not misplaced. It remains, after all, the burden of the field—of psychotherapy's advocates—to demonstrate whether psychotherapy is indicated in treating schizophrenia and, if so, of what it should consist, who should deliver it, and who should receive it. Only by removing the now widespread doubts about the merits of this approach will it be possible to restore psychotherapy's "good name." This much is certain: There is no lack of questions to which psychotherapy's advocates might reasonably address themselves.

REFERENCES

Bookhammer, R. S.; Meyers, R. W.; Schober, C. C.; and Piotrowski, A. Z. A five-year follow-up study of schizophrenics treated by Rosen's "direct analysis": Compared with controls. *American Journal of Psychiatry*, 123:602–604, 1966.

Cole, J. O. A lack of controls. *International Journal of Psychiatry*, 4(2):129–131, 1967.

Cole, J. O. A unique study which may never be repeated. In: May, P. R. A. *Treatment of Schizophrenia: A Comparative Study of Five Treatment Methods*. New York: Science House, 1968, pp. 309–310.

Ewalt, J. Psychotherapy of schizophrenia. In: Katz, M. M.; Littlestone, R.; Mosher, L. R.; Tuma, A. H.; and Roath, M., eds., *Schizophrenia—Implications of Recent Research Findings for Training and Treatment*. New York: Basic Books, Inc., in press.

Fine, S. Psychotherapeutic help through the terrible ordeal of illness. In: May, P. R. A. *Treatment of Schizophrenia: A Comparative Study of Five Treatment Methods*. New York: Science House, 1968, pp. 293–294.

Fiske, D. W.; Hunt, H. F.; Luborsky, L.; Orne, M. T.; Parloff, M. B.; Reiser, M. F.; and Tuma, A. H. Planning of research on effectiveness of psychotherapy. *Archives of General Psychiatry*, 22:12–32, 1970.

Fleiss, J. L. An incomplete report based on possibly faulty statistics. *International Journal of Psychiatry*, 8(4):723–726, 1969.

Fromm-Reichmann, F. Some aspects of psychoanalytic psychotherapy with schizophrenics. In: Brody, E. B., and Redlich, F. C., eds., *Psychotherapy with Schizophrenics*. New York: International Universities Press, 1952, pp. 89–111.

Grinspoon, L. The utility of psychotherapy with schizophrenia. *International Journal of Psychiatry*, 8(4):727–729, 1969.

Grinspoon, L.; Ewalt, J. R.; and Shader, R. Long-term treatment of chronic schizophrenia. *International Journal of Psychiatry*, 4(2):116–128, 1967.

Hamilton, L. A., Jr. May's conclusions are found to be generally confirmed by clinical experience. *International Journal of Psychiatry*, 8(4):730–733, 1969.

Heller, K. Review of Rogers et al.'s *The Therapeutic Relationship and Its Impact: A Study of Psychotherapy with Schizophrenics*. In: *Psychiatry*, 32(3):348–350, 1969.

Karon, B., and O'Grady, P. Intellectual test changes in schizophrenic patients in the first six months of treatment. *Psychotherapy: Theory, Research and Practice*, 6:88–96, 1969.

Karon, B. P., and VandenBos, G. R. Experience, medication, and the effectiveness of psychotherapy with schizophrenics: A note on Drs. May and Tuma's conclusions. *British Journal of Psychiatry*, 116(533):427–428, 1970.

Leavitt, M. It is in the degree of differences, perhaps, where the surprises lie. In: May, P. R. A., *Treatment of Schizophrenia: A Comparative Study of Five Treatment Methods*. New York: Science House, 1968, pp. 301–304.

Ludwig, A. M. Review of Rogers et al.'s *The Therapeutic Relationship and Its Impact: A Study of Psychotherapy with Schizophrenics*. In: *American Journal of Psychotherapy*, 21(4):845–847, 1967.

May, P. R. A. *Treatment of Schizophrenia: A Comparative Study of Five Treatment Methods*. New York: Science House, 1968.

May, P. R. A. Reply to discussants. *International Journal of Psychiatry*, 8(4):763–783, 1969.

May, P. R. A., and Tuma, A. H. Methodological problems in psychotherapy research: Observations on the Karon-VandenBos study of psychotherapy and drugs in schizophrenia. *British Journal of Psychiatry,* 117(540): 569-570, 1970.

Messier, M.; Finnerty, R.; Botuin, C.; and Grinspoon, L. A. A follow-up study of intensively treated chronic schizophrenic patients. *American Journal of Psychiatry,* 125(8):159–163, 1969.

Michels, R. Research design and training programs. *International Journal of Psychiatry,* 8(4):740–743, 1969.

Rogers, C. R. *Counseling and Psychotherapy.* Boston: Houghton Mifflin, 1942.

Rogers, C. R.; Gendlin, E. G.; Kiesler, D. J.; and Truax, C. B., eds. *The Therapeutic Relationship and Its Impact: A Study of Psychotherapy with Schizophrenics.* Madison: University of Wisconsin Press, 1967.

Rosen, J. N. The treatment of schizophrenic psychoses by direct analytic therapy. *Psychiatric Quarterly,* 21:3–37, 117–119, 1947.

Rosen, J. N. *Direct Analysis: Selected Papers.* New York: Grune & Stratton, 1953.

Rosen, J. N. Psychotherapy and schizophrenia. *International Journal of Psychiatry,* 8(4):748–752, 1969.

Shader, R. I.; Grinspoon, L.; Harmatz, J.; and Ewalt, J. R. The therapist variable. *American Journal of Psychiatry,* 127(8):1009–1012, 1971.

Shlien, J. M. Review of Rogers et al.'s *The Therapeutic Relationship and Its Impact: A Study of Psychotherapy with Schizophrenics.* In: *Psychology Today,* September–October, 1967.

Strupp, H. H. On the limitations of psychotherapy. *International Journal of Psychiatry,* 4(2):136–138, 1967.

Vaccaro, M. V. Review of Rogers et al.'s *The Therapeutic Relationship and Its Impact: A Study of Psychotherapy with Schizophrenics.* In: *Journal of the Albert Einstein Medical Center,* October, 1967.

Wexler, M. One path to recovery lies in the development of stable object relationships with someone in the outside world. In May, P. R. A., *Treatment of Schizophrenia: A Comparative Study of Five Treatment Methods.* New York: Science House, 1968, pp. 278–284.

Whitehorn, J. C., and Betz, B. J. A study of psychotherapeutic relationships between physicians and schizophrenic patients. *American Journal of Psychiatry,* 111:321–331, 1954.

Whitehorn, J. C., and Betz, B. J. Further studies of the doctor as a crucial variable in the outcome of treatment with schizophrenic patients. *American Journal of Psychiatry,* 117:214–223, 1960.

Zetzel, E. R. The usefulness—and limitations—of the phenothiazines. *International Journal of Psychiatry,* 4(2):138–139, 1967.

TABLE 1

Summary of Studies Assessing Psychotherapy with Schizophrenic Patients

	Bookhammer et al. (1966) *Direct Analysis*	Rogers et al. (1967) *Client Centered*	May (1968) *Ego Supportive*	Grinspoon, Ewalt, & Shader (1967) *Analytically Oriented*	The Karon Studies (1969 & 1970) *Direct Analysis (DA) & Ego Analysis (EA)*
Diagnosis by	Clinical staff	Clinical staff	Clinical staff & independent psychiatrists	3 independent psychiatrists	Clinical staff & independent psychiatrists
Sample	N=51 first break, age:15–35	N=48;16 matched pairs +16 normal volunteers	N=228 first admission, age:16–45, "average prognosis"	N=41 hospitalized >3 yr., single, male, age:18–35	N=36 first admission, acute
Study group (patients receiving psychotherapy)	N=14	N=24 (8 hospitalized >8 mo., 8 hospitalized <8 mo.) + 8 normal volunteers	+ drugs, N=44 no drugs, N=46	+ drugs, N=10 no drugs, N=10	+drugs, N=24
Comparison groups (selection of, n, & treatment received)	(a) designated biased, N=18 (b) random, N=19 Usual hospital treatment,[1] different setting than study group	Random, matched pairs, N=16 (8 hospitalized >8 mo., 8 hospitalized <8 mo.) + normal volunteers. Usual hospital treatment in same setting as the study groups.	Random (a) active milieu, N=43 (b) drugs, N=48 (c) ECT, N=47	Biased (by self-selection), N=21, usual hospital treatment in different setting than study group	Random, N=12, usual hospital treatment in different setting than study group
Therapists		8 with 1–25 yr. experience, not supervised	41 with 6 mo.–6 yr. experience, supervised 1/2 hr./wk./patient	18 senior analysts, not supervised	2 senior therapists & 10 supervised trainees

Continued on following page

Variables studied		A/B²	A/B, experience & personality	A/B, focus of interviews	Experience
Psychotherapy (intensity & duration)	Probably intense & <2 mo.	2 hr./wk. for 2 mo., 2½ yr.	2 hr./wk. for 1 yr. (7 to 87 hrs.)	2 hr./wk. for 2 yr.	12 patients in each therapy: DA: 5hr./wk. for 8 wk. EA: 3 hr./wk. for 7 wk. then, 1 hr./wk. for total of 1 yr.
Assessments Schedule	Before & 5-5½ yr. after treatment	Before & at 3-mo. intervals during treatment	Before & after treatment	Before & at 2-wk. intervals during treatment	Before & at 3-mo. intervals during treatment
Done by	Investigator	Therapists, patients, & trained non-professionals	Nurses, psychologist, social worker, therapist, & independent analyst	Nurses, therapists & patient's family	Independent professionals
Types	Signs, symptoms, work, attitudes, thinking, & hospital status	Therapist relationship, personality, behavior, hospital status, & projective tests	Signs, symptoms, behavior, mood, thinking, personality, ego functions, cost,& hospital status	Behavior, signs, symptoms, social adjustment, & hospital status	Behavior, signs, symptoms, thinking, & hospital status
Results[3]	No difference between groups at 5-yr. follow-up[4]	Psychotherapy ≧ usual hospital treatment at end of treatment & at 1 yr. follow-up	At end of treatment, psychotherapy alone <<drugs alone; psychotherapy+ drugs ≥ drugs alone	At end of treatment, psychotherapy <<drugs + psychotherapy; at 3-5-yr. follow-up, psychotherapy + milieu± drugs same as usual hospital treatment	At end of treatment, psychotherapy ± drugs>usual hospital treatment; at 2-yr. follow-up, psychotherapy ± drugs approximately the same as usual hospital treatment.

[1] Usual (state) hospital treatment here refers to moderate to minimal staffing and significant, regular drug therapy.
[2] A/B refers to the Whitehorn-Betz A/B ratings for therapists.
[3] Only results pertinent to the efficacy question are cited.
[4] Follow-up may have dated from either the time that treatment began or ended; see text.

28

COMMENT ON THE FIVE
TREATMENT COMPARATIVE STUDY
Milton Wexler, Ph.D.

A Source of Doubt

I would like to comment on Phil May's study. I was part of that study as one of the principal investigators and I've always had a sense of uneasiness about it. Somewhere along the line I left the research group. I quit in the middle of that study not really out of any kind of profound doubt concerning the research. I happened to get terribly involved at the time with other things—and now I wish I had quit out of some deep scientific conviction. I tried to write something in that vein, a brief objection to the total publication, in the hope that I could salvage something of my conscience by raising some doubts about the soundness of the study. I see it didn't do a bit of good, because in the presentation by Drs. Dyrud and Holzman, referring to Dr. May's study, they say, "We do not challenge the validity of these findings." I find that terrible because I, as a participant, and several of the people from California as participants, I think definitely would challenge those findings. I want to say now that I don't have to wait for follow-up findings. Having supervised some of the residents who were working with those patients, and having worked up some of those scales that measured outcomes, and having been involved in many other things connected with the study, I will probably feel as skeptical about the follow-up as about the main findings. Basically, the academic, objective, statistical, clearheaded way in which the findings are

431

reported presents outcomes which I just can't believe. It contradicts my experience, it contradicts my work at Camarillo, it contradicts all those exchanges I've had with colleagues who worked there. These are some of the objections that we had.

Supervisor Variability

We tried to select patients on a random basis, assigning patients to a particular group as they came to the hospital. Then the senior analysts supervised residents in their treatment of patients. In the first place, I must say that the people who were doing the supervising were recruited from the Los Angeles Psychoanalytic Institute and, while they all had a certain kind of high-level achievement in terms of prestige and experience and practice, there was an enormous variation in terms of their experience in the treatment of schizophrenic patients; so you had in that supervising group people with a very wide variety of experience with the treatment of schizophrenia and people with relatively little experience—in fact, in some instances, out of their psychiatric residencies and nothing else.

Resident Variability

In the second place, you had an enormous range, as far as I could see, of experience and talent in terms of the residents who were being supervised. These were people who had very, very little experience with the psychotherapy of schizophrenia, and they not only had very little experience but, just from observation—and that observation was over a fairly long period of time—these people also ranged very, very considerably in what I consider to be aptitude. Even if they didn't range in terms of aptitude, they certainly ranged tremendously in terms of personality type, a factor worth considering, and in their experience in living. So you had here a range that could not be considered as controlled factors in this experimental design. Furthermore, I think that the value of supervision did vary tremendously in terms of who was doing the supervising and how intensive that supervision was.

Lack of Scale Validity

Then, I believe some of the scales that were used for measurement were things that developed off the top of our heads. They had no validation. They scarcely had evaluations as to reliability. They did have internal consistency. I think that that high level of internal consistency has developed basically because when we were first presented with a series of schizophrenic patients, the patients varied so widely in this series that it would have been almost impossible not to have developed a high level of statistical consistency among the raters. I don't think it particularly validated any of those scales.

These are some of my doubts. I have such a very high regard for Philip May and his co-workers that I express these concerns with considerable reluctance. They labored long, hard, and with a decency and dedication that cannot be faulted. I regretfully think they are trapped by a fascination with a questionable methodology and statistics that have more brilliance than substance.

INDEX